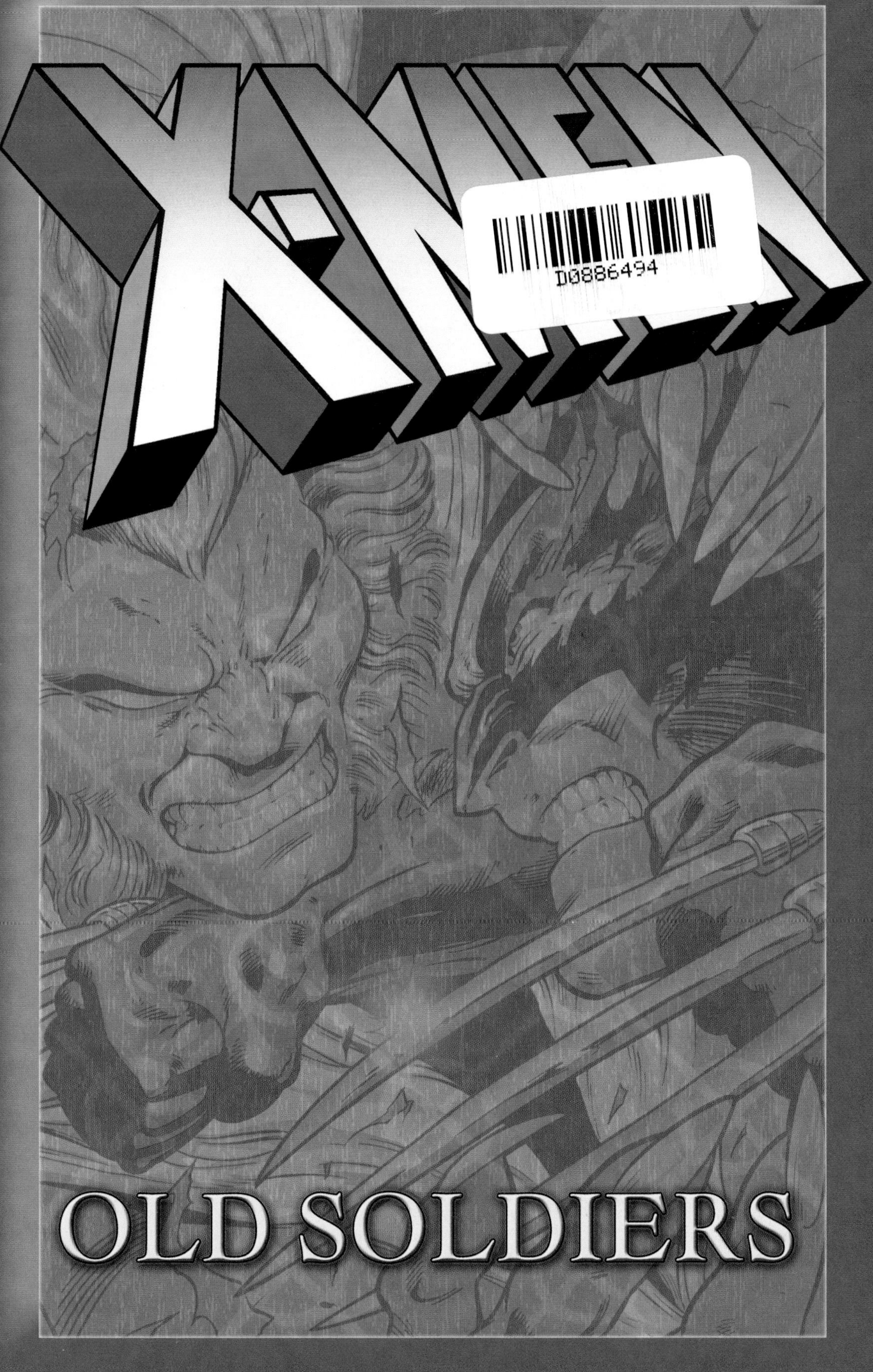
X-MEN
OLD SOLDIERS

OLD SOLDIERS

Writer
Chris Claremont

Pencils
Alan Davis

Inks
Paul Neary with Dan Green

Letters
Tom Orzechowski

Colors
Glynis Oliver

Color Reconstruction
Jerron Quality Color

Cover Art
Alan Davis & Paul Neary

Cover Colors
Avalon's Matt Milla

Editor
Ann Nocenti

Collections Editor: Jeff Youngquist
Assistant Managing Editor: Mark D. Beazley
Assistant Editor: Jennifer Grünwald
Book Designer: Meghan Kerns
Creative Director: Tom Marvelli

Editor in Chief: Joe Quesada
Publisher: Dan Buckley

The New Mutants Annual #2

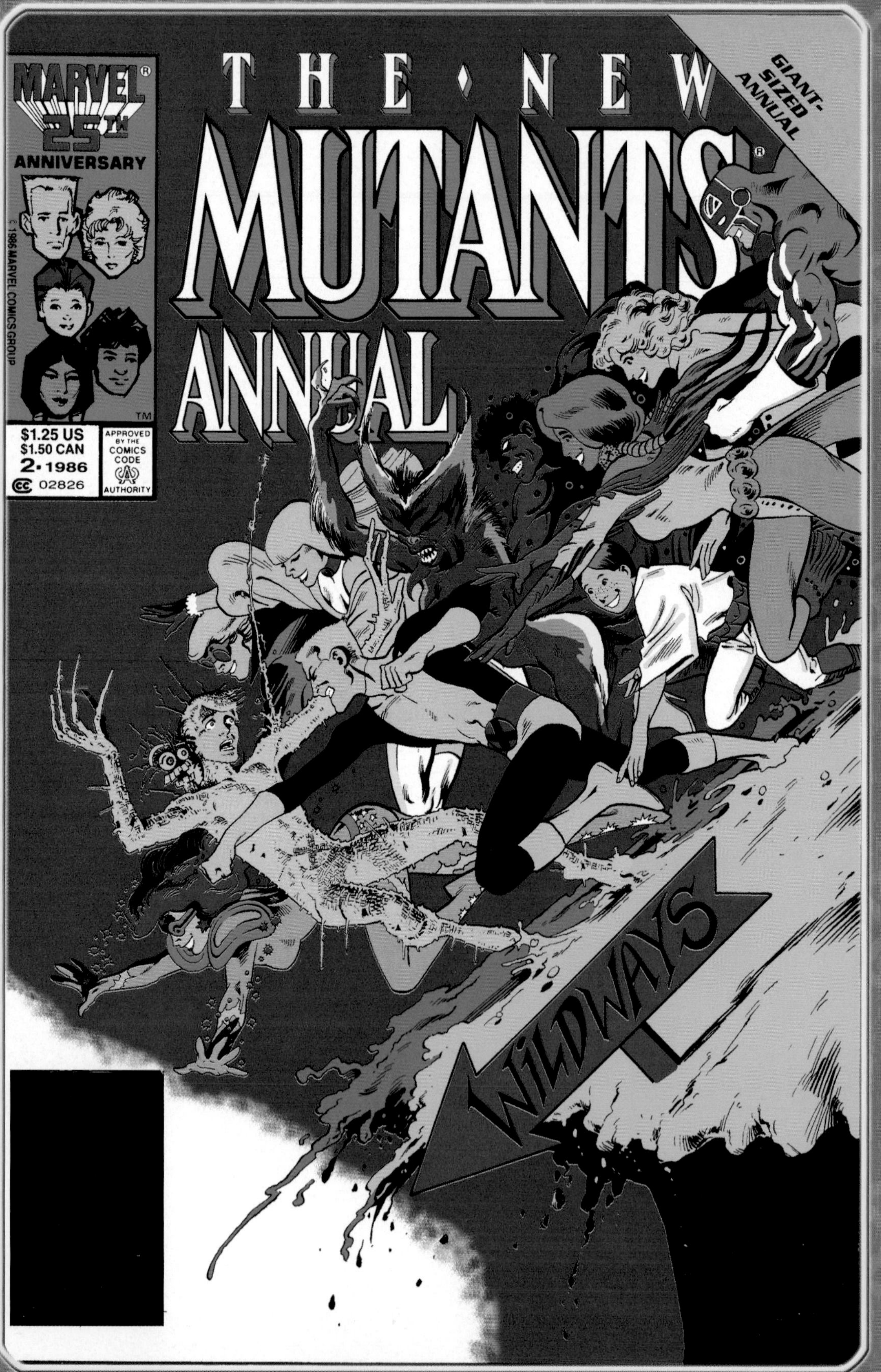

MARVEL®
25TH
ANNIVERSARY
© 1986 MARVEL COMICS GROUP
TM
$1.25 US
$1.50 CAN
2·1986
02826
APPROVED BY THE COMICS CODE AUTHORITY
THE·NEW
MUTANTS®
ANNUAL
GIANT-SIZED ANNUAL
WILDWAYS

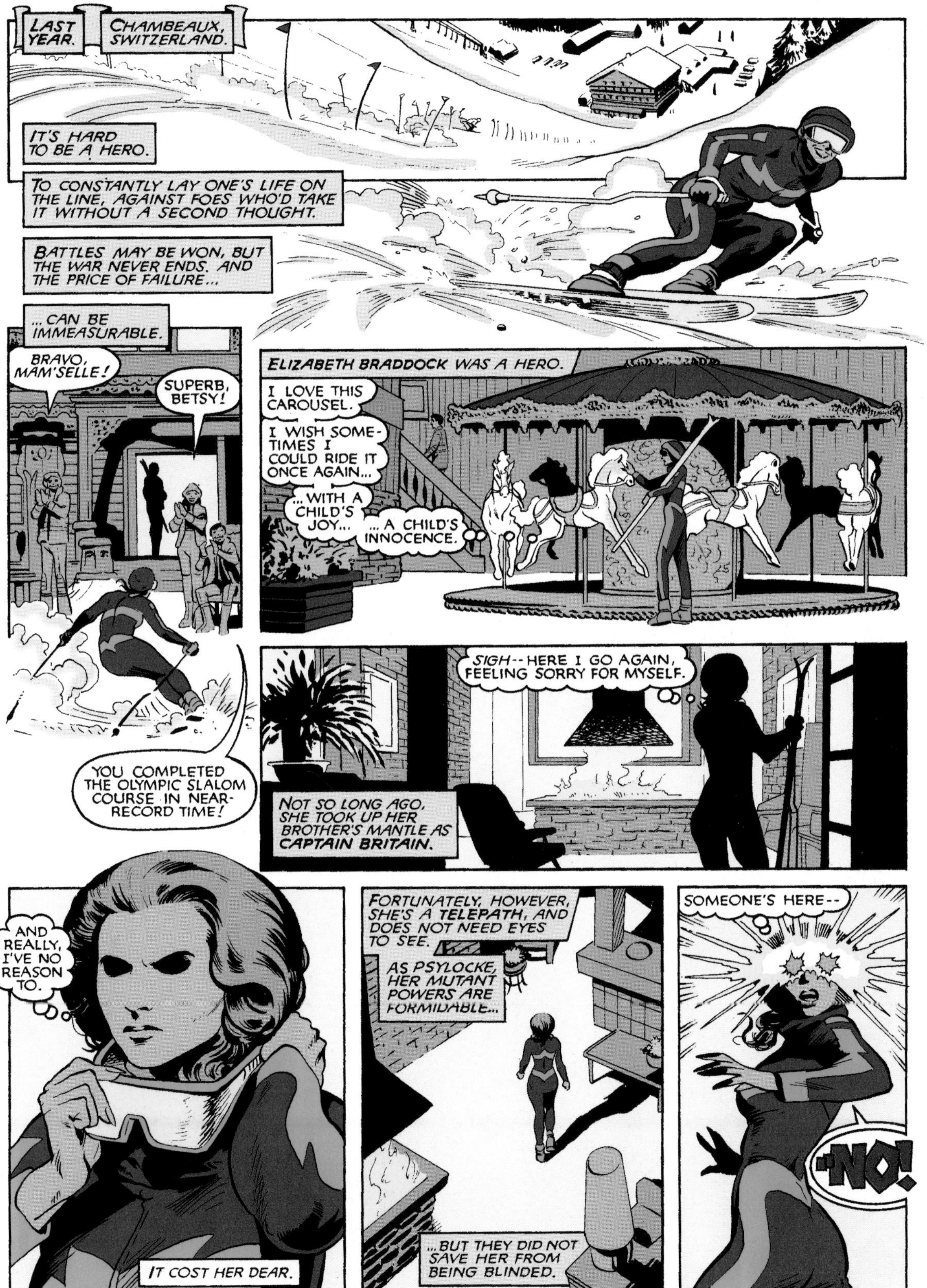
LAST YEAR.
CHAMBEAUX, SWITZERLAND.
IT'S HARD TO BE A HERO.
TO CONSTANTLY LAY ONE'S LIFE ON THE LINE, AGAINST FOES WHO'D TAKE IT WITHOUT A SECOND THOUGHT.
BATTLES MAY BE WON, BUT THE WAR NEVER ENDS. AND THE PRICE OF FAILURE...
...CAN BE IMMEASURABLE.
BRAVO, MAM'SELLE!
SUPERB, BETSY!
YOU COMPLETED THE OLYMPIC SLALOM COURSE IN NEAR-RECORD TIME!
ELIZABETH BRADDOCK WAS A HERO.
I LOVE THIS CAROUSEL.
I WISH SOMETIMES I COULD RIDE IT ONCE AGAIN...
...WITH A CHILD'S JOY...
...A CHILD'S INNOCENCE.
SIGH--HERE I GO AGAIN, FEELING SORRY FOR MYSELF.
NOT SO LONG AGO, SHE TOOK UP HER BROTHER'S MANTLE AS CAPTAIN BRITAIN.
AND REALLY, I'VE NO REASON TO.
IT COST HER DEAR.
FORTUNATELY, HOWEVER, SHE'S A TELEPATH, AND DOES NOT NEED EYES TO SEE.
AS PSYLOCKE, HER MUTANT POWERS ARE FORMIDABLE...
...BUT THEY DID NOT SAVE HER FROM BEING BLINDED.
SOMEONE'S HERE--
--NO!

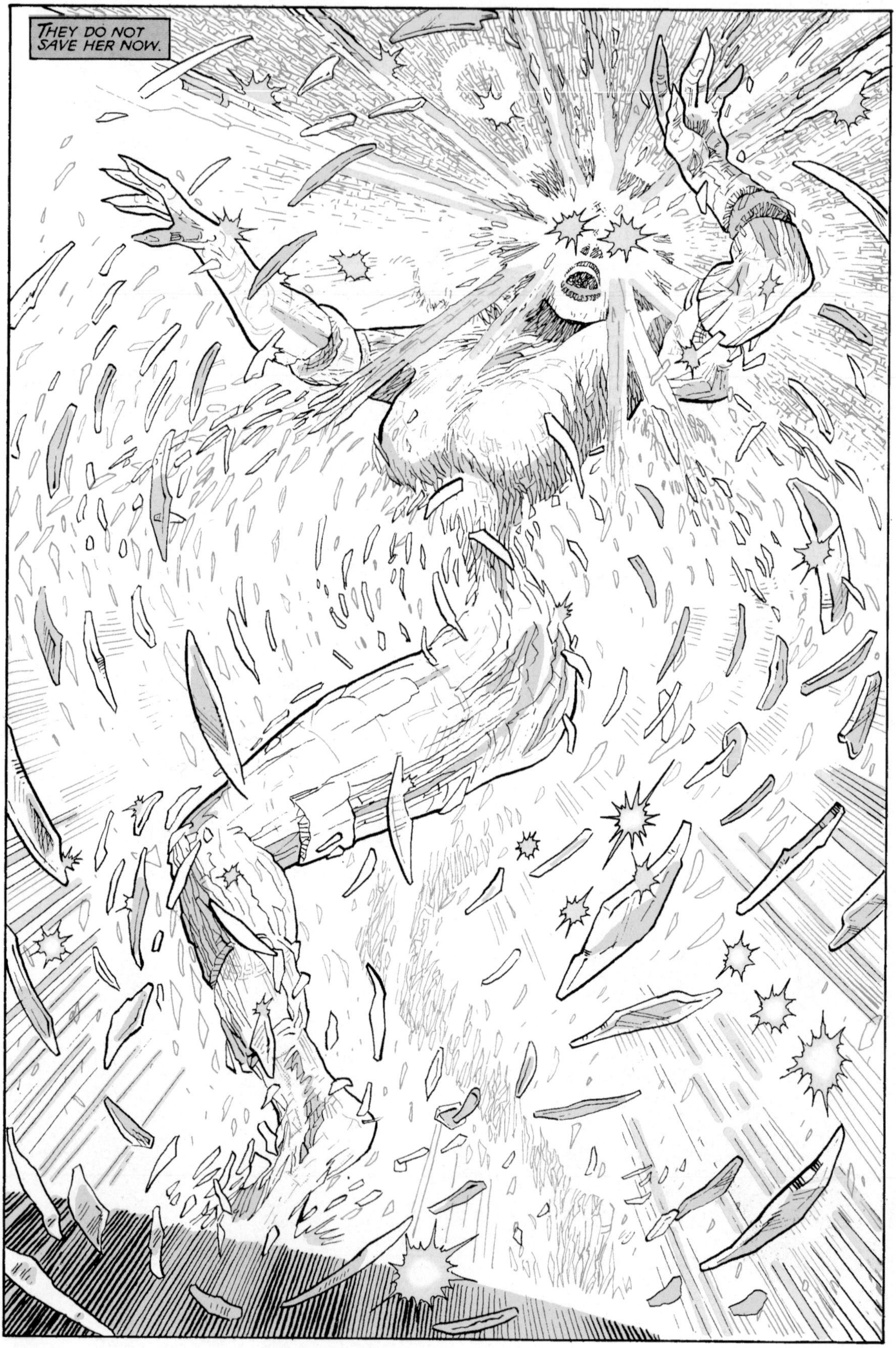
THEY DO NOT SAVE HER NOW.

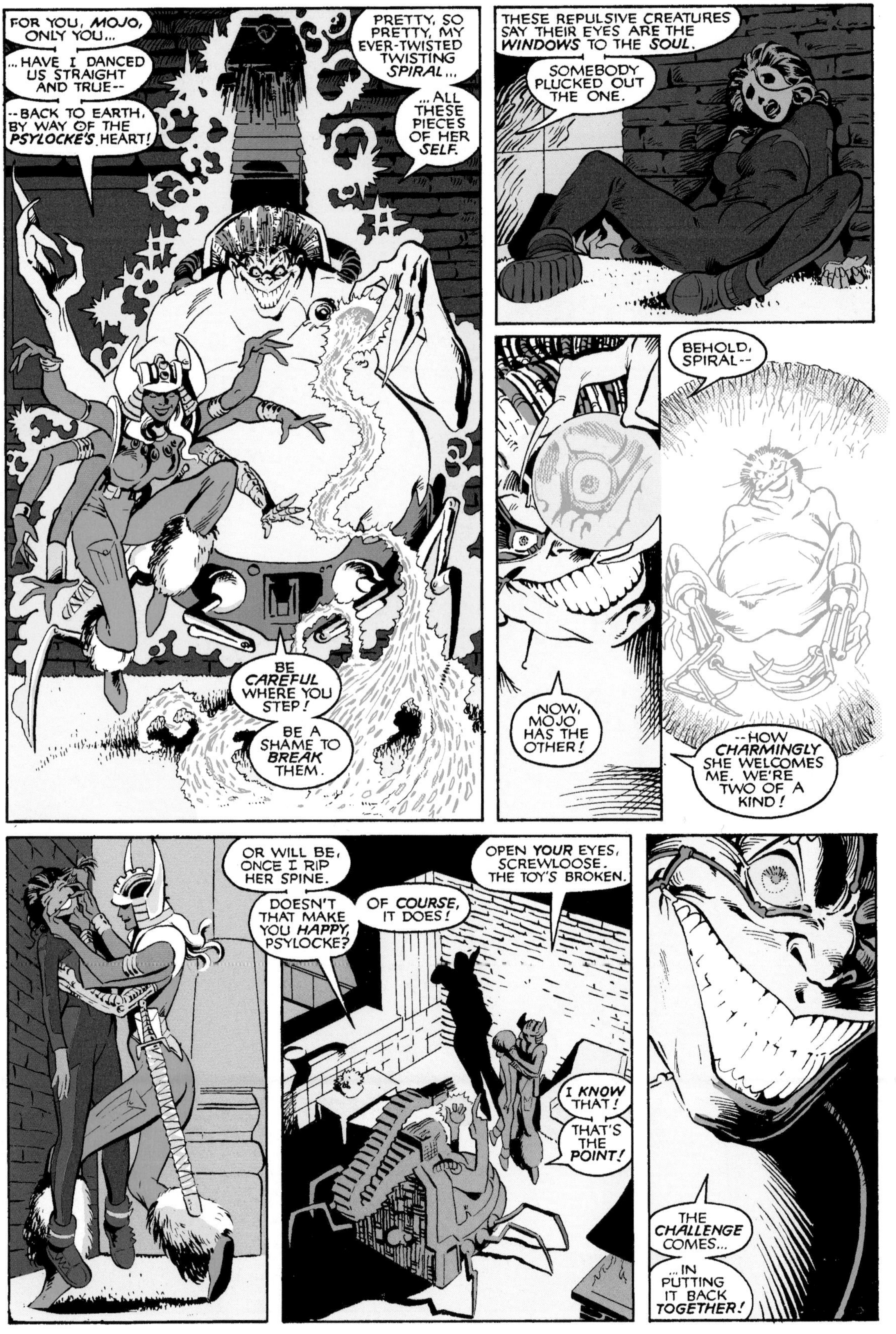
FOR YOU, MOJO, ONLY YOU...
...HAVE I DANCED US STRAIGHT AND TRUE--
--BACK TO EARTH, BY WAY OF THE PSYLOCKE'S HEART!
PRETTY, SO PRETTY, MY EVER-TWISTED TWISTING SPIRAL...
...ALL THESE PIECES OF HER SELF.
BE CAREFUL WHERE YOU STEP!
BE A SHAME TO BREAK THEM.
THESE REPULSIVE CREATURES SAY THEIR EYES ARE THE WINDOWS TO THE SOUL.
SOMEBODY PLUCKED OUT THE ONE.
BEHOLD, SPIRAL--
NOW, MOJO HAS THE OTHER!
--HOW CHARMINGLY SHE WELCOMES ME. WE'RE TWO OF A KIND!
OR WILL BE, ONCE I RIP HER SPINE.
DOESN'T THAT MAKE YOU HAPPY, PSYLOCKE?
OF COURSE, IT DOES!
OPEN YOUR EYES, SCREWLOOSE. THE TOY'S BROKEN.
I KNOW THAT!
THAT'S THE POINT!
THE CHALLENGE COMES...
...IN PUTTING IT BACK TOGETHER!

STAN LEE PRESENTOR · CHRIS CLAREMONT WRITER · ALAN DAVIS ARTIST · TOM ORZECHOWSKI LETTERER · GLYNIS OLIVER COLORIST · ANN NOCENTI EDITOR · JIM SHOOTER EDITOR IN CHIEF · CHRIS CLAREMONT & BOB McLEOD CREATORS

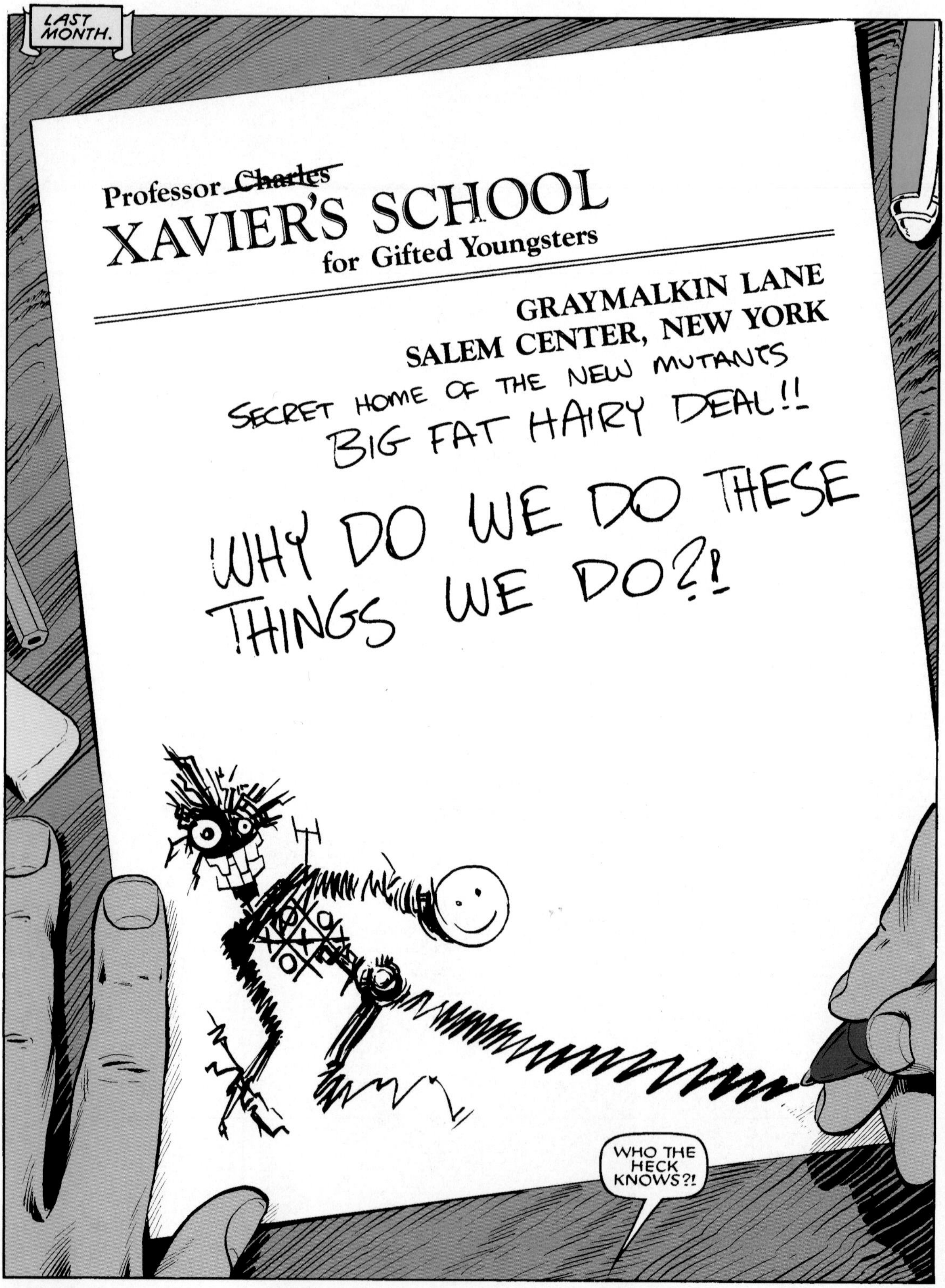

LAST MONTH.
Professor ~~Charles~~ XAVIER'S SCHOOL for Gifted Youngsters
GRAYMALKIN LANE
SALEM CENTER, NEW YORK
SECRET HOME OF THE NEW MUTANTS
BIG FAT HAIRY DEAL!!
WHY DO WE DO THESE THINGS WE DO?!
WHO THE HECK KNOWS?!

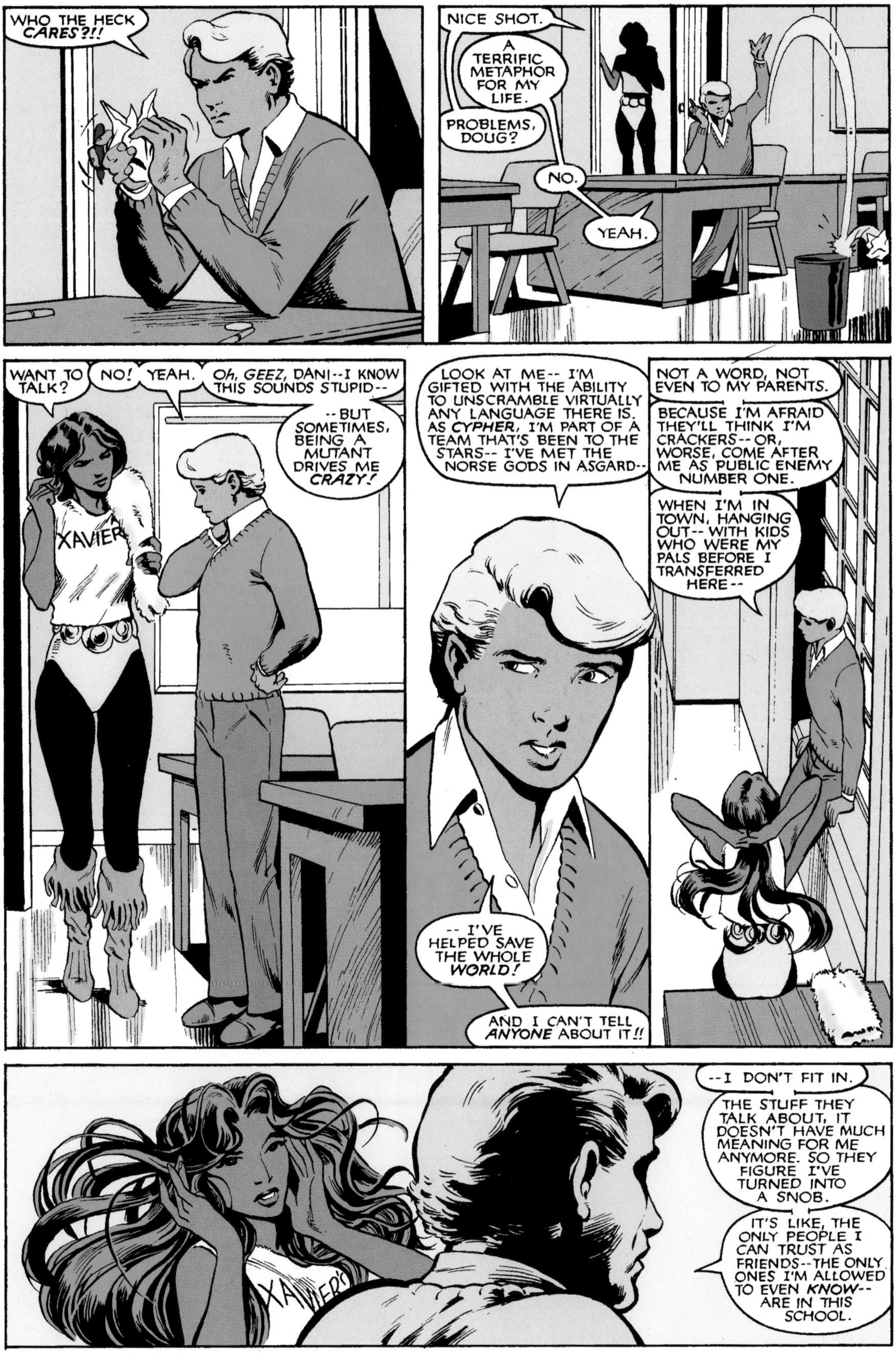

WHO THE HECK *CARES?!!*
NICE SHOT.
A TERRIFIC METAPHOR FOR MY LIFE.
PROBLEMS, DOUG?
NO.
YEAH.
WANT TO TALK?
NO!
YEAH.
Oh, GEEZ, DANI--I KNOW THIS SOUNDS STUPID--
--BUT SOMETIMES, BEING A MUTANT DRIVES ME *CRAZY!*
LOOK AT ME-- I'M GIFTED WITH THE ABILITY TO UNSCRAMBLE VIRTUALLY ANY LANGUAGE THERE IS. AS *CYPHER,* I'M PART OF A TEAM THAT'S BEEN TO THE STARS-- I'VE MET THE NORSE GODS IN ASGARD--
-- I'VE HELPED SAVE THE WHOLE *WORLD!*
AND I CAN'T TELL *ANYONE* ABOUT IT!!
NOT A WORD, NOT EVEN TO MY PARENTS.
BECAUSE I'M AFRAID THEY'LL THINK I'M CRACKERS--OR, WORSE, COME AFTER ME AS PUBLIC ENEMY NUMBER ONE.
WHEN I'M IN TOWN, HANGING OUT-- WITH KIDS WHO WERE MY PALS BEFORE I TRANSFERRED HERE--
--I DON'T FIT IN.
THE STUFF THEY TALK ABOUT, IT DOESN'T HAVE MUCH MEANING FOR ME ANYMORE. SO THEY FIGURE I'VE TURNED INTO A SNOB.
IT'S LIKE, THE ONLY PEOPLE I CAN TRUST AS FRIENDS--THE ONLY ONES I'M ALLOWED TO EVEN *KNOW*-- ARE IN THIS SCHOOL.

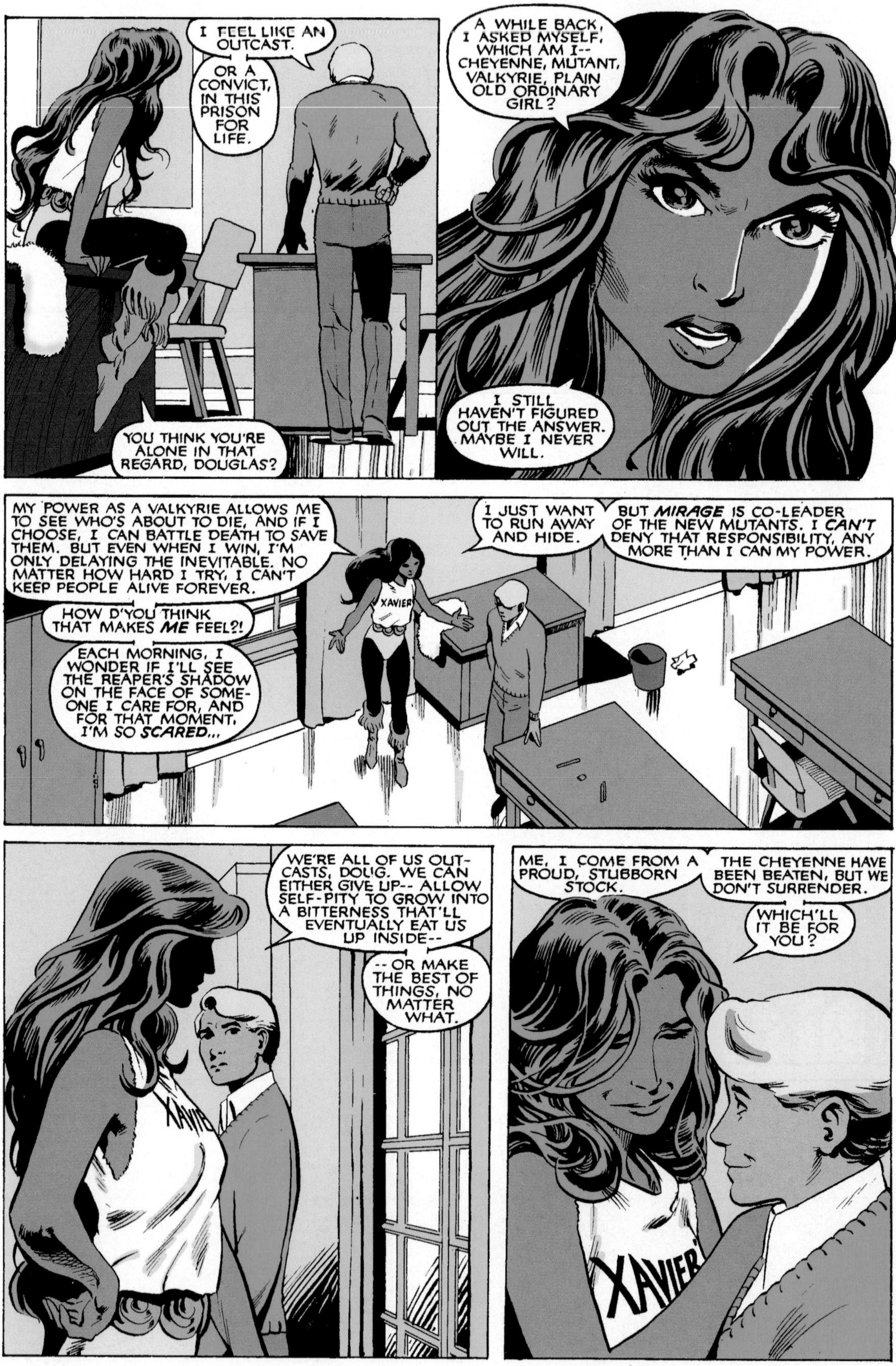
I FEEL LIKE AN OUTCAST.
OR A CONVICT, IN THIS PRISON FOR LIFE.
YOU THINK YOU'RE ALONE IN THAT REGARD, DOUGLAS?
A WHILE BACK, I ASKED MYSELF, WHICH AM I-- CHEYENNE, MUTANT, VALKYRIE, PLAIN OLD ORDINARY GIRL?
I STILL HAVEN'T FIGURED OUT THE ANSWER. MAYBE I NEVER WILL.
MY POWER AS A VALKYRIE ALLOWS ME TO SEE WHO'S ABOUT TO DIE, AND IF I CHOOSE, I CAN BATTLE DEATH TO SAVE THEM. BUT EVEN WHEN I WIN, I'M ONLY DELAYING THE INEVITABLE. NO MATTER HOW HARD I TRY, I CAN'T KEEP PEOPLE ALIVE FOREVER.
HOW D'YOU THINK THAT MAKES ME FEEL?!
EACH MORNING, I WONDER IF I'LL SEE THE REAPER'S SHADOW ON THE FACE OF SOME-ONE I CARE FOR, AND FOR THAT MOMENT, I'M SO SCARED...
XAVIER
I JUST WANT TO RUN AWAY AND HIDE.
BUT MIRAGE IS CO-LEADER OF THE NEW MUTANTS. I CAN'T DENY THAT RESPONSIBILITY, ANY MORE THAN I CAN MY POWER.
WE'RE ALL OF US OUT-CASTS, DOUG. WE CAN EITHER GIVE UP-- ALLOW SELF-PITY TO GROW INTO A BITTERNESS THAT'LL EVENTUALLY EAT US UP INSIDE--
-- OR MAKE THE BEST OF THINGS, NO MATTER WHAT.
ME, I COME FROM A PROUD, STUBBORN STOCK.
THE CHEYENNE HAVE BEEN BEATEN, BUT WE DON'T SURRENDER.
WHICH'LL IT BE FOR YOU?
XAVIER

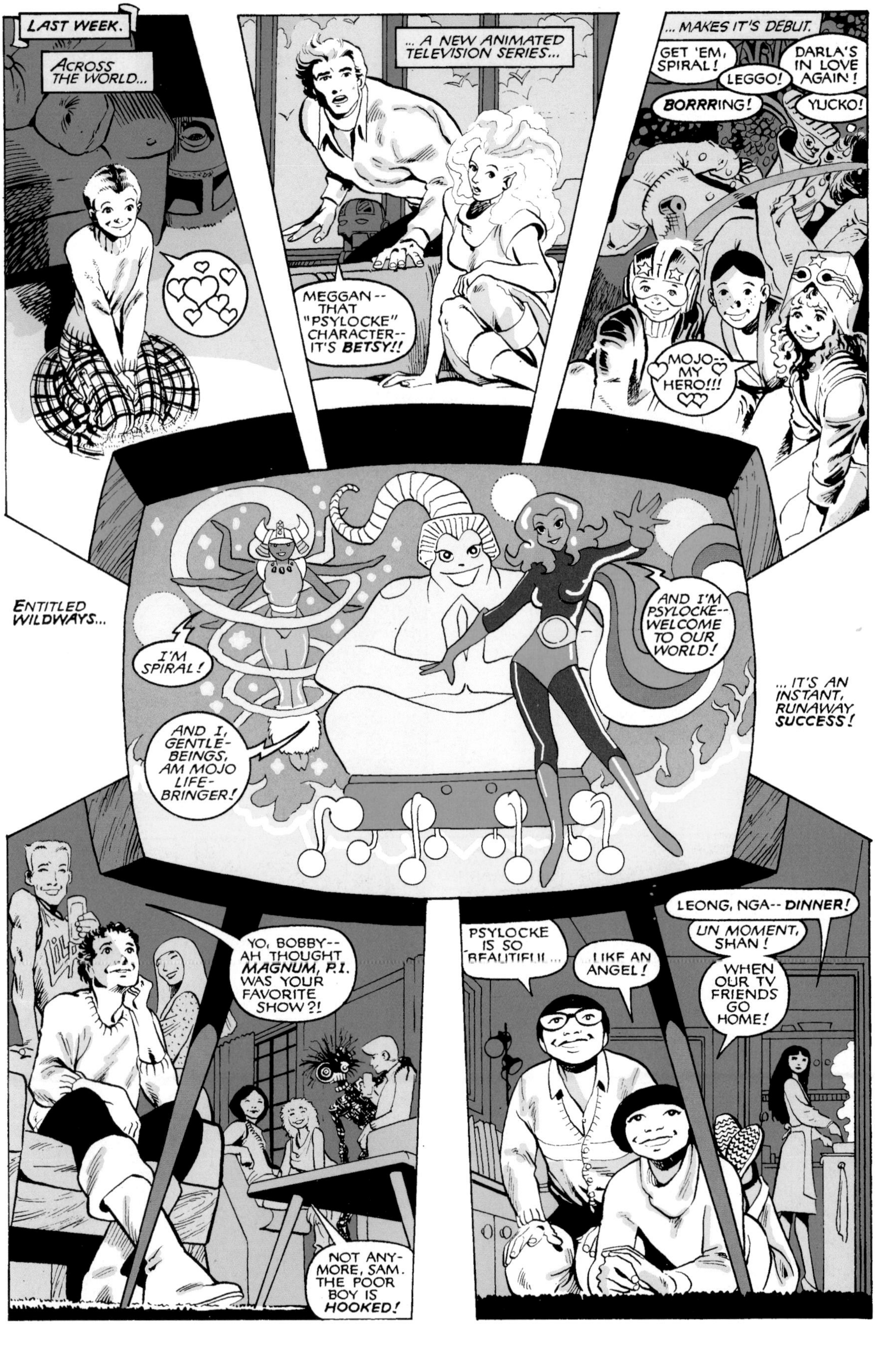
LAST WEEK.
ACROSS THE WORLD...
... A NEW ANIMATED TELEVISION SERIES...
MEGGAN-- THAT "PSYLOCKE" CHARACTER-- IT'S BETSY!!
... MAKES IT'S DEBUT.
GET 'EM, SPIRAL!
LEGGO!
DARLA'S IN LOVE AGAIN!
BORRRING!
YUCKO!
MOJO-- MY HERO!!!
ENTITLED WILDWAYS...
I'M SPIRAL!
AND I, GENTLE-BEINGS, AM MOJO LIFE-BRINGER!
AND I'M PSYLOCKE-- WELCOME TO OUR WORLD!
... IT'S AN INSTANT, RUNAWAY SUCCESS!
YO, BOBBY-- AH THOUGHT MAGNUM, P.I. WAS YOUR FAVORITE SHOW?!
NOT ANY-MORE, SAM. THE POOR BOY IS HOOKED!
PSYLOCKE IS SO BEAUTIFUL...
LIKE AN ANGEL!
LEONG, NGA-- DINNER!
UN MOMENT, SHAN!
WHEN OUR TV FRIENDS GO HOME!

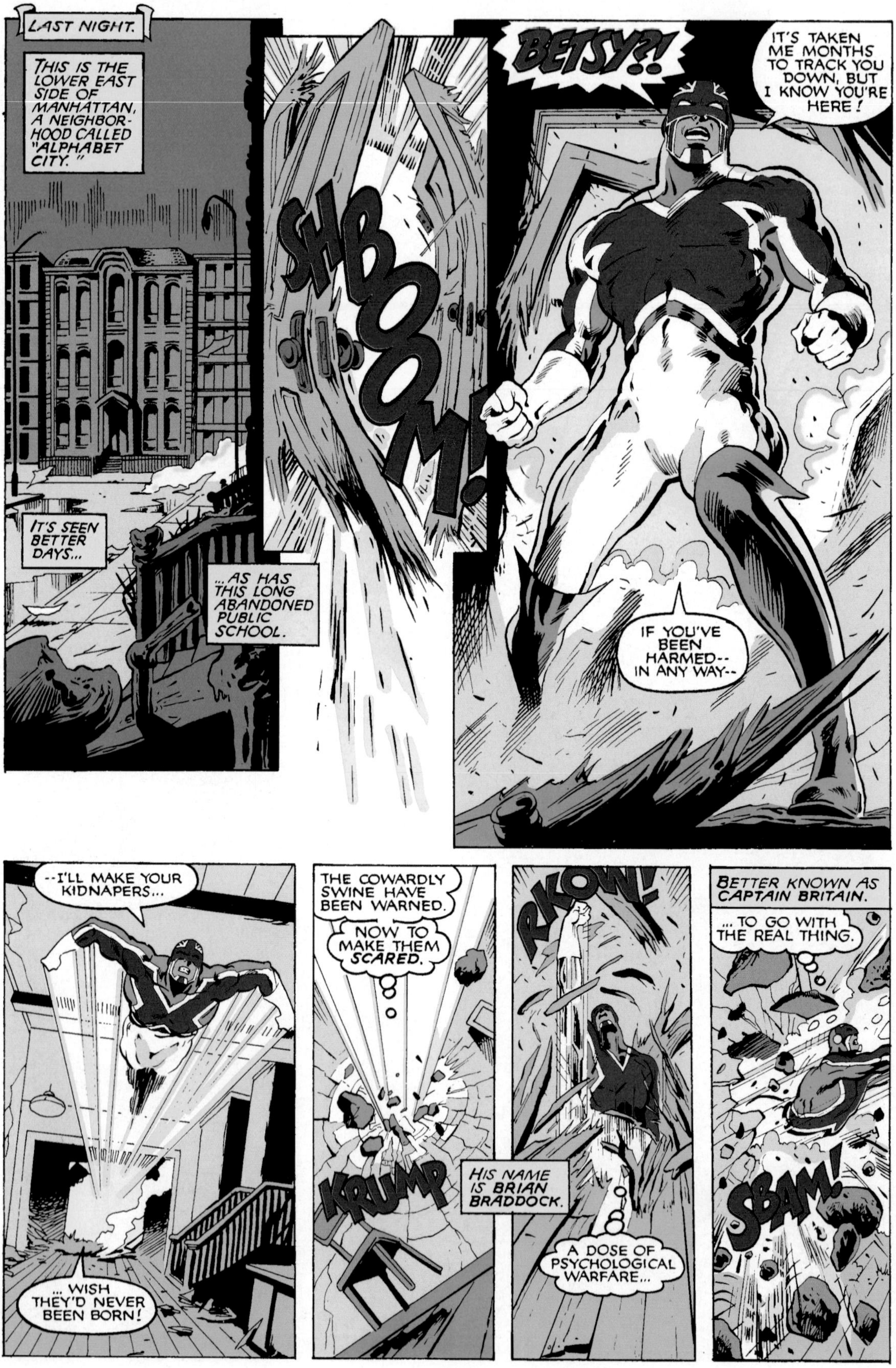
LAST NIGHT.
THIS IS THE LOWER EAST SIDE OF MANHATTAN, A NEIGHBORHOOD CALLED "ALPHABET CITY."
IT'S SEEN BETTER DAYS...
...AS HAS THIS LONG ABANDONED PUBLIC SCHOOL.
SHBOOOM!
BETSY?!
IT'S TAKEN ME MONTHS TO TRACK YOU DOWN, BUT I KNOW YOU'RE HERE!
IF YOU'VE BEEN HARMED-- IN ANY WAY--
--I'LL MAKE YOUR KIDNAPERS...
... WISH THEY'D NEVER BEEN BORN!
THE COWARDLY SWINE HAVE BEEN WARNED.
NOW TO MAKE THEM SCARED.
KRUMP
HIS NAME IS BRIAN BRADDOCK.
RKOW!
A DOSE OF PSYCHOLOGICAL WARFARE...
BETTER KNOWN AS CAPTAIN BRITAIN.
... TO GO WITH THE REAL THING.
SBAM!

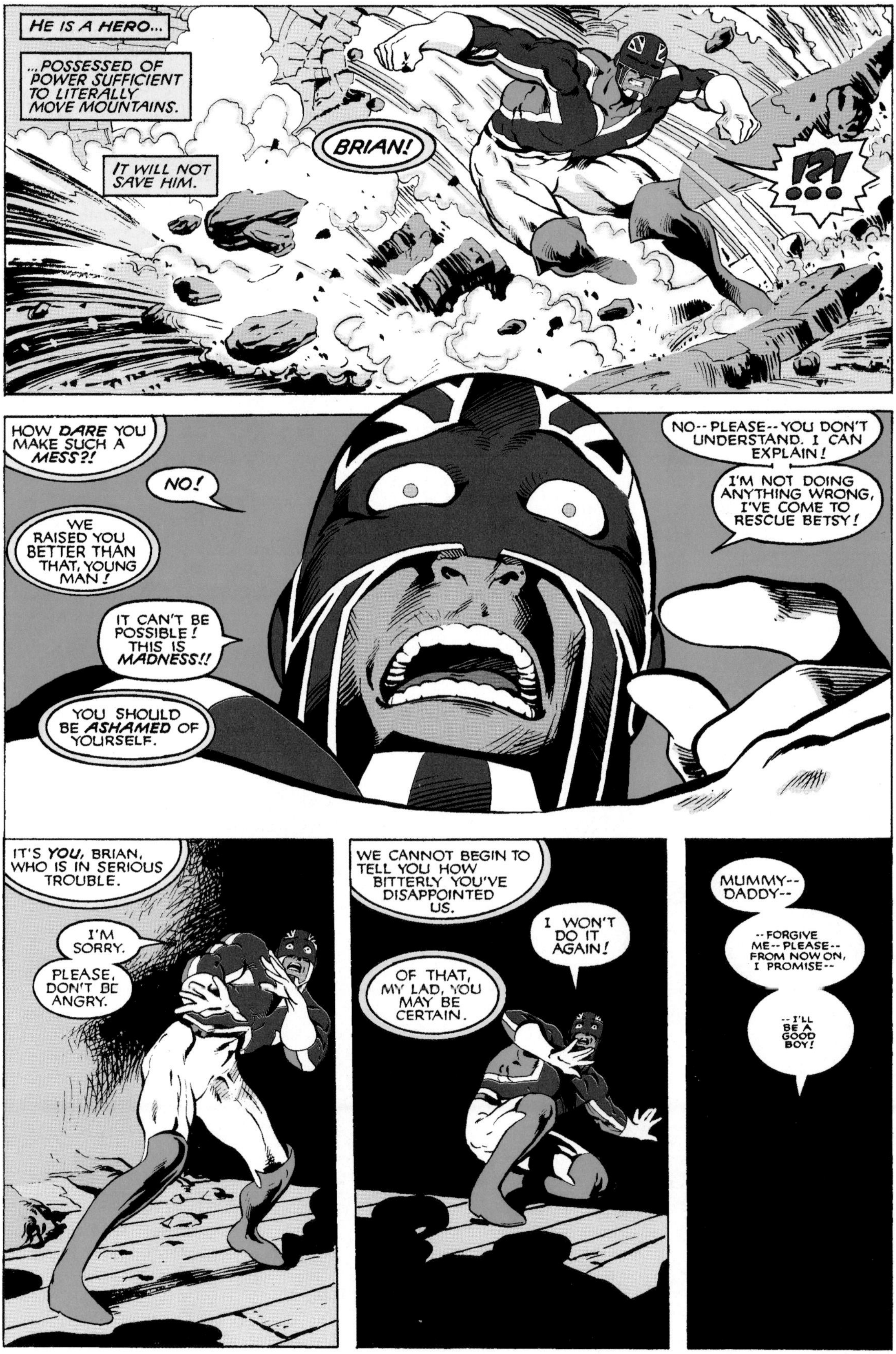

HE IS A HERO...
...POSSESSED OF POWER SUFFICIENT TO LITERALLY MOVE MOUNTAINS.
BRIAN!
IT WILL NOT SAVE HIM.
!?!
HOW DARE YOU MAKE SUCH A MESS?!
NO!
WE RAISED YOU BETTER THAN THAT, YOUNG MAN!
IT CAN'T BE POSSIBLE! THIS IS MADNESS!!
YOU SHOULD BE ASHAMED OF YOURSELF.
NO-- PLEASE-- YOU DON'T UNDERSTAND. I CAN EXPLAIN!
I'M NOT DOING ANYTHING WRONG, I'VE COME TO RESCUE BETSY!
IT'S YOU, BRIAN, WHO IS IN SERIOUS TROUBLE.
I'M SORRY.
PLEASE, DON'T BE ANGRY.
WE CANNOT BEGIN TO TELL YOU HOW BITTERLY YOU'VE DISAPPOINTED US.
I WON'T DO IT AGAIN!
OF THAT, MY LAD, YOU MAY BE CERTAIN.
MUMMY-- DADDY--
--FORGIVE ME--PLEASE-- FROM NOW ON, I PROMISE--
--I'LL BE A GOOD BOY!

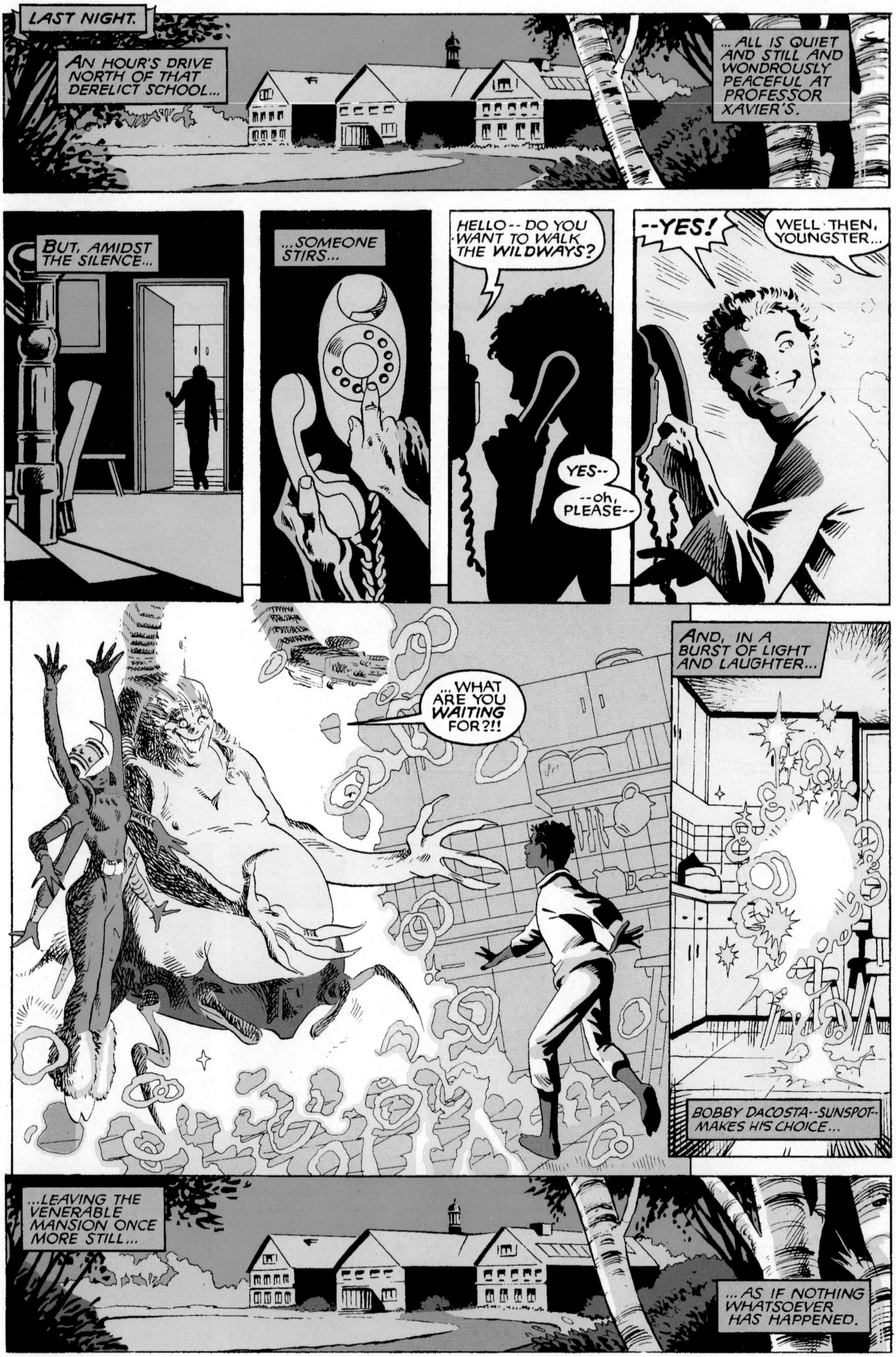
LAST NIGHT.
AN HOUR'S DRIVE NORTH OF THAT DERELICT SCHOOL...
...ALL IS QUIET AND STILL AND WONDROUSLY PEACEFUL AT PROFESSOR XAVIER'S.
BUT, AMIDST THE SILENCE...
...SOMEONE STIRS...
HELLO-- DO YOU WANT TO WALK THE WILDWAYS?
YES--
--oh, PLEASE--
--YES!
WELL THEN, YOUNGSTER...
...WHAT ARE YOU WAITING FOR?!!
AND, IN A BURST OF LIGHT AND LAUGHTER...
BOBBY DACOSTA--SUNSPOT--MAKES HIS CHOICE...
...LEAVING THE VENERABLE MANSION ONCE MORE STILL...
...AS IF NOTHING WHATSOEVER HAS HAPPENED.

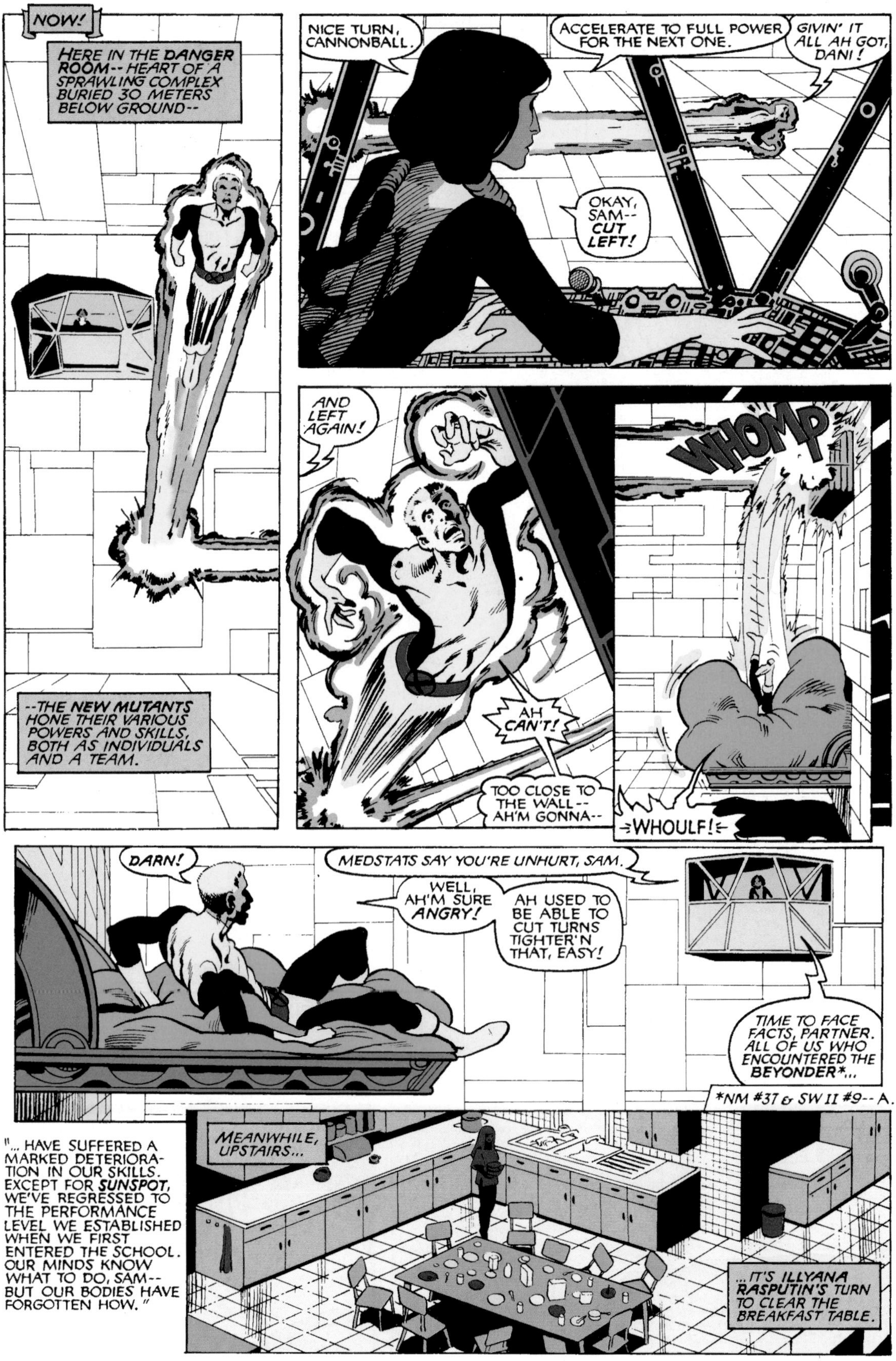
NOW!
HERE IN THE DANGER ROOM-- HEART OF A SPRAWLING COMPLEX BURIED 30 METERS BELOW GROUND--
--THE NEW MUTANTS HONE THEIR VARIOUS POWERS AND SKILLS, BOTH AS INDIVIDUALS AND A TEAM.
NICE TURN, CANNONBALL.
ACCELERATE TO FULL POWER FOR THE NEXT ONE.
GIVIN' IT ALL AH GOT, DANI!
OKAY, SAM-- CUT LEFT!
AND LEFT AGAIN!
AH CAN'T!
TOO CLOSE TO THE WALL-- AH'M GONNA--
WHOMP
WHOULF!
DARN!
MEDSTATS SAY YOU'RE UNHURT, SAM.
WELL, AH'M SURE ANGRY!
AH USED TO BE ABLE TO CUT TURNS TIGHTER'N THAT, EASY!
TIME TO FACE FACTS, PARTNER. ALL OF US WHO ENCOUNTERED THE BEYONDER*...
*NM #37 & SW II #9-- A.
"... HAVE SUFFERED A MARKED DETERIORATION IN OUR SKILLS. EXCEPT FOR SUNSPOT, WE'VE REGRESSED TO THE PERFORMANCE LEVEL WE ESTABLISHED WHEN WE FIRST ENTERED THE SCHOOL. OUR MINDS KNOW WHAT TO DO, SAM-- BUT OUR BODIES HAVE FORGOTTEN HOW."
MEANWHILE, UPSTAIRS...
...IT'S ILLYANA RASPUTIN'S TURN TO CLEAR THE BREAKFAST TABLE.

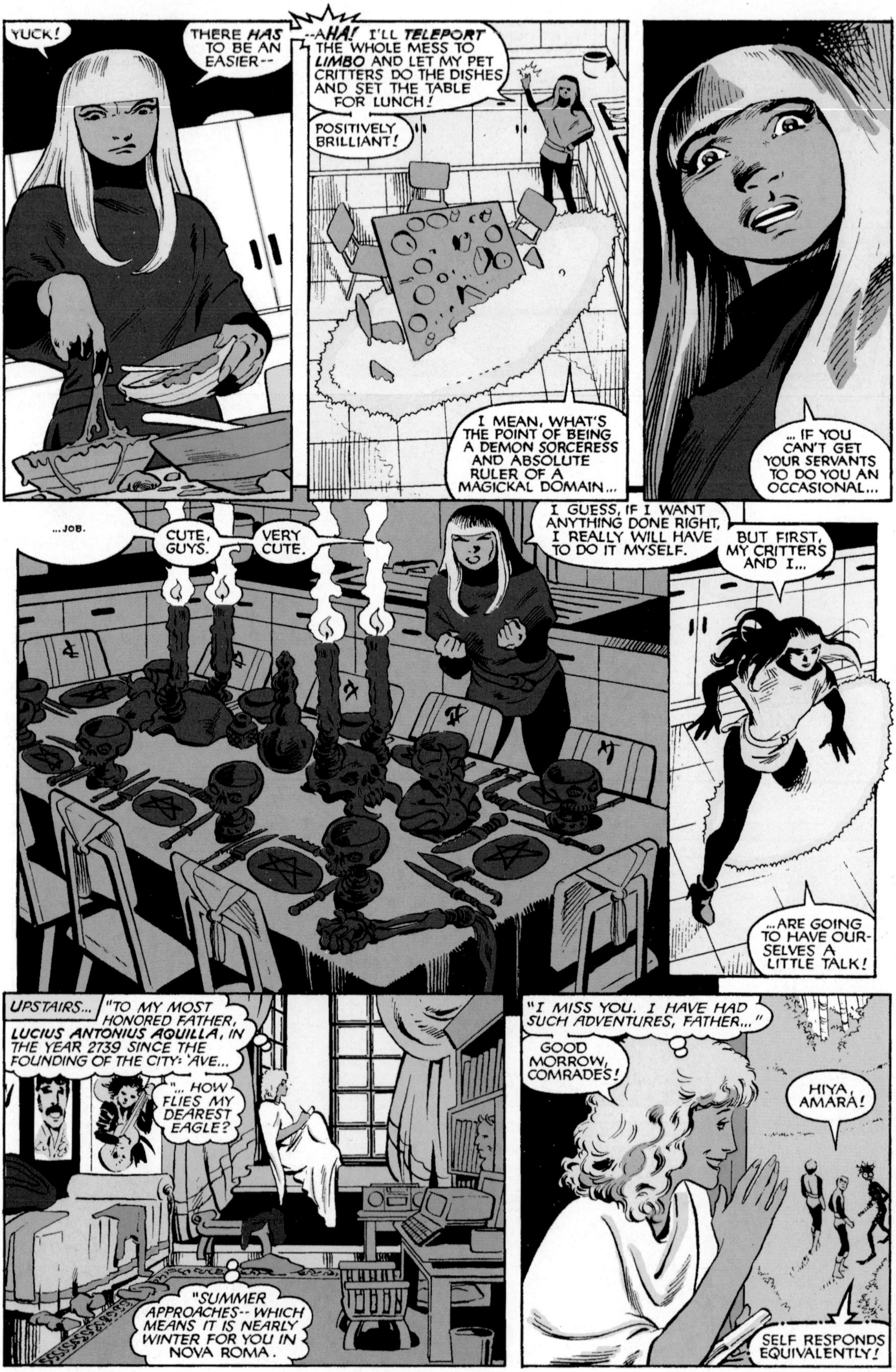
YUCK!
THERE HAS TO BE AN EASIER--
--AHA! I'LL TELEPORT THE WHOLE MESS TO LIMBO AND LET MY PET CRITTERS DO THE DISHES AND SET THE TABLE FOR LUNCH!
POSITIVELY BRILLIANT!
I MEAN, WHAT'S THE POINT OF BEING A DEMON SORCERESS AND ABSOLUTE RULER OF A MAGICKAL DOMAIN...
...IF YOU CAN'T GET YOUR SERVANTS TO DO YOU AN OCCASIONAL...
...JOB.
CUTE, GUYS.
VERY CUTE.
I GUESS, IF I WANT ANYTHING DONE RIGHT, I REALLY WILL HAVE TO DO IT MYSELF.
BUT FIRST, MY CRITTERS AND I...
...ARE GOING TO HAVE OURSELVES A LITTLE TALK!
UPSTAIRS...
"TO MY MOST HONORED FATHER, LUCIUS ANTONIUS AQUILLA, IN THE YEAR 2739 SINCE THE FOUNDING OF THE CITY: 'AVE...
"...HOW FLIES MY DEAREST EAGLE?
"SUMMER APPROACHES-- WHICH MEANS IT IS NEARLY WINTER FOR YOU IN NOVA ROMA.
"I MISS YOU. I HAVE HAD SUCH ADVENTURES, FATHER..."
GOOD MORROW, COMRADES!
HIYA, AMARA!
SELF RESPONDS EQUIVALENTLY!

WHAT ARE YOU ABOUT?

GONNA CLEAR SOME DEAD TREES. WANT TO HELP?

WHEN I HAVE FINISHED MY LETTER.

SEE YOU LATER, THEN!

GIVE YOUR FATHER MY BEST WISHES, AMARA!

IS WORKSUIT SATISFACTORY, SELFRIENDDOUG?

LOOKS GOOD, WARLOCK, AND FEELS BETTER!

IS IT MY IMAGINATION, PAL...

...OR IS BOBBY ACTING NICE AS CAN BE TO EVERYONE TODAY?

QUERY: IS SUCH BEHAVIOR UNDESIRABLE?

UNCHARACTERISTIC.

YOU GRAB THE ROOTS, BOBBY.

I'LL TAKE THE CROWN...

SELFSENSORS REGISTER MINOR ANOMALIES IN SUNSPOT'S PHYSIOLOGY.

YOU MEAN HE'S SICK?

HEY, BOBBY, YOU SURE YOU'RE UP TO THIS?

OF COURSE, DOUGLAS. READY WHEN YOU ARE.

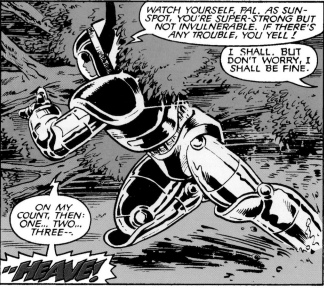

WATCH YOURSELF, PAL. AS SUNSPOT, YOU'RE SUPER-STRONG BUT NOT INVULNERABLE. IF THERE'S ANY TROUBLE, YOU YELL!

I SHALL. BUT DON'T WORRY, I SHALL BE FINE.

ON MY COUNT, THEN: ONE... TWO... THREE--

"HEAVE!

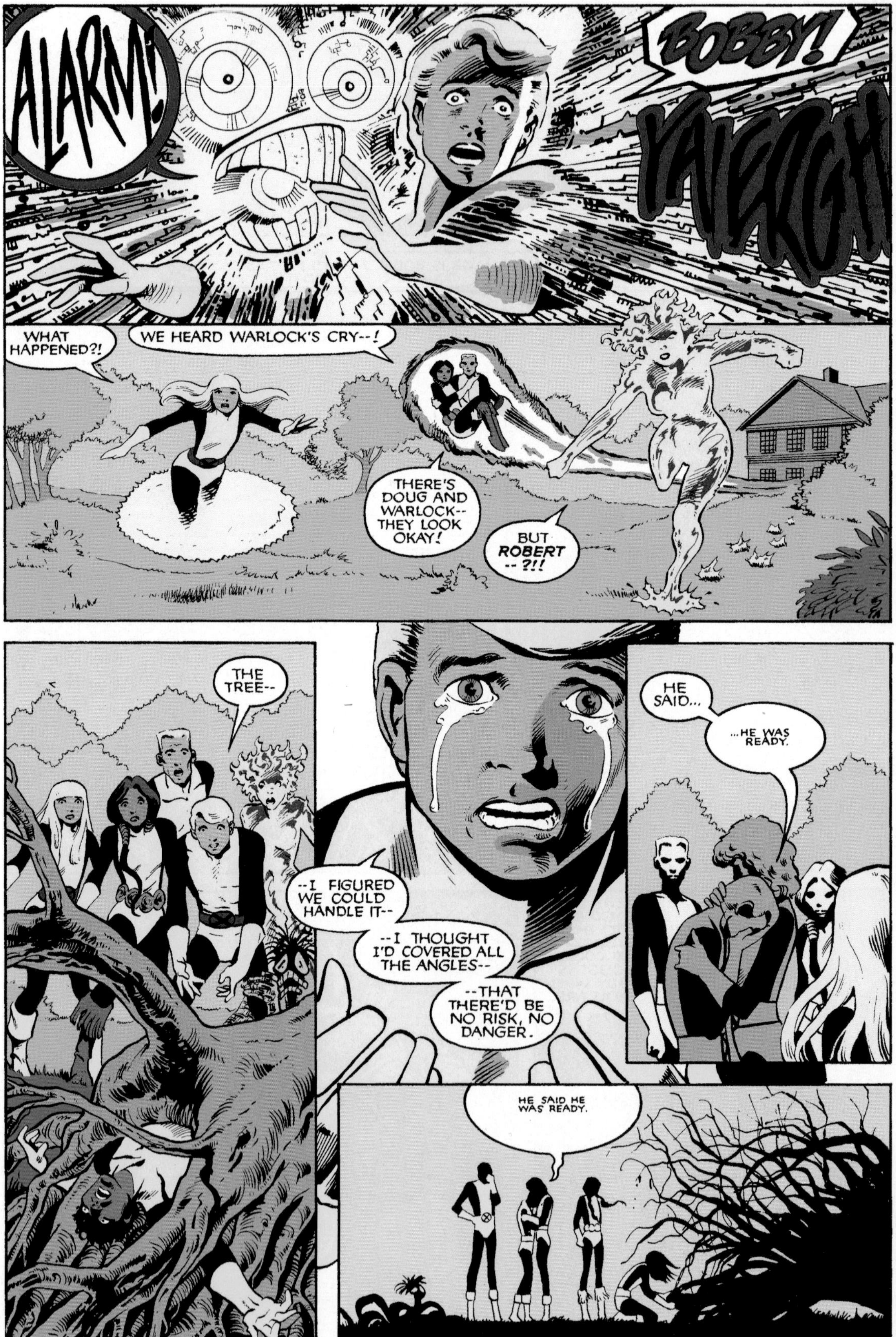
ALARM!
BOBBY!
YAAAAGH!
WHAT HAPPENED?!
WE HEARD WARLOCK'S CRY--!
THERE'S DOUG AND WARLOCK-- THEY LOOK OKAY!
BUT ROBERT --?!!
THE TREE--
--I FIGURED WE COULD HANDLE IT--
--I THOUGHT I'D COVERED ALL THE ANGLES--
--THAT THERE'D BE NO RISK, NO DANGER.
HE SAID...
...HE WAS READY.
HE SAID HE WAS READY.

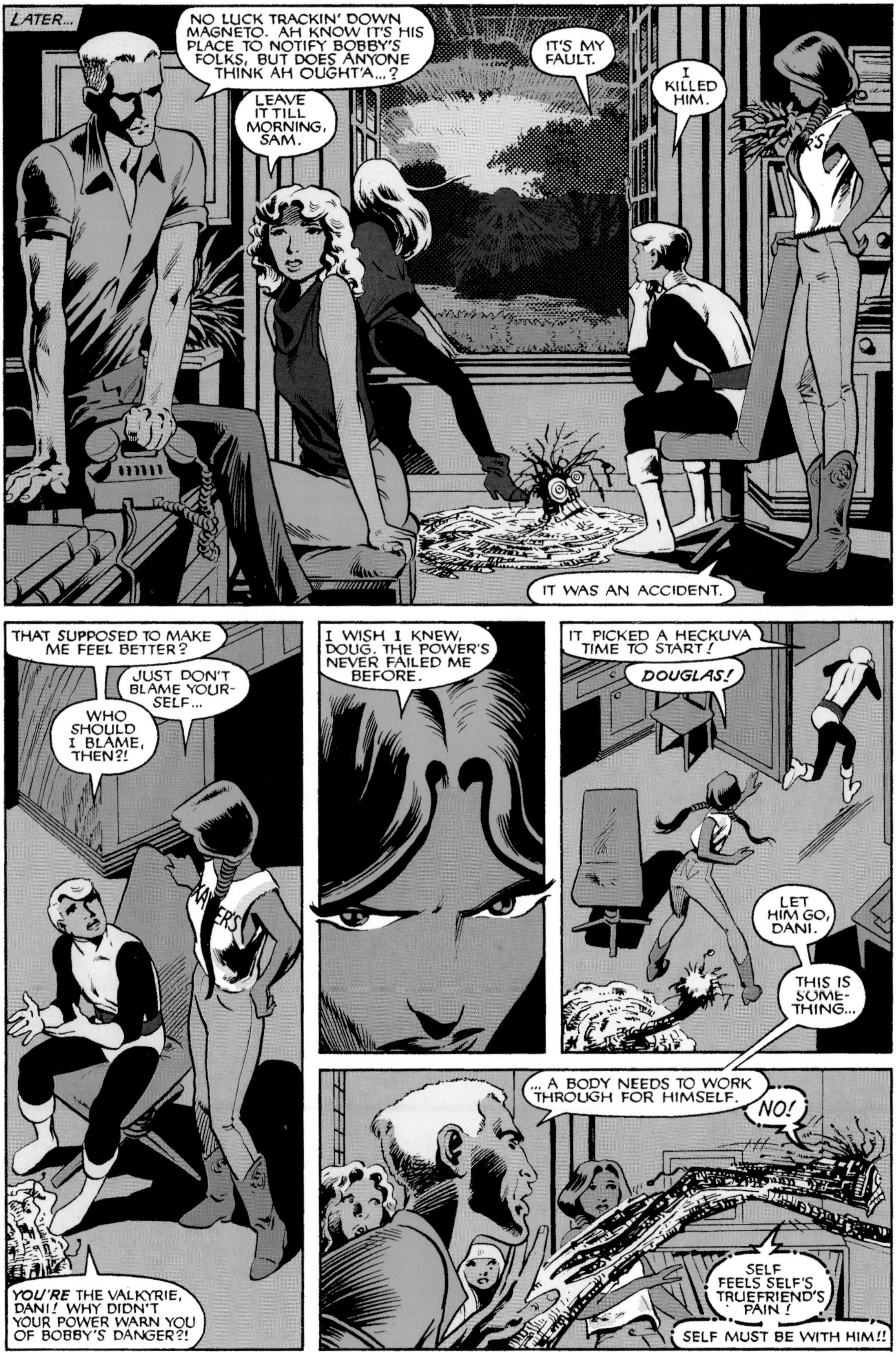
LATER...
NO LUCK TRACKIN' DOWN MAGNETO. AH KNOW IT'S HIS PLACE TO NOTIFY BOBBY'S FOLKS, BUT DOES ANYONE THINK AH OUGHT'A...?
LEAVE IT TILL MORNING, SAM.
IT'S MY FAULT.
I KILLED HIM.
IT WAS AN ACCIDENT.
THAT SUPPOSED TO MAKE ME FEEL BETTER?
JUST DON'T BLAME YOURSELF...
WHO SHOULD I BLAME, THEN?!
YOU'RE THE VALKYRIE, DANI! WHY DIDN'T YOUR POWER WARN YOU OF BOBBY'S DANGER?!
I WISH I KNEW, DOUG. THE POWER'S NEVER FAILED ME BEFORE.
IT PICKED A HECKUVA TIME TO START!
DOUGLAS!
LET HIM GO, DANI.
THIS IS SOMETHING...
... A BODY NEEDS TO WORK THROUGH FOR HIMSELF.
NO!
SELF FEELS SELF'S TRUEFRIEND'S PAIN!
SELF MUST BE WITH HIM!!

BOBBY'S IN HERE. FUNNY, INFIRMARY NEVER FELT SO COLD-- OR SCARY-- BEFORE.

HI, PAL.

THIS IS CRAZY.

I KNOW...

GHOULISH.

...WE NEVER REALLY GOT ON.

DON'T DO THIS TO YOURSELF! I...

...I'M SORRY, ROBERTO.

PLEASE...

...I NEVER MEANT...

...I'M REALLY...

I TRIED...

...FORGIVE ME!

FRIENDOUG?

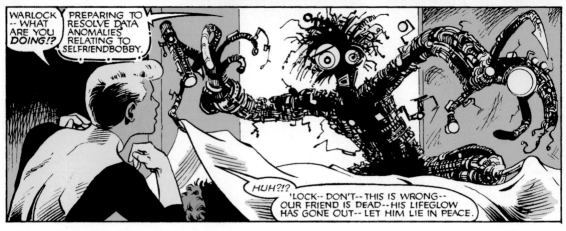

WARLOCK -- WHAT ARE YOU DOING!?

PREPARING TO RESOLVE DATA ANOMALIES RELATING TO SELFRIENDBOBBY.

HUH?!?

'LOCK-- DON'T-- THIS IS WRONG-- OUR FRIEND IS DEAD-- HIS LIFEGLOW HAS GONE OUT-- LET HIM LIE IN PEACE.

STATEMENT ERROR. FRIENDBOBBYSUNSPOT'S LIFE-GLOW CANNOT HAVE BEEN EXTINGUISHED BECAUSE PROPER LIFEGLOW DID NOT PREVIOUSLY EXIST. RADIANCE SIMILAR BUT DIFFERENT.

WHAT ARE YOU SAYING...

...THAT THIS ISN'T BOBBY?!

UNKNOWN. REMAINS TO BE ESTABLISHED. WILL SELFFRIENDOUG AID SELF IN PERFORMING ANALYSIS?

YOU'RE REALLY DETERMINED.

FRIENDOUG ALWAYS STATES: "WHEN SOMETHING FEELS FUNNY, YA GOTTA WORK IT OUT."

ALL RIGHT, PARTNER. I'LL FOLLOW YOUR LEAD.

AND...

UNBELIEVABLE!

WE HAD TO PROBE DOWN TO THE SUB-ATOMIC LEVEL TO BE SURE-- BUT THERE'S NO MORE DENYING IT. HE'S A FAKE!

AN ALMOST PERFECT DUPLICATE. AN INCREDIBLY SOPHISTICATED ANDROID!

IT MIRRORED BOBBY'S FORM, BUT EVIDENTLY NOT HIS SUBSTANCE. ITS SIMULATED GENES COULDN'T MIMIC HIS MUTANT TRANSFORMATION TO SUNSPOT. THAT'S WHAT TRIPPED HIM. OTHERWISE, WE'D NEVER HAVE GUESSED-- ESPECIALLY IF HE RESIGNED FROM THE SCHOOL.

LOGICAL CONCLUSION.

COLD COMFORT, BUDDY.

SOMEONE WENT TO A LOT OF TROUBLE TO PULL THIS SWITCH.

CAN'T BE FOR A GOOD REASON.

THEN, SELF AND SELFFRIENDTEAMMATES SHALL LEARN REASON, FIND MISSING SELFFRIEND BOBBYSUNSPOT AND RESCUE HIM.

JUST LIKE THAT? YOU MAKE IT SOUND SO EASY.

DOUG! WARLOCK?!

WHAT THE DEVIL DO YOU BOYS THINK YOU'RE DOING?!!

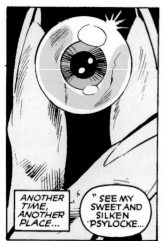

ANOTHER TIME, ANOTHER PLACE...

" SEE MY SWEET AND SILKEN PSYLOCKE...

"...HOW GENEROUS IS YOUR LORD AND MASTER, MOJO.

"NEW EYES-- *WONDROUS* EYES-- HAVE I MADE FOR YOU...

"... WHOSE SUBSTANCE BLENDS YOUR SOUL WITH MINE.

NOW WE'LL *NEVER* BE APART!

SHE'S THRILLED.

OF COURSE.

JUST AS *YOU* WERE, DANCER...

... WHEN I MADE YOU WHAT YOU ARE.

WHAT I AM, MOJO, IS NOT WHAT I WAS...

...NOR WHAT I WILL BE--

--WHEN I DANCE YOU OFF YOUR THRONE AND MAKE IT *MINE!*

YOU HAVE YOUR PRECIOUS TOYS, SCREWLOOSE. WHAT COMES NEXT?

DO YOU INTEND TO STAND HERE WATCHING, 'TILL THEY ROT?

ROT? *ROT?!*

NOBODY ROTS, UNLESS *I* SAY SO!

AND ANYONE WHO TRIES...

...WILL DIE TO REGRET IT.

AN ARTISTE, SPIRAL, CANNOT CREATE *EPICS* WITHOUT PROPER TOOLS

I'M *BORED* WITH THE ONES AT HOME.

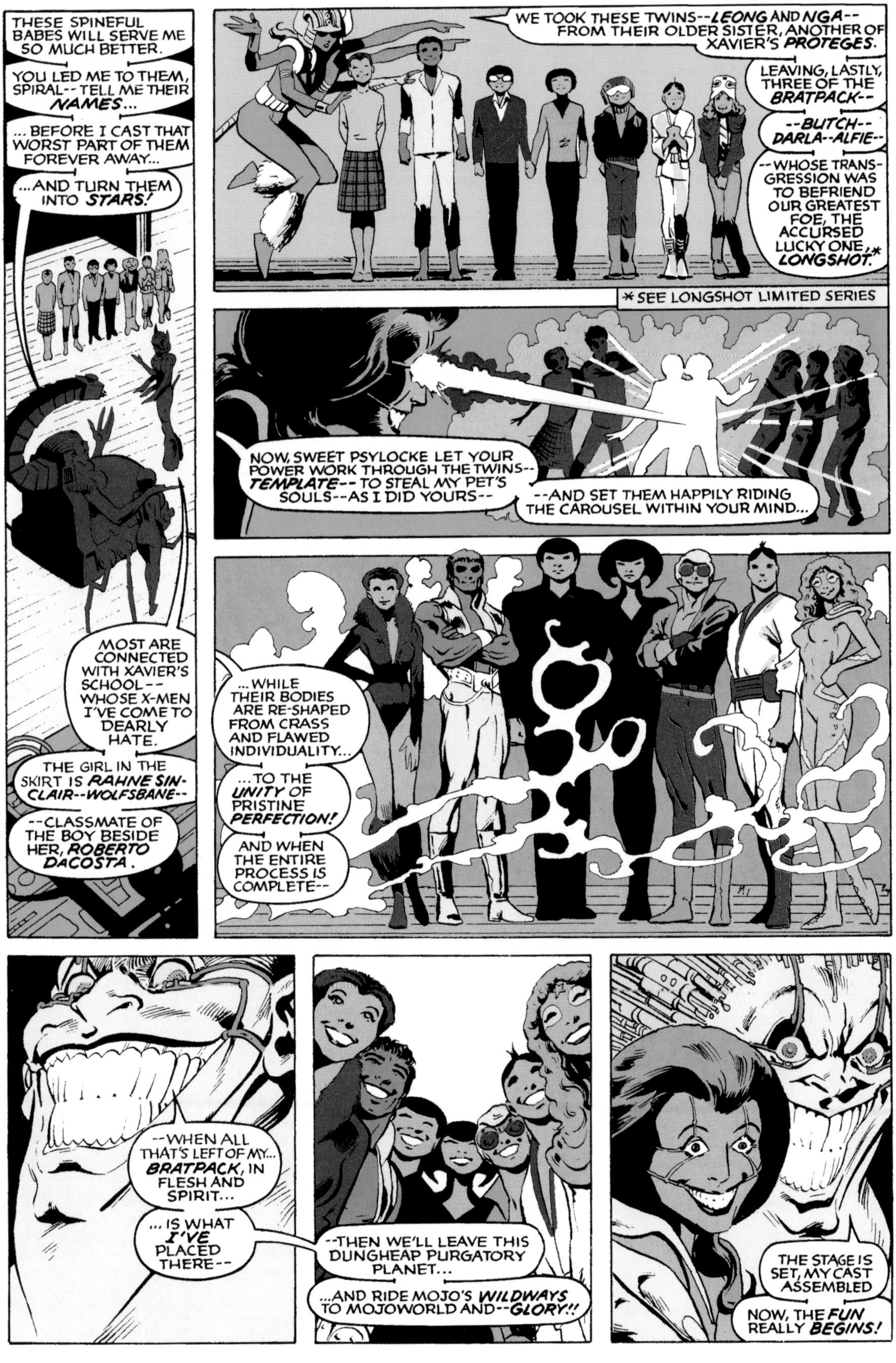
THESE SPINEFUL BABES WILL SERVE ME SO MUCH BETTER.
YOU LED ME TO THEM, SPIRAL-- TELL ME THEIR NAMES...
... BEFORE I CAST THAT WORST PART OF THEM FOREVER AWAY...
...AND TURN THEM INTO STARS!
WE TOOK THESE TWINS--LEONG AND NGA-- FROM THEIR OLDER SISTER, ANOTHER OF XAVIER'S PROTEGES.
LEAVING, LASTLY, THREE OF THE BRATPACK--
--BUTCH-- DARLA--ALFIE--
--WHOSE TRANSGRESSION WAS TO BEFRIEND OUR GREATEST FOE, THE ACCURSED LUCKY ONE, LONGSHOT.*
*SEE LONGSHOT LIMITED SERIES
NOW, SWEET PSYLOCKE LET YOUR POWER WORK THROUGH THE TWINS-- TEMPLATE-- TO STEAL MY PET'S SOULS--AS I DID YOURS--
--AND SET THEM HAPPILY RIDING THE CAROUSEL WITHIN YOUR MIND...
MOST ARE CONNECTED WITH XAVIER'S SCHOOL-- WHOSE X-MEN I'VE COME TO DEARLY HATE.
THE GIRL IN THE SKIRT IS RAHNE SINCLAIR--WOLFSBANE--
--CLASSMATE OF THE BOY BESIDE HER, ROBERTO DACOSTA.
...WHILE THEIR BODIES ARE RE-SHAPED FROM CRASS AND FLAWED INDIVIDUALITY...
...TO THE UNITY OF PRISTINE PERFECTION!
AND WHEN THE ENTIRE PROCESS IS COMPLETE--
--WHEN ALL THAT'S LEFT OF MY... BRATPACK, IN FLESH AND SPIRIT...
...IS WHAT I'VE PLACED THERE--
--THEN WE'LL LEAVE THIS DUNGHEAP PURGATORY PLANET...
...AND RIDE MOJO'S WILDWAYS TO MOJOWORLD AND--GLORY!!
THE STAGE IS SET, MY CAST ASSEMBLED
NOW, THE FUN REALLY BEGINS!

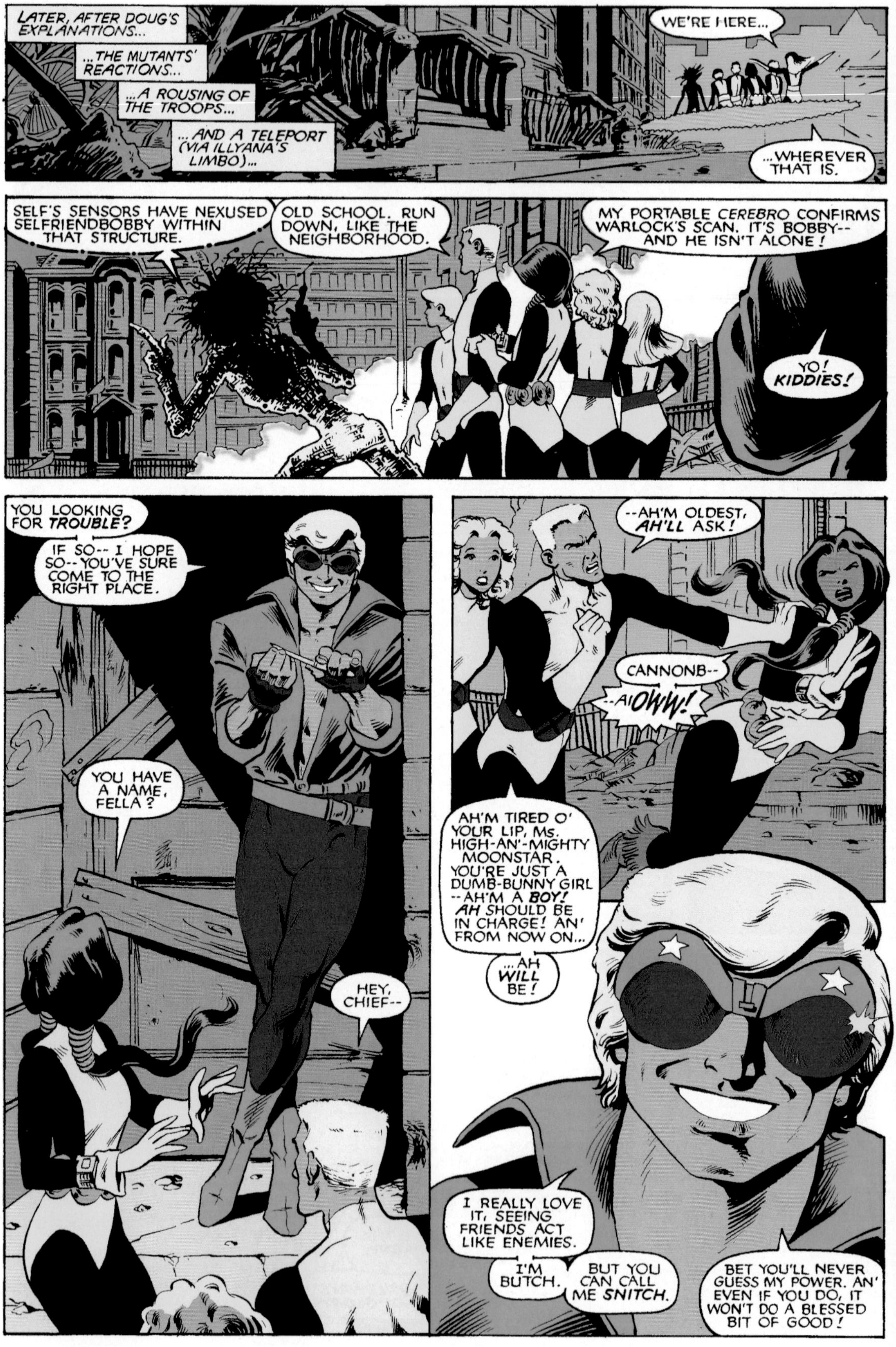
LATER, AFTER DOUG'S EXPLANATIONS...
...THE MUTANTS' REACTIONS...
...A ROUSING OF THE TROOPS...
...AND A TELEPORT (VIA ILLYANA'S LIMBO)...
WE'RE HERE...
...WHEREVER THAT IS.
SELF'S SENSORS HAVE NEXUSED SELFRIENDBOBBY WITHIN THAT STRUCTURE.
OLD SCHOOL. RUN DOWN, LIKE THE NEIGHBORHOOD.
MY PORTABLE CEREBRO CONFIRMS WARLOCK'S SCAN. IT'S BOBBY-- AND HE ISN'T ALONE!
YO! KIDDIES!
YOU LOOKING FOR TROUBLE?
IF SO-- I HOPE SO-- YOU'VE SURE COME TO THE RIGHT PLACE.
YOU HAVE A NAME, FELLA?
HEY, CHIEF--
--AH'M OLDEST, AH'LL ASK!
CANNONB--
--AIOWW!
AH'M TIRED O' YOUR LIP, Ms. HIGH-AN'-MIGHTY MOONSTAR. YOU'RE JUST A DUMB-BUNNY GIRL --AH'M A BOY! AH SHOULD BE IN CHARGE! AN' FROM NOW ON...
...AH WILL BE!
I REALLY LOVE IT, SEEING FRIENDS ACT LIKE ENEMIES.
I'M BUTCH.
BUT YOU CAN CALL ME SNITCH.
BET YOU'LL NEVER GUESS MY POWER. AN' EVEN IF YOU DO, IT WON'T DO A BLESSED BIT OF GOOD!

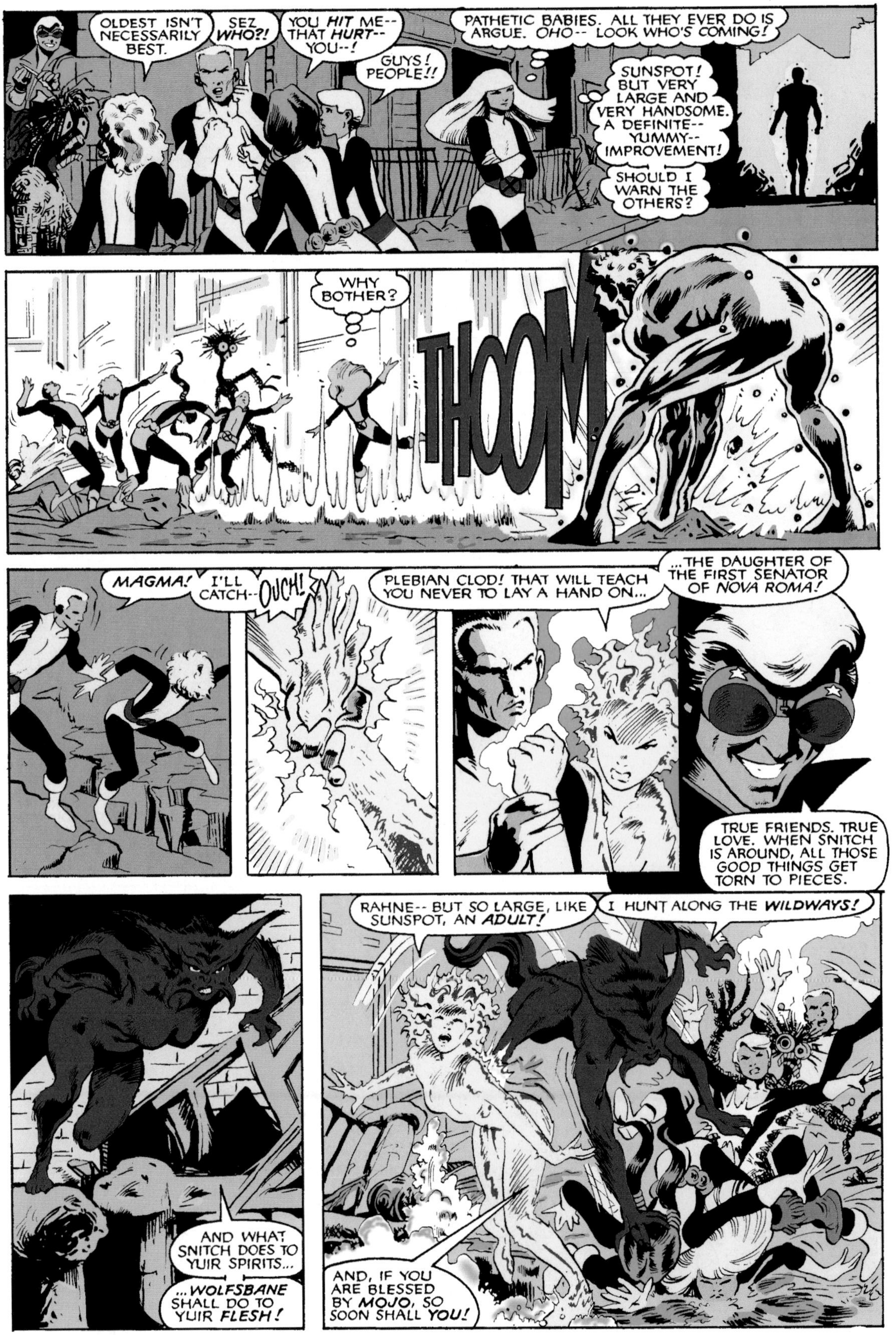
OLDEST ISN'T NECESSARILY BEST.
SEZ WHO?!
YOU HIT ME-- THAT HURT-- YOU--!
GUYS! PEOPLE!!
PATHETIC BABIES. ALL THEY EVER DO IS ARGUE. OHO-- LOOK WHO'S COMING!
SUNSPOT! BUT VERY LARGE AND VERY HANDSOME. A DEFINITE-- YUMMY-- IMPROVEMENT!
SHOULD I WARN THE OTHERS?
WHY BOTHER?
THOOM
MAGMA!
I'LL CATCH--
OUCH!
PLEBIAN CLOD! THAT WILL TEACH YOU NEVER TO LAY A HAND ON...
...THE DAUGHTER OF THE FIRST SENATOR OF NOVA ROMA!
TRUE FRIENDS. TRUE LOVE. WHEN SNITCH IS AROUND, ALL THOSE GOOD THINGS GET TORN TO PIECES.
AND WHAT SNITCH DOES TO YUIR SPIRITS...
...WOLFSBANE SHALL DO TO YUIR FLESH!
RAHNE-- BUT SO LARGE, LIKE SUNSPOT, AN ADULT!
I HUNT ALONG THE WILDWAYS!
AND, IF YOU ARE BLESSED BY MOJO, SO SOON SHALL YOU!

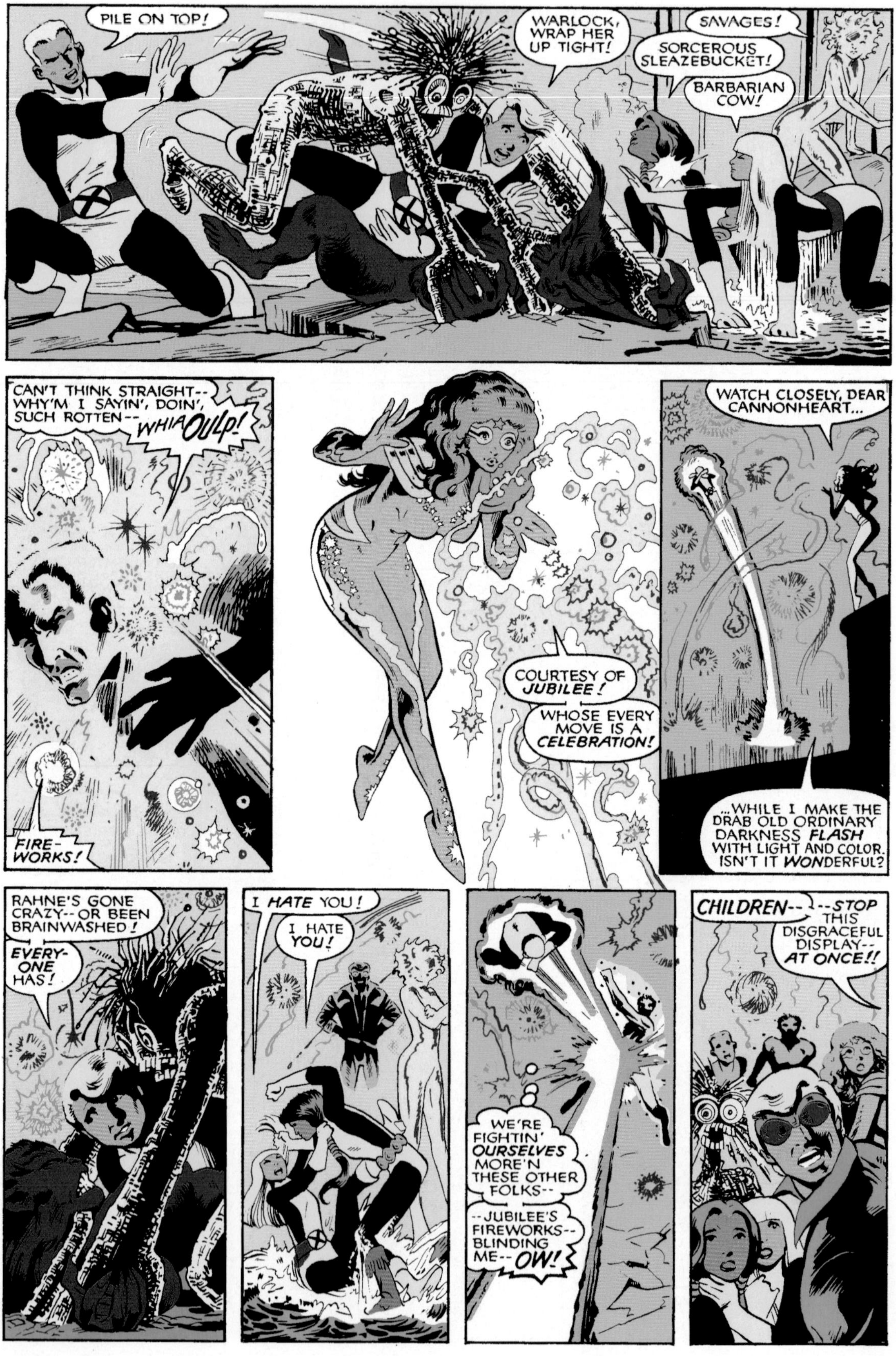
PILE ON TOP!
WARLOCK, WRAP HER UP TIGHT!
SAVAGES!
SORCEROUS SLEAZEBUCKET!
BARBARIAN COW!
CAN'T THINK STRAIGHT-- WHY'M I SAYIN', DOIN', SUCH ROTTEN--
WHIAOULP!
FIRE-WORKS!
COURTESY OF JUBILEE!
WHOSE EVERY MOVE IS A CELEBRATION!
WATCH CLOSELY, DEAR CANNONHEART...
...WHILE I MAKE THE DRAB OLD ORDINARY DARKNESS FLASH WITH LIGHT AND COLOR. ISN'T IT WONDERFUL?
RAHNE'S GONE CRAZY--OR BEEN BRAINWASHED!
EVERY-ONE HAS!
I HATE YOU!
I HATE YOU!
WE'RE FIGHTIN' OURSELVES MORE'N THESE OTHER FOLKS--
--JUBILEE'S FIREWORKS-- BLINDING ME--OW!
CHILDREN--
--STOP THIS DISGRACEFUL DISPLAY-- AT ONCE!!

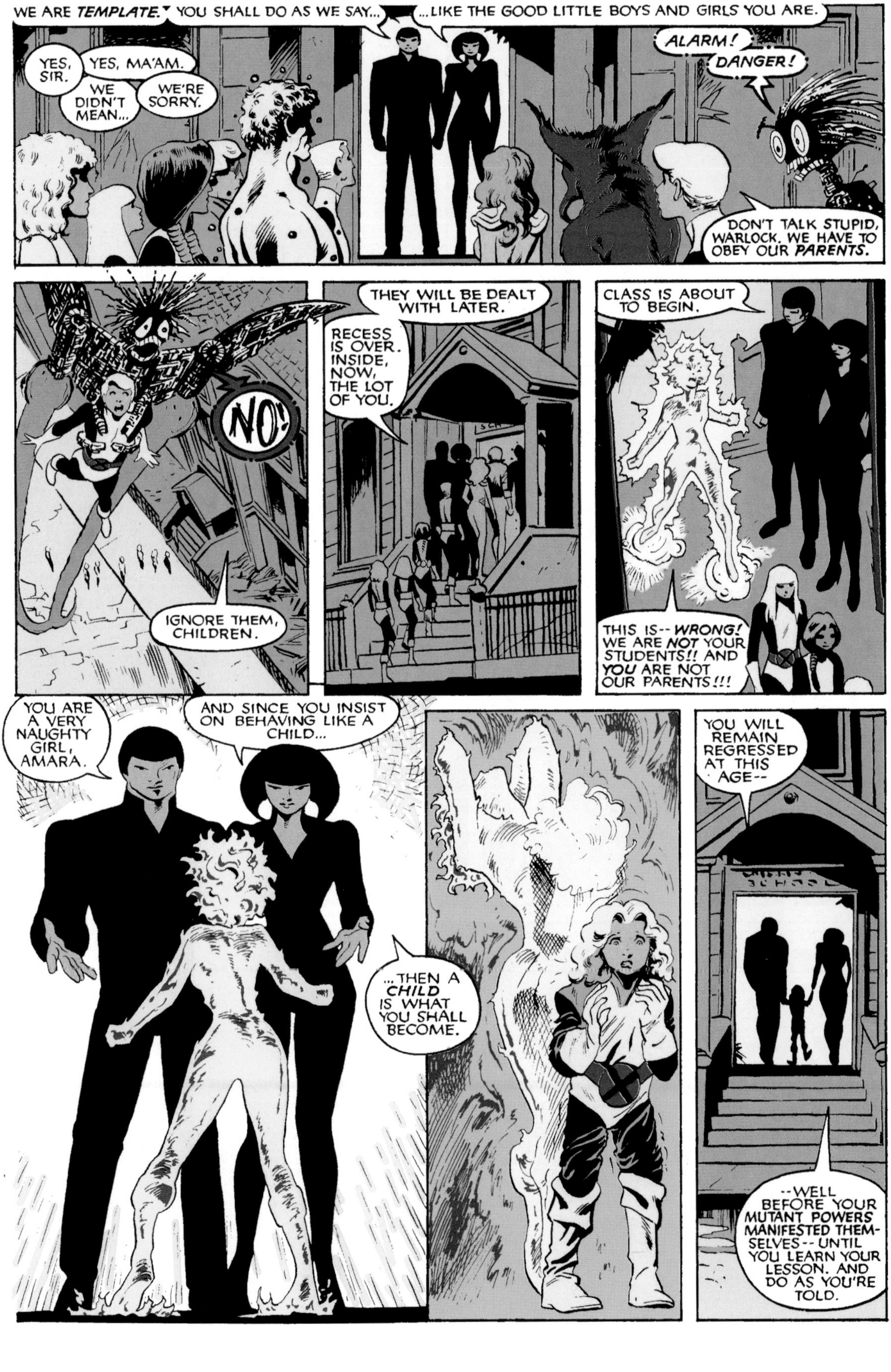
WE ARE TEMPLATE.* YOU SHALL DO AS WE SAY...
...LIKE THE GOOD LITTLE BOYS AND GIRLS YOU ARE.
YES, SIR.
YES, MA'AM.
WE DIDN'T MEAN...
WE'RE SORRY.
ALARM!
DANGER!
DON'T TALK STUPID, WARLOCK. WE HAVE TO OBEY OUR PARENTS.
NO!
IGNORE THEM, CHILDREN.
THEY WILL BE DEALT WITH LATER.
RECESS IS OVER. INSIDE, NOW, THE LOT OF YOU.
CLASS IS ABOUT TO BEGIN.
THIS IS--WRONG! WE ARE NOT YOUR STUDENTS!! AND YOU ARE NOT OUR PARENTS!!!
YOU ARE A VERY NAUGHTY GIRL, AMARA.
AND SINCE YOU INSIST ON BEHAVING LIKE A CHILD...
...THEN A CHILD IS WHAT YOU SHALL BECOME.
YOU WILL REMAIN REGRESSED AT THIS AGE--
--WELL BEFORE YOUR MUTANT POWERS MANIFESTED THEMSELVES--UNTIL YOU LEARN YOUR LESSON. AND DO AS YOU'RE TOLD.

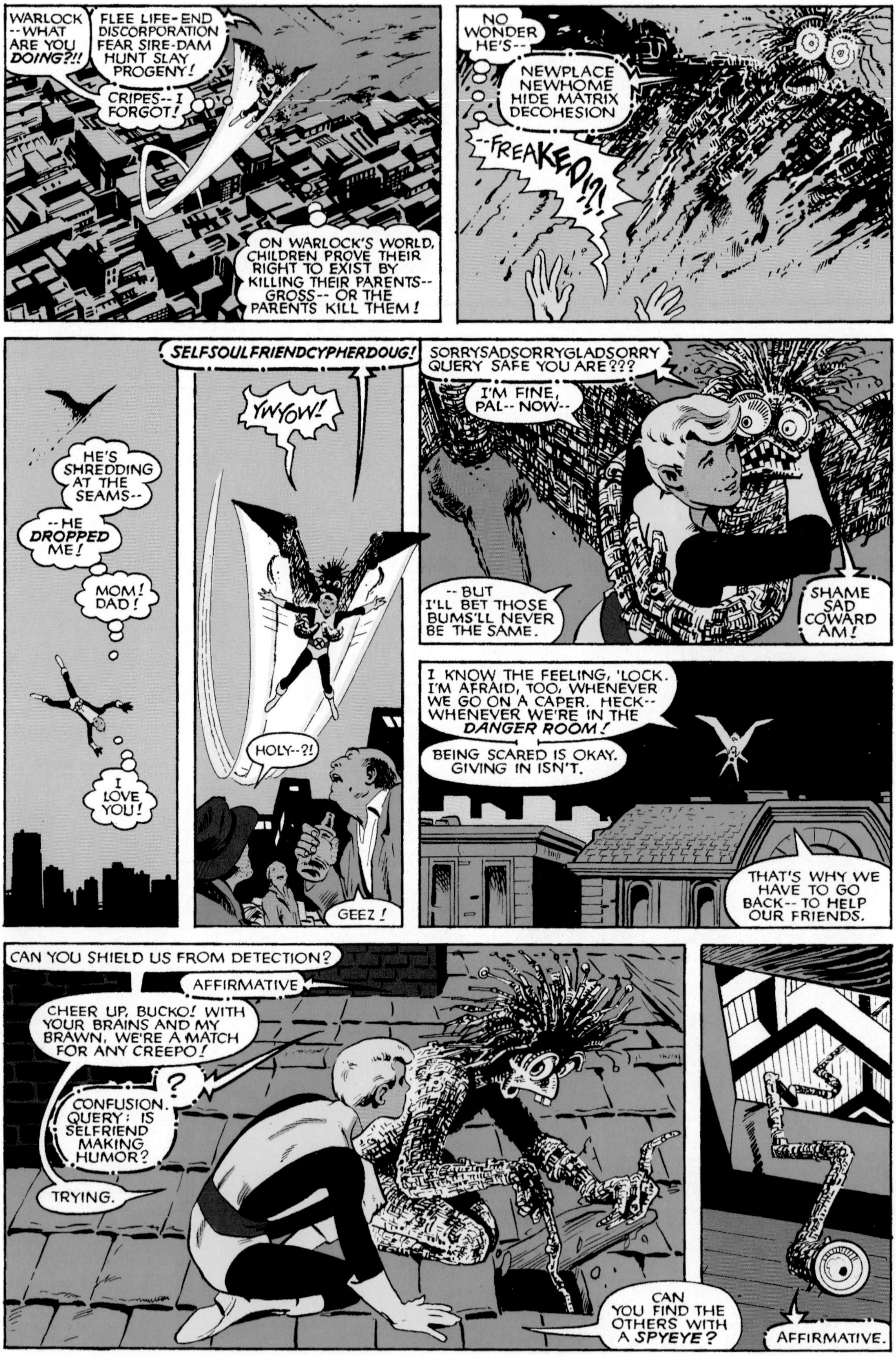
WARLOCK --WHAT ARE YOU DOING?!!
FLEE LIFE-END DISCORPORATION FEAR SIRE-DAM HUNT SLAY PROGENY!
CRIPES-- I FORGOT!
ON WARLOCK'S WORLD, CHILDREN PROVE THEIR RIGHT TO EXIST BY KILLING THEIR PARENTS-- GROSS-- OR THE PARENTS KILL THEM!
NO WONDER HE'S--
NEWPLACE NEWHOME HIDE MATRIX DECOHESION
--FREAKED!?!
HE'S SHREDDING AT THE SEAMS--
--HE DROPPED ME!
MOM! DAD!
I LOVE YOU!
SELFSOULFRIENDCYPHERDOUG!
YWYOW!
HOLY--?!
GEEZ!
SORRYSADSORRYGLADSORRY QUERY SAFE YOU ARE???
I'M FINE, PAL-- NOW--
--BUT I'LL BET THOSE BUMS'LL NEVER BE THE SAME.
SHAME SAD COWARD AM!
I KNOW THE FEELING, 'LOCK. I'M AFRAID, TOO, WHENEVER WE GO ON A CAPER. HECK-- WHENEVER WE'RE IN THE DANGER ROOM!
BEING SCARED IS OKAY. GIVING IN ISN'T.
THAT'S WHY WE HAVE TO GO BACK-- TO HELP OUR FRIENDS.
CAN YOU SHIELD US FROM DETECTION?
AFFIRMATIVE
CHEER UP, BUCKO! WITH YOUR BRAINS AND MY BRAWN, WE'RE A MATCH FOR ANY CREEPO!
?
CONFUSION. QUERY: IS SELFRIEND MAKING HUMOR?
TRYING.
CAN YOU FIND THE OTHERS WITH A SPYEYE?
AFFIRMATIVE.

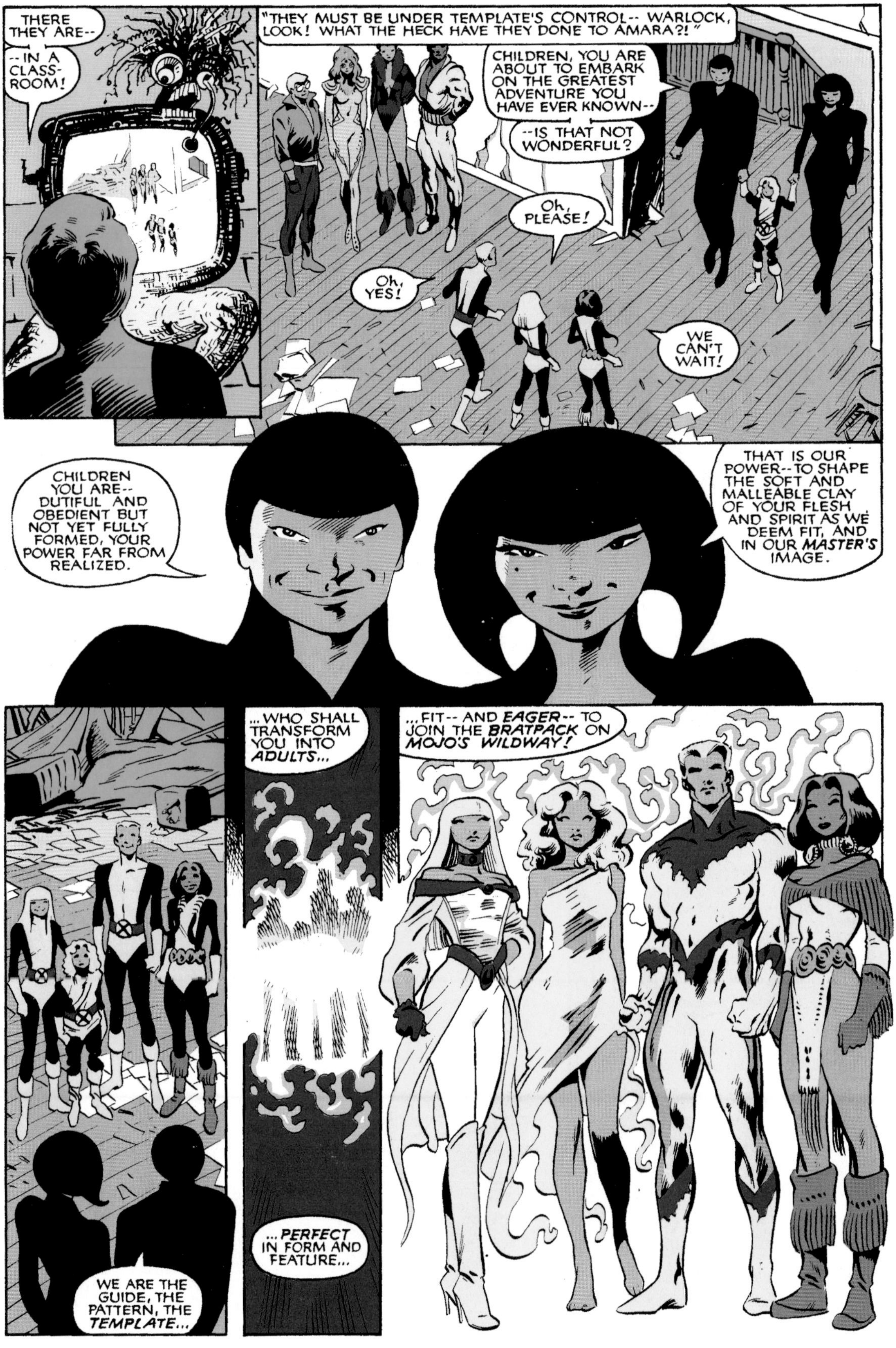
THERE THEY ARE--
--IN A CLASSROOM!
"THEY MUST BE UNDER TEMPLATE'S CONTROL-- WARLOCK, LOOK! WHAT THE HECK HAVE THEY DONE TO AMARA?!"
CHILDREN, YOU ARE ABOUT TO EMBARK ON THE GREATEST ADVENTURE YOU HAVE EVER KNOWN--
--IS THAT NOT WONDERFUL?
Oh, PLEASE!
Oh, YES!
WE CAN'T WAIT!
CHILDREN YOU ARE-- DUTIFUL AND OBEDIENT BUT NOT YET FULLY FORMED, YOUR POWER FAR FROM REALIZED.
THAT IS OUR POWER--TO SHAPE THE SOFT AND MALLEABLE CLAY OF YOUR FLESH AND SPIRIT AS WE DEEM FIT, AND IN OUR MASTER'S IMAGE.
WE ARE THE GUIDE, THE PATTERN, THE TEMPLATE...
...WHO SHALL TRANSFORM YOU INTO ADULTS...
...PERFECT IN FORM AND FEATURE...
...FIT-- AND EAGER-- TO JOIN THE BRATPACK ON MOJO'S WILDWAY!

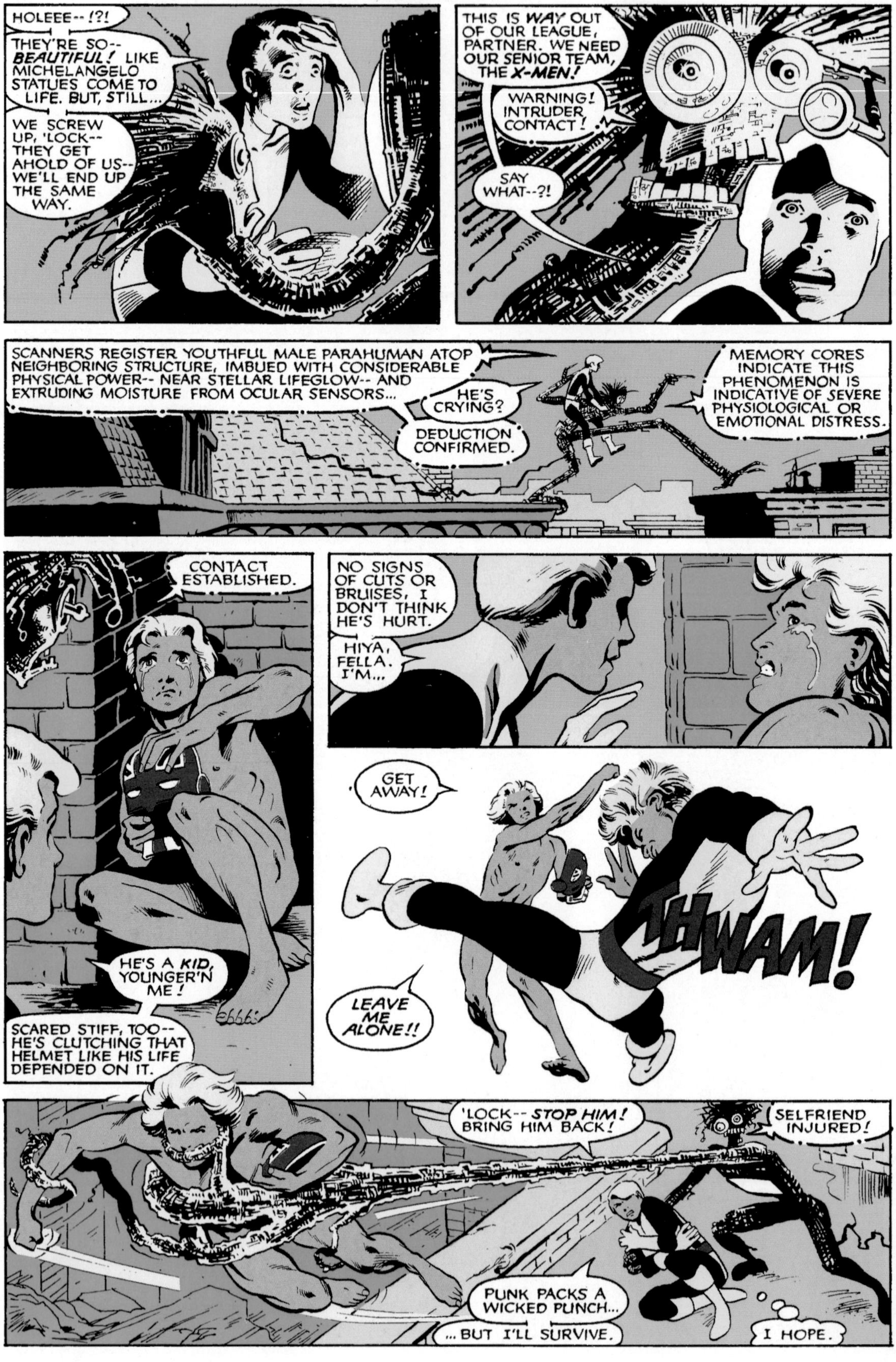
HOLEEE--!?!
THEY'RE SO-- BEAUTIFUL! LIKE MICHELANGELO STATUES COME TO LIFE. BUT, STILL...
WE SCREW UP, 'LOCK-- THEY GET AHOLD OF US-- WE'LL END UP THE SAME WAY.
THIS IS WAY OUT OF OUR LEAGUE, PARTNER. WE NEED OUR SENIOR TEAM, THE X-MEN!
WARNING! INTRUDER CONTACT!
SAY WHAT--?!
SCANNERS REGISTER YOUTHFUL MALE PARAHUMAN ATOP NEIGHBORING STRUCTURE, IMBUED WITH CONSIDERABLE PHYSICAL POWER-- NEAR STELLAR LIFEGLOW-- AND EXTRUDING MOISTURE FROM OCULAR SENSORS...
HE'S CRYING?
DEDUCTION CONFIRMED.
MEMORY CORES INDICATE THIS PHENOMENON IS INDICATIVE OF SEVERE PHYSIOLOGICAL OR EMOTIONAL DISTRESS.
CONTACT ESTABLISHED.
HE'S A KID, YOUNGER'N ME!
SCARED STIFF, TOO-- HE'S CLUTCHING THAT HELMET LIKE HIS LIFE DEPENDED ON IT.
NO SIGNS OF CUTS OR BRUISES, I DON'T THINK HE'S HURT.
HIYA, FELLA. I'M...
GET AWAY!
THWAM!
LEAVE ME ALONE!!
'LOCK-- STOP HIM! BRING HIM BACK!
SELFRIEND INJURED!
PUNK PACKS A WICKED PUNCH...
... BUT I'LL SURVIVE.
I HOPE.

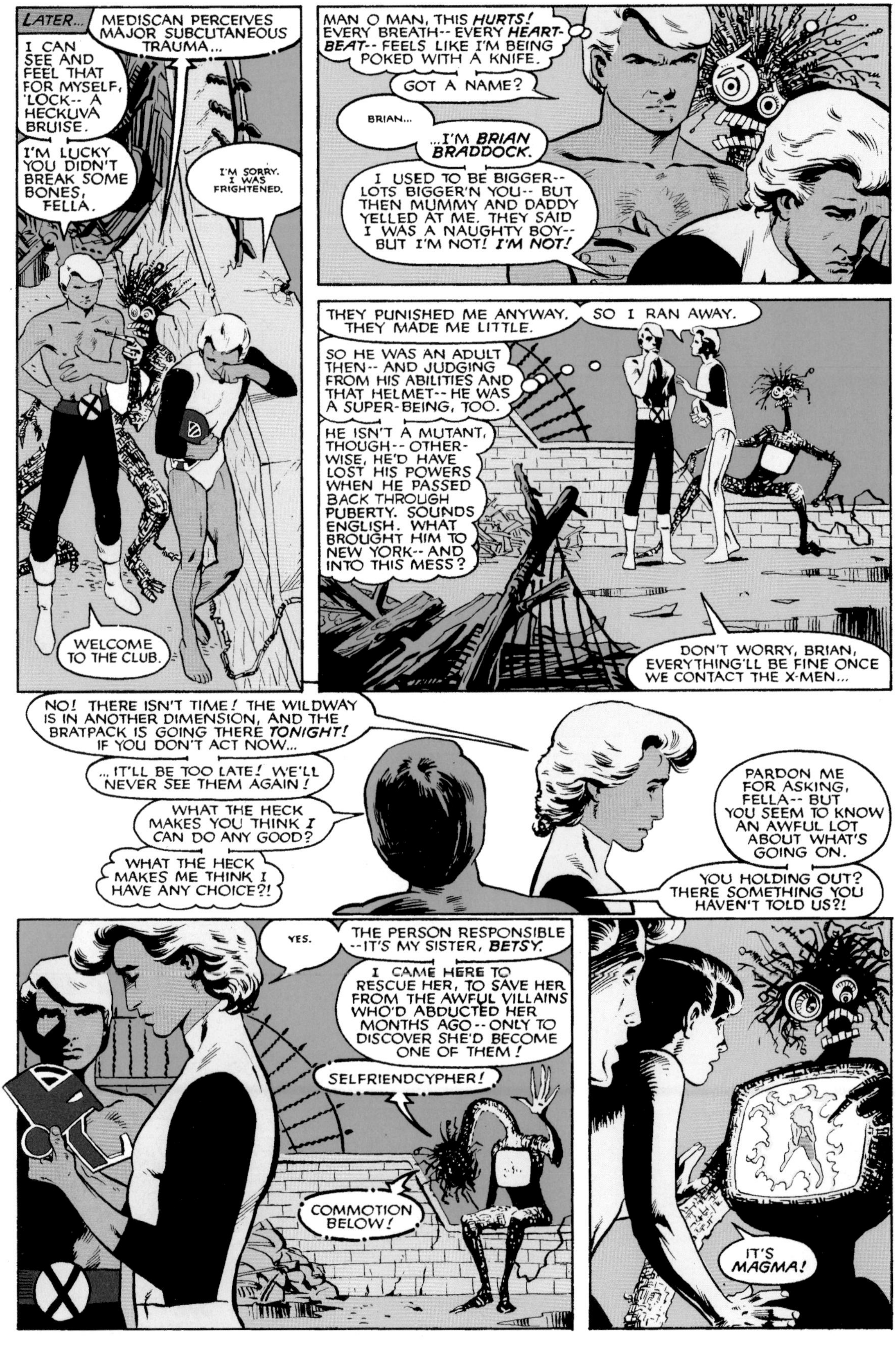
LATER...
MEDISCAN PERCEIVES MAJOR SUBCUTANEOUS TRAUMA...
I CAN SEE AND FEEL THAT FOR MYSELF, 'LOCK-- A HECKUVA BRUISE.
I'M LUCKY YOU DIDN'T BREAK SOME BONES, FELLA.
I'M SORRY. I WAS FRIGHTENED.
WELCOME TO THE CLUB.
MAN O MAN, THIS HURTS! EVERY BREATH-- EVERY HEART-BEAT-- FEELS LIKE I'M BEING POKED WITH A KNIFE.
GOT A NAME?
BRIAN...
...I'M BRIAN BRADDOCK.
I USED TO BE BIGGER-- LOTS BIGGER'N YOU-- BUT THEN MUMMY AND DADDY YELLED AT ME. THEY SAID I WAS A NAUGHTY BOY-- BUT I'M NOT! I'M NOT!
THEY PUNISHED ME ANYWAY. THEY MADE ME LITTLE.
SO I RAN AWAY.
SO HE WAS AN ADULT THEN-- AND JUDGING FROM HIS ABILITIES AND THAT HELMET-- HE WAS A SUPER-BEING, TOO.
HE ISN'T A MUTANT, THOUGH-- OTHERWISE, HE'D HAVE LOST HIS POWERS WHEN HE PASSED BACK THROUGH PUBERTY. SOUNDS ENGLISH. WHAT BROUGHT HIM TO NEW YORK-- AND INTO THIS MESS?
DON'T WORRY, BRIAN, EVERYTHING'LL BE FINE ONCE WE CONTACT THE X-MEN...
NO! THERE ISN'T TIME! THE WILDWAY IS IN ANOTHER DIMENSION, AND THE BRATPACK IS GOING THERE TONIGHT! IF YOU DON'T ACT NOW...
...IT'LL BE TOO LATE! WE'LL NEVER SEE THEM AGAIN!
WHAT THE HECK MAKES YOU THINK I CAN DO ANY GOOD?
WHAT THE HECK MAKES ME THINK I HAVE ANY CHOICE?!
PARDON ME FOR ASKING, FELLA-- BUT YOU SEEM TO KNOW AN AWFUL LOT ABOUT WHAT'S GOING ON.
YOU HOLDING OUT? THERE SOMETHING YOU HAVEN'T TOLD US?!
YES.
THE PERSON RESPONSIBLE --IT'S MY SISTER, BETSY.
I CAME HERE TO RESCUE HER, TO SAVE HER FROM THE AWFUL VILLAINS WHO'D ABDUCTED HER MONTHS AGO-- ONLY TO DISCOVER SHE'D BECOME ONE OF THEM!
SELFRIENDCYPHER!
COMMOTION BELOW!
IT'S MAGMA!

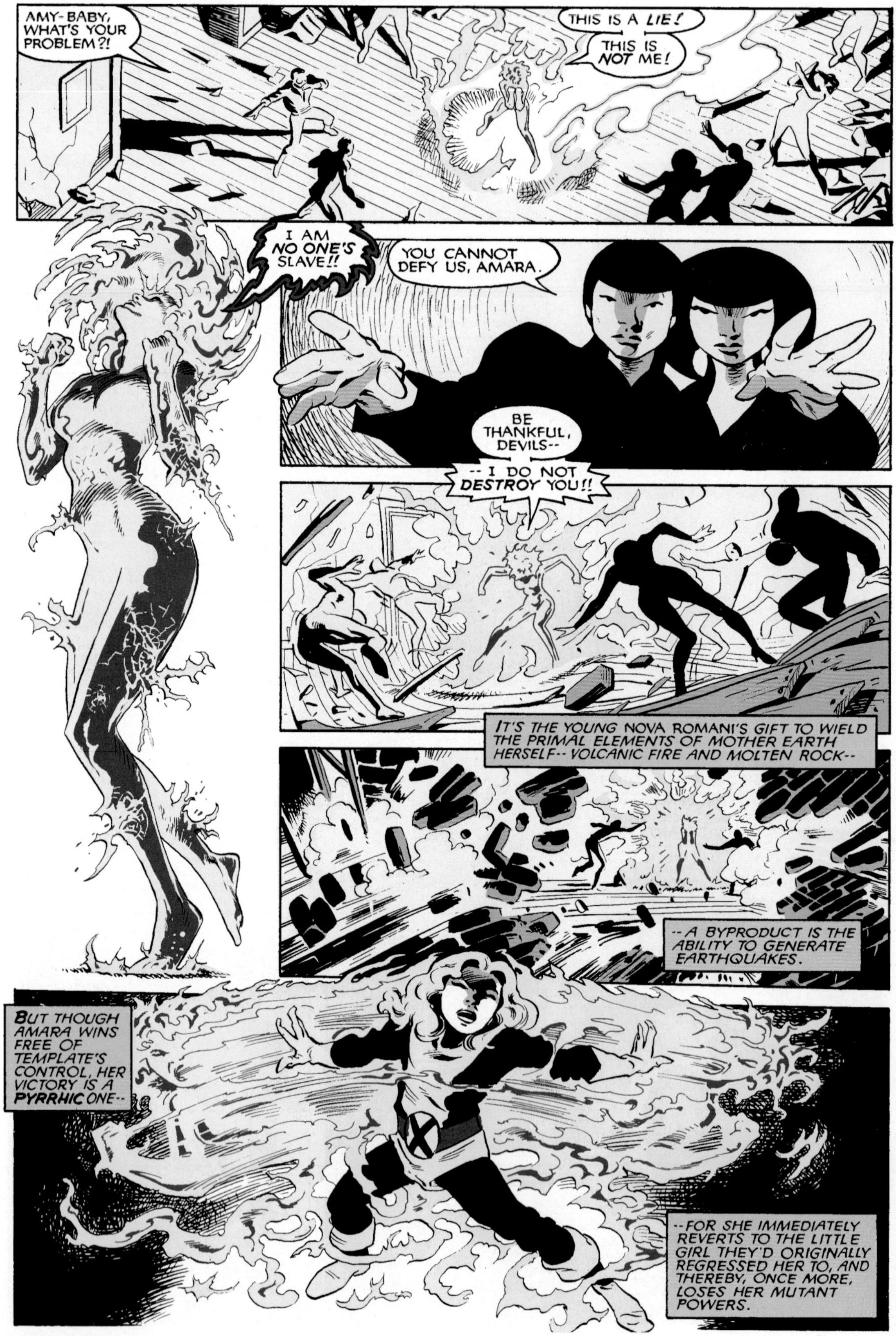
AMY-BABY, WHAT'S YOUR PROBLEM?!
THIS IS A *LIE!*
THIS IS *NOT* ME!
I AM *NO ONE'S* SLAVE!!
YOU CANNOT DEFY US, AMARA.
BE THANKFUL, DEVILS--
-- I DO NOT *DESTROY* YOU!!
IT'S THE YOUNG NOVA ROMANI'S GIFT TO WIELD THE PRIMAL ELEMENTS OF MOTHER EARTH HERSELF-- VOLCANIC FIRE AND MOLTEN ROCK--
--A BYPRODUCT IS THE ABILITY TO GENERATE EARTHQUAKES.
BUT THOUGH AMARA WINS FREE OF TEMPLATE'S CONTROL, HER VICTORY IS A ***PYRRHIC*** *ONE--*
--FOR SHE IMMEDIATELY REVERTS TO THE LITTLE GIRL THEY'D ORIGINALLY REGRESSED HER TO, AND THEREBY, ONCE MORE, LOSES HER MUTANT POWERS.

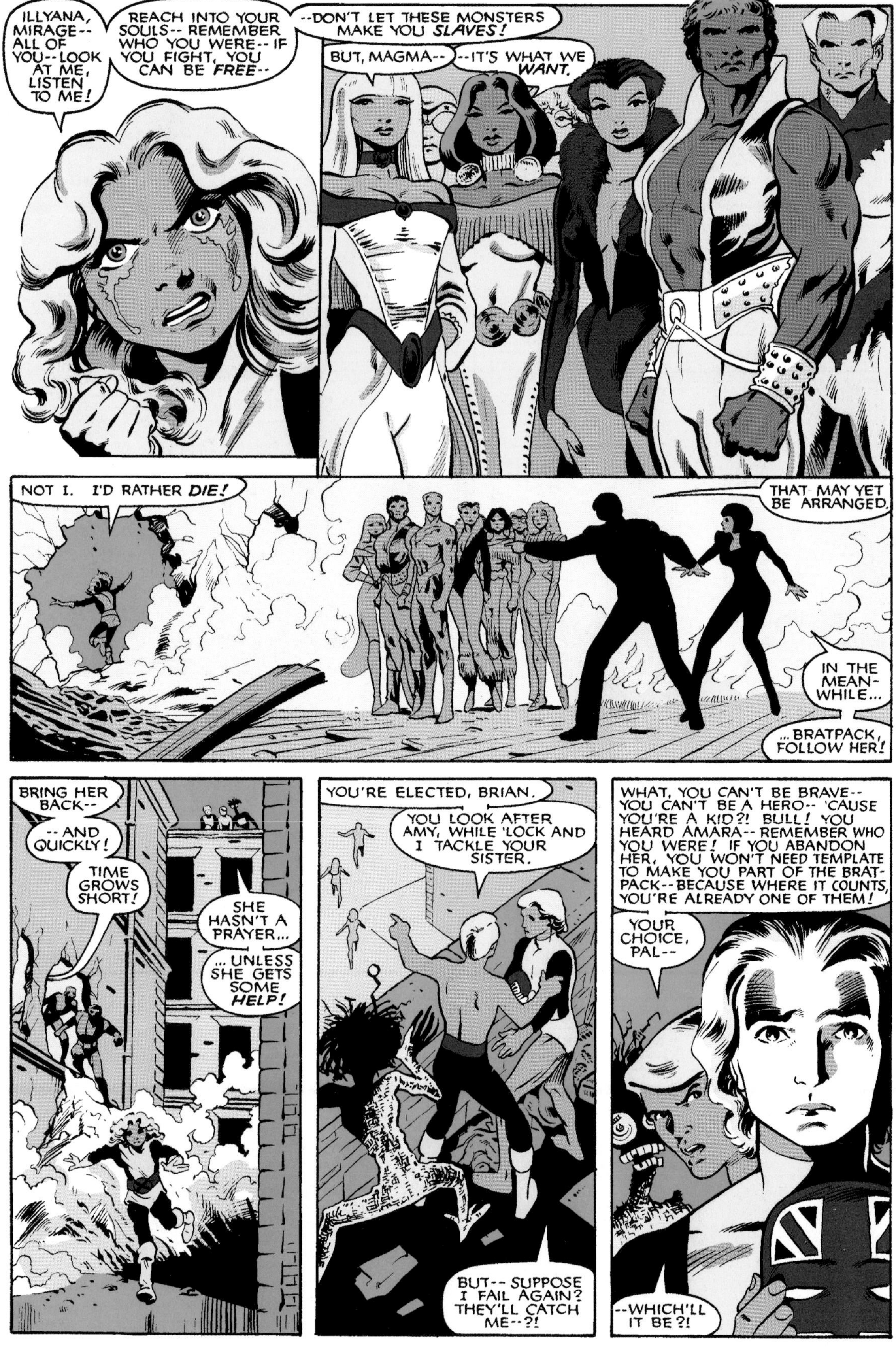
ILLYANA, MIRAGE-- ALL OF YOU--LOOK AT ME, LISTEN TO ME!
REACH INTO YOUR SOULS-- REMEMBER WHO YOU WERE-- IF YOU FIGHT, YOU CAN BE FREE--
--DON'T LET THESE MONSTERS MAKE YOU SLAVES!
BUT, MAGMA--
--IT'S WHAT WE WANT.
NOT I. I'D RATHER DIE!
THAT MAY YET BE ARRANGED.
IN THE MEAN-WHILE...
...BRATPACK, FOLLOW HER!
BRING HER BACK--
--AND QUICKLY!
TIME GROWS SHORT!
SHE HASN'T A PRAYER...
...UNLESS SHE GETS SOME HELP!
YOU'RE ELECTED, BRIAN.
YOU LOOK AFTER AMY, WHILE 'LOCK AND I TACKLE YOUR SISTER.
BUT-- SUPPOSE I FAIL AGAIN? THEY'LL CATCH ME--?!
WHAT, YOU CAN'T BE BRAVE-- YOU CAN'T BE A HERO-- 'CAUSE YOU'RE A KID?! BULL! YOU HEARD AMARA-- REMEMBER WHO YOU WERE! IF YOU ABANDON HER, YOU WON'T NEED TEMPLATE TO MAKE YOU PART OF THE BRAT-PACK--BECAUSE WHERE IT COUNTS, YOU'RE ALREADY ONE OF THEM!
YOUR CHOICE, PAL--
--WHICH'LL IT BE?!

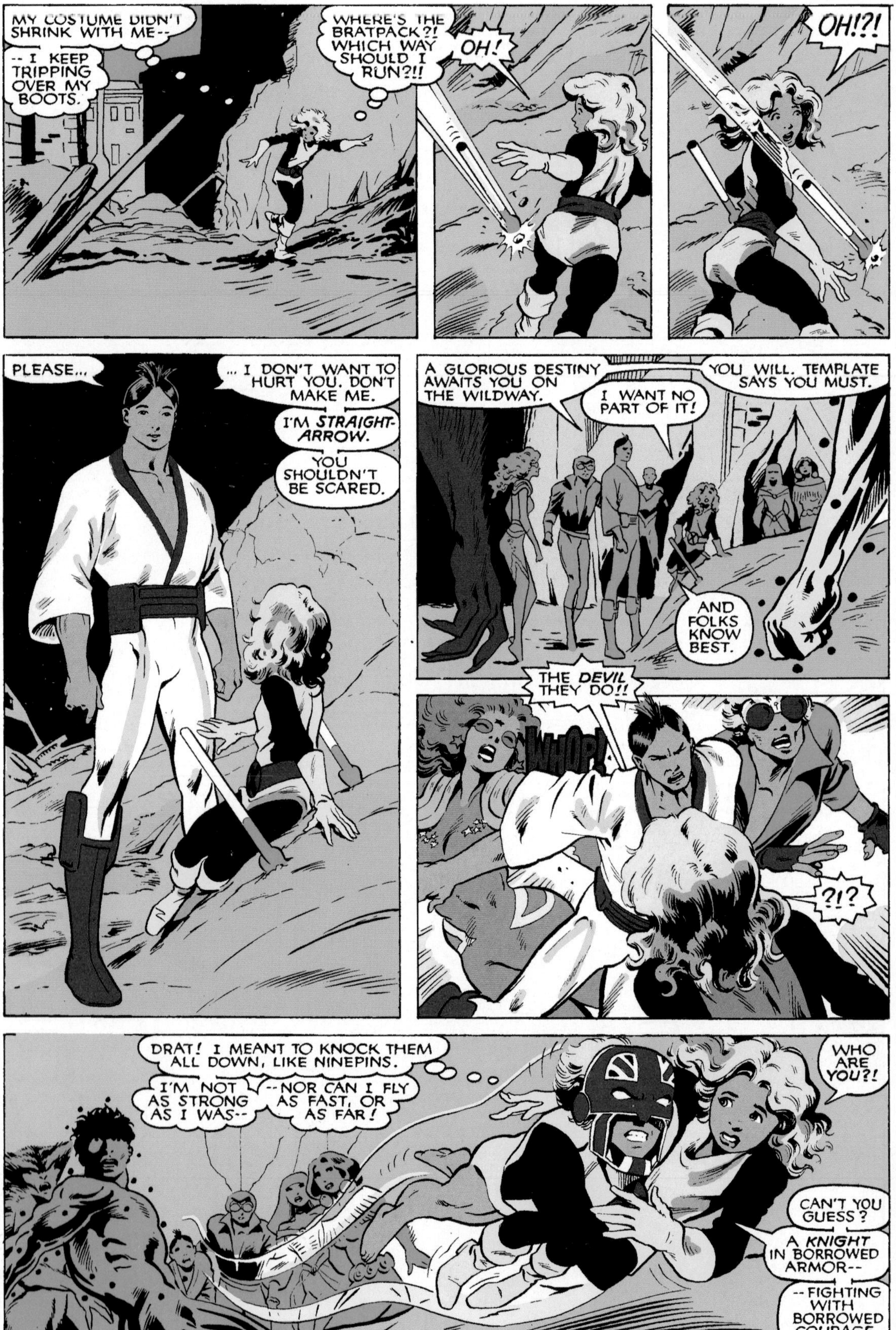
MY COSTUME DIDN'T SHRINK WITH ME--
-- I KEEP TRIPPING OVER MY BOOTS.
WHERE'S THE BRATPACK?! WHICH WAY SHOULD I RUN?!!
OH!
OH!?!
PLEASE...
... I DON'T WANT TO HURT YOU. DON'T MAKE ME.
I'M STRAIGHT-ARROW.
YOU SHOULDN'T BE SCARED.
A GLORIOUS DESTINY AWAITS YOU ON THE WILDWAY.
I WANT NO PART OF IT!
YOU WILL. TEMPLATE SAYS YOU MUST.
AND FOLKS KNOW BEST.
THE DEVIL THEY DO!!
WHOP!
?!?
DRAT! I MEANT TO KNOCK THEM ALL DOWN, LIKE NINEPINS.
I'M NOT AS STRONG AS I WAS--
--NOR CAN I FLY AS FAST, OR AS FAR!
WHO ARE YOU?!
CAN'T YOU GUESS?
A KNIGHT IN BORROWED ARMOR--
--FIGHTING WITH BORROWED COURAGE.

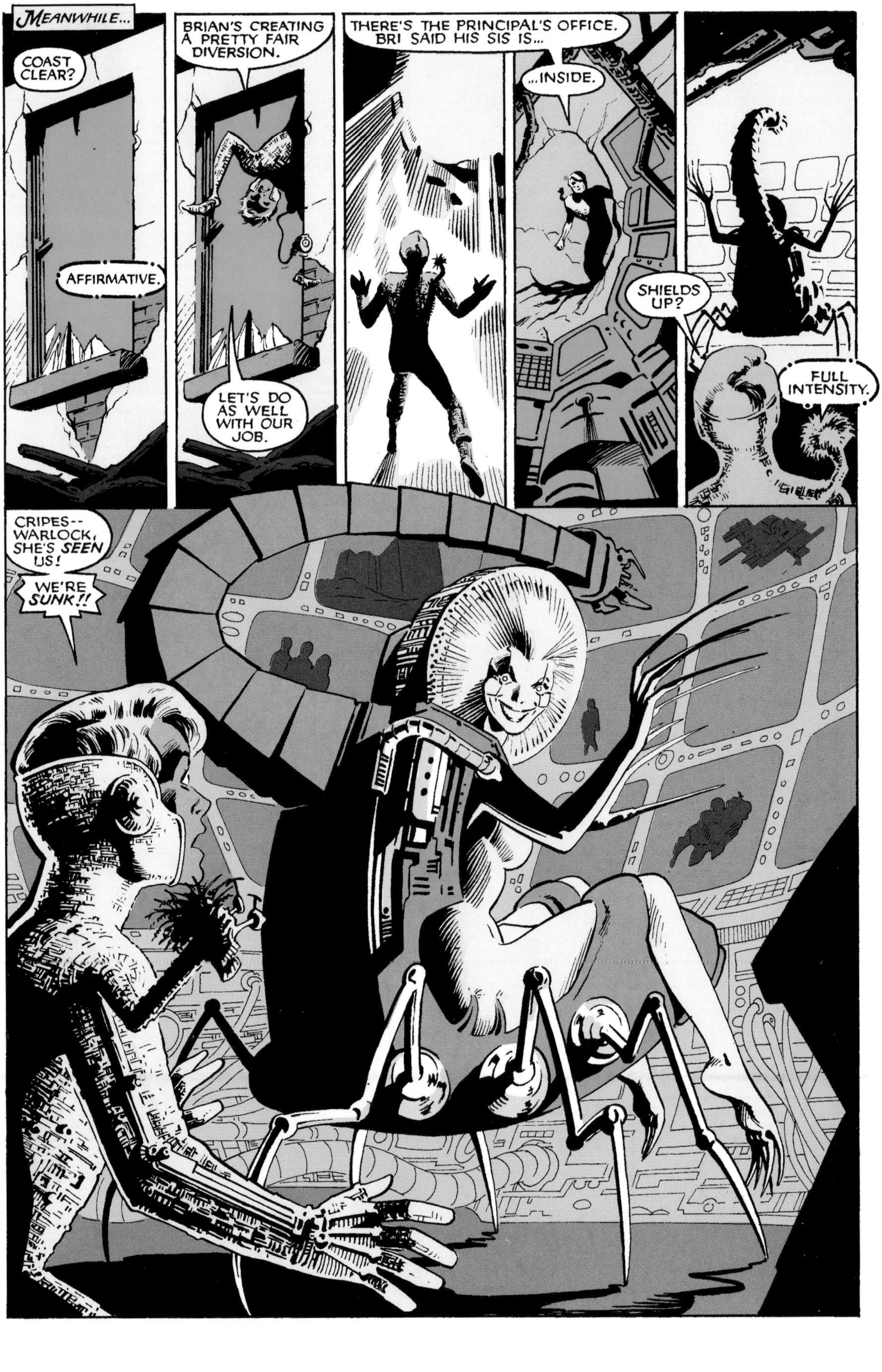
MEANWHILE...
COAST CLEAR?
AFFIRMATIVE.
BRIAN'S CREATING A PRETTY FAIR DIVERSION.
LET'S DO AS WELL WITH OUR JOB.
THERE'S THE PRINCIPAL'S OFFICE. BRI SAID HIS SIS IS...
...INSIDE.
SHIELDS UP?
FULL INTENSITY.
CRIPES-- WARLOCK, SHE'S SEEN US!
WE'RE SUNK!!

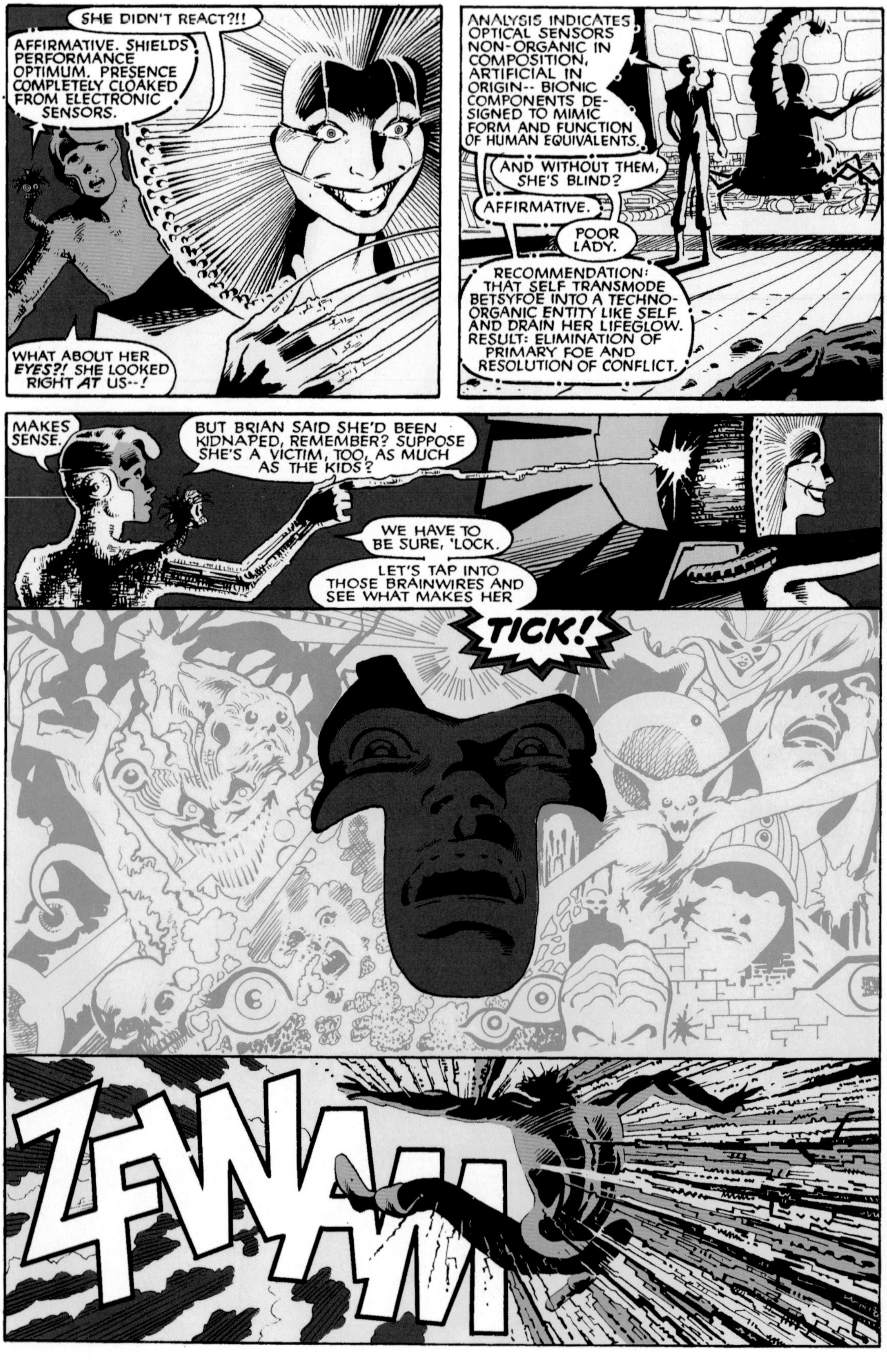
SHE DIDN'T REACT?!!
AFFIRMATIVE. SHIELDS PERFORMANCE OPTIMUM. PRESENCE COMPLETELY CLOAKED FROM ELECTRONIC SENSORS.
WHAT ABOUT HER EYES?! SHE LOOKED RIGHT AT US--!
ANALYSIS INDICATES OPTICAL SENSORS NON-ORGANIC IN COMPOSITION, ARTIFICIAL IN ORIGIN-- BIONIC COMPONENTS DESIGNED TO MIMIC FORM AND FUNCTION OF HUMAN EQUIVALENTS.
AND WITHOUT THEM, SHE'S BLIND?
AFFIRMATIVE.
POOR LADY.
RECOMMENDATION: THAT SELF TRANSMODE BETSYFOE INTO A TECHNO-ORGANIC ENTITY LIKE SELF AND DRAIN HER LIFEGLOW. RESULT: ELIMINATION OF PRIMARY FOE AND RESOLUTION OF CONFLICT.
MAKES SENSE.
BUT BRIAN SAID SHE'D BEEN KIDNAPED, REMEMBER? SUPPOSE SHE'S A VICTIM, TOO, AS MUCH AS THE KIDS?
WE HAVE TO BE SURE, 'LOCK.
LET'S TAP INTO THOSE BRAINWIRES AND SEE WHAT MAKES HER
TICK!
ZFWAMM

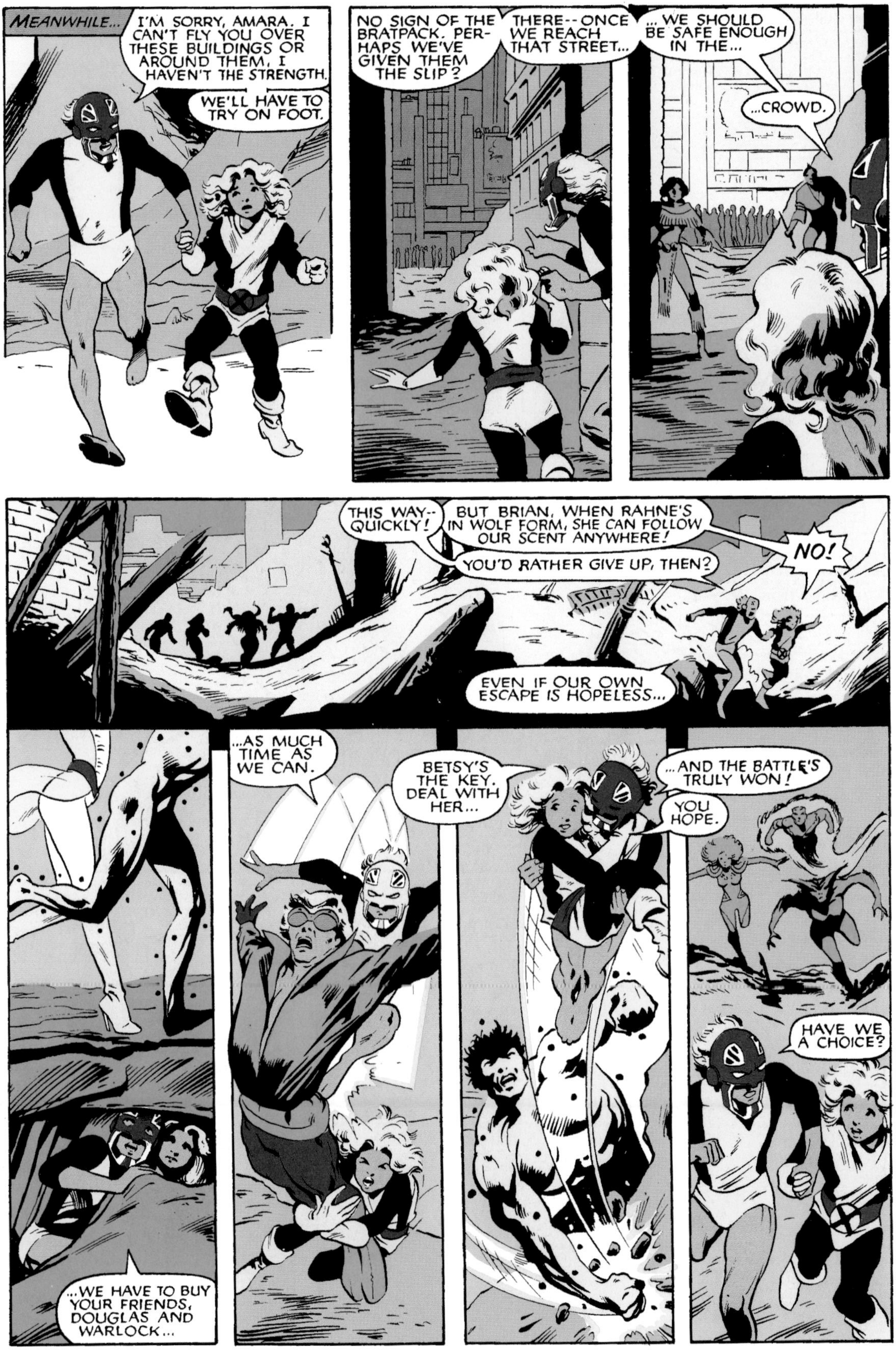
MEANWHILE...
I'M SORRY, AMARA. I CAN'T FLY YOU OVER THESE BUILDINGS OR AROUND THEM, I HAVEN'T THE STRENGTH.
WE'LL HAVE TO TRY ON FOOT.
NO SIGN OF THE BRATPACK. PERHAPS WE'VE GIVEN THEM THE SLIP?
THERE--ONCE WE REACH THAT STREET...
...WE SHOULD BE SAFE ENOUGH IN THE...
...CROWD.
THIS WAY--QUICKLY!
BUT BRIAN, WHEN RAHNE'S IN WOLF FORM, SHE CAN FOLLOW OUR SCENT ANYWHERE!
YOU'D RATHER GIVE UP, THEN?
NO!
EVEN IF OUR OWN ESCAPE IS HOPELESS...
...WE HAVE TO BUY YOUR FRIENDS, DOUGLAS AND WARLOCK...
...AS MUCH TIME AS WE CAN.
BETSY'S THE KEY. DEAL WITH HER...
...AND THE BATTLE'S TRULY WON!
YOU HOPE.
HAVE WE A CHOICE?

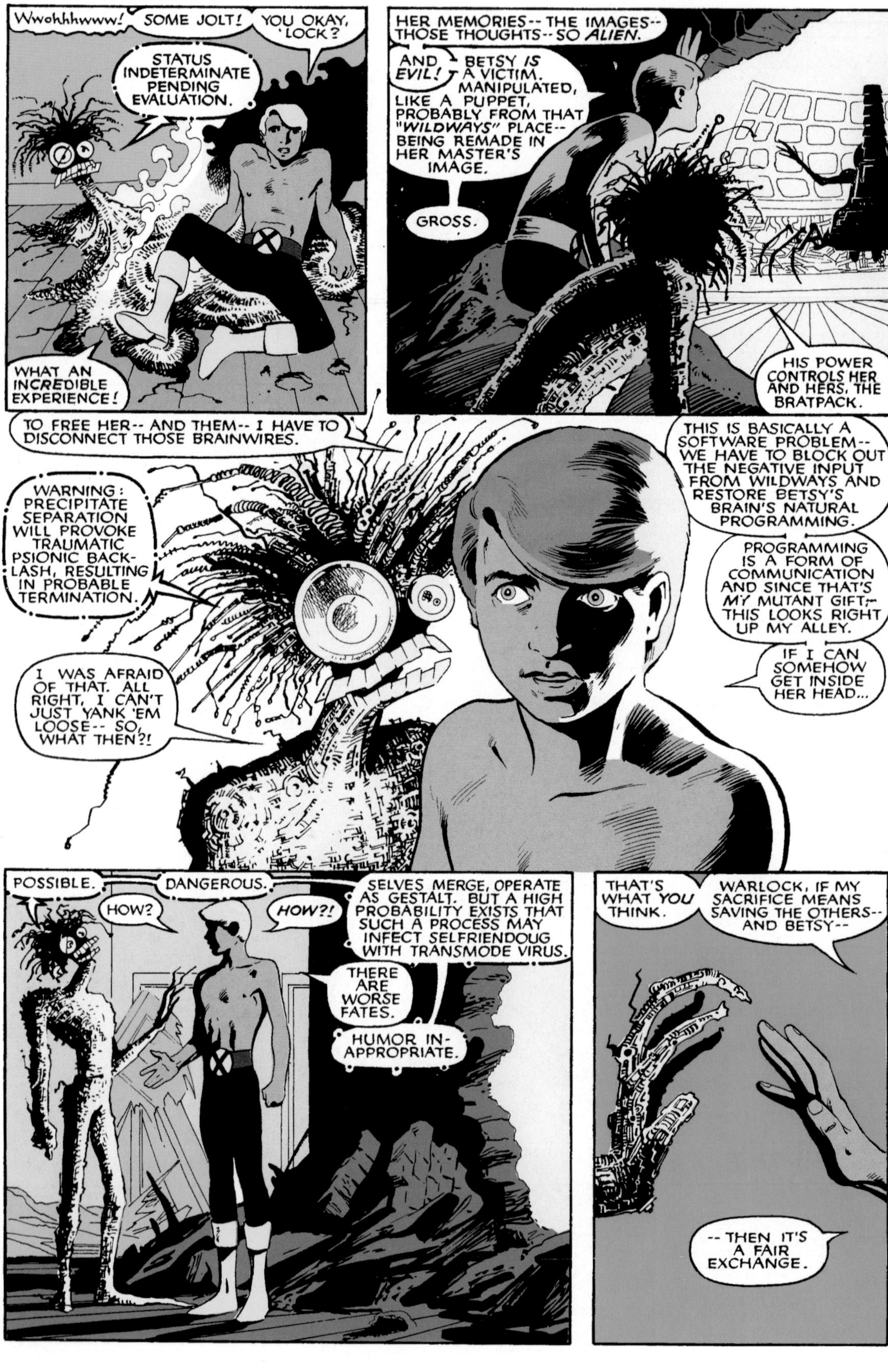
Wwohhhwww!
SOME JOLT!
YOU OKAY, 'LOCK?
STATUS INDETERMINATE PENDING EVALUATION.
WHAT AN INCREDIBLE EXPERIENCE!
HER MEMORIES-- THE IMAGES-- THOSE THOUGHTS-- SO ALIEN.
AND EVIL!
BETSY IS A VICTIM. MANIPULATED, LIKE A PUPPET, PROBABLY FROM THAT "WILDWAYS" PLACE-- BEING REMADE IN HER MASTER'S IMAGE.
GROSS.
HIS POWER CONTROLS HER AND HERS, THE BRATPACK.
TO FREE HER-- AND THEM-- I HAVE TO DISCONNECT THOSE BRAINWIRES.
WARNING: PRECIPITATE SEPARATION WILL PROVOKE TRAUMATIC PSIONIC BACK-LASH, RESULTING IN PROBABLE TERMINATION.
I WAS AFRAID OF THAT. ALL RIGHT, I CAN'T JUST YANK 'EM LOOSE-- SO, WHAT THEN?!
THIS IS BASICALLY A SOFTWARE PROBLEM-- WE HAVE TO BLOCK OUT THE NEGATIVE INPUT FROM WILDWAYS AND RESTORE BETSY'S BRAIN'S NATURAL PROGRAMMING.
PROGRAMMING IS A FORM OF COMMUNICATION AND SINCE THAT'S MY MUTANT GIFT-- THIS LOOKS RIGHT UP MY ALLEY.
IF I CAN SOMEHOW GET INSIDE HER HEAD...
POSSIBLE.
DANGEROUS.
HOW?
HOW?!
SELVES MERGE, OPERATE AS GESTALT. BUT A HIGH PROBABILITY EXISTS THAT SUCH A PROCESS MAY INFECT SELFRIENDOUG WITH TRANSMODE VIRUS.
THERE ARE WORSE FATES.
HUMOR IN-APPROPRIATE.
THAT'S WHAT YOU THINK.
WARLOCK, IF MY SACRIFICE MEANS SAVING THE OTHERS-- AND BETSY--
-- THEN IT'S A FAIR EXCHANGE.

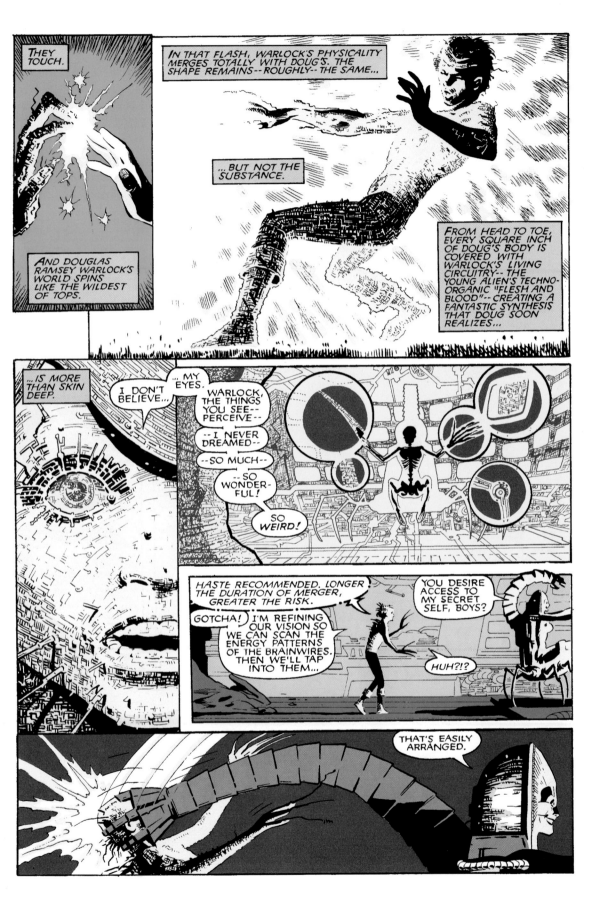

THEY TOUCH.

IN THAT FLASH, WARLOCK'S PHYSICALITY MERGES TOTALLY WITH DOUG'S. THE SHAPE REMAINS--ROUGHLY--THE SAME...

...BUT NOT THE SUBSTANCE.

FROM HEAD TO TOE, EVERY SQUARE INCH OF DOUG'S BODY IS COVERED WITH WARLOCK'S LIVING CIRCUITRY-- THE YOUNG ALIEN'S TECHNO-ORGANIC "FLESH AND BLOOD"-- CREATING A FANTASTIC SYNTHESIS THAT DOUG SOON REALIZES...

AND DOUGLAS RAMSEY WARLOCK'S WORLD SPINS LIKE THE WILDEST OF TOPS.

...IS MORE THAN SKIN DEEP.

I DON'T BELIEVE...

...MY EYES.

WARLOCK, THE THINGS YOU SEE--PERCEIVE--

--I NEVER DREAMED--

--SO MUCH--

--SO WONDER-FUL!

SO WEIRD!

HASTE RECOMMENDED. LONGER THE DURATION OF MERGER, GREATER THE RISK.

GOTCHA! I'M REFINING OUR VISION SO WE CAN SCAN THE ENERGY PATTERNS OF THE BRAINWIRES. THEN WE'LL TAP INTO THEM...

YOU DESIRE ACCESS TO MY SECRET SELF, BOYS?

HUH?!?

THAT'S EASILY ARRANGED.

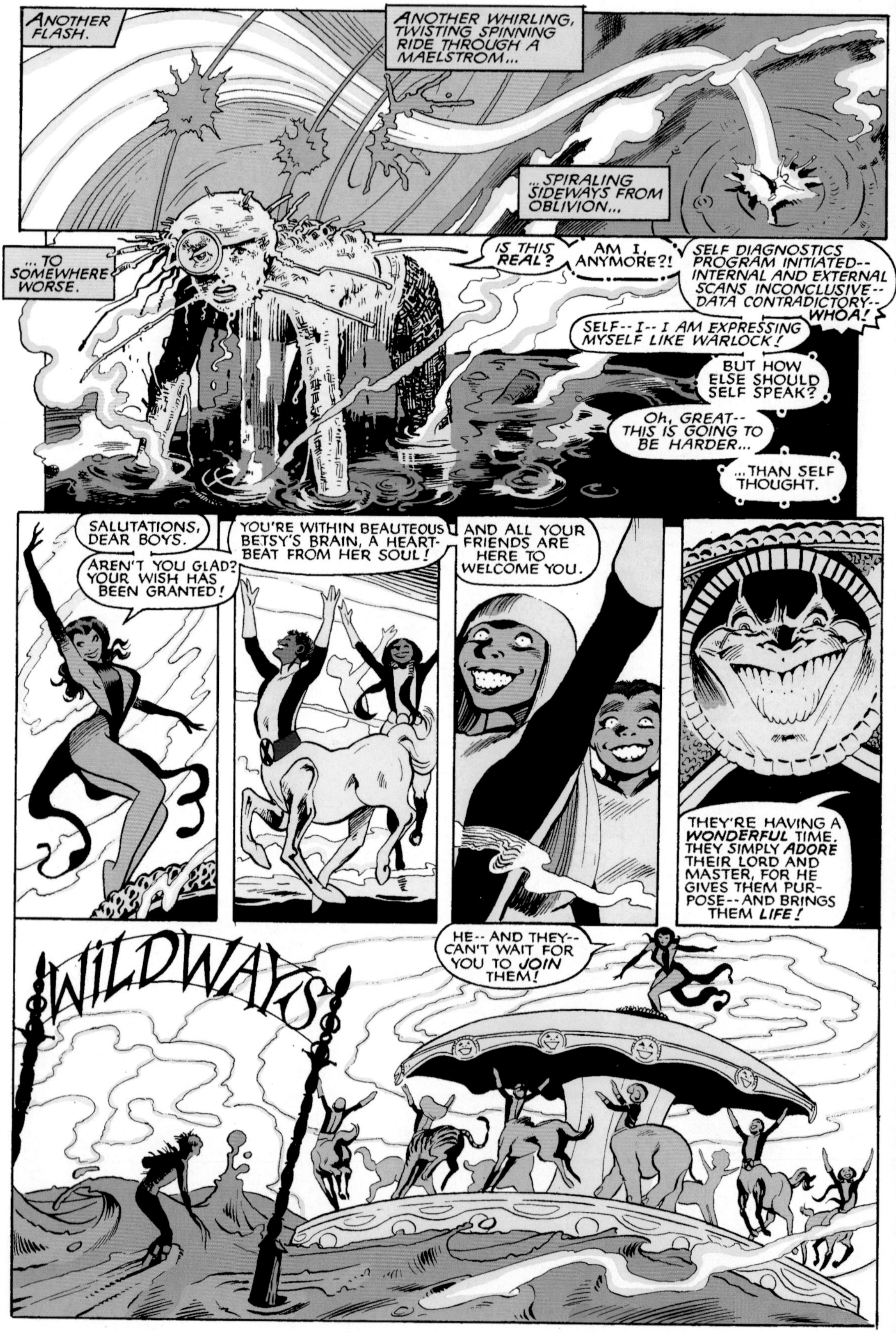
ANOTHER FLASH.
ANOTHER WHIRLING, TWISTING SPINNING RIDE THROUGH A MAELSTROM...
...SPIRALING SIDEWAYS FROM OBLIVION...
...TO SOMEWHERE WORSE.
IS THIS REAL?
AM I, ANYMORE?!
SELF DIAGNOSTICS PROGRAM INITIATED-- INTERNAL AND EXTERNAL SCANS INCONCLUSIVE-- DATA CONTRADICTORY-- WHOA!
SELF-- I-- I AM EXPRESSING MYSELF LIKE WARLOCK!
BUT HOW ELSE SHOULD SELF SPEAK?
Oh, GREAT-- THIS IS GOING TO BE HARDER...
...THAN SELF THOUGHT.
SALUTATIONS, DEAR BOYS.
AREN'T YOU GLAD? YOUR WISH HAS BEEN GRANTED!
YOU'RE WITHIN BEAUTEOUS BETSY'S BRAIN, A HEART-BEAT FROM HER SOUL!
AND ALL YOUR FRIENDS ARE HERE TO WELCOME YOU.
THEY'RE HAVING A WONDERFUL TIME. THEY SIMPLY ADORE THEIR LORD AND MASTER, FOR HE GIVES THEM PUR-POSE--AND BRINGS THEM LIFE!
WILDWAYS
HE-- AND THEY-- CAN'T WAIT FOR YOU TO JOIN THEM!

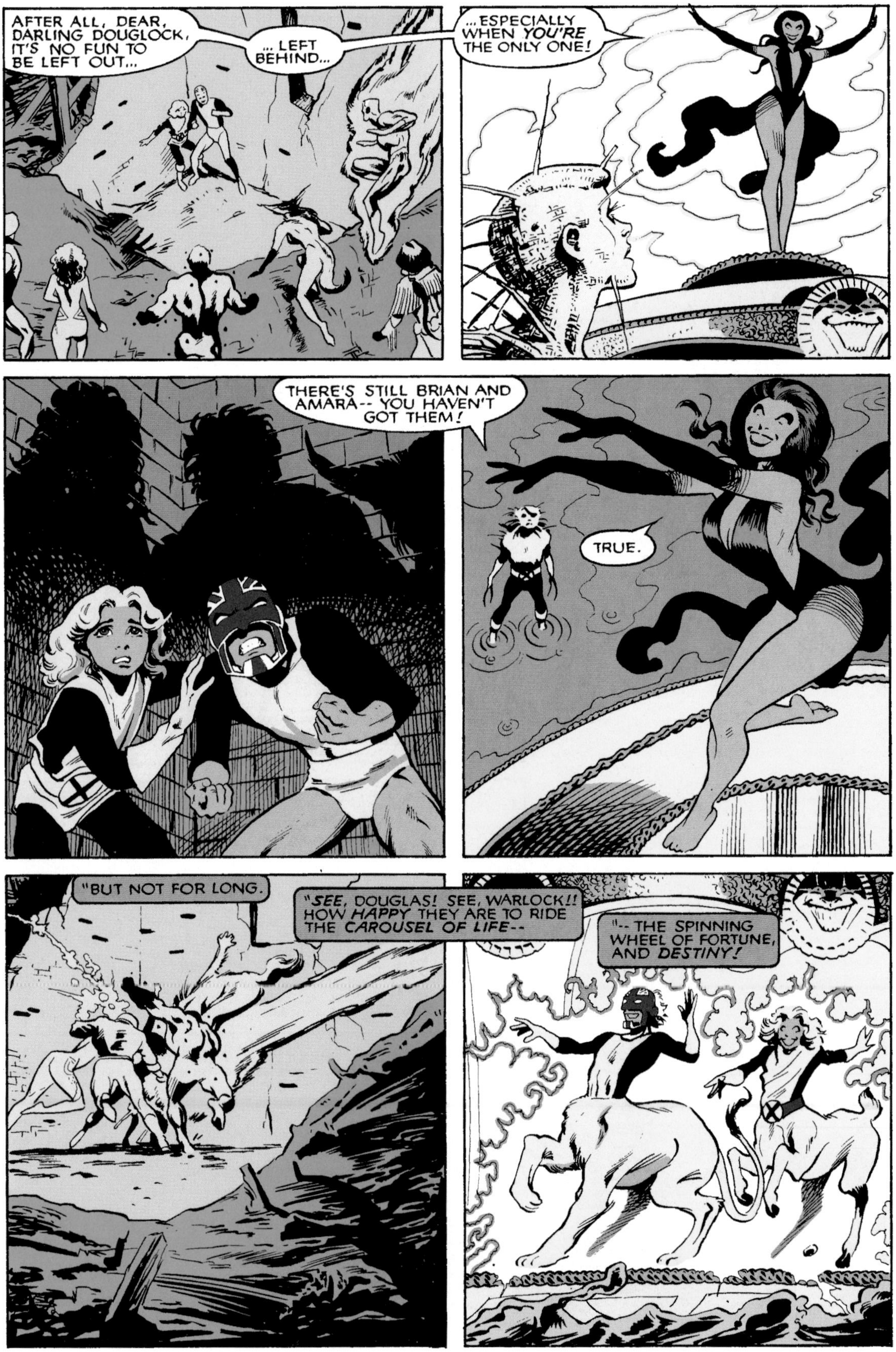
AFTER ALL, DEAR, DARLING DOUGLOCK, IT'S NO FUN TO BE LEFT OUT...
... LEFT BEHIND...
... ESPECIALLY WHEN YOU'RE THE ONLY ONE!
THERE'S STILL BRIAN AND AMARA-- YOU HAVEN'T GOT THEM!
TRUE.
"BUT NOT FOR LONG.
"SEE, DOUGLAS! SEE, WARLOCK!! HOW HAPPY THEY ARE TO RIDE THE CAROUSEL OF LIFE--
"-- THE SPINNING WHEEL OF FORTUNE, AND DESTINY!

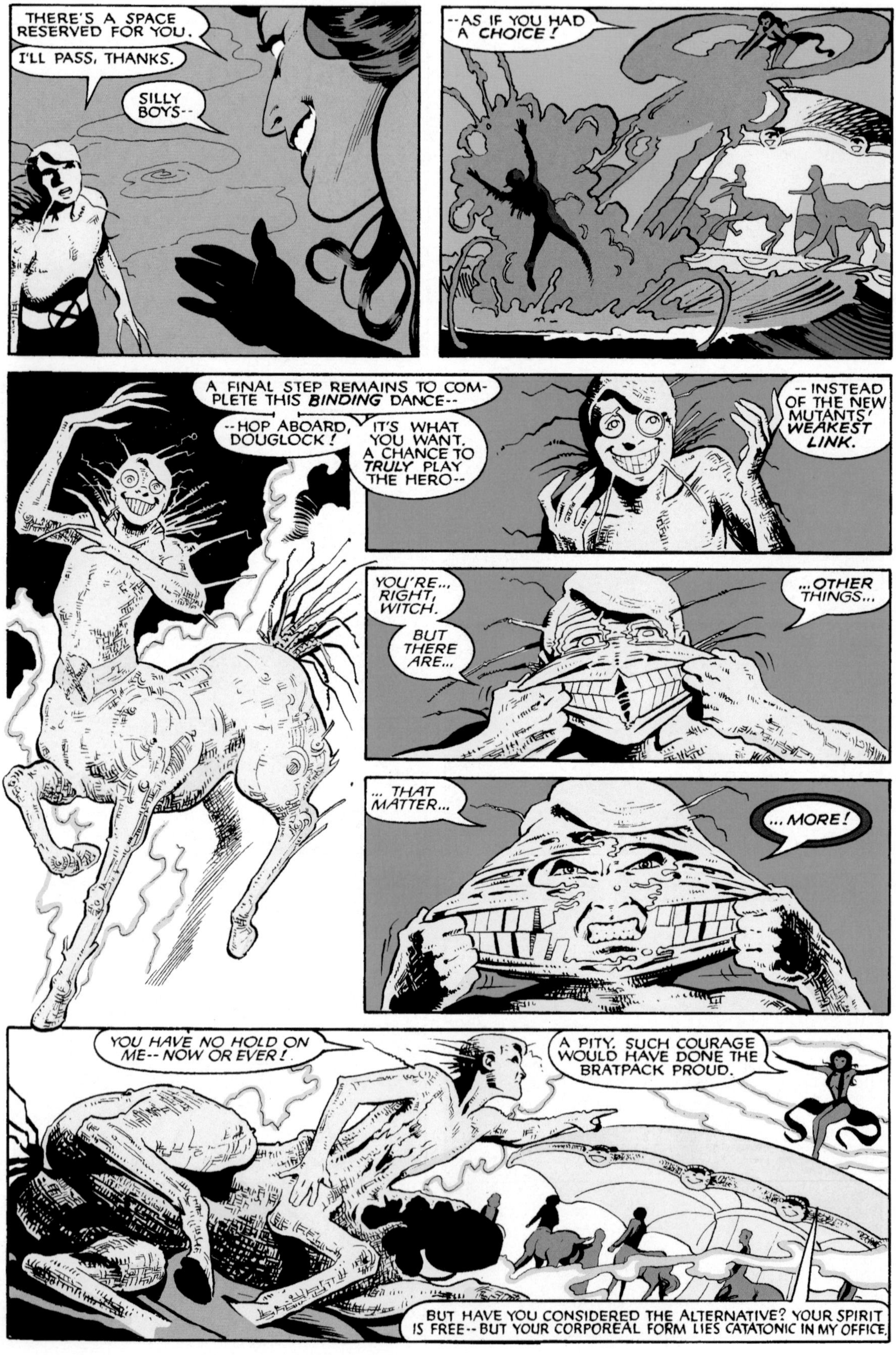
THERE'S A SPACE RESERVED FOR YOU.
I'LL PASS, THANKS.
SILLY BOYS--
--AS IF YOU HAD A CHOICE!
A FINAL STEP REMAINS TO COMPLETE THIS BINDING DANCE--
--HOP ABOARD, DOUGLOCK!
IT'S WHAT YOU WANT. A CHANCE TO TRULY PLAY THE HERO--
--INSTEAD OF THE NEW MUTANTS' WEAKEST LINK.
YOU'RE... RIGHT, WITCH.
BUT THERE ARE...
...OTHER THINGS...
...THAT MATTER...
...MORE!
YOU HAVE NO HOLD ON ME--NOW OR EVER!
A PITY. SUCH COURAGE WOULD HAVE DONE THE BRATPACK PROUD.
BUT HAVE YOU CONSIDERED THE ALTERNATIVE? YOUR SPIRIT IS FREE--BUT YOUR CORPOREAL FORM LIES CATATONIC IN MY OFFICE.

A SIMPLE--*HELPLESS*--THING FOR THE *BRAT-PACK* TO SLAY!

NOT IF I GET YOU *FIRST*!

A TOUCH IS ALL IT TAKES. THE TRANSMODE VIRUS IS INCURABLE, ITS EFFECTS IRREVERSABLE!

IF YOU'RE A MANIFESTATION OF MISS BRADDOCK--

--YOU'RE DONE FOR!

BUT I AM *NOT*.

SNAP

SCREAM

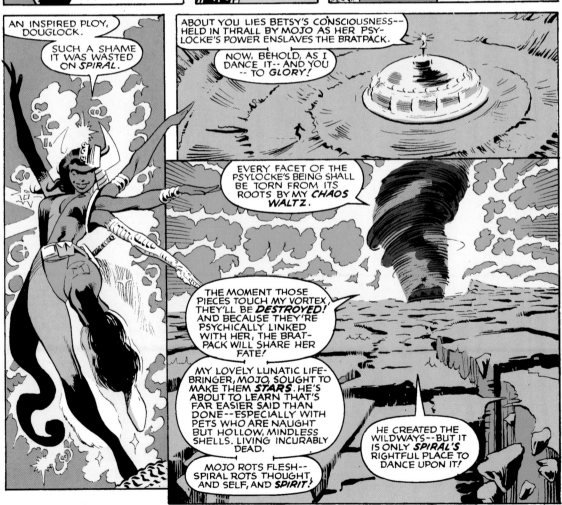

AN INSPIRED PLOY, DOUGLOCK.

SUCH A SHAME IT WAS WASTED ON *SPIRAL*.

ABOUT YOU LIES BETSY'S CONSCIOUSNESS-- HELD IN THRALL BY MOJO AS HER PSY-LOCKE'S POWER ENSLAVES THE BRATPACK.

NOW, BEHOLD, AS I DANCE IT-- AND YOU -- TO GLORY!

EVERY FACET OF THE PSYLOCKE'S BEING SHALL BE TORN FROM ITS ROOTS BY MY *CHAOS WALTZ*.

THE MOMENT THOSE PIECES TOUCH MY VORTEX, THEY'LL BE *DESTROYED*! AND BECAUSE THEY'RE PSYCHICALLY LINKED WITH HER, THE BRAT-PACK WILL SHARE HER *FATE*!

MY LOVELY LUNATIC LIFE-BRINGER, MOJO, SOUGHT TO MAKE THEM *STARS*. HE'S ABOUT TO LEARN THAT'S FAR EASIER SAID THAN DONE--ESPECIALLY WITH PETS WHO ARE NAUGHT BUT HOLLOW, MINDLESS SHELLS. LIVING INCURABLY DEAD.

MOJO ROTS FLESH-- SPIRAL ROTS THOUGHT AND SELF, AND *SPIRIT*!

HE CREATED THE WILDWAYS--BUT IT IS ONLY *SPIRAL'S* RIGHTFUL PLACE TO DANCE UPON IT!

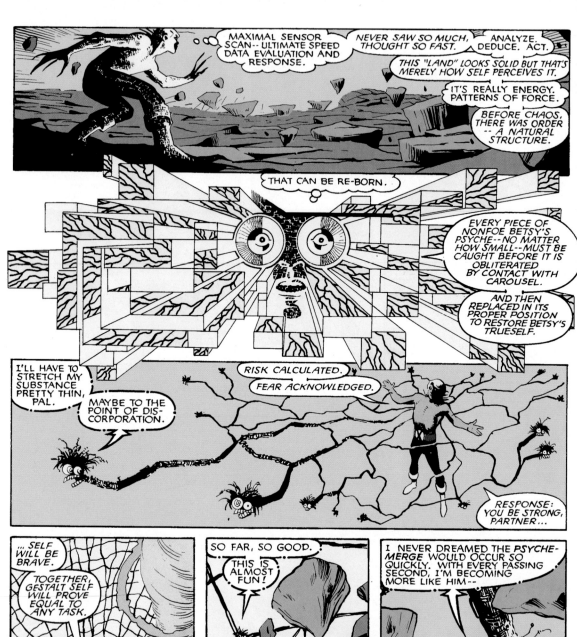

MAXIMAL SENSOR SCAN-- ULTIMATE SPEED DATA EVALUATION AND RESPONSE.

NEVER SAW SO MUCH, THOUGHT SO FAST.

ANALYZE. DEDUCE. ACT.

THIS "LAND" LOOKS SOLID BUT THAT'S MERELY HOW SELF PERCEIVES IT.

IT'S REALLY ENERGY. PATTERNS OF FORCE.

BEFORE CHAOS, THERE WAS ORDER -- A NATURAL STRUCTURE.

THAT CAN BE RE-BORN.

EVERY PIECE OF NONFOE BETSY'S PSYCHE--NO MATTER HOW SMALL--MUST BE CAUGHT BEFORE IT IS OBLITERATED BY CONTACT WITH CAROUSEL.

AND THEN REPLACED IN ITS PROPER POSITION TO RESTORE BETSY'S TRUESELF.

I'LL HAVE TO STRETCH MY SUBSTANCE PRETTY THIN, PAL.

MAYBE TO THE POINT OF DIS-CORPORATION.

RISK CALCULATED.

FEAR ACKNOWLEDGED.

RESPONSE: YOU BE STRONG, PARTNER...

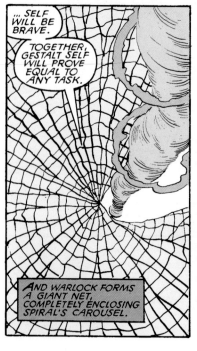

... SELF WILL BE BRAVE.

TOGETHER, GESTALT SELF WILL PROVE EQUAL TO ANY TASK.

AND WARLOCK FORMS A GIANT NET, COMPLETELY ENCLOSING SPIRAL'S CAROUSEL.

SO FAR, SO GOOD.

THIS IS ALMOST FUN!

I'M MORE WORRIED ABOUT DOUG.

I NEVER DREAMED THE PSYCHE-MERGE WOULD OCCUR SO QUICKLY. WITH EVERY PASSING SECOND, I'M BECOMING MORE LIKE HIM--

-- AND HIM, LIKE SELF!

WORSE, WE'RE BOTH STARTING TO THINK THIS IS THE WAY THINGS SHOULD BE!

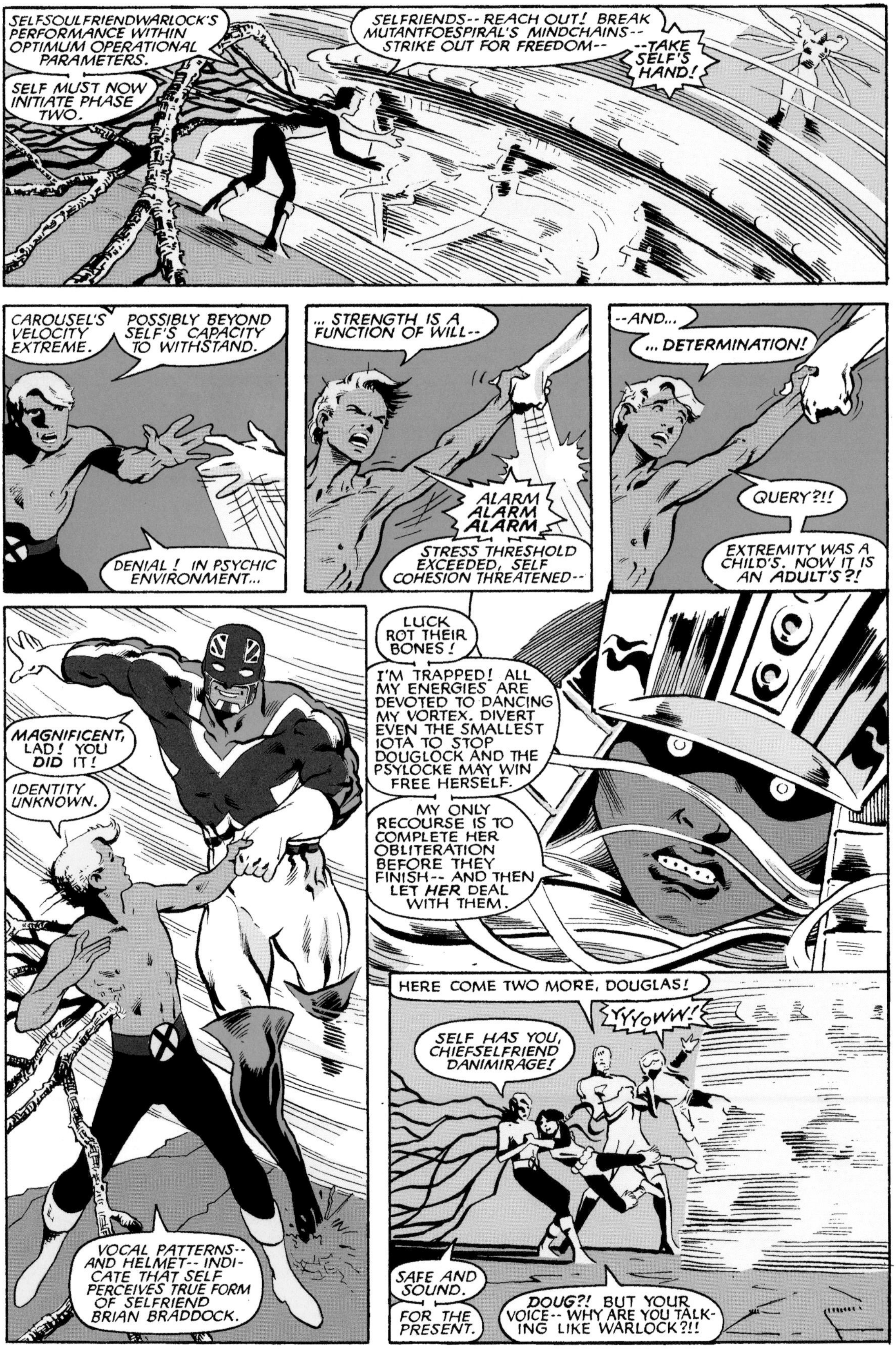
SELFSOULFRIENDWARLOCK'S PERFORMANCE WITHIN OPTIMUM OPERATIONAL PARAMETERS.
SELF MUST NOW INITIATE PHASE TWO.
SELFRIENDS-- REACH OUT! BREAK MUTANTFOESPIRAL'S MINDCHAINS-- STRIKE OUT FOR FREEDOM--
--TAKE SELF'S HAND!
CAROUSEL'S VELOCITY EXTREME.
POSSIBLY BEYOND SELF'S CAPACITY TO WITHSTAND.
DENIAL! IN PSYCHIC ENVIRONMENT...
... STRENGTH IS A FUNCTION OF WILL--
ALARM ALARM ALARM
STRESS THRESHOLD EXCEEDED, SELF COHESION THREATENED--
--AND...
... DETERMINATION!
QUERY?!!
EXTREMITY WAS A CHILD'S. NOW IT IS AN ADULT'S?!
MAGNIFICENT, LAD! YOU DID IT!
IDENTITY UNKNOWN.
VOCAL PATTERNS-- AND HELMET-- INDI-CATE THAT SELF PERCEIVES TRUE FORM OF SELFRIEND BRIAN BRADDOCK.
LUCK ROT THEIR BONES!
I'M TRAPPED! ALL MY ENERGIES ARE DEVOTED TO DANCING MY VORTEX. DIVERT EVEN THE SMALLEST IOTA TO STOP DOUGLOCK AND THE PSYLOCKE MAY WIN FREE HERSELF.
MY ONLY RECOURSE IS TO COMPLETE HER OBLITERATION BEFORE THEY FINISH-- AND THEN LET HER DEAL WITH THEM.
HERE COME TWO MORE, DOUGLAS!
YYYOWW!
SELF HAS YOU, CHIEFSELFRIEND DANIMIRAGE!
SAFE AND SOUND.
FOR THE PRESENT.
DOUG?! BUT YOUR VOICE-- WHY ARE YOU TALK-ING LIKE WARLOCK?!!

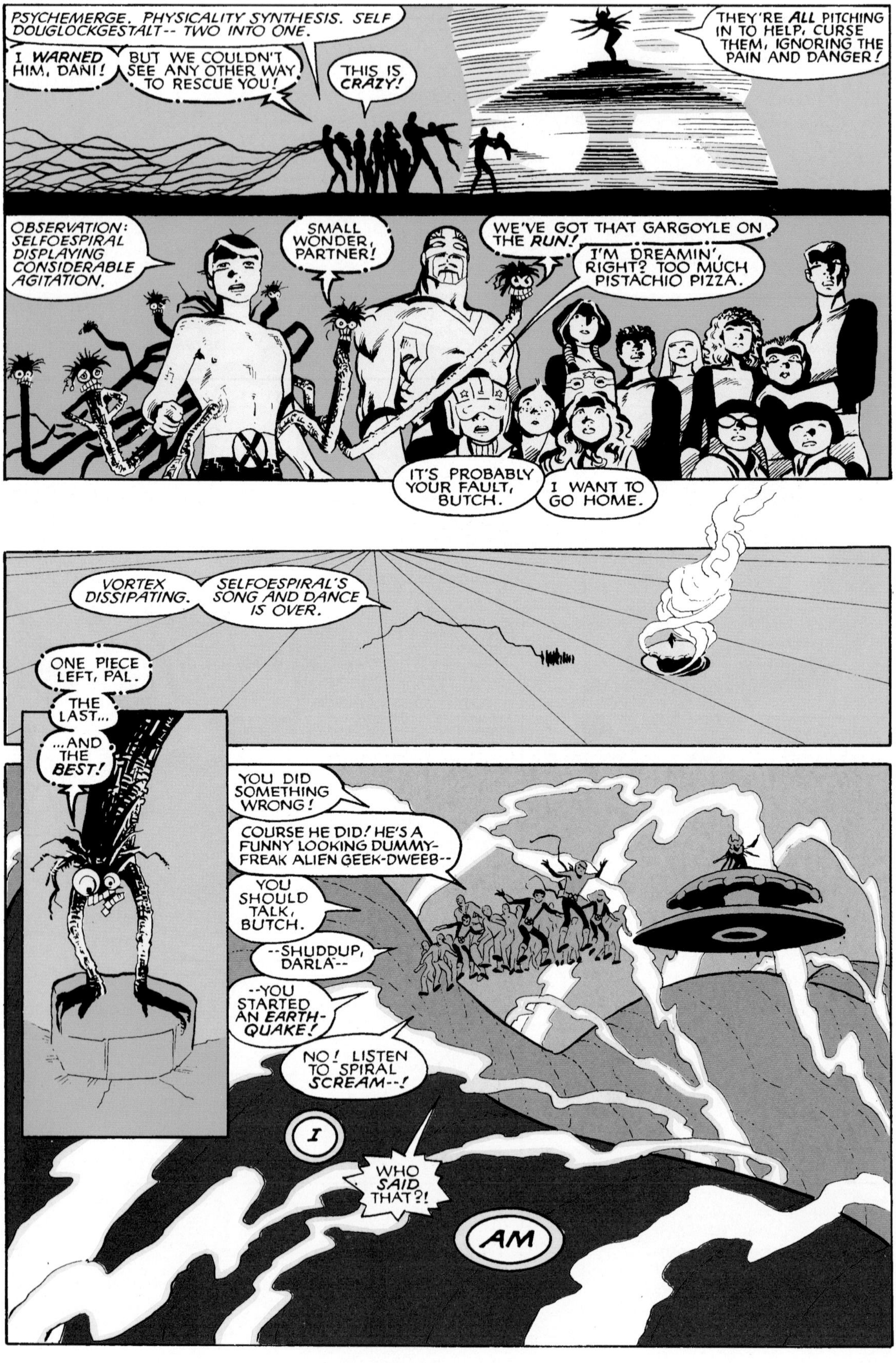
PSYCHEMERGE. PHYSICALITY SYNTHESIS. SELF DOUGLOCKGESTALT-- TWO INTO ONE.
I WARNED HIM, DANI!
BUT WE COULDN'T SEE ANY OTHER WAY TO RESCUE YOU!
THIS IS CRAZY!
THEY'RE ALL PITCHING IN TO HELP, CURSE THEM, IGNORING THE PAIN AND DANGER!
OBSERVATION: SELFOESPIRAL DISPLAYING CONSIDERABLE AGITATION.
SMALL WONDER, PARTNER!
WE'VE GOT THAT GARGOYLE ON THE RUN!
I'M DREAMIN', RIGHT? TOO MUCH PISTACHIO PIZZA.
IT'S PROBABLY YOUR FAULT, BUTCH.
I WANT TO GO HOME.
VORTEX DISSIPATING.
SELFOESPIRAL'S SONG AND DANCE IS OVER.
ONE PIECE LEFT, PAL.
THE LAST...
...AND THE BEST!
YOU DID SOMETHING WRONG!
COURSE HE DID! HE'S A FUNNY LOOKING DUMMY-FREAK ALIEN GEEK-DWEEB--
YOU SHOULD TALK, BUTCH.
--SHUDDUP, DARLA--
--YOU STARTED AN EARTHQUAKE!
NO! LISTEN TO SPIRAL SCREAM--!
I
WHO SAID THAT?!
AM

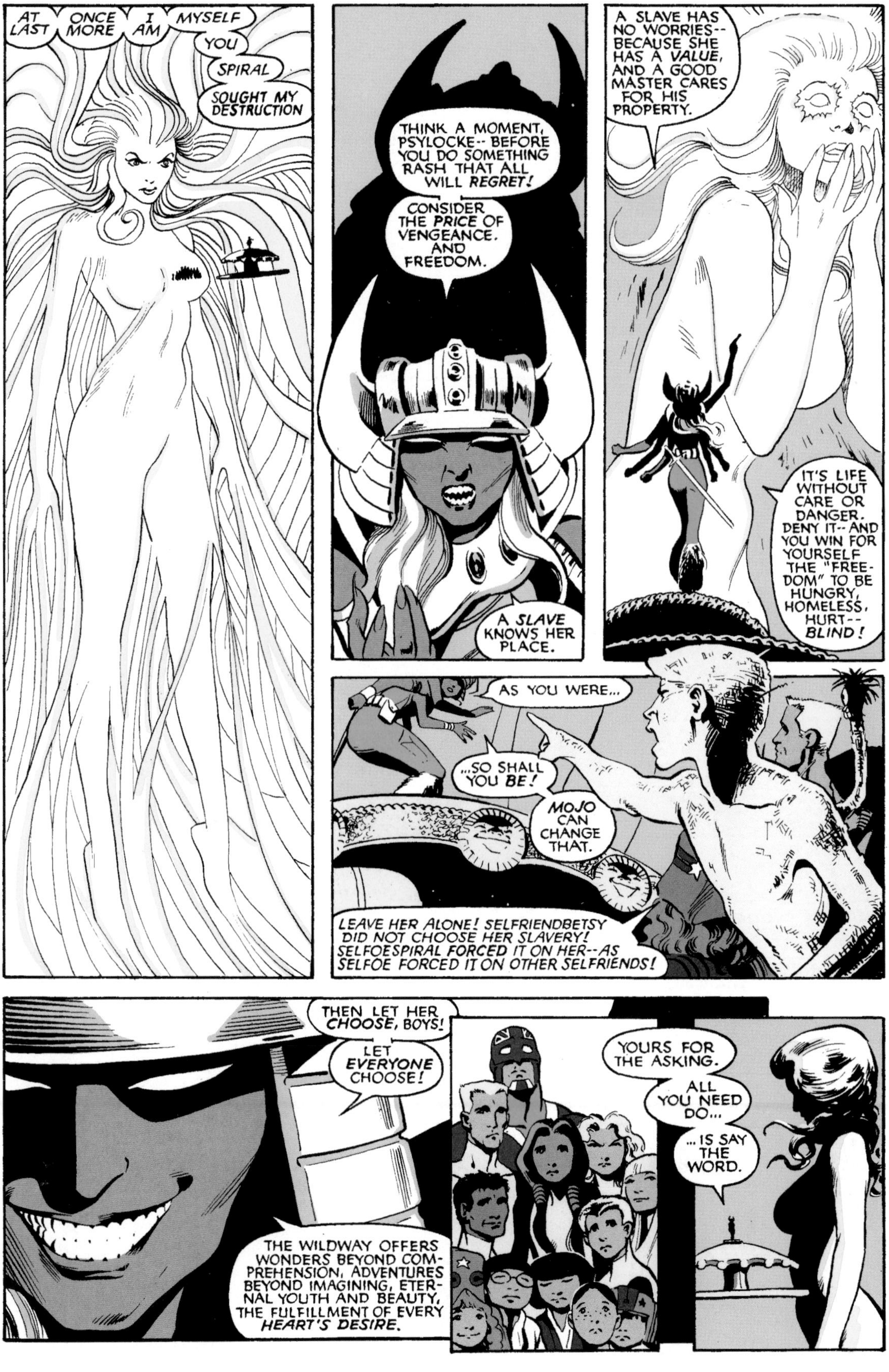

AT LAST
ONCE MORE
I AM
MYSELF
YOU
SPIRAL
SOUGHT MY DESTRUCTION
THINK A MOMENT, PSYLOCKE-- BEFORE YOU DO SOMETHING RASH THAT ALL WILL REGRET!
CONSIDER THE PRICE OF VENGEANCE. AND FREEDOM.
A SLAVE KNOWS HER PLACE.
A SLAVE HAS NO WORRIES-- BECAUSE SHE HAS A VALUE, AND A GOOD MASTER CARES FOR HIS PROPERTY.
IT'S LIFE WITHOUT CARE OR DANGER. DENY IT--AND YOU WIN FOR YOURSELF THE "FREE-DOM" TO BE HUNGRY, HOMELESS, HURT-- BLIND!
AS YOU WERE...
...SO SHALL YOU BE!
MOJO CAN CHANGE THAT.
LEAVE HER ALONE! SELFRIENDBETSY DID NOT CHOOSE HER SLAVERY! SELFOESPIRAL FORCED IT ON HER--AS SELFOE FORCED IT ON OTHER SELFRIENDS!
THEN LET HER CHOOSE, BOYS!
LET EVERYONE CHOOSE!
THE WILDWAY OFFERS WONDERS BEYOND COM-PREHENSION, ADVENTURES BEYOND IMAGINING, ETER-NAL YOUTH AND BEAUTY, THE FULFILLMENT OF EVERY HEART'S DESIRE.
YOURS FOR THE ASKING.
ALL YOU NEED DO...
...IS SAY THE WORD.

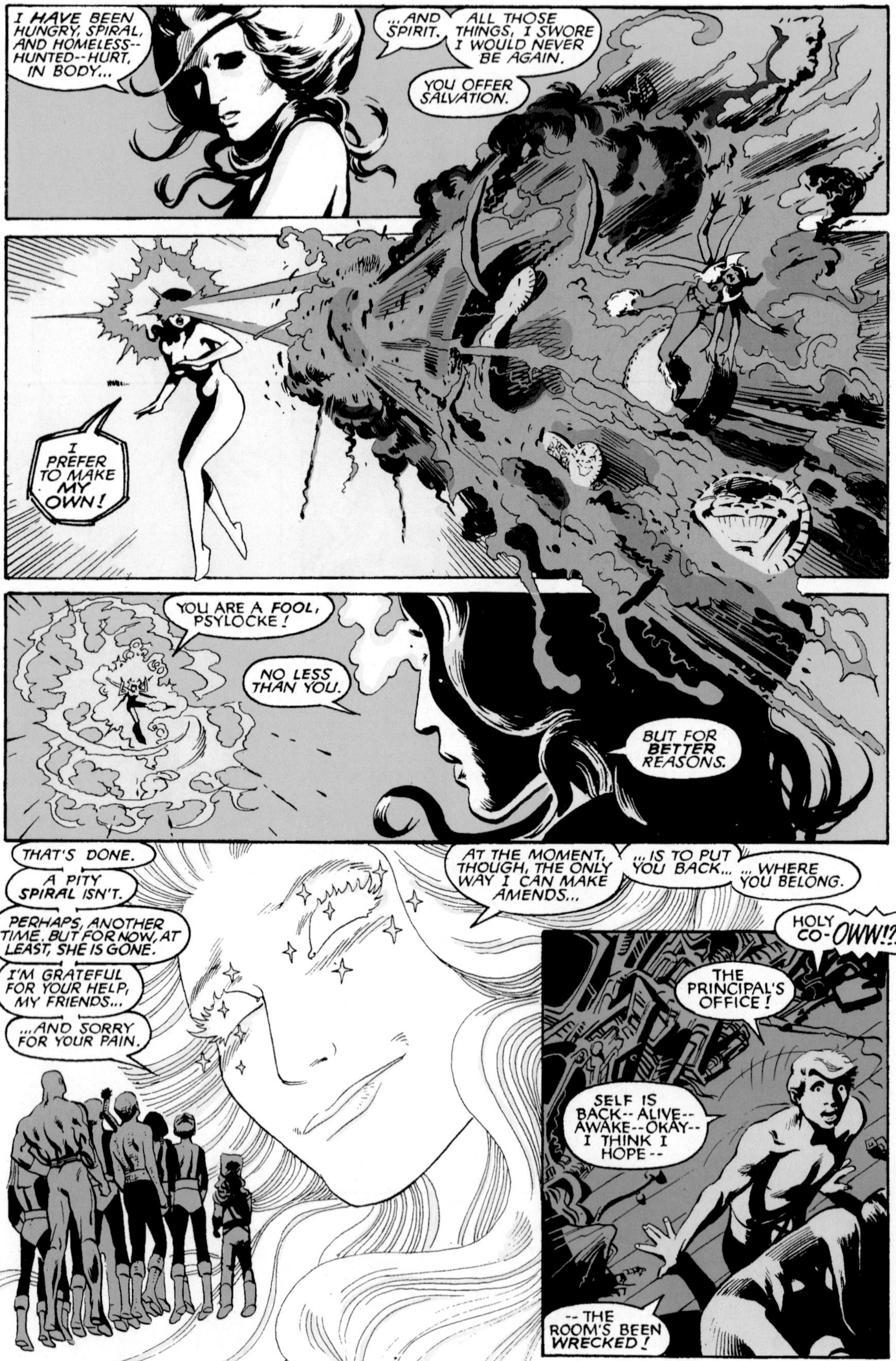
I HAVE BEEN HUNGRY, SPIRAL, AND HOMELESS-- HUNTED--HURT, IN BODY...
...AND SPIRIT.
ALL THOSE THINGS, I SWORE I WOULD NEVER BE AGAIN.
YOU OFFER SALVATION.
I PREFER TO MAKE MY OWN!
YOU ARE A FOOL, PSYLOCKE!
NO LESS THAN YOU.
BUT FOR BETTER REASONS.
THAT'S DONE.
A PITY SPIRAL ISN'T.
PERHAPS, ANOTHER TIME. BUT FOR NOW, AT LEAST, SHE IS GONE.
I'M GRATEFUL FOR YOUR HELP, MY FRIENDS...
...AND SORRY FOR YOUR PAIN.
AT THE MOMENT, THOUGH, THE ONLY WAY I CAN MAKE AMENDS...
...IS TO PUT YOU BACK...
...WHERE YOU BELONG.
HOLY CO-OWW!?!
THE PRINCIPAL'S OFFICE!
SELF IS BACK-- ALIVE-- AWAKE--OKAY-- I THINK I HOPE--
-- THE ROOM'S BEEN WRECKED!

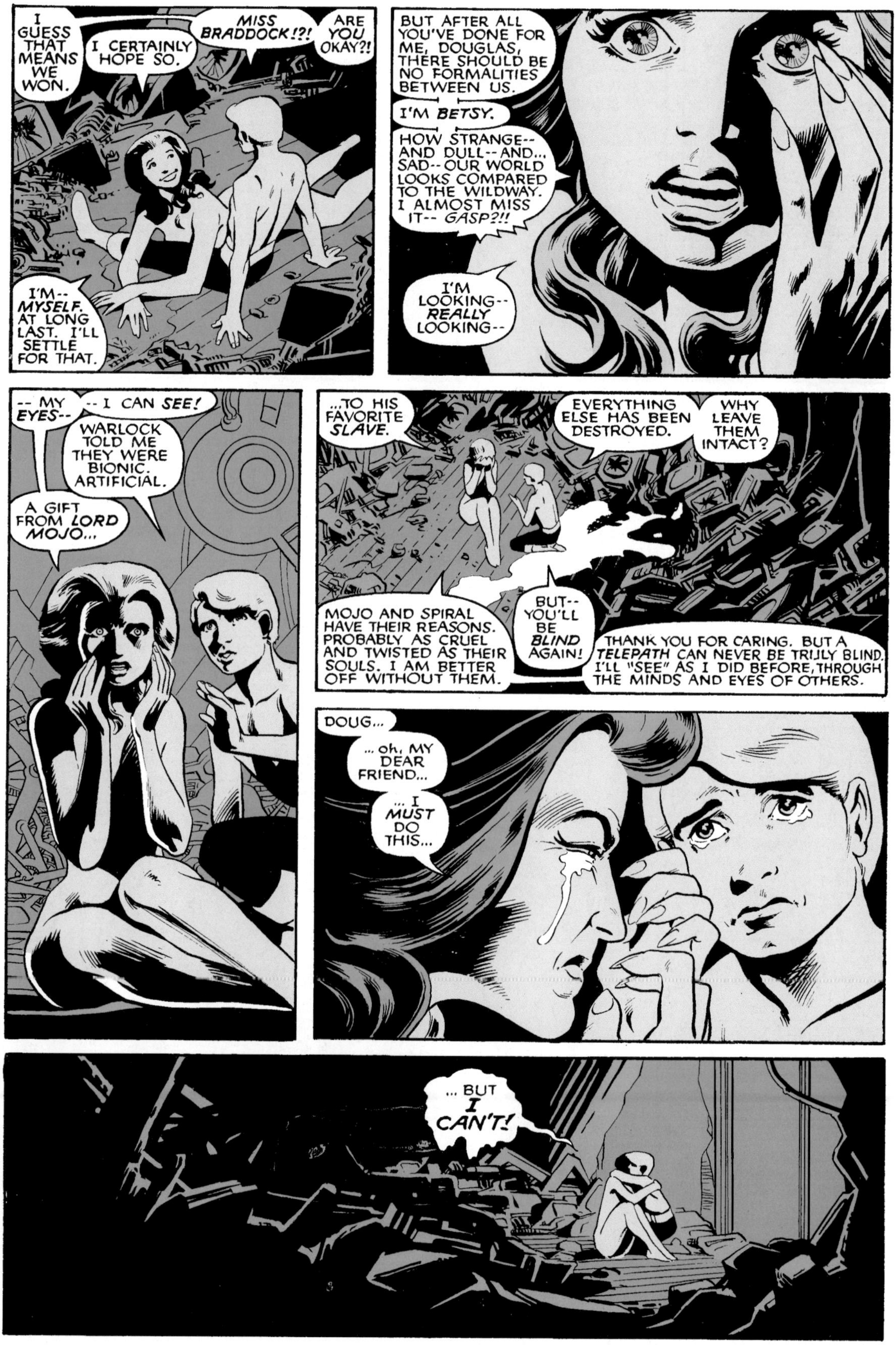
I GUESS THAT MEANS WE WON.
I CERTAINLY HOPE SO.
MISS BRADDOCK!?!
ARE YOU OKAY?!
I'M-- MYSELF. AT LONG LAST. I'LL SETTLE FOR THAT.
BUT AFTER ALL YOU'VE DONE FOR ME, DOUGLAS, THERE SHOULD BE NO FORMALITIES BETWEEN US.
I'M BETSY.
HOW STRANGE-- AND DULL--AND... SAD--OUR WORLD LOOKS COMPARED TO THE WILDWAY. I ALMOST MISS IT-- GASP?!!
I'M LOOKING-- REALLY LOOKING--
-- MY EYES--
-- I CAN SEE!
WARLOCK TOLD ME THEY WERE BIONIC. ARTIFICIAL.
A GIFT FROM LORD MOJO...
...TO HIS FAVORITE SLAVE.
EVERYTHING ELSE HAS BEEN DESTROYED.
WHY LEAVE THEM INTACT?
MOJO AND SPIRAL HAVE THEIR REASONS. PROBABLY AS CRUEL AND TWISTED AS THEIR SOULS. I AM BETTER OFF WITHOUT THEM.
BUT-- YOU'LL BE BLIND AGAIN!
THANK YOU FOR CARING. BUT A TELEPATH CAN NEVER BE TRULY BLIND. I'LL "SEE" AS I DID BEFORE, THROUGH THE MINDS AND EYES OF OTHERS.
DOUG...
... oh, MY DEAR FRIEND...
... I MUST DO THIS...
... BUT I CAN'T!

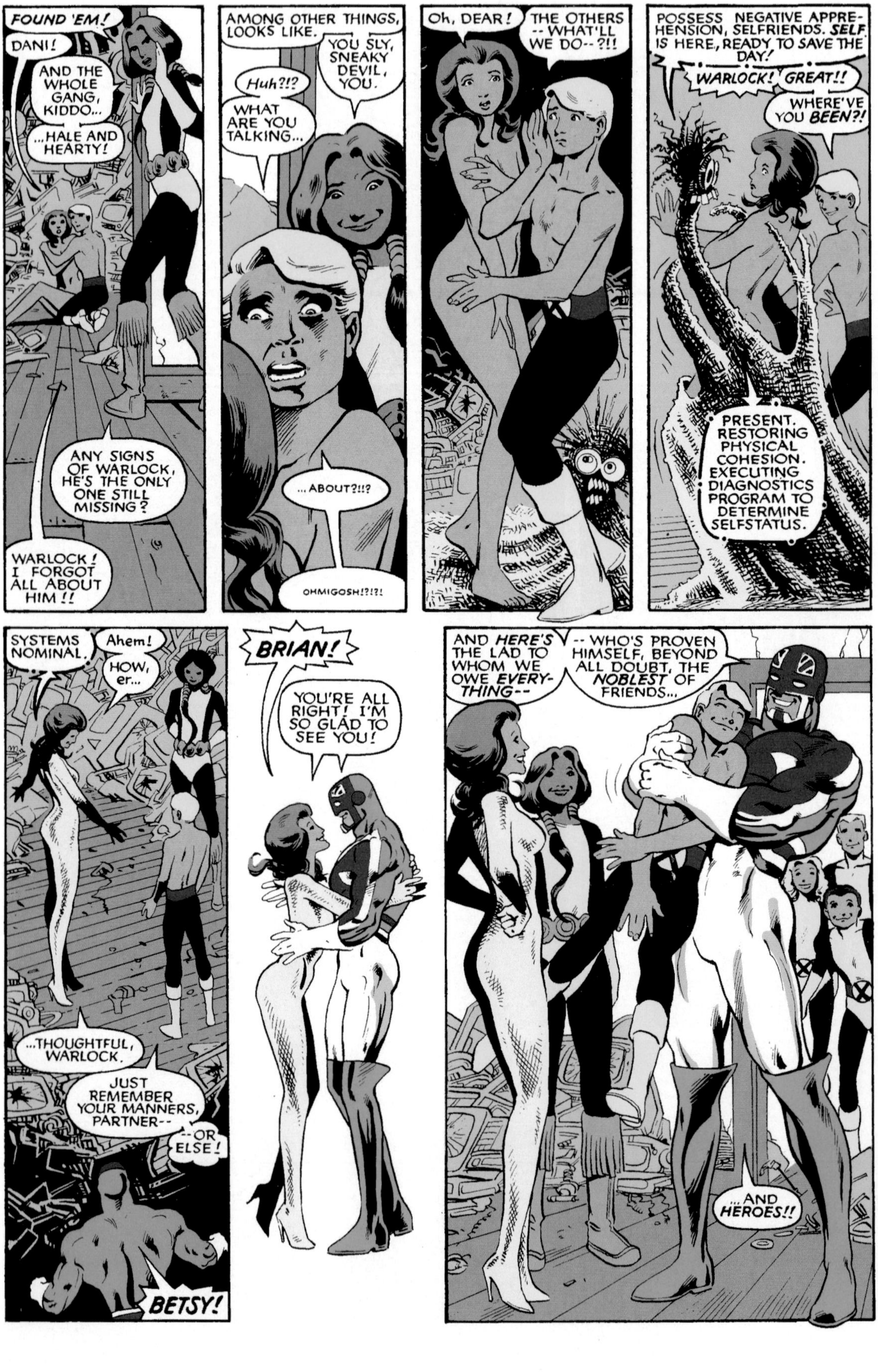
FOUND 'EM!
DANI!
AND THE WHOLE GANG, KIDDO...
...HALE AND HEARTY!
ANY SIGNS OF WARLOCK, HE'S THE ONLY ONE STILL MISSING?
WARLOCK! I FORGOT ALL ABOUT HIM!!
AMONG OTHER THINGS, LOOKS LIKE.
YOU SLY, SNEAKY DEVIL, YOU.
Huh?!?
WHAT ARE YOU TALKING...
...ABOUT?!!?
OHMIGOSH!?!?!
Oh, DEAR!
THE OTHERS -- WHAT'LL WE DO--?!!
POSSESS NEGATIVE APPREHENSION, SELFFRIENDS. SELF IS HERE, READY TO SAVE THE DAY!
WARLOCK!
GREAT!!
WHERE'VE YOU BEEN?!
PRESENT. RESTORING PHYSICAL COHESION. EXECUTING DIAGNOSTICS PROGRAM TO DETERMINE SELFSTATUS.
SYSTEMS NOMINAL.
Ahem!
HOW, er...
...THOUGHTFUL, WARLOCK.
JUST REMEMBER YOUR MANNERS, PARTNER--
--OR ELSE!
BETSY!
BRIAN!
YOU'RE ALL RIGHT! I'M SO GLAD TO SEE YOU!
AND HERE'S THE LAD TO WHOM WE OWE EVERYTHING--
-- WHO'S PROVEN HIMSELF, BEYOND ALL DOUBT, THE NOBLEST OF FRIENDS...
...AND HEROES!!

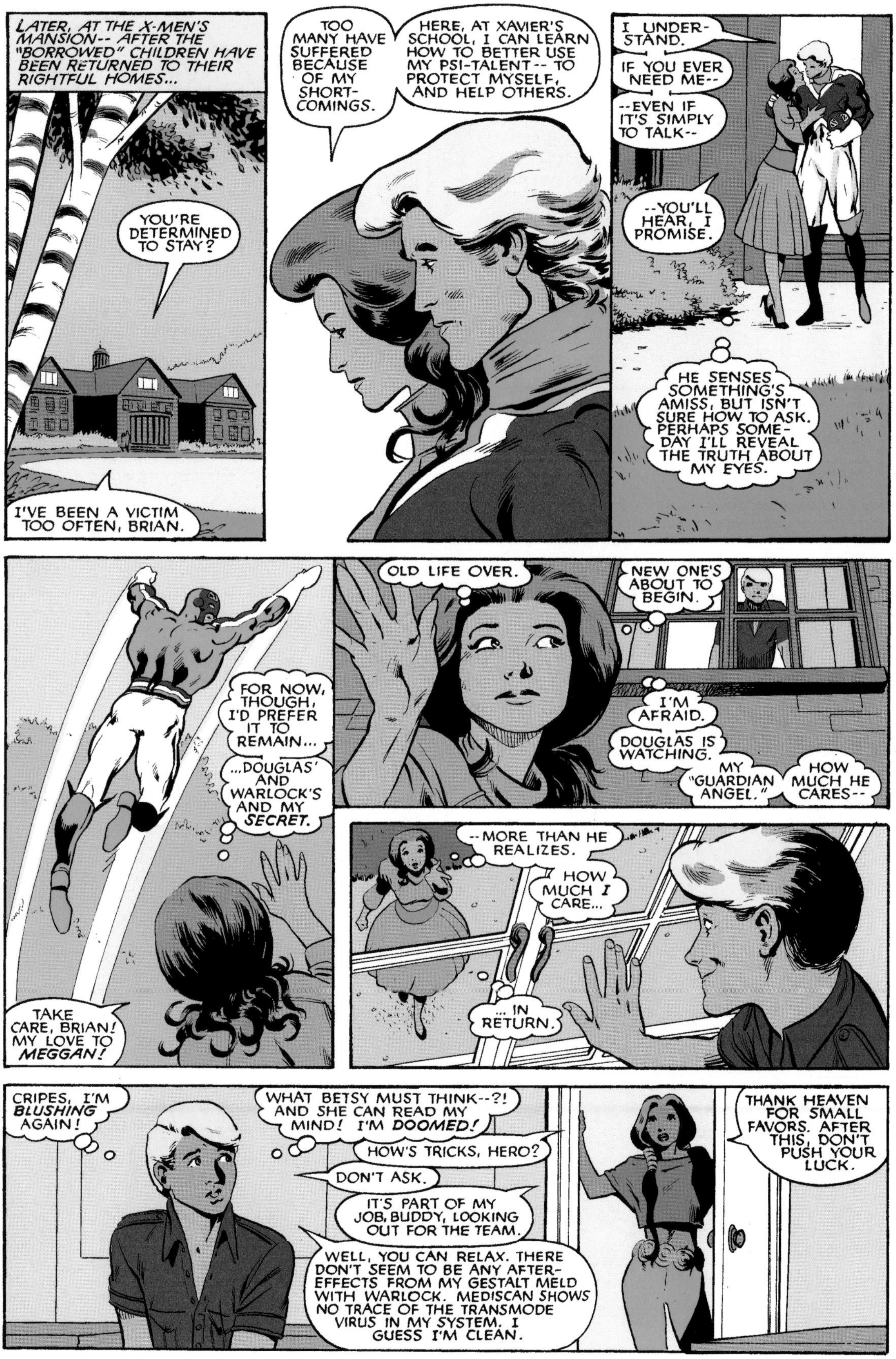
LATER, AT THE X-MEN'S MANSION-- AFTER THE "BORROWED" CHILDREN HAVE BEEN RETURNED TO THEIR RIGHTFUL HOMES...
YOU'RE DETERMINED TO STAY?
I'VE BEEN A VICTIM TOO OFTEN, BRIAN.
TOO MANY HAVE SUFFERED BECAUSE OF MY SHORT-COMINGS.
HERE, AT XAVIER'S SCHOOL, I CAN LEARN HOW TO BETTER USE MY PSI-TALENT-- TO PROTECT MYSELF, AND HELP OTHERS.
I UNDER-STAND.
IF YOU EVER NEED ME--
--EVEN IF IT'S SIMPLY TO TALK--
--YOU'LL HEAR, I PROMISE.
HE SENSES SOMETHING'S AMISS, BUT ISN'T SURE HOW TO ASK. PERHAPS SOME-DAY I'LL REVEAL THE TRUTH ABOUT MY EYES.
FOR NOW, THOUGH, I'D PREFER IT TO REMAIN...
...DOUGLAS' AND WARLOCK'S AND MY SECRET.
TAKE CARE, BRIAN! MY LOVE TO MEGGAN!
OLD LIFE OVER.
NEW ONE'S ABOUT TO BEGIN.
I'M AFRAID.
DOUGLAS IS WATCHING.
MY "GUARDIAN ANGEL."
HOW MUCH HE CARES--
--MORE THAN HE REALIZES.
HOW MUCH I CARE...
... IN RETURN.
CRIPES, I'M BLUSHING AGAIN!
WHAT BETSY MUST THINK--?! AND SHE CAN READ MY MIND! I'M DOOMED!
HOW'S TRICKS, HERO?
DON'T ASK.
IT'S PART OF MY JOB, BUDDY, LOOKING OUT FOR THE TEAM.
WELL, YOU CAN RELAX. THERE DON'T SEEM TO BE ANY AFTER-EFFECTS FROM MY GESTALT MELD WITH WARLOCK. MEDISCAN SHOWS NO TRACE OF THE TRANSMODE VIRUS IN MY SYSTEM. I GUESS I'M CLEAN.
THANK HEAVEN FOR SMALL FAVORS. AFTER THIS, DON'T PUSH YOUR LUCK.

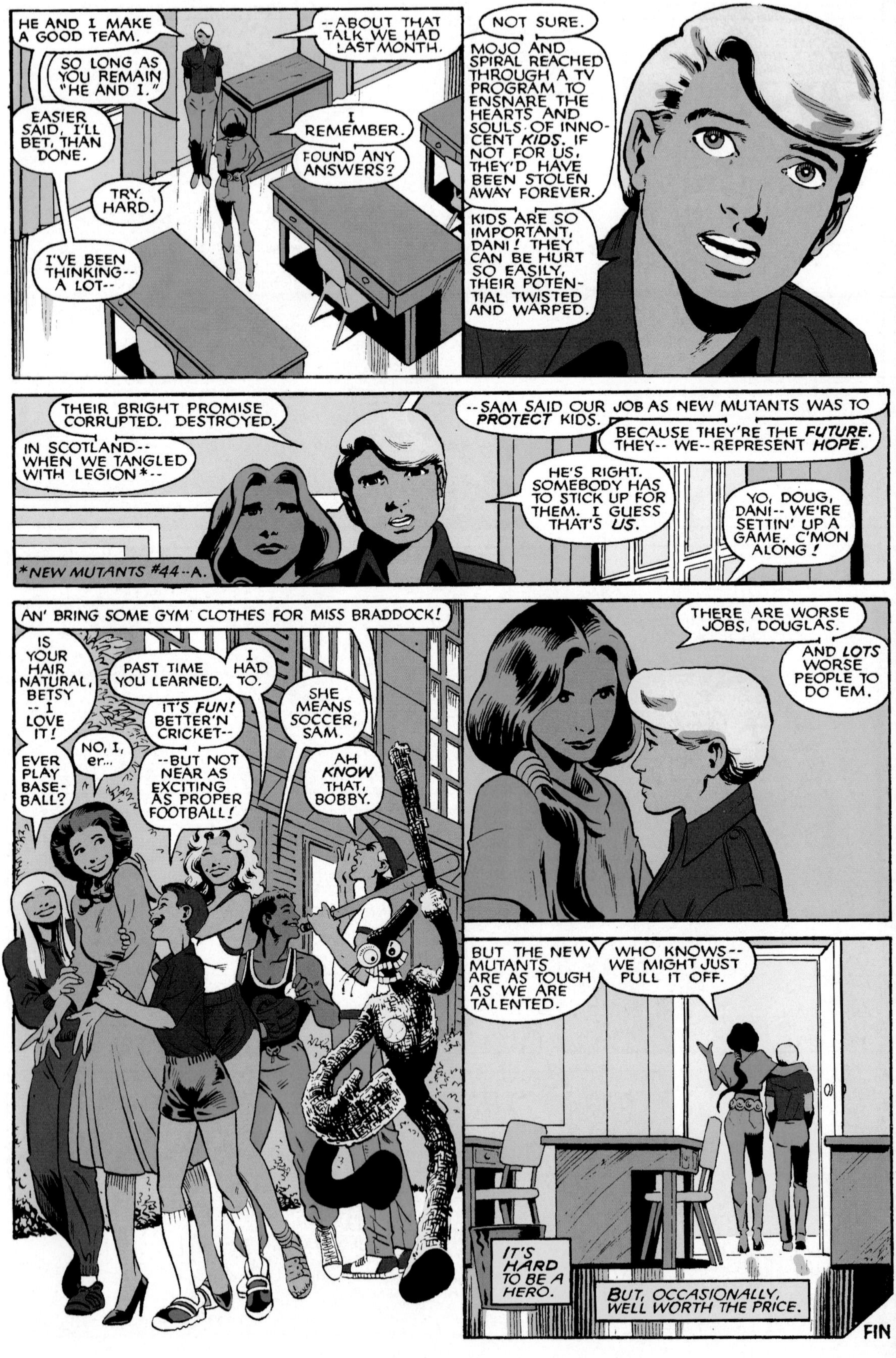
HE AND I MAKE A GOOD TEAM.
SO LONG AS YOU REMAIN "HE AND I."
EASIER SAID, I'LL BET, THAN DONE.
TRY. HARD.
I'VE BEEN THINKING-- A LOT--
--ABOUT THAT TALK WE HAD LAST MONTH.
I REMEMBER.
FOUND ANY ANSWERS?
NOT SURE.
MOJO AND SPIRAL REACHED THROUGH A TV PROGRAM TO ENSNARE THE HEARTS AND SOULS OF INNOCENT KIDS. IF NOT FOR US, THEY'D HAVE BEEN STOLEN AWAY FOREVER.
KIDS ARE SO IMPORTANT, DANI! THEY CAN BE HURT SO EASILY, THEIR POTENTIAL TWISTED AND WARPED.
THEIR BRIGHT PROMISE CORRUPTED. DESTROYED.
IN SCOTLAND-- WHEN WE TANGLED WITH LEGION*--
--SAM SAID OUR JOB AS NEW MUTANTS WAS TO PROTECT KIDS.
BECAUSE THEY'RE THE FUTURE. THEY-- WE-- REPRESENT HOPE.
HE'S RIGHT. SOMEBODY HAS TO STICK UP FOR THEM. I GUESS THAT'S US.
YO, DOUG, DANI-- WE'RE SETTIN' UP A GAME. C'MON ALONG!
*NEW MUTANTS #44--A.
AN' BRING SOME GYM CLOTHES FOR MISS BRADDOCK!
IS YOUR HAIR NATURAL, BETSY -- I LOVE IT!
EVER PLAY BASE-BALL?
NO, I, er...
PAST TIME YOU LEARNED.
I HAD TO.
IT'S FUN! BETTER'N CRICKET--
--BUT NOT NEAR AS EXCITING AS PROPER FOOTBALL!
SHE MEANS SOCCER, SAM.
AH KNOW THAT, BOBBY.
THERE ARE WORSE JOBS, DOUGLAS.
AND LOTS WORSE PEOPLE TO DO 'EM.
BUT THE NEW MUTANTS ARE AS TOUGH AS WE ARE TALENTED.
WHO KNOWS-- WE MIGHT JUST PULL IT OFF.
IT'S HARD TO BE A HERO.
BUT, OCCASIONALLY, WELL WORTH THE PRICE.
FIN

The New Mutants Annual #3

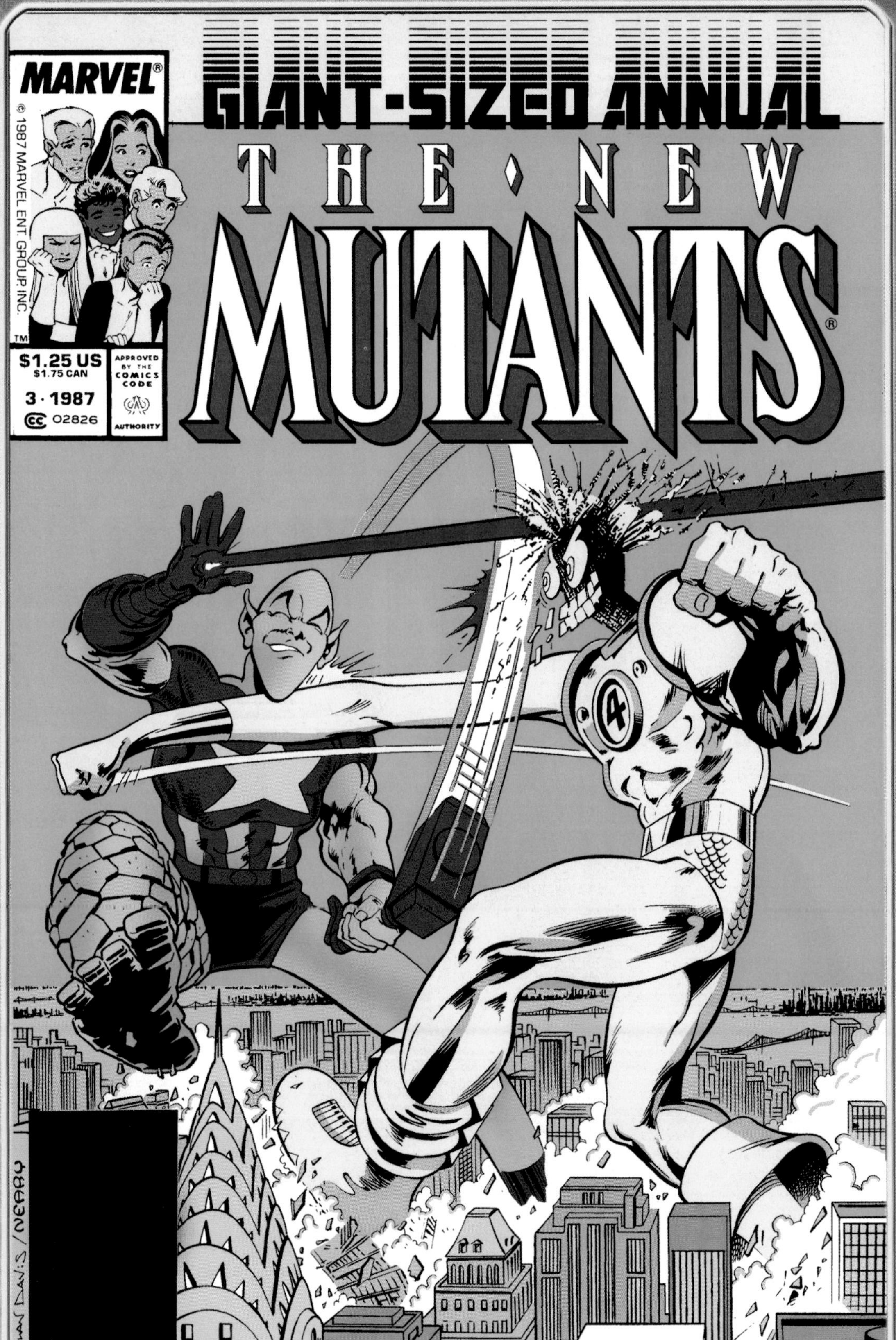

MARVEL®
© 1987 MARVEL ENT. GROUP, INC.
TM
$1.25 US
$1.75 CAN
3 · 1987
CC 02826
APPROVED BY THE COMICS CODE AUTHORITY
GIANT-SIZED ANNUAL
THE · NEW
MUTANTS®
ALAN DAVIS / NEARY

ANYTHING YOU CAN DO...!

AWHILE AGO, IN HAPPIER DAYS, AT PROFESSOR XAVIER'S SCHOOL FOR GIFTED YOUNGSTERS-- SALEM CENTER, NEW YORK.

"BANGLES" BOOMING ON THE TAPE DECK, WALKING LIKE EGYPTIANS.

MUSIC WITH A BEAT, TO SCHEME BY-- HARD, DRIVING, HOT, FIRING HIS BLOOD, SPARKING HIS MIND THE NASTIEST OF WAYS.

"BEASTIE BOYS" ARE NEXT, CLASHING WITH JOAN JETT, THEN LILA AND TINA AND ALI-DAZZLER--TOPPED OFF BY THE "BOSS"-- THE BROO, BRUCE, LIVE!

MASTER OF THE MUSIC-- AND THE COMPUTERS THAT HUM AND WHIR ABOUT HIM IN THIS OBSERVATION CONTROL BOOTH-- IS DOUGLAS RAMSEY...

...ALSO KNOWN AS CYPHER (BECAUSE OF HIS PARAHUMAN ABILITY TO VIRTUALLY INSTANTLY COMPREHEND ANY LANGUAGE, SPOKEN OR WRITTEN, LIVING OR MACHINE.)

AND HE HOLDS THE FATE OF HIS FELLOW NEW MUTANTS IN THE PALMS OF HIS HANDS.

| STAN LEE PRESENTOR | CHRIS CLAREMONT WRITER | ALAN DAVIS PENCILER | PAUL NEARY INKER | TOM ORZECHOWSKI LETTERER | GLYNIS OLIVER COLORIST | ANN NOCENTI EDITOR | JIM SHOOTER CHIEF | CHRIS CLAREMONT & BOB McLEOD CREATORS |

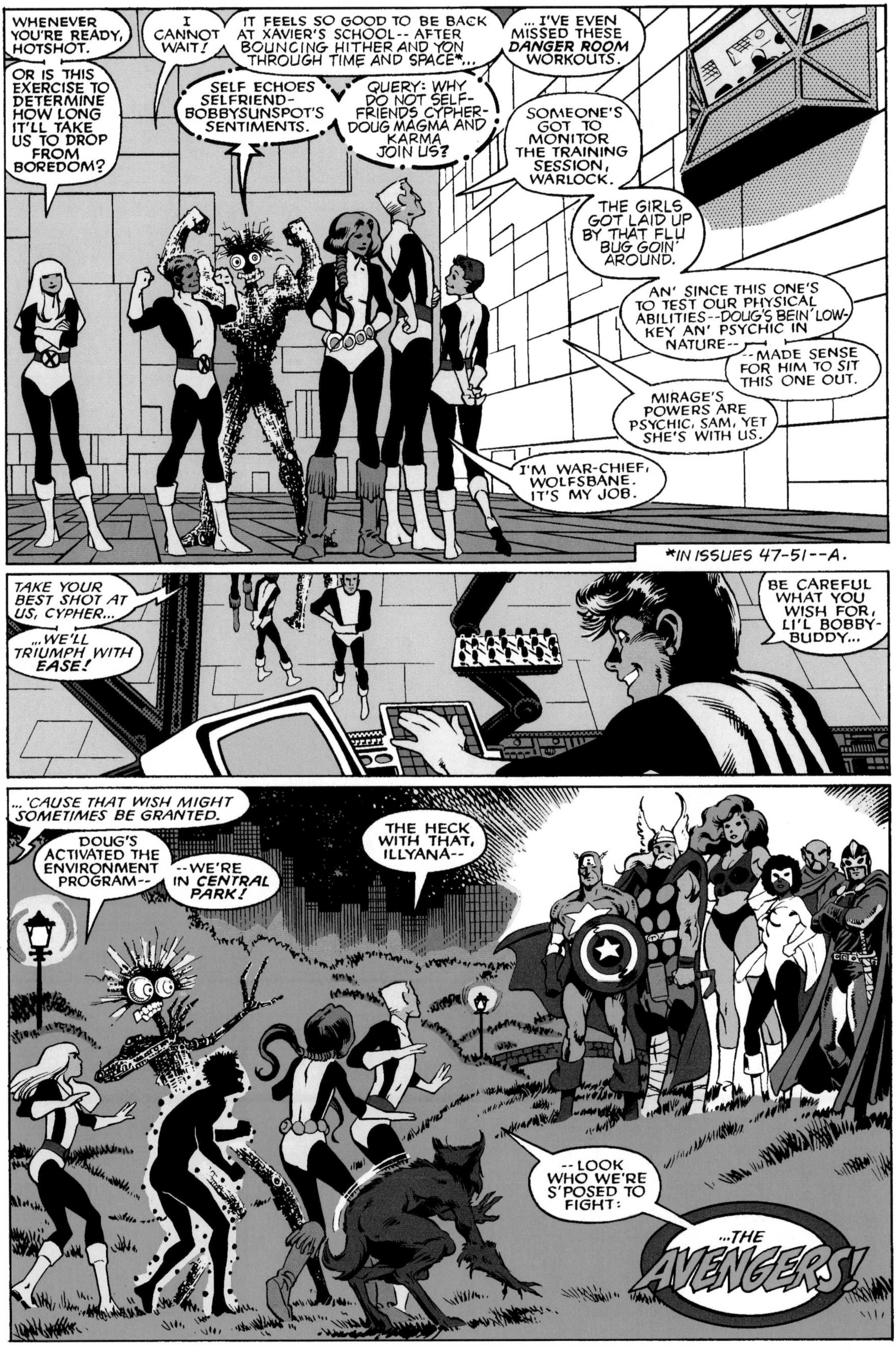
WHENEVER YOU'RE READY, HOTSHOT.
OR IS THIS EXERCISE TO DETERMINE HOW LONG IT'LL TAKE US TO DROP FROM BOREDOM?
I CANNOT WAIT!
IT FEELS SO GOOD TO BE BACK AT XAVIER'S SCHOOL-- AFTER BOUNCING HITHER AND YON THROUGH TIME AND SPACE*...
...I'VE EVEN MISSED THESE DANGER ROOM WORKOUTS.
SELF ECHOES SELFRIEND-BOBBYSUNSPOT'S SENTIMENTS.
QUERY: WHY DO NOT SELF-FRIENDS CYPHER-DOUG MAGMA AND KARMA JOIN US?
SOMEONE'S GOT TO MONITOR THE TRAINING SESSION, WARLOCK.
THE GIRLS GOT LAID UP BY THAT FLU BUG GOIN' AROUND.
AN' SINCE THIS ONE'S TO TEST OUR PHYSICAL ABILITIES--DOUG'S BEIN' LOW-KEY AN' PSYCHIC IN NATURE--
--MADE SENSE FOR HIM TO SIT THIS ONE OUT.
MIRAGE'S POWERS ARE PSYCHIC, SAM, YET SHE'S WITH US.
I'M WAR-CHIEF, WOLFSBANE. IT'S MY JOB.
*IN ISSUES 47-51--A.
TAKE YOUR BEST SHOT AT US, CYPHER...
...WE'LL TRIUMPH WITH EASE!
BE CAREFUL WHAT YOU WISH FOR, LI'L BOBBY-BUDDY...
...'CAUSE THAT WISH MIGHT SOMETIMES BE GRANTED.
DOUG'S ACTIVATED THE ENVIRONMENT PROGRAM--
--WE'RE IN CENTRAL PARK!
THE HECK WITH THAT, ILLYANA--
--LOOK WHO WE'RE S'POSED TO FIGHT:
...THE AVENGERS!

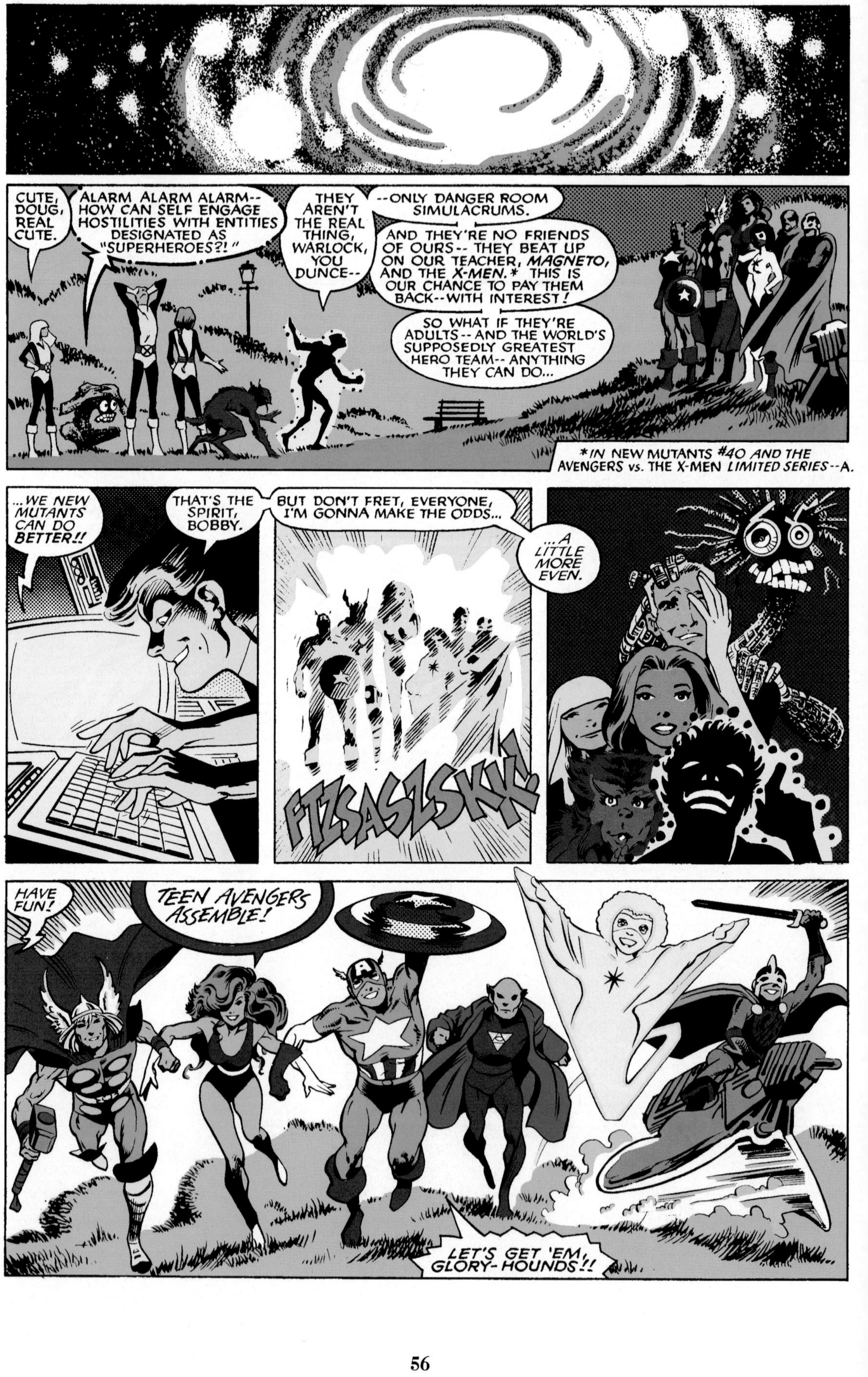
CUTE, DOUG, REAL CUTE.
ALARM ALARM ALARM-- HOW CAN SELF ENGAGE HOSTILITIES WITH ENTITIES DESIGNATED AS "SUPERHEROES?!"
THEY AREN'T THE REAL THING, WARLOCK, YOU DUNCE--
--ONLY DANGER ROOM SIMULACRUMS.
AND THEY'RE NO FRIENDS OF OURS-- THEY BEAT UP ON OUR TEACHER, MAGNETO, AND THE X-MEN.* THIS IS OUR CHANCE TO PAY THEM BACK--WITH INTEREST!
SO WHAT IF THEY'RE ADULTS--AND THE WORLD'S SUPPOSEDLY GREATEST HERO TEAM--ANYTHING THEY CAN DO...
*IN NEW MUTANTS #40 AND THE AVENGERS vs. THE X-MEN LIMITED SERIES--A.
...WE NEW MUTANTS CAN DO BETTER!!
THAT'S THE SPIRIT, BOBBY.
BUT DON'T FRET, EVERYONE, I'M GONNA MAKE THE ODDS...
...A LITTLE MORE EVEN.
FTZSASZSKK!
HAVE FUN!
TEEN AVENGERS ASSEMBLE!
LET'S GET 'EM, GLORY-HOUNDS!!

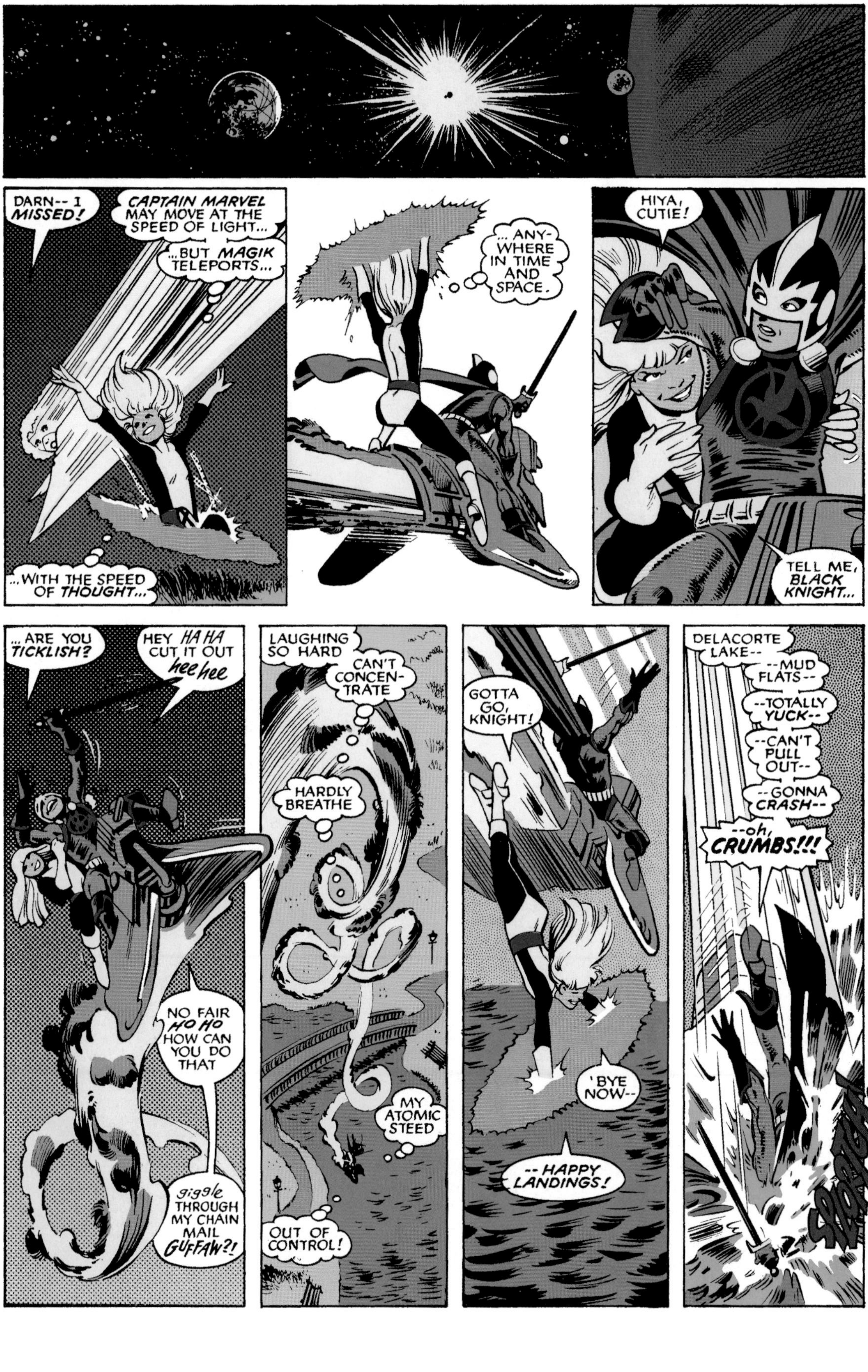
DARN-- I MISSED!
CAPTAIN MARVEL MAY MOVE AT THE SPEED OF LIGHT...
...BUT MAGIK TELEPORTS...
...WITH THE SPEED OF THOUGHT...
... ANY-WHERE IN TIME AND SPACE.
HIYA, CUTIE!
TELL ME, BLACK KNIGHT...
...ARE YOU TICKLISH?
HEY HA HA CUT IT OUT hee hee
NO FAIR HO HO HOW CAN YOU DO THAT
giggle THROUGH MY CHAIN MAIL GUFFAW?!
LAUGHING SO HARD
CAN'T CONCEN-TRATE
HARDLY BREATHE
MY ATOMIC STEED
OUT OF CONTROL!
GOTTA GO, KNIGHT!
'BYE NOW--
--HAPPY LANDINGS!
DELACORTE LAKE--
--MUD FLATS--
--TOTALLY YUCK--
--CAN'T PULL OUT--
--GONNA CRASH--
--oh, CRUMBS!!!
SPLOOSH!

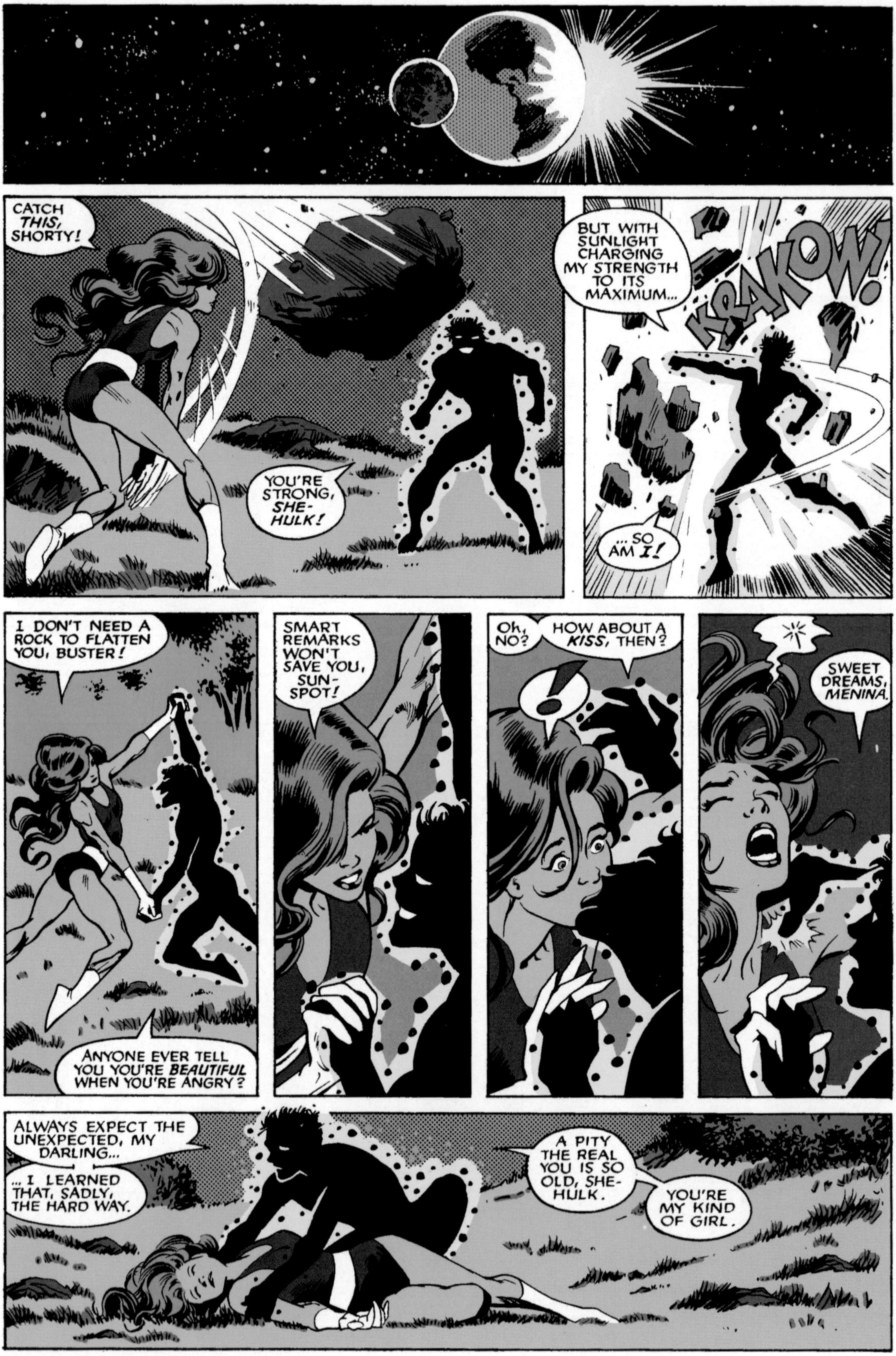

CATCH THIS, SHORTY!
YOU'RE STRONG, SHE-HULK!
BUT WITH SUNLIGHT CHARGING MY STRENGTH TO ITS MAXIMUM...
KRAKOW!
...SO AM I!
I DON'T NEED A ROCK TO FLATTEN YOU, BUSTER!
ANYONE EVER TELL YOU YOU'RE BEAUTIFUL WHEN YOU'RE ANGRY?
SMART REMARKS WON'T SAVE YOU, SUN-SPOT!
Oh, NO?
HOW ABOUT A KISS, THEN?
SWEET DREAMS, MENINA.
ALWAYS EXPECT THE UNEXPECTED, MY DARLING...
...I LEARNED THAT, SADLY, THE HARD WAY.
A PITY THE REAL YOU IS SO OLD, SHE-HULK.
YOU'RE MY KIND OF GIRL.

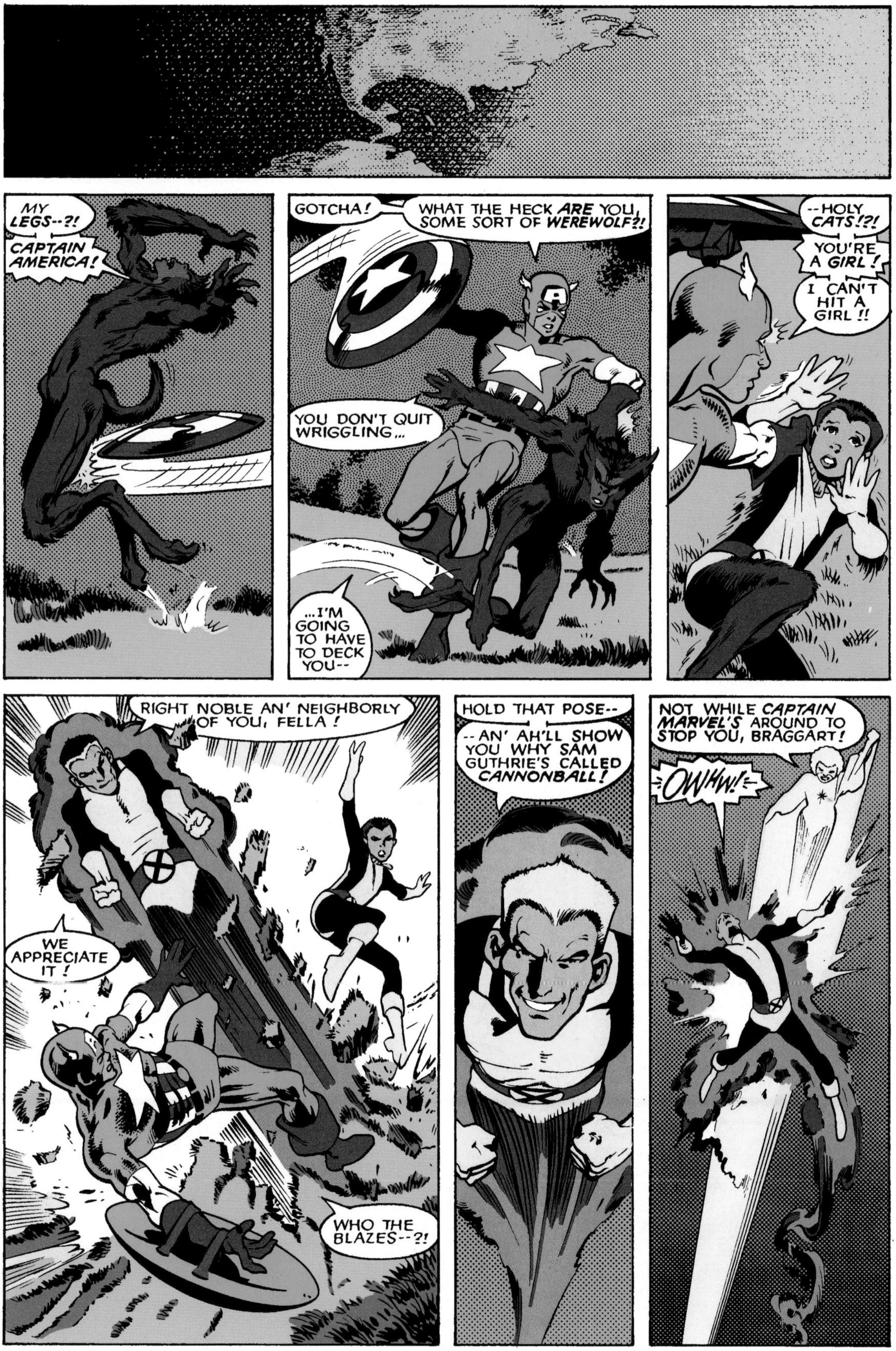
MY LEGS--?!
CAPTAIN AMERICA!
GOTCHA!
WHAT THE HECK ARE YOU, SOME SORT OF WEREWOLF?!
YOU DON'T QUIT WRIGGLING...
...I'M GOING TO HAVE TO DECK YOU--
--HOLY CATS!?!
YOU'RE A GIRL!
I CAN'T HIT A GIRL!!
RIGHT NOBLE AN' NEIGHBORLY OF YOU, FELLA!
WE APPRECIATE IT!
WHO THE BLAZES--?!
HOLD THAT POSE--
--AN' AH'LL SHOW YOU WHY SAM GUTHRIE'S CALLED CANNONBALL!
NOT WHILE CAPTAIN MARVEL'S AROUND TO STOP YOU, BRAGGART!
OWHW!

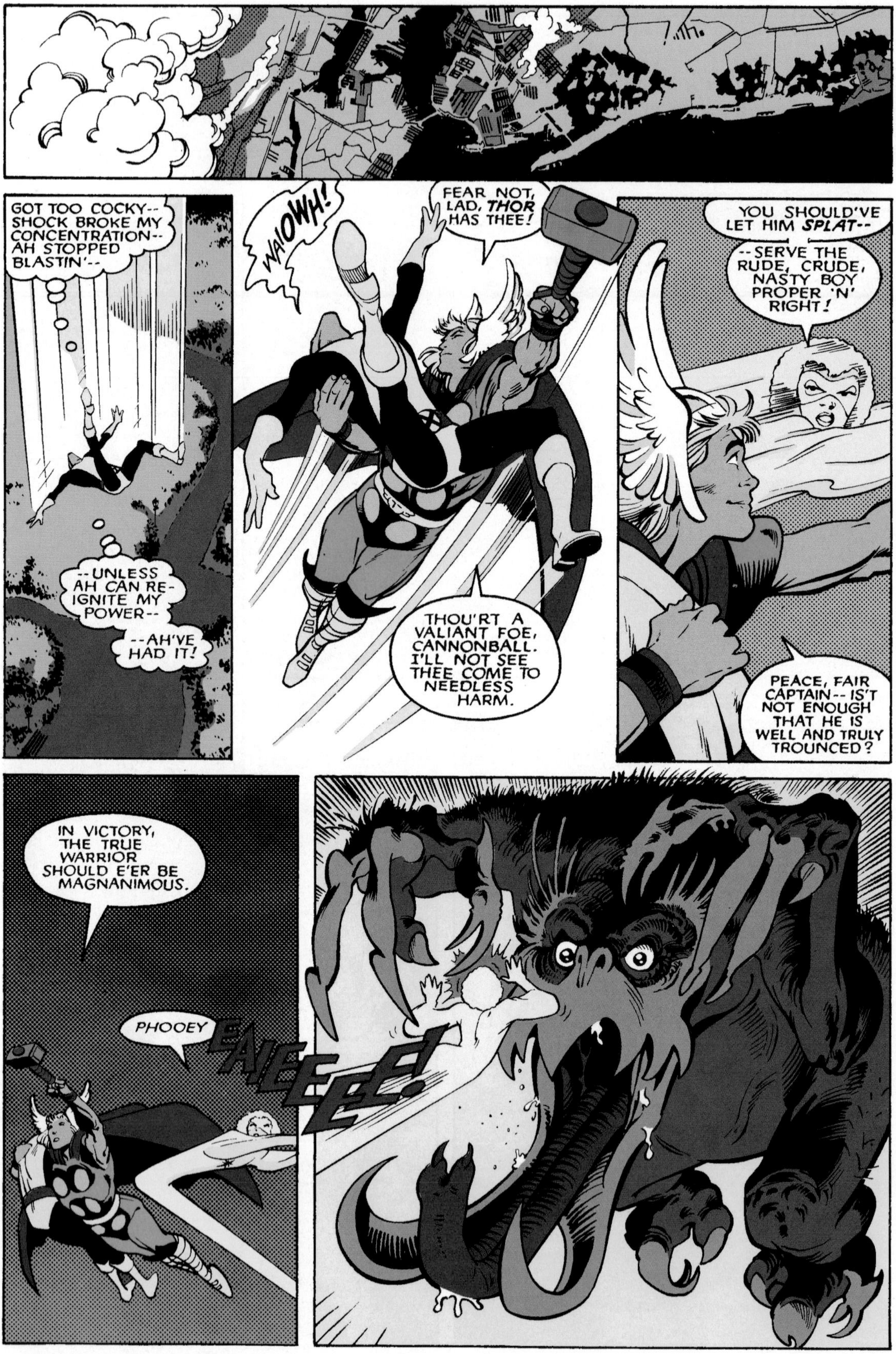
GOT TOO COCKY--
SHOCK BROKE MY CONCENTRATION--
AH STOPPED BLASTIN'--
--UNLESS AH CAN RE-IGNITE MY POWER--
--AH'VE HAD IT!
WAIOWH!
FEAR NOT, LAD, THOR HAS THEE!
THOU'RT A VALIANT FOE, CANNONBALL. I'LL NOT SEE THEE COME TO NEEDLESS HARM.
YOU SHOULD'VE LET HIM SPLAT--
--SERVE THE RUDE, CRUDE, NASTY BOY PROPER 'N' RIGHT!
PEACE, FAIR CAPTAIN-- IS'T NOT ENOUGH THAT HE IS WELL AND TRULY TROUNCED?
IN VICTORY, THE TRUE WARRIOR SHOULD E'ER BE MAGNANIMOUS.
PHOOEY
EAIEEEEE!

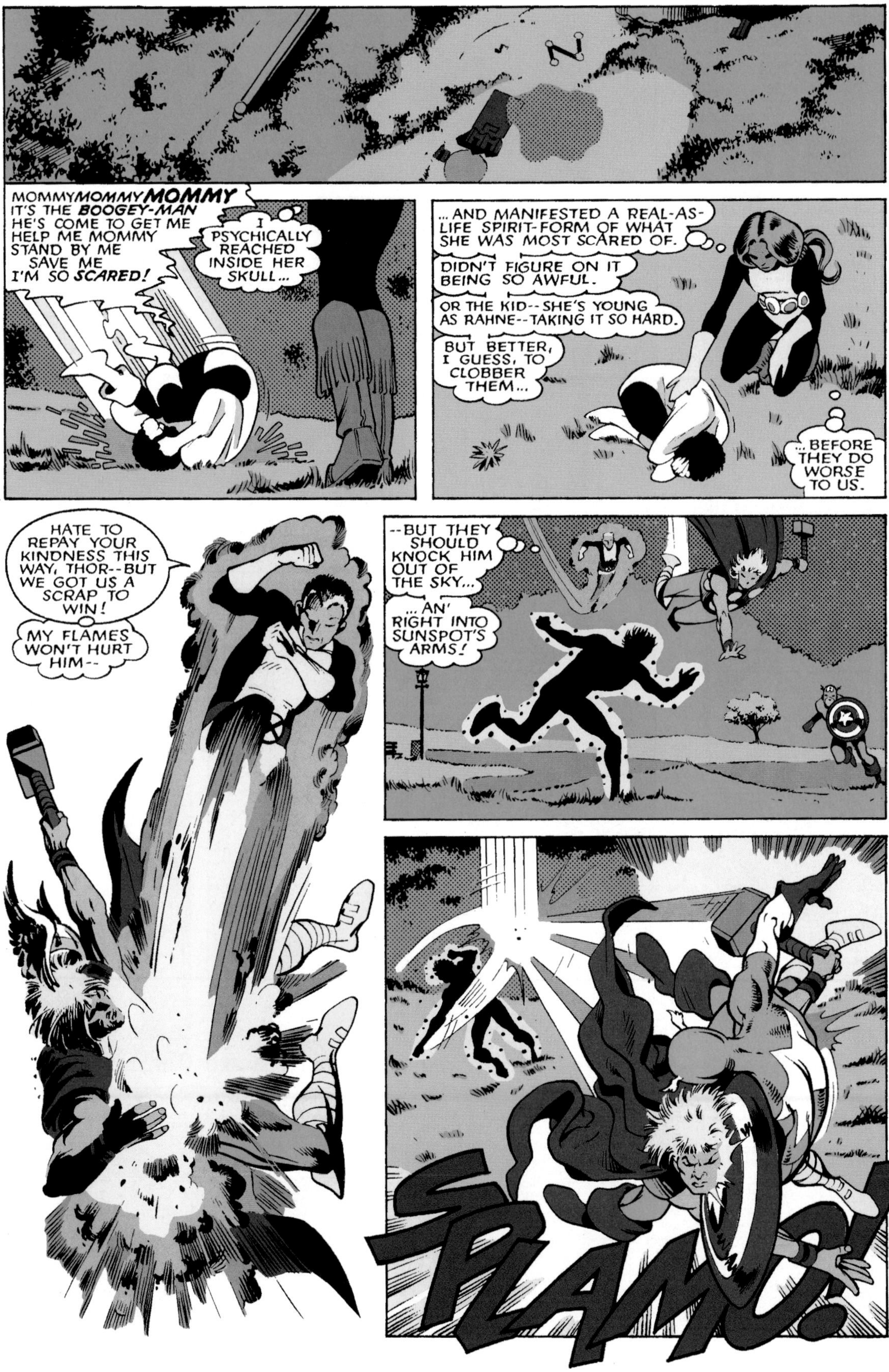
MOMMYMOMMYMOMMY IT'S THE BOOGEY-MAN HE'S COME TO GET ME HELP ME MOMMY STAND BY ME SAVE ME I'M SO SCARED!
I PSYCHICALLY REACHED INSIDE HER SKULL...
...AND MANIFESTED A REAL-AS-LIFE SPIRIT-FORM OF WHAT SHE WAS MOST SCARED OF.
DIDN'T FIGURE ON IT BEING SO AWFUL.
OR THE KID--SHE'S YOUNG AS RAHNE--TAKING IT SO HARD.
BUT BETTER, I GUESS, TO CLOBBER THEM...
...BEFORE THEY DO WORSE TO US.
HATE TO REPAY YOUR KINDNESS THIS WAY, THOR--BUT WE GOT US A SCRAP TO WIN!
MY FLAMES WON'T HURT HIM--
--BUT THEY SHOULD KNOCK HIM OUT OF THE SKY...
...AN' RIGHT INTO SUNSPOT'S ARMS!
SPLAMM!

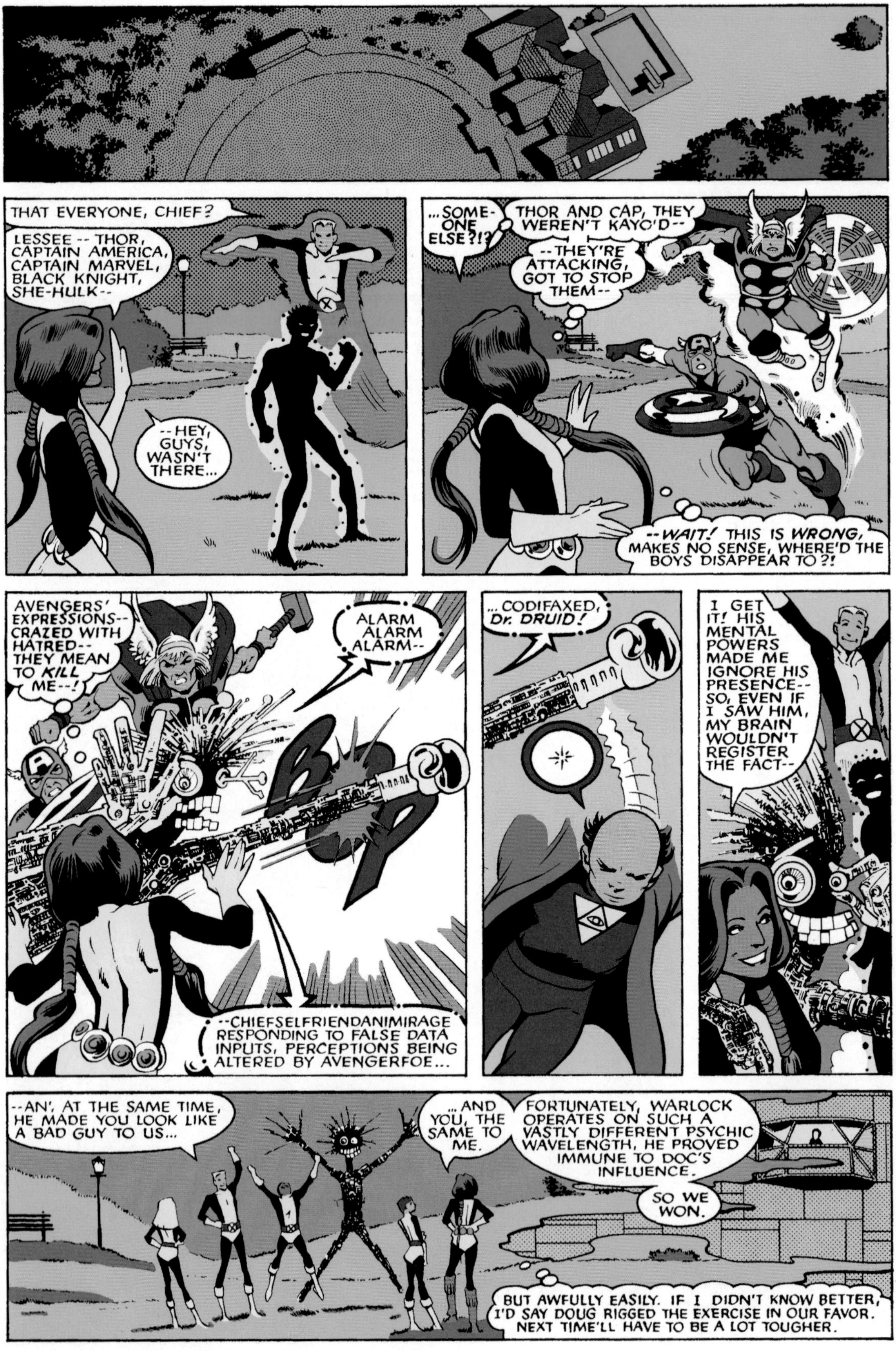
THAT EVERYONE, CHIEF?
LESSEE -- THOR, CAPTAIN AMERICA, CAPTAIN MARVEL, BLACK KNIGHT, SHE-HULK--
--HEY, GUYS, WASN'T THERE...
...SOME-ONE ELSE?!?
THOR AND CAP, THEY WEREN'T KAYO'D--
--THEY'RE ATTACKING, GOT TO STOP THEM--
--WAIT! THIS IS WRONG, MAKES NO SENSE, WHERE'D THE BOYS DISAPPEAR TO?!
AVENGERS' EXPRESSIONS--CRAZED WITH HATRED--THEY MEAN TO KILL ME--!
ALARM ALARM ALARM--
BOP
--CHIEFSELFRIENDANIMIRAGE RESPONDING TO FALSE DATA INPUTS, PERCEPTIONS BEING ALTERED BY AVENGERFOE...
...CODIFAXED, Dr. DRUID!
I GET IT! HIS MENTAL POWERS MADE ME IGNORE HIS PRESENCE--SO, EVEN IF I SAW HIM, MY BRAIN WOULDN'T REGISTER THE FACT--
--AN', AT THE SAME TIME, HE MADE YOU LOOK LIKE A BAD GUY TO US...
...AND YOU, THE SAME TO ME.
FORTUNATELY, WARLOCK OPERATES ON SUCH A VASTLY DIFFERENT PSYCHIC WAVELENGTH, HE PROVED IMMUNE TO DOC'S INFLUENCE.
SO WE WON.
BUT AWFULLY EASILY. IF I DIDN'T KNOW BETTER, I'D SAY DOUG RIGGED THE EXERCISE IN OUR FAVOR. NEXT TIME'LL HAVE TO BE A LOT TOUGHER.

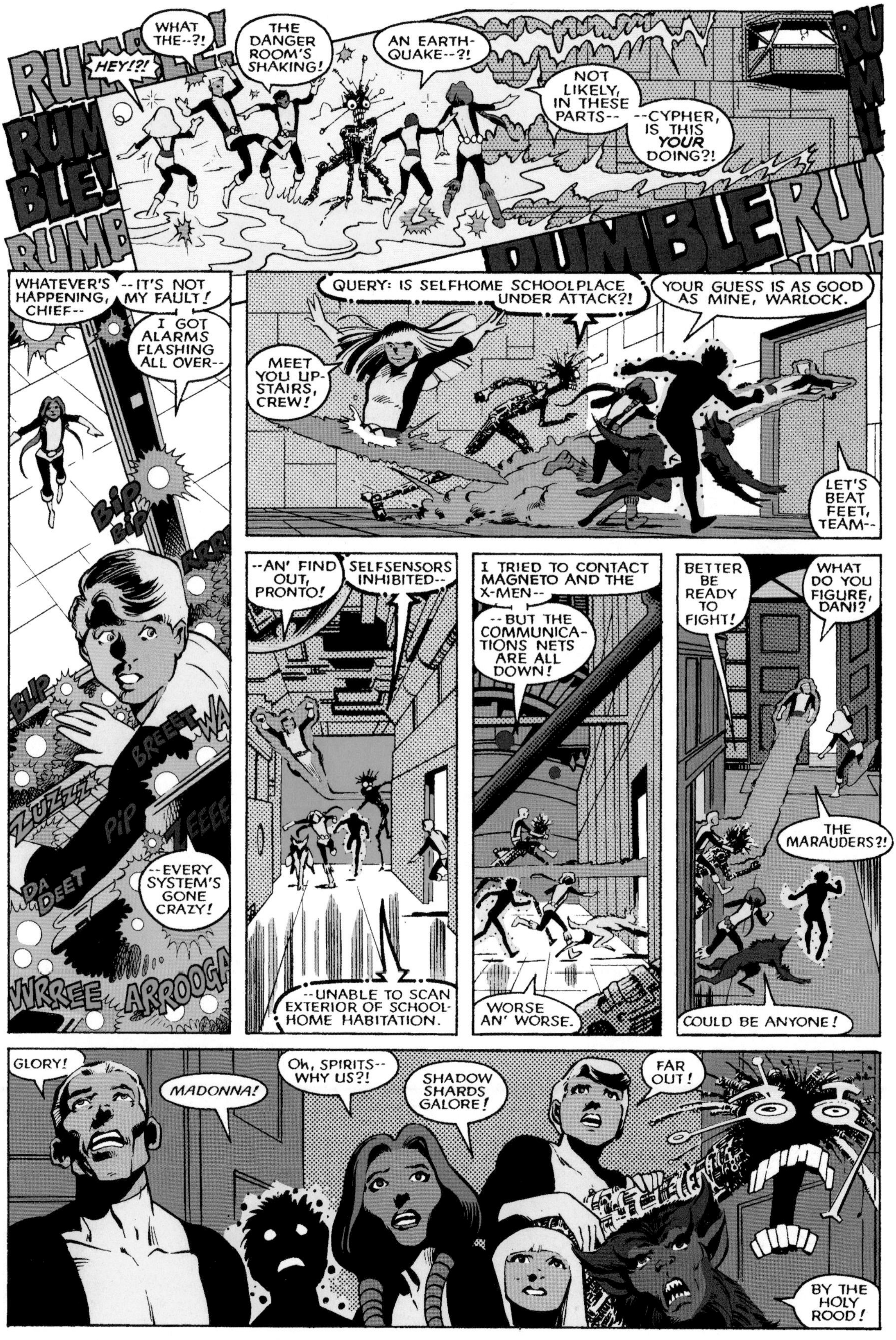
RUMBLE!
RUMBLE!
RUMBLE!
WHAT THE--?!
HEY!?!
THE DANGER ROOM'S SHAKING!
AN EARTH-QUAKE--?!
NOT LIKELY, IN THESE PARTS--
--CYPHER, IS THIS YOUR DOING?!
RUMBLE
WHATEVER'S HAPPENING, CHIEF--
--IT'S NOT MY FAULT!
I GOT ALARMS FLASHING ALL OVER--
BIP BIP
BLIP
BREEET
ZUZZZ
PIP
DA DEET
--EVERY SYSTEM'S GONE CRAZY!
WRREE ARROOGA
QUERY: IS SELFHOME SCHOOLPLACE UNDER ATTACK?!
YOUR GUESS IS AS GOOD AS MINE, WARLOCK.
MEET YOU UP-STAIRS, CREW!
LET'S BEAT FEET, TEAM--
--AN' FIND OUT, PRONTO!
SELFSENSORS INHIBITED--
--UNABLE TO SCAN EXTERIOR OF SCHOOL-HOME HABITATION.
I TRIED TO CONTACT MAGNETO AND THE X-MEN--
--BUT THE COMMUNICA-TIONS NETS ARE ALL DOWN!
WORSE AN' WORSE.
BETTER BE READY TO FIGHT!
WHAT DO YOU FIGURE, DANI?
THE MARAUDERS?!
COULD BE ANYONE!
GLORY!
MADONNA!
Oh, SPIRITS-- WHY US?!
SHADOW SHARDS GALORE!
FAR OUT!
BY THE HOLY ROOD!

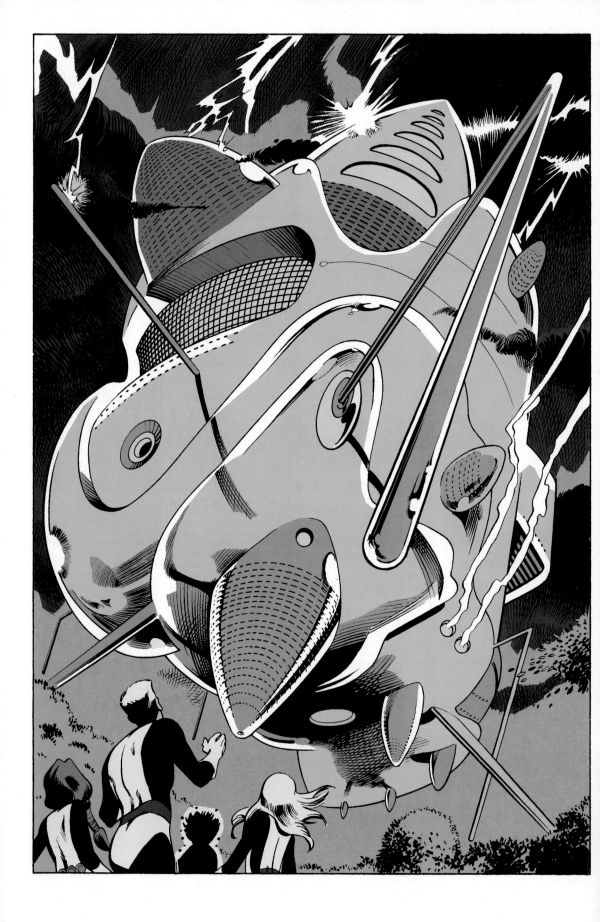

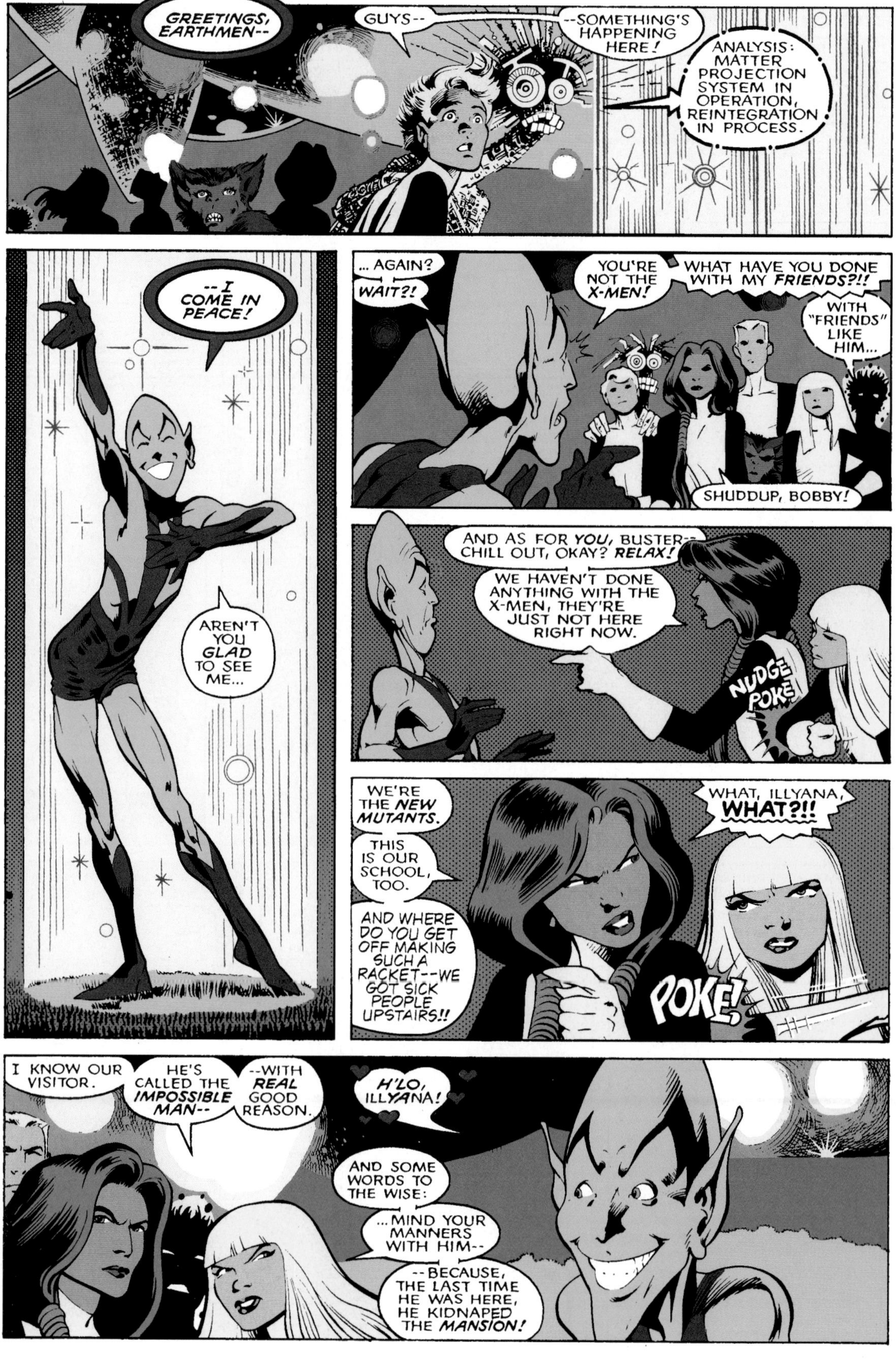
GREETINGS, EARTHMEN--
GUYS--
--SOMETHING'S HAPPENING HERE!
ANALYSIS: MATTER PROJECTION SYSTEM IN OPERATION, REINTEGRATION IN PROCESS.
--I COME IN PEACE!
AREN'T YOU GLAD TO SEE ME...
... AGAIN?
WAIT?!
YOU'RE NOT THE X-MEN!
WHAT HAVE YOU DONE WITH MY FRIENDS?!!
WITH "FRIENDS" LIKE HIM...
SHUDDUP, BOBBY!
AND AS FOR YOU, BUSTER--
CHILL OUT, OKAY? RELAX!
WE HAVEN'T DONE ANYTHING WITH THE X-MEN, THEY'RE JUST NOT HERE RIGHT NOW.
NUDGE
POKE
WE'RE THE NEW MUTANTS.
THIS IS OUR SCHOOL, TOO.
AND WHERE DO YOU GET OFF MAKING SUCH A RACKET--WE GOT SICK PEOPLE UPSTAIRS!!
WHAT, ILLYANA, WHAT?!!
POKE!
I KNOW OUR VISITOR.
HE'S CALLED THE IMPOSSIBLE MAN--
--WITH REAL GOOD REASON.
H'LO, ILLYANA!
AND SOME WORDS TO THE WISE:
...MIND YOUR MANNERS WITH HIM--
--BECAUSE, THE LAST TIME HE WAS HERE, HE KIDNAPED THE MANSION!

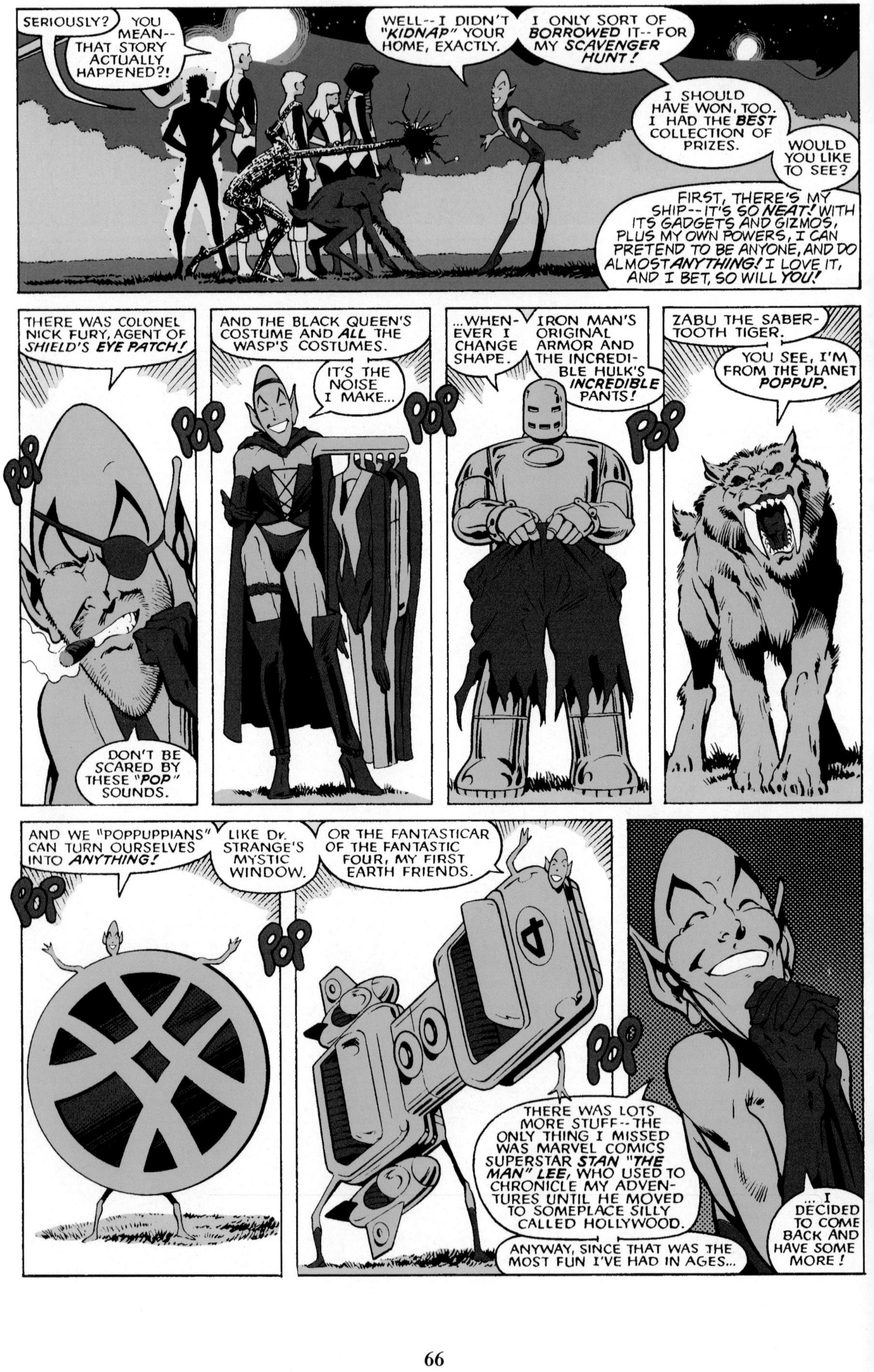

SERIOUSLY? YOU MEAN-- THAT STORY ACTUALLY HAPPENED?!
WELL--I DIDN'T "KIDNAP" YOUR HOME, EXACTLY.
I ONLY SORT OF BORROWED IT-- FOR MY SCAVENGER HUNT!
I SHOULD HAVE WON, TOO. I HAD THE BEST COLLECTION OF PRIZES.
WOULD YOU LIKE TO SEE?
FIRST, THERE'S MY SHIP--IT'S SO NEAT! WITH ITS GADGETS AND GIZMOS, PLUS MY OWN POWERS, I CAN PRETEND TO BE ANYONE, AND DO ALMOST ANYTHING! I LOVE IT, AND I BET, SO WILL YOU!
THERE WAS COLONEL NICK FURY, AGENT OF SHIELD'S EYE PATCH!
POP
POP
DON'T BE SCARED BY THESE "POP" SOUNDS.
AND THE BLACK QUEEN'S COSTUME AND ALL THE WASP'S COSTUMES.
IT'S THE NOISE I MAKE...
POP
...WHEN-EVER I CHANGE SHAPE.
IRON MAN'S ORIGINAL ARMOR AND THE INCREDI-BLE HULK'S INCREDIBLE PANTS!
POP
ZABU THE SABER-TOOTH TIGER.
YOU SEE, I'M FROM THE PLANET POPPUP.
AND WE "POPPUPPIANS" CAN TURN OURSELVES INTO ANYTHING!
POP
LIKE Dr. STRANGE'S MYSTIC WINDOW.
POP
OR THE FANTASTICAR OF THE FANTASTIC FOUR, MY FIRST EARTH FRIENDS.
POP
THERE WAS LOTS MORE STUFF--THE ONLY THING I MISSED WAS MARVEL COMICS SUPERSTAR STAN "THE MAN" LEE, WHO USED TO CHRONICLE MY ADVEN-TURES UNTIL HE MOVED TO SOMEPLACE SILLY CALLED HOLLYWOOD.
ANYWAY, SINCE THAT WAS THE MOST FUN I'VE HAD IN AGES...
...I DECIDED TO COME BACK AND HAVE SOME MORE!

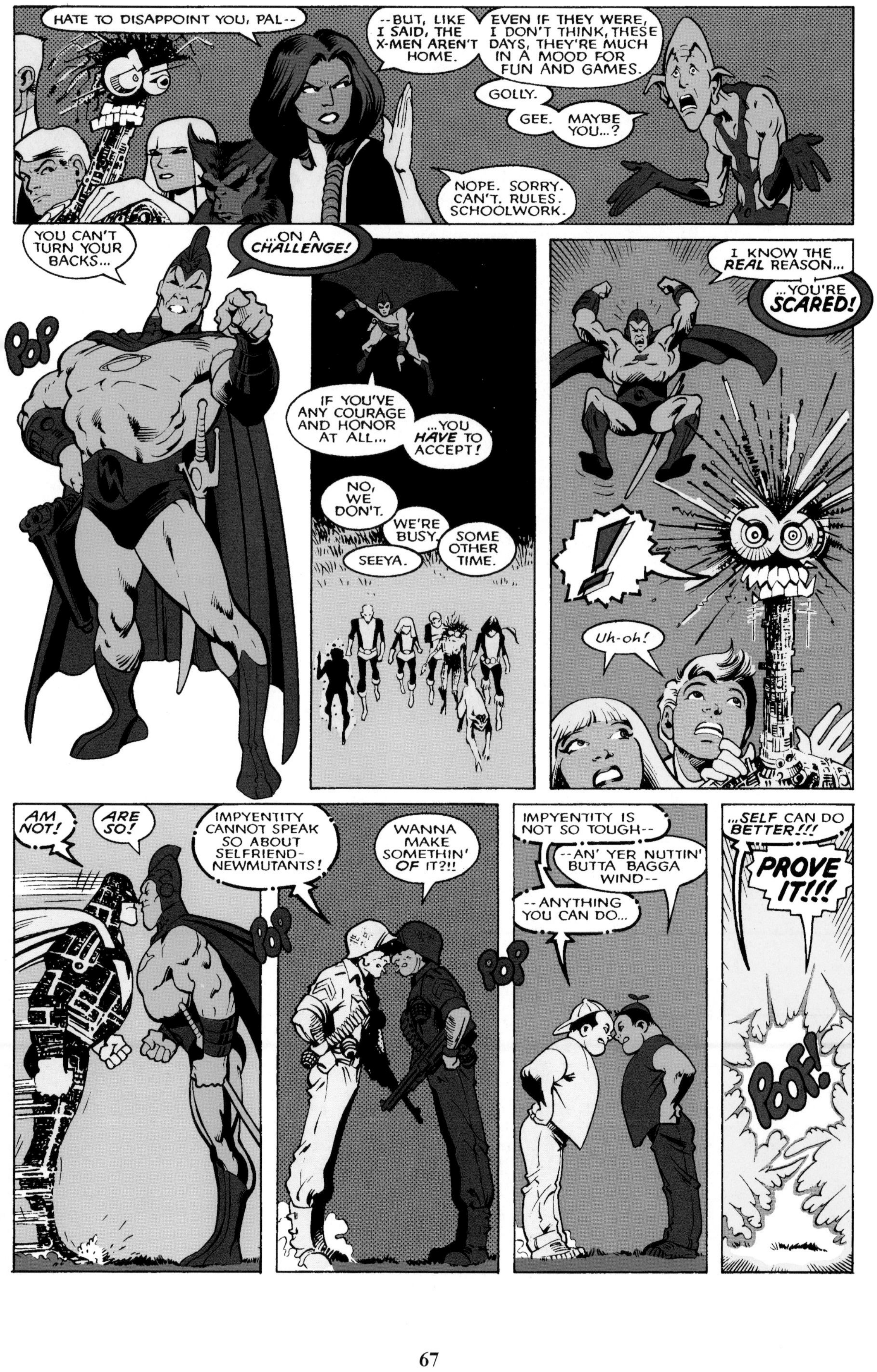
HATE TO DISAPPOINT YOU, PAL--
--BUT, LIKE I SAID, THE X-MEN AREN'T HOME.
EVEN IF THEY WERE, I DON'T THINK, THESE DAYS, THEY'RE MUCH IN A MOOD FOR FUN AND GAMES.
GOLLY.
GEE.
MAYBE YOU...?
NOPE. SORRY. CAN'T. RULES. SCHOOLWORK.
YOU CAN'T TURN YOUR BACKS...
...ON A CHALLENGE!
POP
IF YOU'VE ANY COURAGE AND HONOR AT ALL...
...YOU HAVE TO ACCEPT!
NO, WE DON'T.
WE'RE BUSY.
SOME OTHER TIME.
SEEYA.
I KNOW THE REAL REASON...
...YOU'RE SCARED!
Uh-oh!
AM NOT!
ARE SO!
IMPYENTITY CANNOT SPEAK SO ABOUT SELFRIEND-NEWMUTANTS!
POP
WANNA MAKE SOMETHIN' OF IT?!!
POP
IMPYENTITY IS NOT SO TOUGH--
--AN' YER NUTTIN' BUTTA BAGGA WIND--
--ANYTHING YOU CAN DO...
...SELF CAN DO BETTER!!!
PROVE IT!!!
POOF!

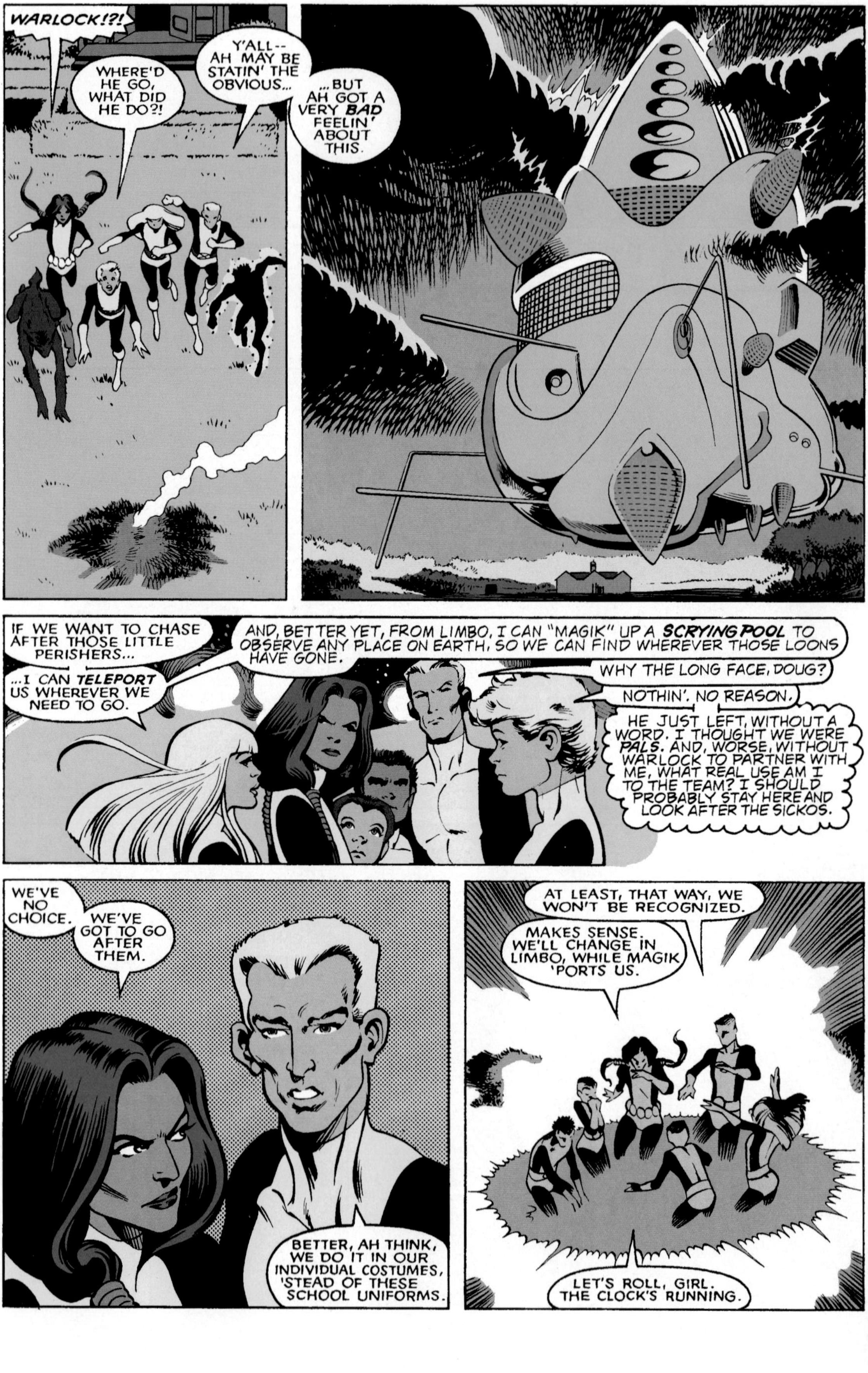
WARLOCK!?!
WHERE'D HE GO, WHAT DID HE DO?!
Y'ALL-- AH MAY BE STATIN' THE OBVIOUS...
...BUT AH GOT A VERY BAD FEELIN' ABOUT THIS.
IF WE WANT TO CHASE AFTER THOSE LITTLE PERISHERS...
...I CAN TELEPORT US WHEREVER WE NEED TO GO.
AND, BETTER YET, FROM LIMBO, I CAN "MAGIK" UP A SCRYING POOL TO OBSERVE ANY PLACE ON EARTH, SO WE CAN FIND WHEREVER THOSE LOONS HAVE GONE.
WHY THE LONG FACE, DOUG?
NOTHIN'. NO REASON.
HE JUST LEFT, WITHOUT A WORD. I THOUGHT WE WERE PALS. AND, WORSE, WITHOUT WARLOCK TO PARTNER WITH ME, WHAT REAL USE AM I TO THE TEAM? I SHOULD PROBABLY STAY HERE AND LOOK AFTER THE SICKOS.
WE'VE NO CHOICE.
WE'VE GOT TO GO AFTER THEM.
BETTER, AH THINK, WE DO IT IN OUR INDIVIDUAL COSTUMES, 'STEAD OF THESE SCHOOL UNIFORMS.
AT LEAST, THAT WAY, WE WON'T BE RECOGNIZED.
MAKES SENSE. WE'LL CHANGE IN LIMBO, WHILE MAGIK 'PORTS US.
LET'S ROLL, GIRL. THE CLOCK'S RUNNING.

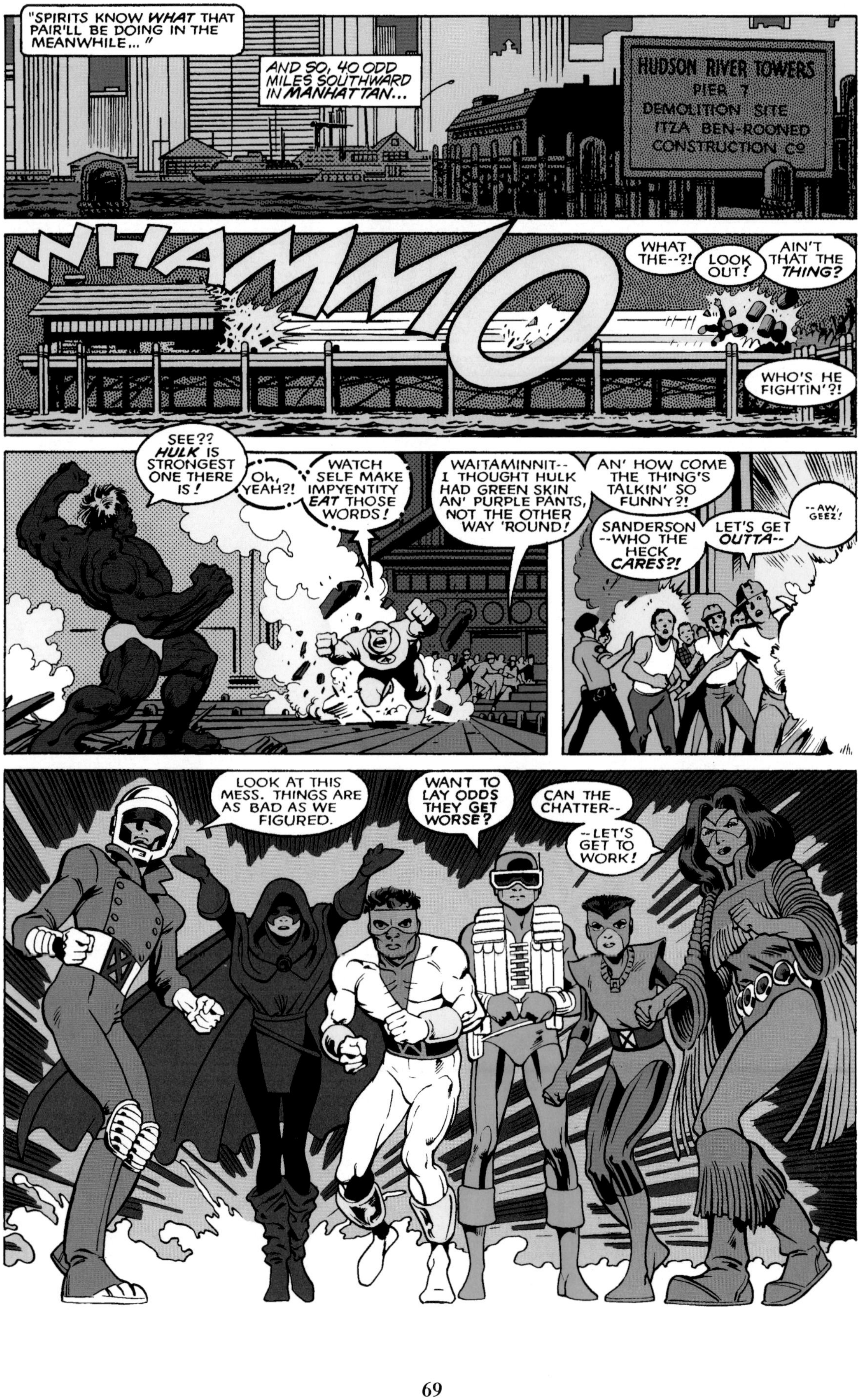
"SPIRITS KNOW WHAT THAT PAIR'LL BE DOING IN THE MEANWHILE..."
AND SO, 40 ODD MILES SOUTHWARD IN MANHATTAN...
HUDSON RIVER TOWERS
PIER 7
DEMOLITION SITE
ITZA BEN-ROONED
CONSTRUCTION Co
WHAMMO
WHAT THE--?!
LOOK OUT!
AIN'T THAT THE THING?
WHO'S HE FIGHTIN'?!
SEE?? HULK IS STRONGEST ONE THERE IS!
Oh, YEAH?!
WATCH SELF MAKE IMPYENTITY EAT THOSE WORDS!
WAITAMINNIT-- I THOUGHT HULK HAD GREEN SKIN AN' PURPLE PANTS, NOT THE OTHER WAY 'ROUND!
AN' HOW COME THE THING'S TALKIN' SO FUNNY?!
SANDERSON --WHO THE HECK CARES?!
LET'S GET OUTTA--
--AW, GEEZ!
LOOK AT THIS MESS. THINGS ARE AS BAD AS WE FIGURED.
WANT TO LAY ODDS THEY GET WORSE?
CAN THE CHATTER--
--LET'S GET TO WORK!

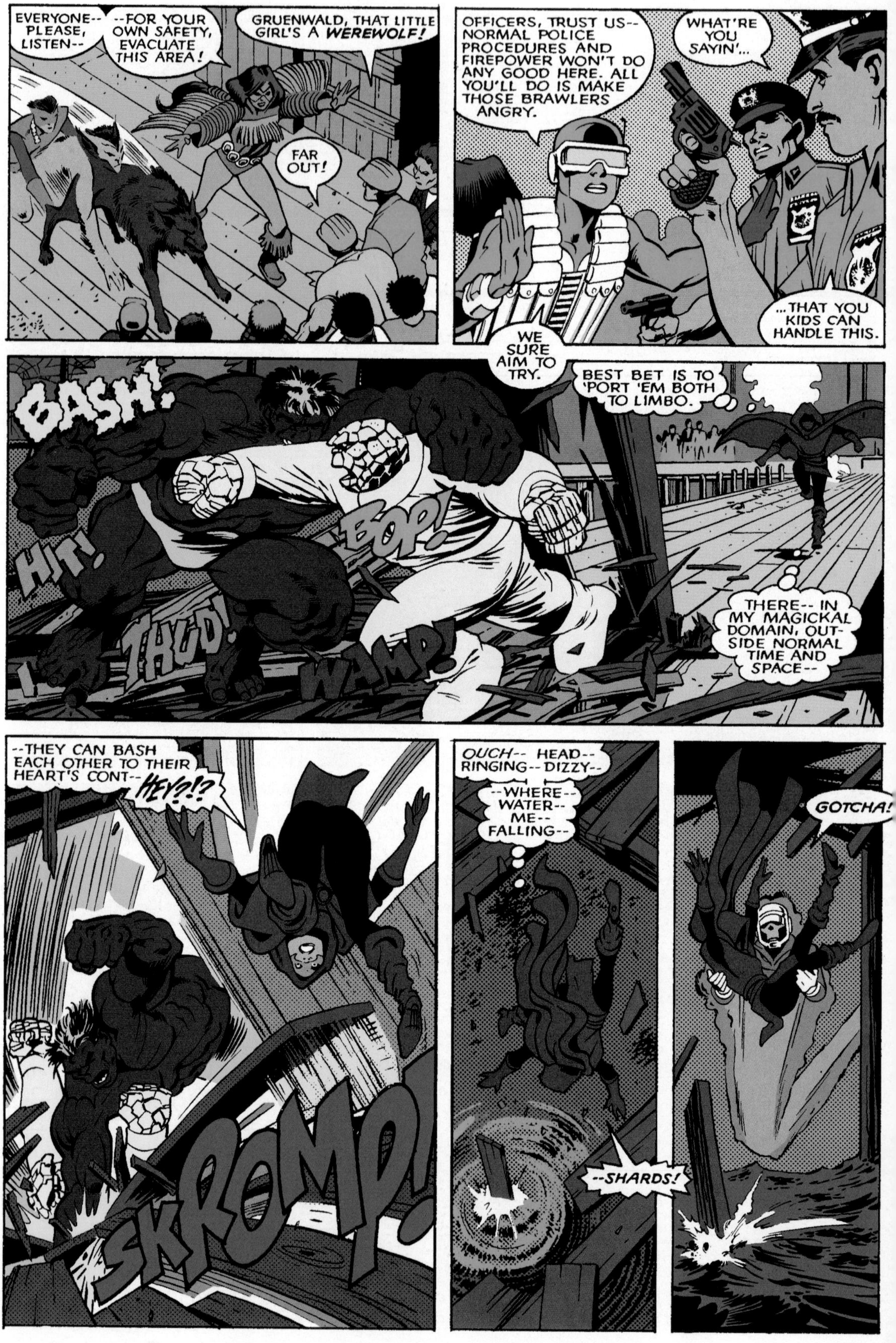
EVERYONE-- PLEASE, LISTEN--
--FOR YOUR OWN SAFETY, EVACUATE THIS AREA!
GRUENWALD, THAT LITTLE GIRL'S A *WEREWOLF!*
FAR OUT!
OFFICERS, TRUST US-- NORMAL POLICE PROCEDURES AND FIREPOWER WON'T DO ANY GOOD HERE. ALL YOU'LL DO IS MAKE THOSE BRAWLERS ANGRY.
WHAT'RE YOU SAYIN'...
...THAT YOU KIDS CAN HANDLE THIS.
WE SURE AIM TO TRY.
BASH!
HIT!
BOP!
THUD!
WAMP!
BEST BET IS TO 'PORT 'EM BOTH TO LIMBO.
THERE-- IN MY MAGICKAL DOMAIN, OUTSIDE NORMAL TIME AND SPACE--
--THEY CAN BASH EACH OTHER TO THEIR HEART'S CONT--
HEY?!?
SKROMP!
OUCH-- HEAD-- RINGING-- DIZZY--
--WHERE-- WATER-- ME-- FALLING--
--SHARDS!
GOTCHA!

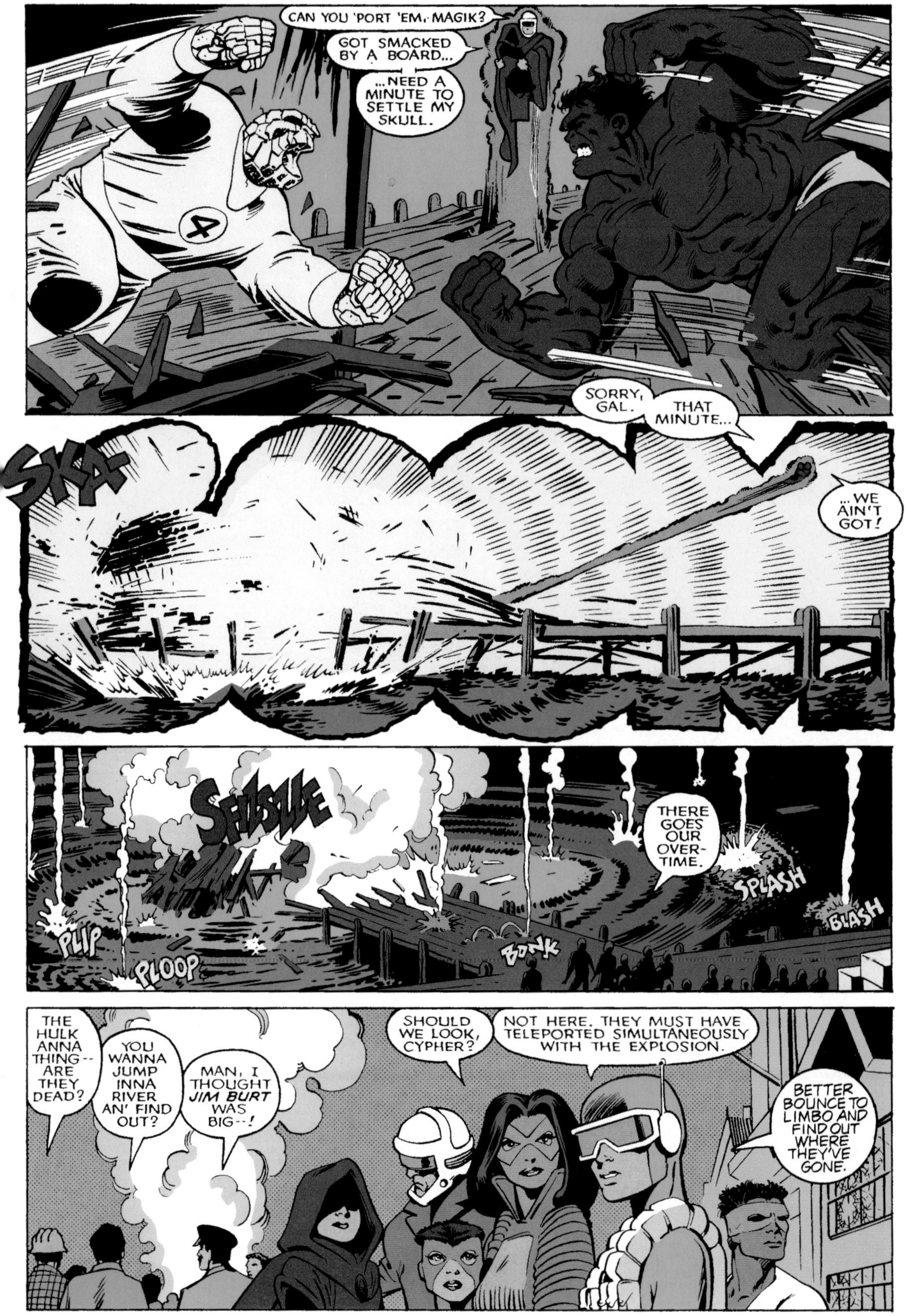

CAN YOU 'PORT 'EM, MAGIK?
GOT SMACKED BY A BOARD...
...NEED A MINUTE TO SETTLE MY SKULL.
SORRY, GAL.
THAT MINUTE...
SKA
...WE AIN'T GOT!
THERE GOES OUR OVER-TIME.
SPLASH
BLASH
PLIP
PLOOP
BONK
THE HULK ANNA THING-- ARE THEY DEAD?
YOU WANNA JUMP INNA RIVER AN' FIND OUT?
MAN, I THOUGHT JIM BURT WAS BIG--!
SHOULD WE LOOK, CYPHER?
NOT HERE. THEY MUST HAVE TELEPORTED SIMULTANEOUSLY WITH THE EXPLOSION.
BETTER BOUNCE TO LIMBO AND FIND OUT WHERE THEY'VE GONE.

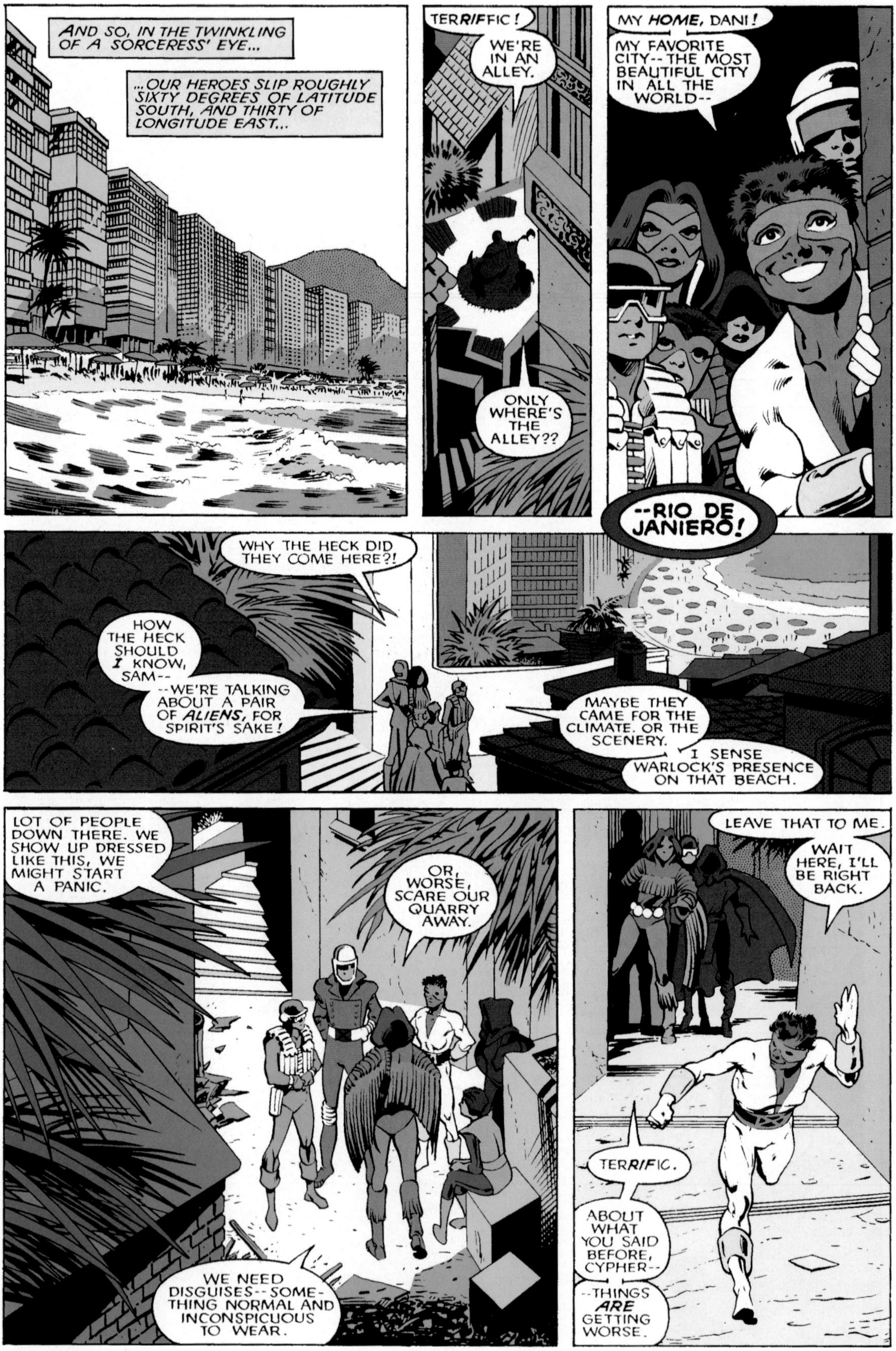
AND SO, IN THE TWINKLING OF A SORCERESS' EYE...
...OUR HEROES SLIP ROUGHLY SIXTY DEGREES OF LATITUDE SOUTH, AND THIRTY OF LONGITUDE EAST...
TERRIFIC!
WE'RE IN AN ALLEY.
ONLY WHERE'S THE ALLEY??
MY HOME, DANI!
MY FAVORITE CITY-- THE MOST BEAUTIFUL CITY IN ALL THE WORLD--
--RIO DE JANIERO!
WHY THE HECK DID THEY COME HERE?!
HOW THE HECK SHOULD I KNOW, SAM--
--WE'RE TALKING ABOUT A PAIR OF ALIENS, FOR SPIRIT'S SAKE!
MAYBE THEY CAME FOR THE CLIMATE. OR THE SCENERY.
I SENSE WARLOCK'S PRESENCE ON THAT BEACH.
LOT OF PEOPLE DOWN THERE. WE SHOW UP DRESSED LIKE THIS, WE MIGHT START A PANIC.
OR, WORSE, SCARE OUR QUARRY AWAY.
WE NEED DISGUISES-- SOMETHING NORMAL AND INCONSPICUOUS TO WEAR.
LEAVE THAT TO ME.
WAIT HERE, I'LL BE RIGHT BACK.
TERRIFIC.
ABOUT WHAT YOU SAID BEFORE, CYPHER--
--THINGS ARE GETTING WORSE.

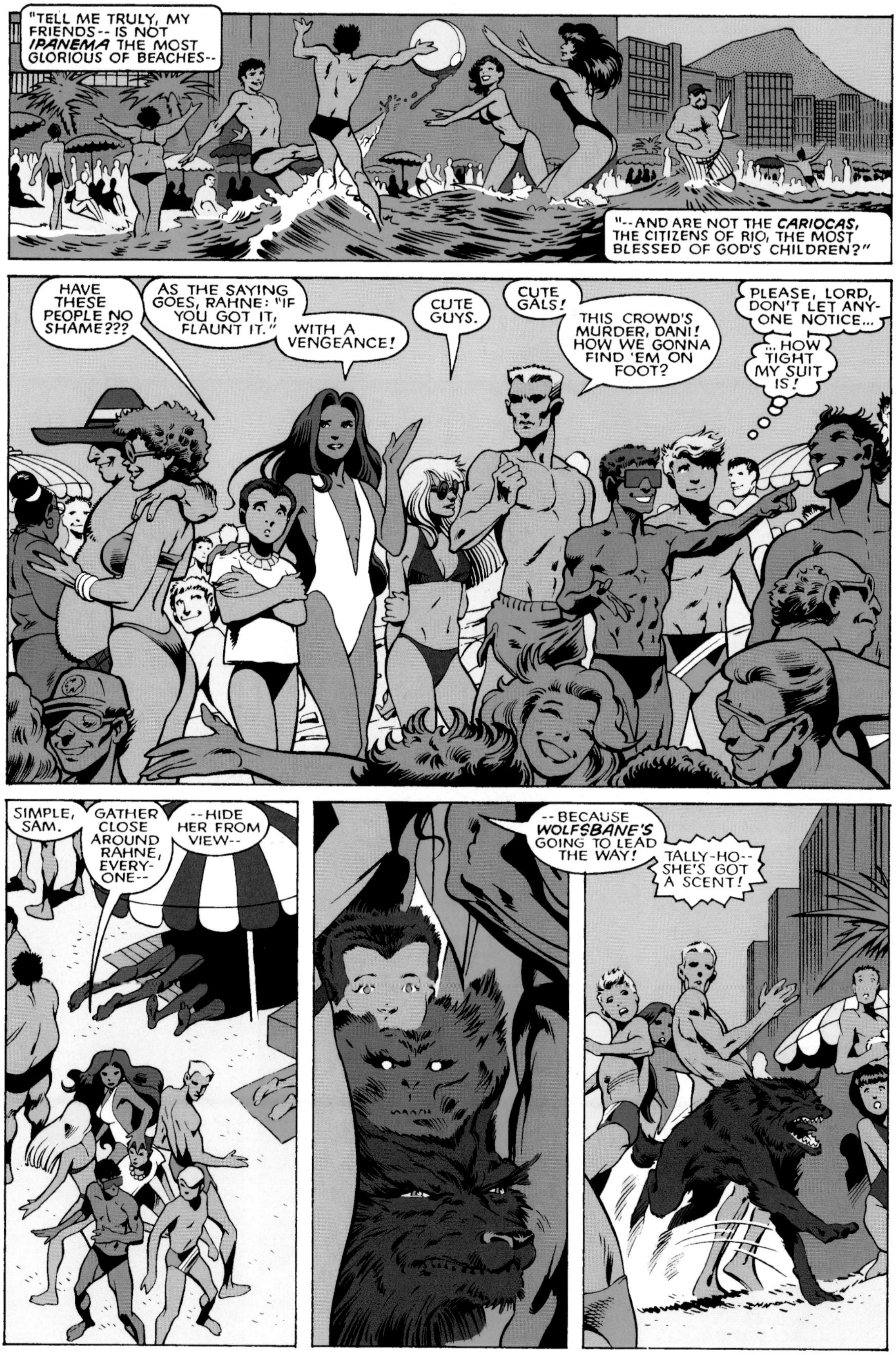
"TELL ME TRULY, MY FRIENDS-- IS NOT IPANEMA THE MOST GLORIOUS OF BEACHES--
"--AND ARE NOT THE CARIOCAS, THE CITIZENS OF RIO, THE MOST BLESSED OF GOD'S CHILDREN?"
HAVE THESE PEOPLE NO SHAME???
AS THE SAYING GOES, RAHNE: "IF YOU GOT IT, FLAUNT IT."
WITH A VENGEANCE!
CUTE GUYS.
CUTE GALS!
THIS CROWD'S MURDER, DANI! HOW WE GONNA FIND 'EM ON FOOT?
PLEASE, LORD, DON'T LET ANY-ONE NOTICE...
...HOW TIGHT MY SUIT IS!
SIMPLE, SAM.
GATHER CLOSE AROUND RAHNE, EVERY-ONE--
--HIDE HER FROM VIEW--
--BECAUSE WOLFSBANE'S GOING TO LEAD THE WAY!
TALLY-HO-- SHE'S GOT A SCENT!

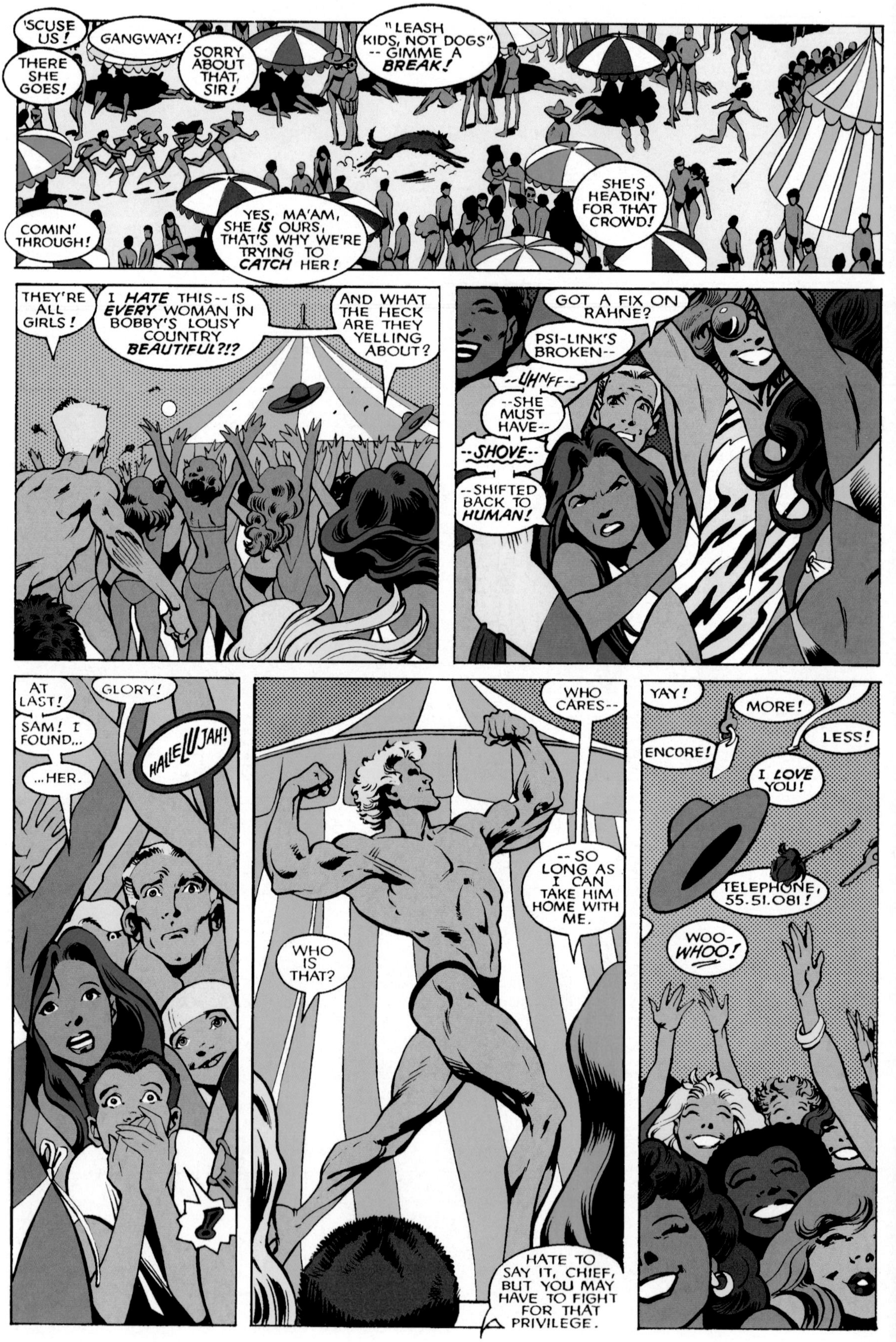
'SCUSE US!
THERE SHE GOES!
GANGWAY!
SORRY ABOUT THAT, SIR!
"LEASH KIDS, NOT DOGS" -- GIMME A BREAK!
COMIN' THROUGH!
YES, MA'AM, SHE IS OURS, THAT'S WHY WE'RE TRYING TO CATCH HER!
SHE'S HEADIN' FOR THAT CROWD!
THEY'RE ALL GIRLS!
I HATE THIS-- IS EVERY WOMAN IN BOBBY'S LOUSY COUNTRY BEAUTIFUL?!?
AND WHAT THE HECK ARE THEY YELLING ABOUT?
GOT A FIX ON RAHNE?
PSI-LINK'S BROKEN--
--UHNFF--
--SHE MUST HAVE--
--SHOVE--
--SHIFTED BACK TO HUMAN!
AT LAST!
SAM! I FOUND...
...HER.
GLORY!
HALLELUJAH!
WHO CARES--
--SO LONG AS I CAN TAKE HIM HOME WITH ME.
WHO IS THAT?
HATE TO SAY IT, CHIEF, BUT YOU MAY HAVE TO FIGHT FOR THAT PRIVILEGE.
YAY!
MORE!
ENCORE!
LESS!
I LOVE YOU!
TELEPHONE, 55.51.081!
WOO-WHOO!

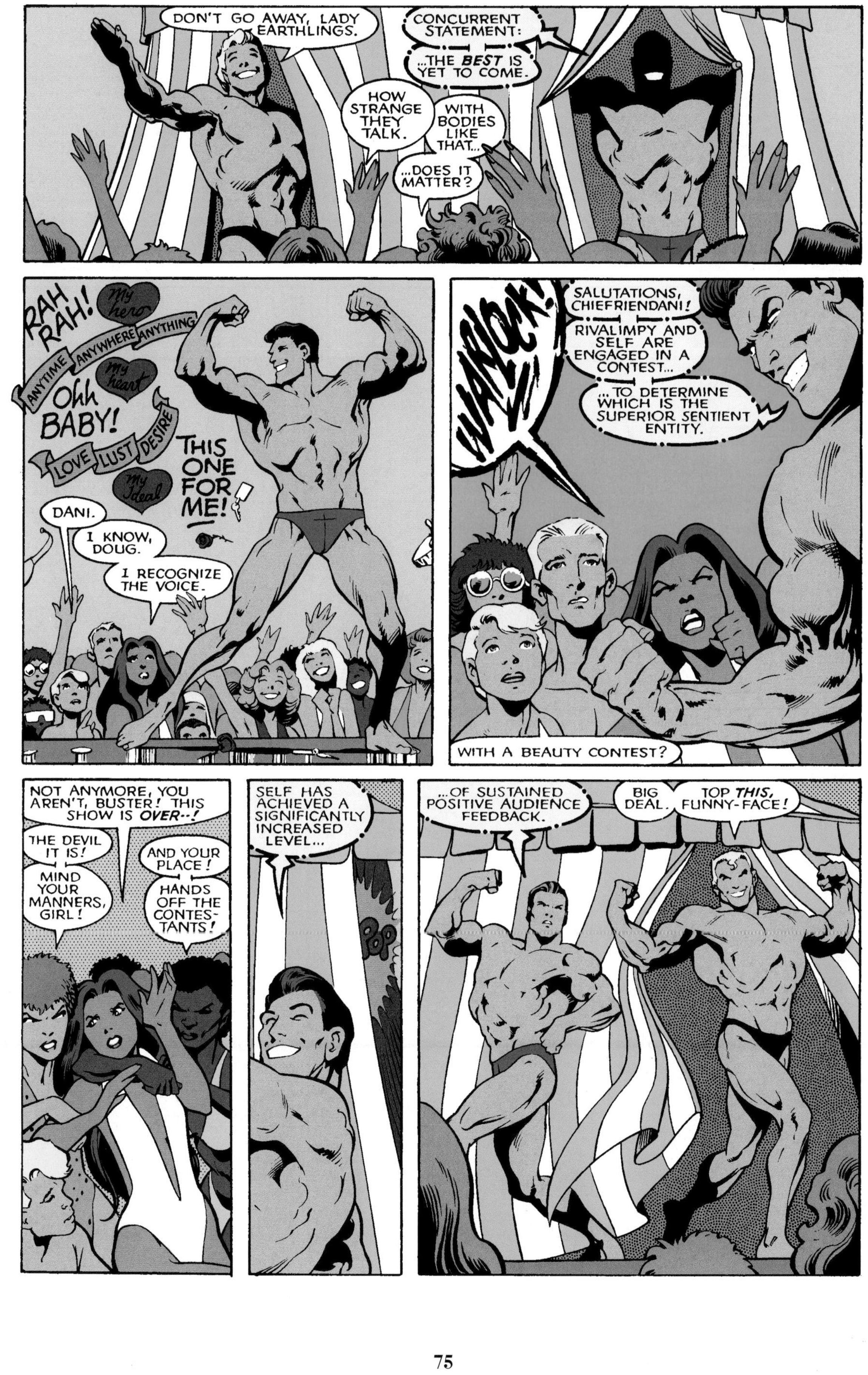
DON'T GO AWAY, LADY EARTHLINGS.
CONCURRENT STATEMENT:
...THE *BEST* IS YET TO COME.
HOW STRANGE THEY TALK.
WITH BODIES LIKE THAT...
...DOES IT MATTER?
RAH RAH!
My hero
ANYTIME ANYWHERE ANYTHING
My heart
Ohh BABY!
LOVE LUST DESIRE
My Ideal
THIS ONE FOR ME!
DANI.
I KNOW, DOUG.
I RECOGNIZE THE VOICE.
WARLOCK!
SALUTATIONS, CHIEFRIENDANI!
RIVALIMPY AND SELF ARE ENGAGED IN A CONTEST...
...TO DETERMINE WHICH IS THE SUPERIOR SENTIENT ENTITY.
WITH A BEAUTY CONTEST?
NOT ANYMORE, YOU AREN'T, BUSTER! THIS SHOW IS *OVER*--!
THE DEVIL IT IS!
MIND YOUR MANNERS, GIRL!
AND YOUR PLACE!
HANDS OFF THE CONTESTANTS!
SELF HAS ACHIEVED A SIGNIFICANTLY INCREASED LEVEL...
POP
...OF SUSTAINED POSITIVE AUDIENCE FEEDBACK.
BIG DEAL.
TOP *THIS*, FUNNY-FACE!

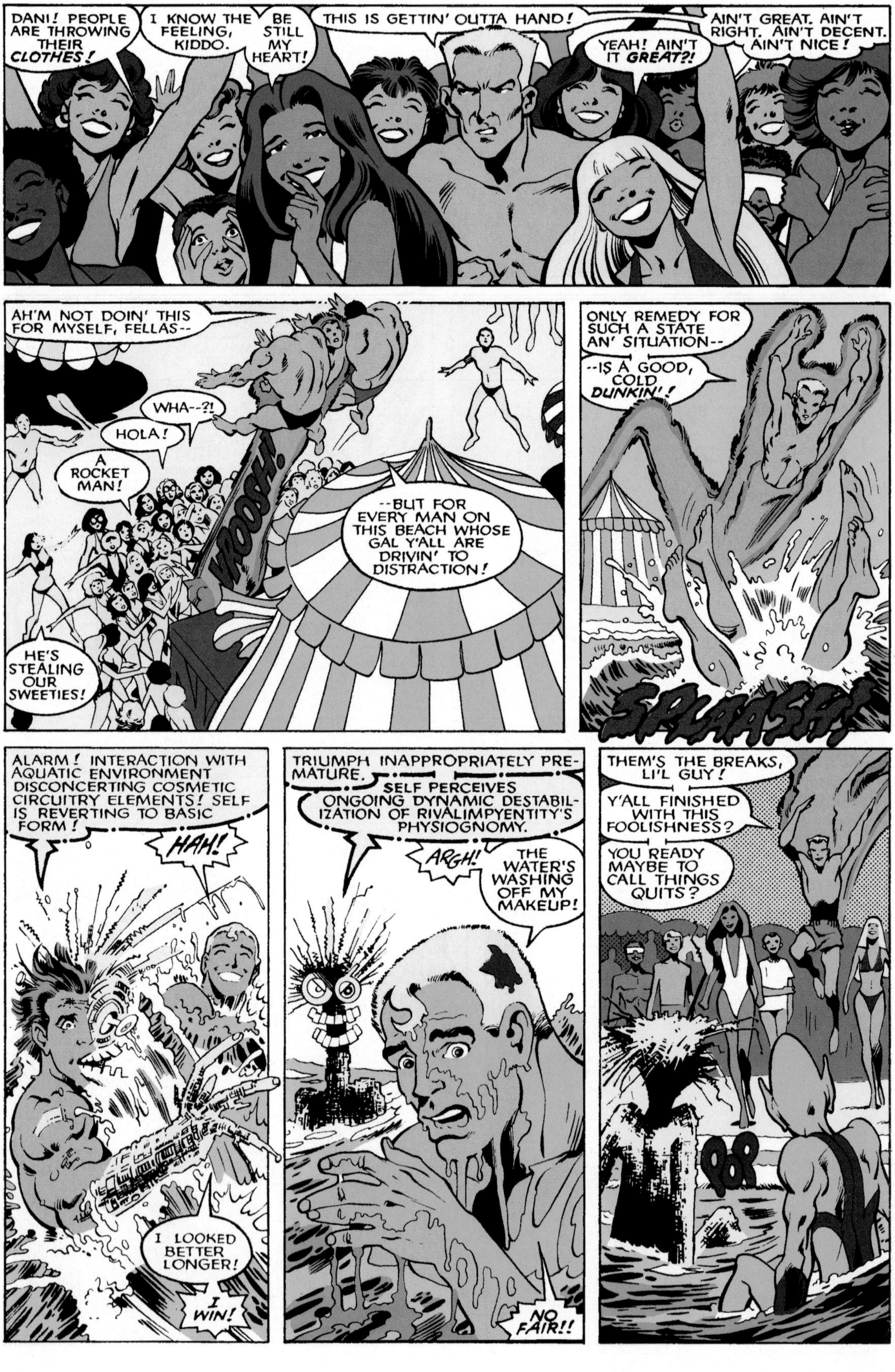

DANI! PEOPLE ARE THROWING THEIR CLOTHES!
I KNOW THE FEELING, KIDDO.
BE STILL MY HEART!
THIS IS GETTIN' OUTTA HAND!
YEAH! AIN'T IT GREAT?!
AIN'T GREAT. AIN'T RIGHT. AIN'T DECENT. AIN'T NICE!
AH'M NOT DOIN' THIS FOR MYSELF, FELLAS--
WHA--?!
HOLA!
A ROCKET MAN!
VROOSH!
--BUT FOR EVERY MAN ON THIS BEACH WHOSE GAL Y'ALL ARE DRIVIN' TO DISTRACTION!
HE'S STEALING OUR SWEETIES!
ONLY REMEDY FOR SUCH A STATE AN' SITUATION--
--IS A GOOD, COLD DUNKIN'!
SPLAASH!
ALARM! INTERACTION WITH AQUATIC ENVIRONMENT DISCONCERTING COSMETIC CIRCUITRY ELEMENTS! SELF IS REVERTING TO BASIC FORM!
HAH!
I LOOKED BETTER LONGER!
I WIN!
TRIUMPH INAPPROPRIATELY PREMATURE.
SELF PERCEIVES ONGOING DYNAMIC DESTABILIZATION OF RIVALIMPYENTITY'S PHYSIOGNOMY.
ARGH!
THE WATER'S WASHING OFF MY MAKEUP!
NO FAIR!!
THEM'S THE BREAKS, LI'L GUY!
Y'ALL FINISHED WITH THIS FOOLISHNESS?
YOU READY MAYBE TO CALL THINGS QUITS?
POP

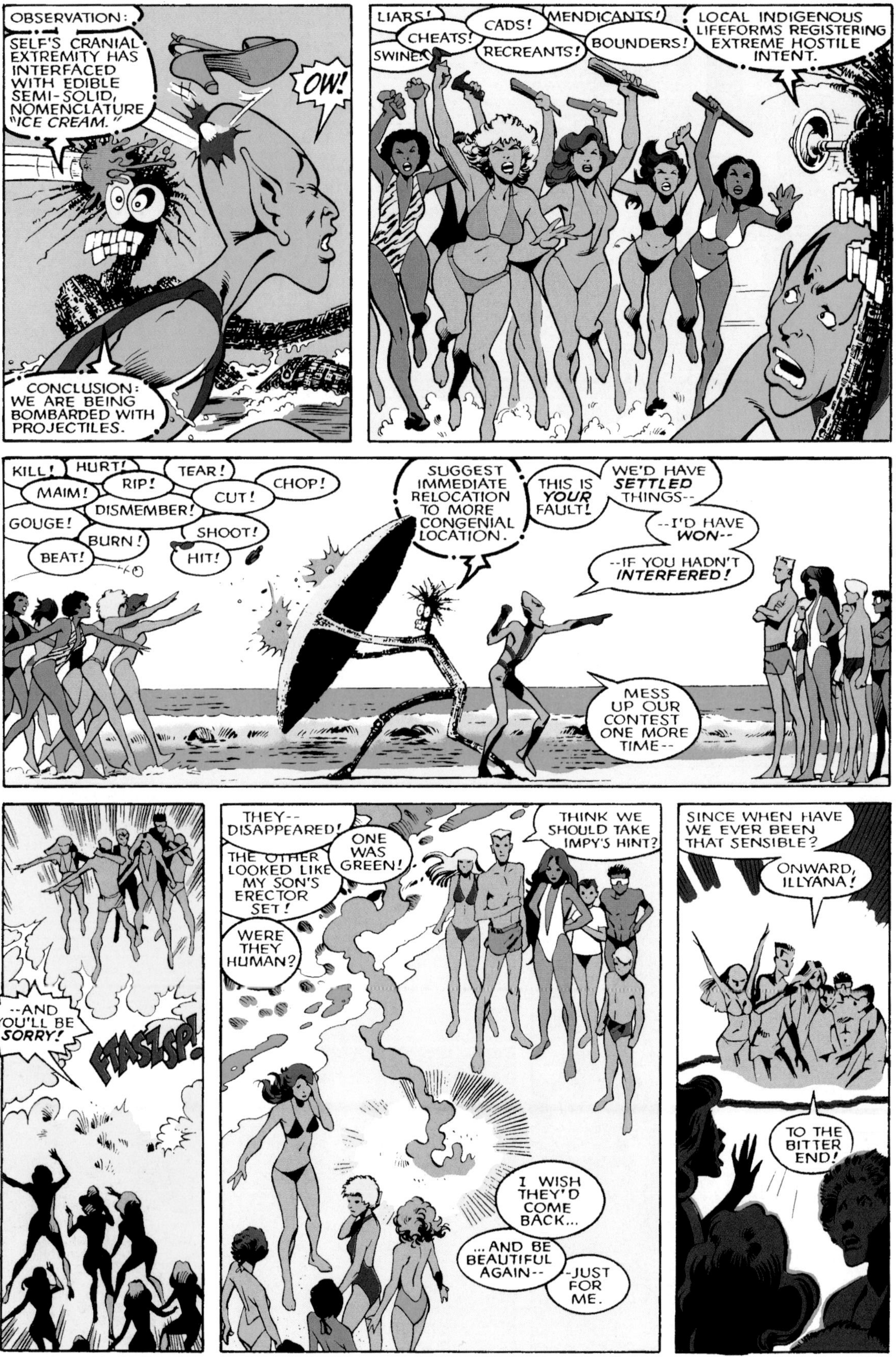
OBSERVATION:
SELF'S CRANIAL EXTREMITY HAS INTERFACED WITH EDIBLE SEMI-SOLID, NOMENCLATURE "ICE CREAM."
OW!
CONCLUSION: WE ARE BEING BOMBARDED WITH PROJECTILES.
LIARS!
CHEATS!
SWINE!
CADS!
RECREANTS!
MENDICANTS!
BOUNDERS!
LOCAL INDIGENOUS LIFEFORMS REGISTERING EXTREME HOSTILE INTENT.
KILL!
HURT!
MAIM!
RIP!
TEAR!
CUT!
CHOP!
DISMEMBER!
GOUGE!
BURN!
SHOOT!
BEAT!
HIT!
SUGGEST IMMEDIATE RELOCATION TO MORE CONGENIAL LOCATION.
THIS IS YOUR FAULT!
WE'D HAVE SETTLED THINGS--
--I'D HAVE WON--
--IF YOU HADN'T INTERFERED!
MESS UP OUR CONTEST ONE MORE TIME--
--AND YOU'LL BE SORRY!
FTASZSP!
THEY--DISAPPEARED!
THE OTHER LOOKED LIKE MY SON'S ERECTOR SET!
ONE WAS GREEN!
WERE THEY HUMAN?
THINK WE SHOULD TAKE IMPY'S HINT?
I WISH THEY'D COME BACK...
...AND BE BEAUTIFUL AGAIN--
--JUST FOR ME.
SINCE WHEN HAVE WE EVER BEEN THAT SENSIBLE?
ONWARD, ILLYANA!
TO THE BITTER END!

LONDON.

HOME TO THE MOTHER OF PARLIAMENTS.

AND, AS WELL, EVERY SUMMER, IN THE BOROUGH OF WIMBLEDON...

...TO THE ALL-ENGLAND LAWN TENNIS CHAMPIONSHIPS.

ADVANTAGE, Mr. MACCHIO.

Mr. LENDL TO SERVE.

HERE, THE BEST PLAY THE BEST, IN A TOURNAMENT THAT IS RARELY DULL AND OFTEN MEMORABLE.

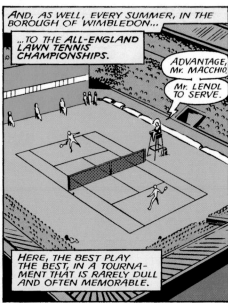

TODAY...

...PROVES ONE OF THE LATTER.

ISN'T IT NICE AND CONSIDERATE OF THEM...

...TO LEAVE CENTER COURT TO US?

SELF EXPRESSES GRATITUDE, THANK YOU.

QUERY: DOES SELFRIVALIMPYENTITY KNOW HOW TO PLAY SPORT, NOMENCLATURE "TENNIS?"

OF COURSE!

I'VE WATCHED IT LOTS OF TIMES ON TELEVISION.

GOOD-- SO HAS SELF!

SELF WILL SERVE!

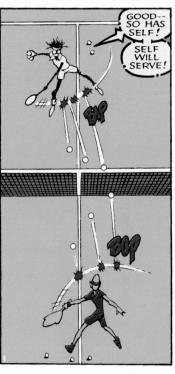

SOME MATCH.

SOME PLAYERS.

WHO'S WINNING?

THE FUNNY LOOKING ONE.

Oh.

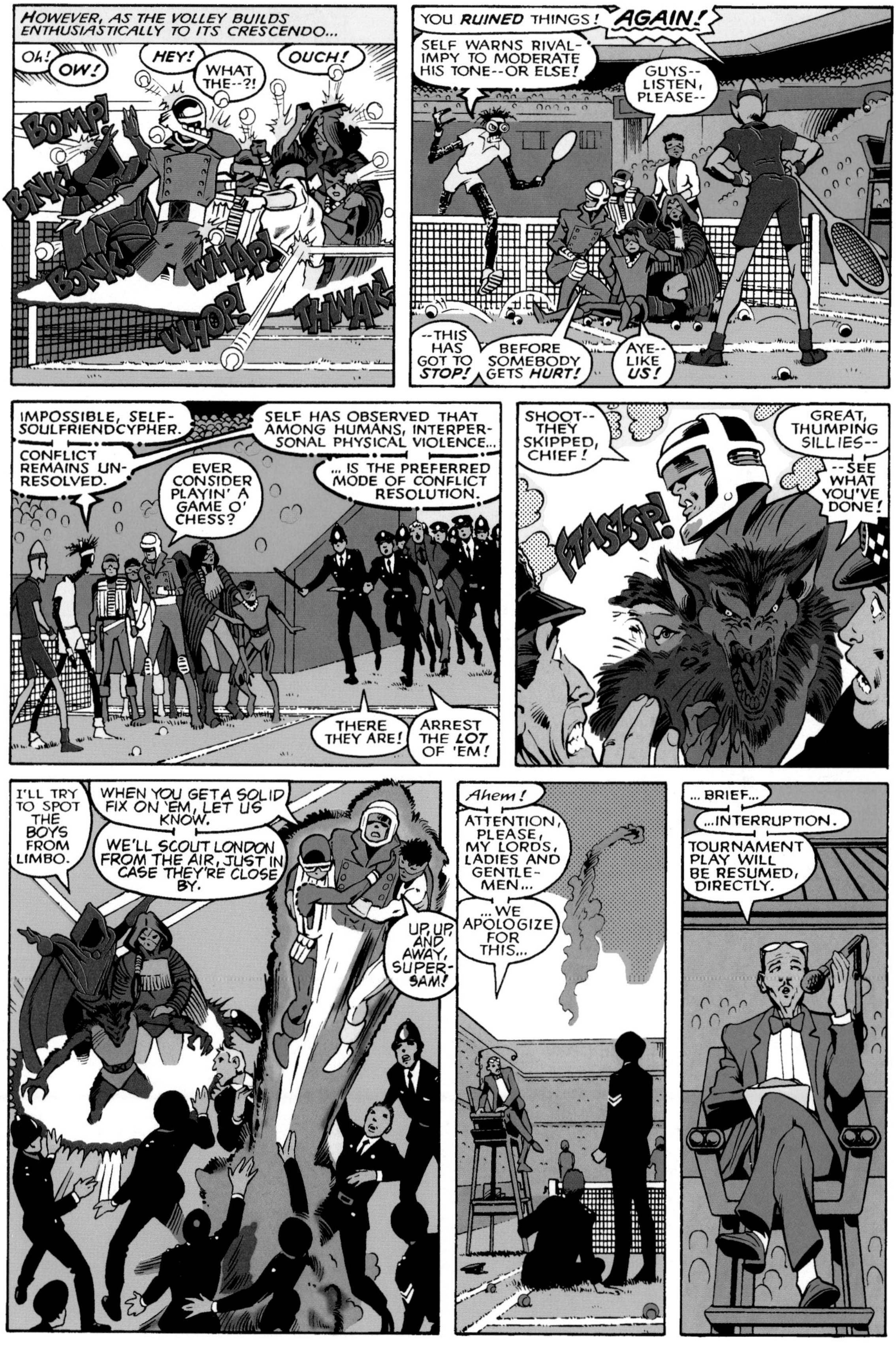
HOWEVER, AS THE VOLLEY BUILDS ENTHUSIASTICALLY TO ITS CRESCENDO...
Oh!
OW!
HEY!
WHAT THE--?!
OUCH!
BOMP!
BINK!
BONK!
WHAP!
WHOP!
THWAK!
YOU RUINED THINGS! AGAIN!
SELF WARNS RIVAL-IMPY TO MODERATE HIS TONE--OR ELSE!
GUYS--LISTEN, PLEASE--
--THIS HAS GOT TO STOP!
BEFORE SOMEBODY GETS HURT!
AYE--LIKE US!
IMPOSSIBLE, SELF-SOULFRIENDCYPHER.
CONFLICT REMAINS UNRESOLVED.
SELF HAS OBSERVED THAT AMONG HUMANS, INTERPERSONAL PHYSICAL VIOLENCE...
... IS THE PREFERRED MODE OF CONFLICT RESOLUTION.
EVER CONSIDER PLAYIN' A GAME O' CHESS?
THERE THEY ARE!
ARREST THE LOT OF 'EM!
SHOOT--THEY SKIPPED, CHIEF!
GREAT, THUMPING SILLIES--
--SEE WHAT YOU'VE DONE!
FTASZSP!
I'LL TRY TO SPOT THE BOYS FROM LIMBO.
WHEN YOU GET A SOLID FIX ON 'EM, LET US KNOW.
WE'LL SCOUT LONDON FROM THE AIR, JUST IN CASE THEY'RE CLOSE BY.
UP, UP, AND AWAY, SUPER-SAM!
Ahem!
ATTENTION, PLEASE, MY LORDS, LADIES AND GENTLE-MEN...
...WE APOLOGIZE FOR THIS...
... BRIEF...
...INTERRUPTION.
TOURNAMENT PLAY WILL BE RESUMED, DIRECTLY.

ALWAYS WANTED TO SEE THE WORLD.

NEVER FIGURED IT'D BE LIKE THIS.

I WONDER WHAT DISASTER'LL HIT US NEXT?

YOU SOUND LIKE YOU WANT TO QUIT AND RUN AWAY HOME.

FACE FACTS, BOBBY. EVERY TIME WE COME CLOSE...

...THOSE TWO GIVE US THE SLIP.

AN' EVEN IF WE MANAGE TO CATCH 'EM...

...HOW THE HECK ARE WE SUPPOSED TO *STOP* THEM?!

HEY, GUYS, LOOK DOWN THERE!

SOMETHING'S HAPPENING ON THAT LITTLE SIDE STREET.

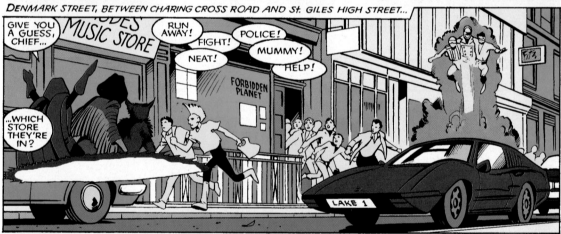

DENMARK STREET, BETWEEN CHARING CROSS ROAD AND St. GILES HIGH STREET...

GIVE YOU A GUESS, CHIEF...

...WHICH STORE THEY'RE IN?

MUSIC STORE

RUN AWAY!

FIGHT!

NEAT!

POLICE!

MUMMY!

HELP!

FORBIDDEN PLANET

LAKE 1

MOVE IN FAST, MUTANTS...

...WHILE THE SETTING'S STILL...

...PEACEFUL.

FORBIDDEN PLANET

WHAMMO!

LAKE 1

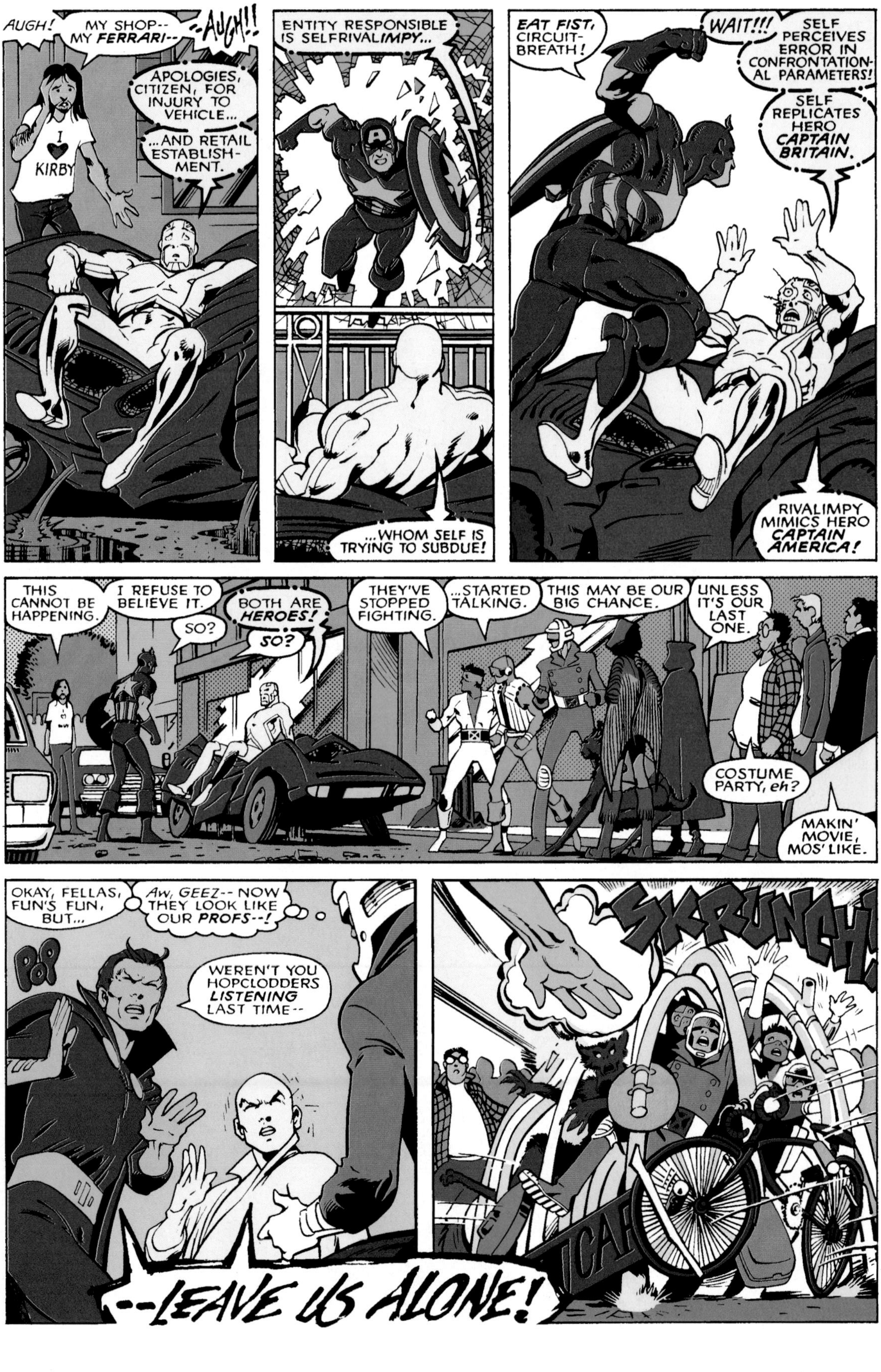
AUGH!
MY SHOP-- MY FERRARI--
AUGH!!
APOLOGIES, CITIZEN, FOR INJURY TO VEHICLE...
...AND RETAIL ESTABLISH-MENT.
I ♥ KIRBY
ENTITY RESPONSIBLE IS SELFRIVALIMPY...
...WHOM SELF IS TRYING TO SUBDUE!
EAT FIST, CIRCUIT-BREATH!
WAIT!!!
SELF PERCEIVES ERROR IN CONFRONTATION-AL PARAMETERS!
SELF REPLICATES HERO CAPTAIN BRITAIN.
RIVALIMPY MIMICS HERO CAPTAIN AMERICA!
THIS CANNOT BE HAPPENING.
I REFUSE TO BELIEVE IT.
SO?
BOTH ARE HEROES!
SO?
THEY'VE STOPPED FIGHTING.
...STARTED TALKING.
THIS MAY BE OUR BIG CHANCE.
UNLESS IT'S OUR LAST ONE.
COSTUME PARTY, eh?
MAKIN' MOVIE, MOS' LIKE.
OKAY, FELLAS, FUN'S FUN, BUT...
Aw, GEEZ-- NOW THEY LOOK LIKE OUR PROFS--!
POP
WEREN'T YOU HOPCLODDERS LISTENING LAST TIME--
SKRUNCH!
--LEAVE US ALONE!

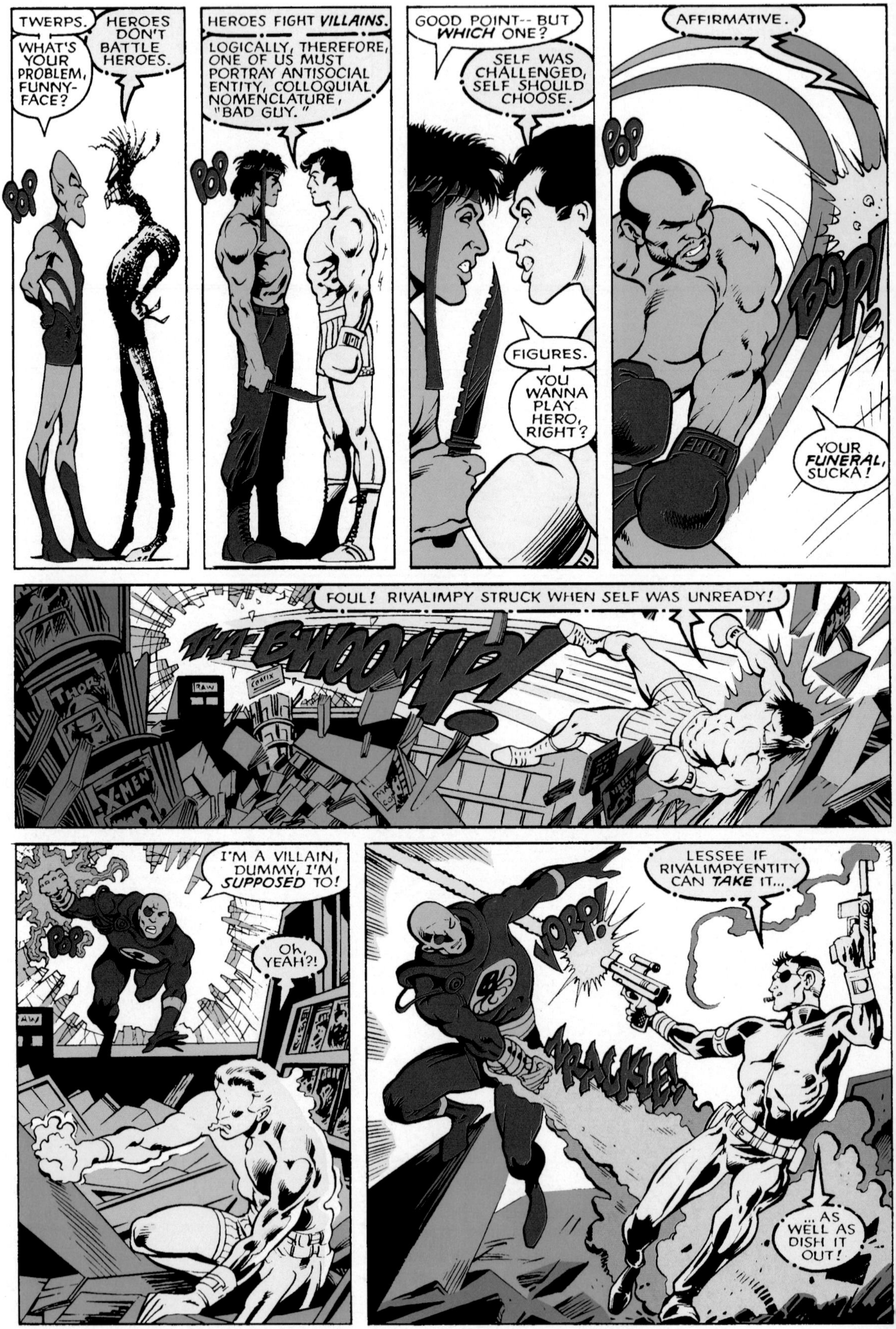
TWERPS.
WHAT'S YOUR PROBLEM, FUNNY-FACE?
HEROES DON'T BATTLE HEROES.
POP
HEROES FIGHT VILLAINS.
LOGICALLY, THEREFORE, ONE OF US MUST PORTRAY ANTISOCIAL ENTITY, COLLOQUIAL NOMENCLATURE, "BAD GUY."
POP
GOOD POINT-- BUT WHICH ONE?
SELF WAS CHALLENGED, SELF SHOULD CHOOSE.
FIGURES.
YOU WANNA PLAY HERO, RIGHT?
AFFIRMATIVE.
POP
BOP!
YOUR FUNERAL, SUCKA!
FOUL! RIVALIMPY STRUCK WHEN SELF WAS UNREADY!
THA-BWOOMPH
THOR
X-MEN
I'M A VILLAIN, DUMMY, I'M SUPPOSED TO!
POP
Oh, YEAH?!
LESSEE IF RIVALIMPYENTITY CAN TAKE IT...
VORP!
KRACKLE!
... AS WELL AS DISH IT OUT!

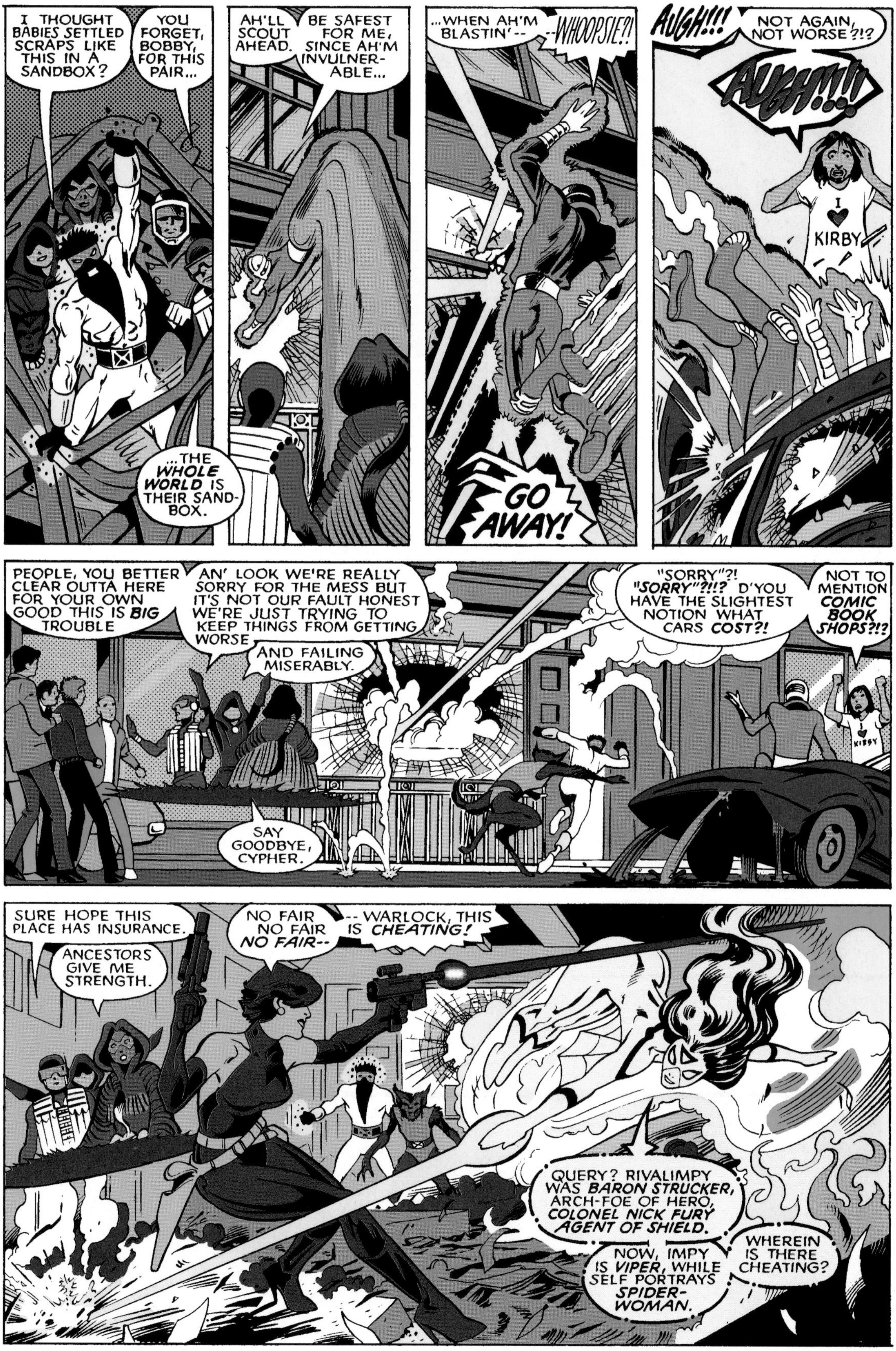
I THOUGHT BABIES SETTLED SCRAPS LIKE THIS IN A SANDBOX?
YOU FORGET, BOBBY, FOR THIS PAIR...
...THE WHOLE WORLD IS THEIR SANDBOX.
AH'LL SCOUT AHEAD.
BE SAFEST FOR ME, SINCE AH'M INVULNERABLE...
...WHEN AH'M BLASTIN'--
--WHOOPSIE?!
GO AWAY!
AUGH!!!
NOT AGAIN, NOT WORSE?!?
AUGH!!!
I ♥ KIRBY
PEOPLE, YOU BETTER CLEAR OUTTA HERE FOR YOUR OWN GOOD THIS IS BIG TROUBLE
AN' LOOK WE'RE REALLY SORRY FOR THE MESS BUT IT'S NOT OUR FAULT HONEST WE'RE JUST TRYING TO KEEP THINGS FROM GETTING WORSE
AND FAILING MISERABLY.
SAY GOODBYE, CYPHER.
"SORRY"?! "SORRY"?!!? D'YOU HAVE THE SLIGHTEST NOTION WHAT CARS COST?!
NOT TO MENTION COMIC BOOK SHOPS?!?
I ♥ KIBBY
SURE HOPE THIS PLACE HAS INSURANCE.
ANCESTORS GIVE ME STRENGTH.
NO FAIR NO FAIR NO FAIR--
--WARLOCK, THIS IS CHEATING!
QUERY? RIVALIMPY WAS BARON STRUCKER, ARCH-FOE OF HERO, COLONEL NICK FURY AGENT OF SHIELD.
NOW, IMPY IS VIPER, WHILE SELF PORTRAYS SPIDER-WOMAN.
WHEREIN IS THERE CHEATING?

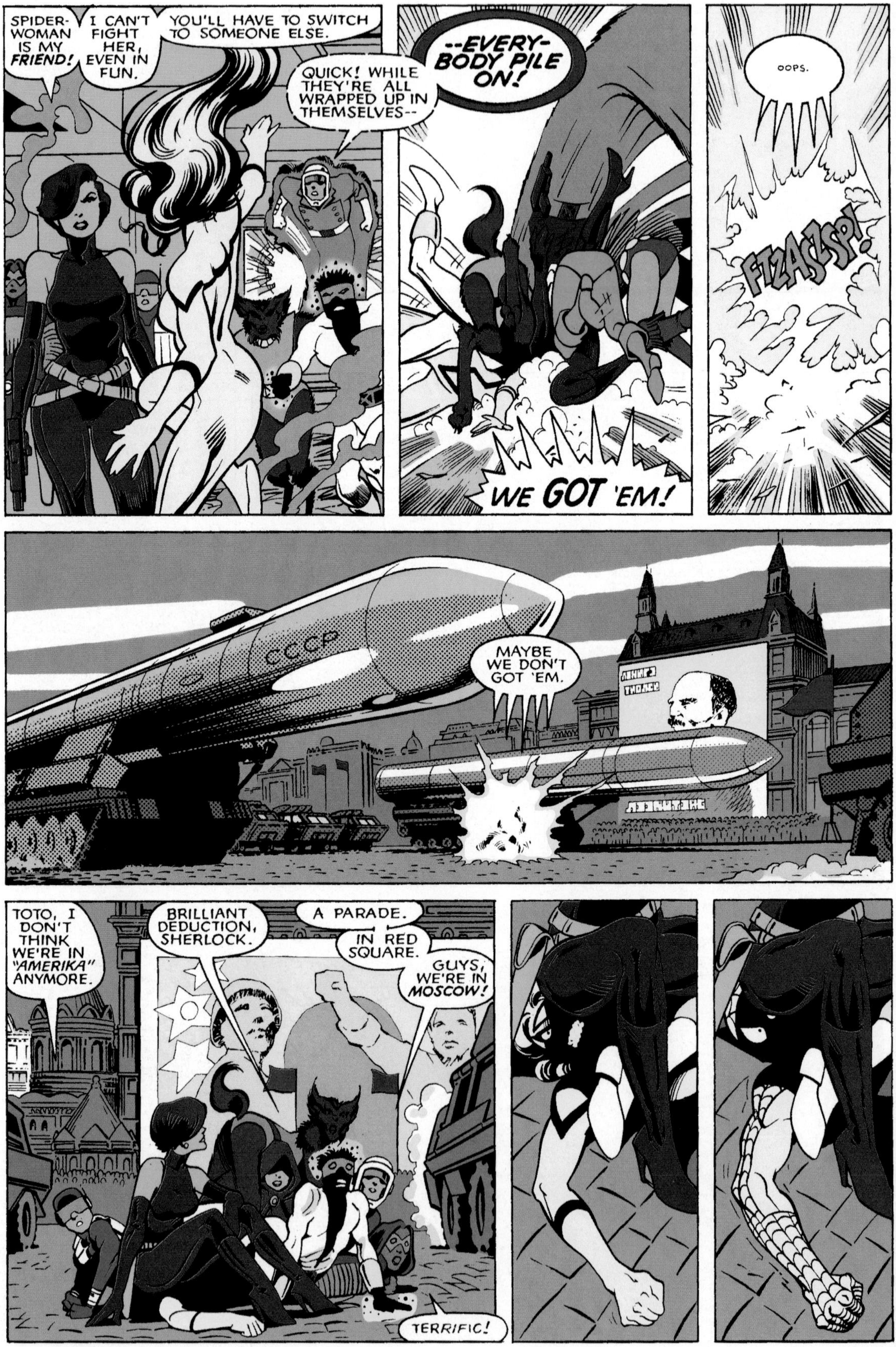
SPIDER-WOMAN IS MY *FRIEND!*
I CAN'T FIGHT HER, EVEN IN FUN.
YOU'LL HAVE TO SWITCH TO SOMEONE ELSE.
QUICK! WHILE THEY'RE ALL WRAPPED UP IN THEMSELVES--
--EVERY-BODY PILE ON!
WE GOT 'EM!
OOPS.
FTZASZSP!
MAYBE WE DON'T GOT 'EM.
CCCP
TOTO, I DON'T THINK WE'RE IN *"AMERIKA"* ANYMORE.
BRILLIANT DEDUCTION, SHERLOCK.
A PARADE.
IN RED SQUARE.
GUYS, WE'RE IN *MOSCOW!*
TERRIFIC!

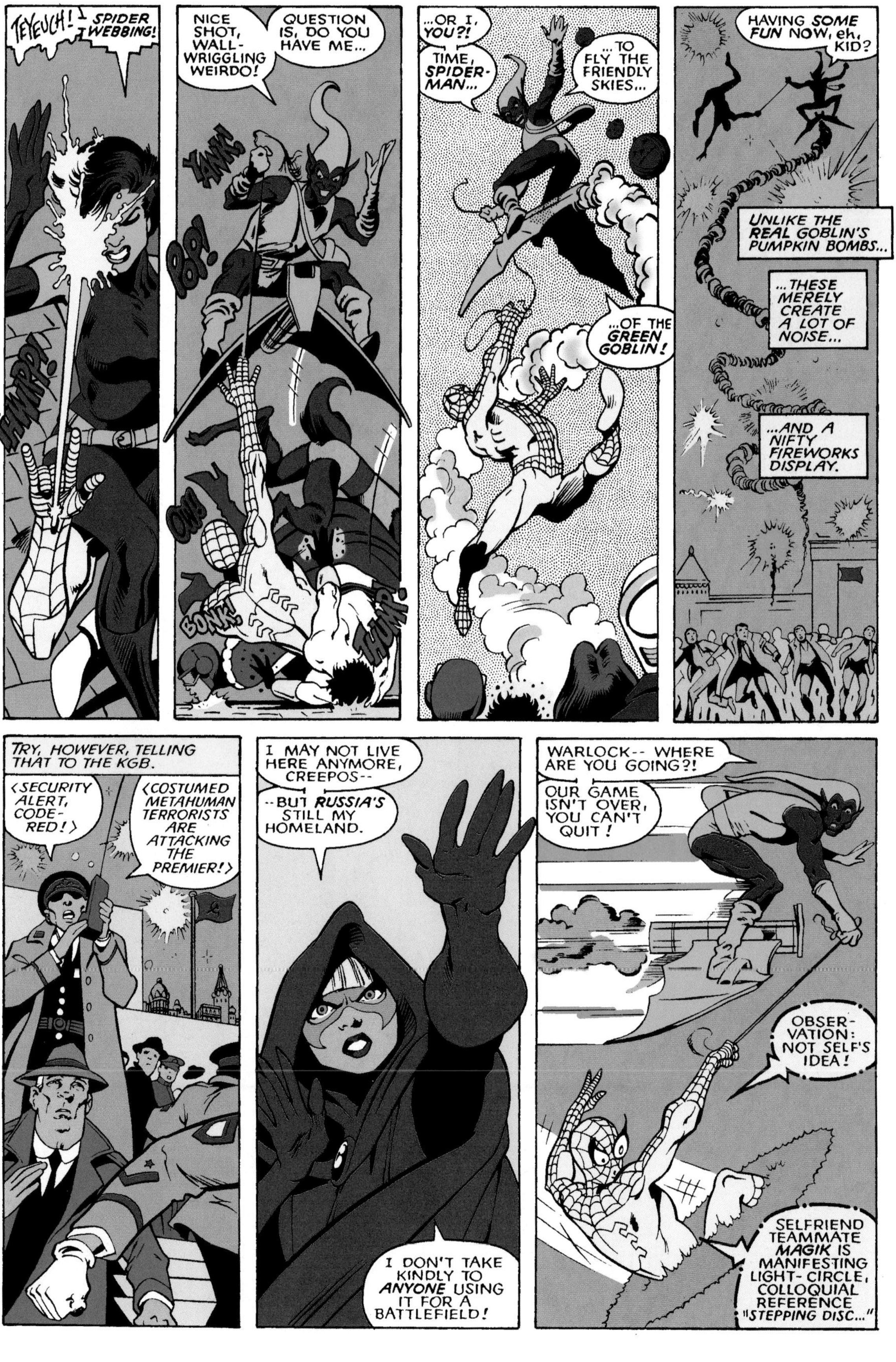
TEYEUCH!
SPIDER WEBBING!
THWIPP!
NICE SHOT, WALL-WRIGGLING WEIRDO!
QUESTION IS, DO YOU HAVE ME...
YANK!
POP!
OW!
BONK!
THUMP!
...OR I, YOU?!
TIME, SPIDER-MAN...
...TO FLY THE FRIENDLY SKIES...
...OF THE GREEN GOBLIN!
HAVING SOME FUN NOW, eh, KID?
UNLIKE THE REAL GOBLIN'S PUMPKIN BOMBS...
...THESE MERELY CREATE A LOT OF NOISE...
...AND A NIFTY FIREWORKS DISPLAY.
TRY, HOWEVER, TELLING THAT TO THE KGB.
<SECURITY ALERT, CODE-RED!>
<COSTUMED METAHUMAN TERRORISTS ARE ATTACKING THE PREMIER!>
I MAY NOT LIVE HERE ANYMORE, CREEPOS--
--BUT RUSSIA'S STILL MY HOMELAND.
I DON'T TAKE KINDLY TO ANYONE USING IT FOR A BATTLEFIELD!
WARLOCK-- WHERE ARE YOU GOING?!
OUR GAME ISN'T OVER, YOU CAN'T QUIT!
OBSERVATION: NOT SELF'S IDEA!
SELFRIEND TEAMMATE MAGIK IS MANIFESTING LIGHT-CIRCLE, COLLOQUIAL REFERENCE "STEPPING DISC..."

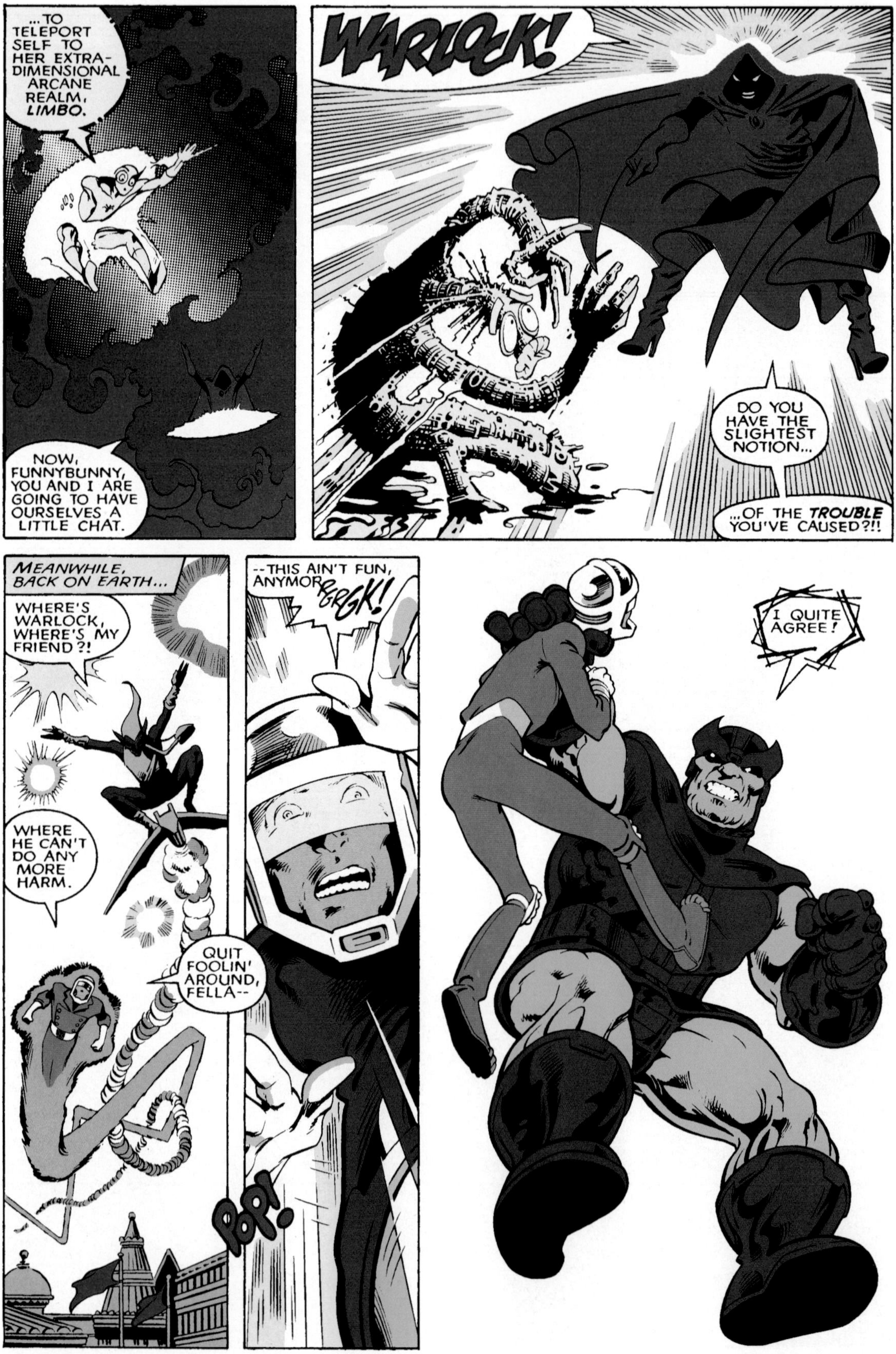
...TO TELEPORT SELF TO HER EXTRA-DIMENSIONAL ARCANE REALM, LIMBO.
NOW, FUNNYBUNNY, YOU AND I ARE GOING TO HAVE OURSELVES A LITTLE CHAT.
WARLOCK!
DO YOU HAVE THE SLIGHTEST NOTION...
...OF THE TROUBLE YOU'VE CAUSED?!!
MEANWHILE, BACK ON EARTH...
WHERE'S WARLOCK, WHERE'S MY FRIEND?!
WHERE HE CAN'T DO ANY MORE HARM.
QUIT FOOLIN' AROUND, FELLA--
POP!
--THIS AIN'T FUN, ANYMOR
GRGK!
I QUITE AGREE!

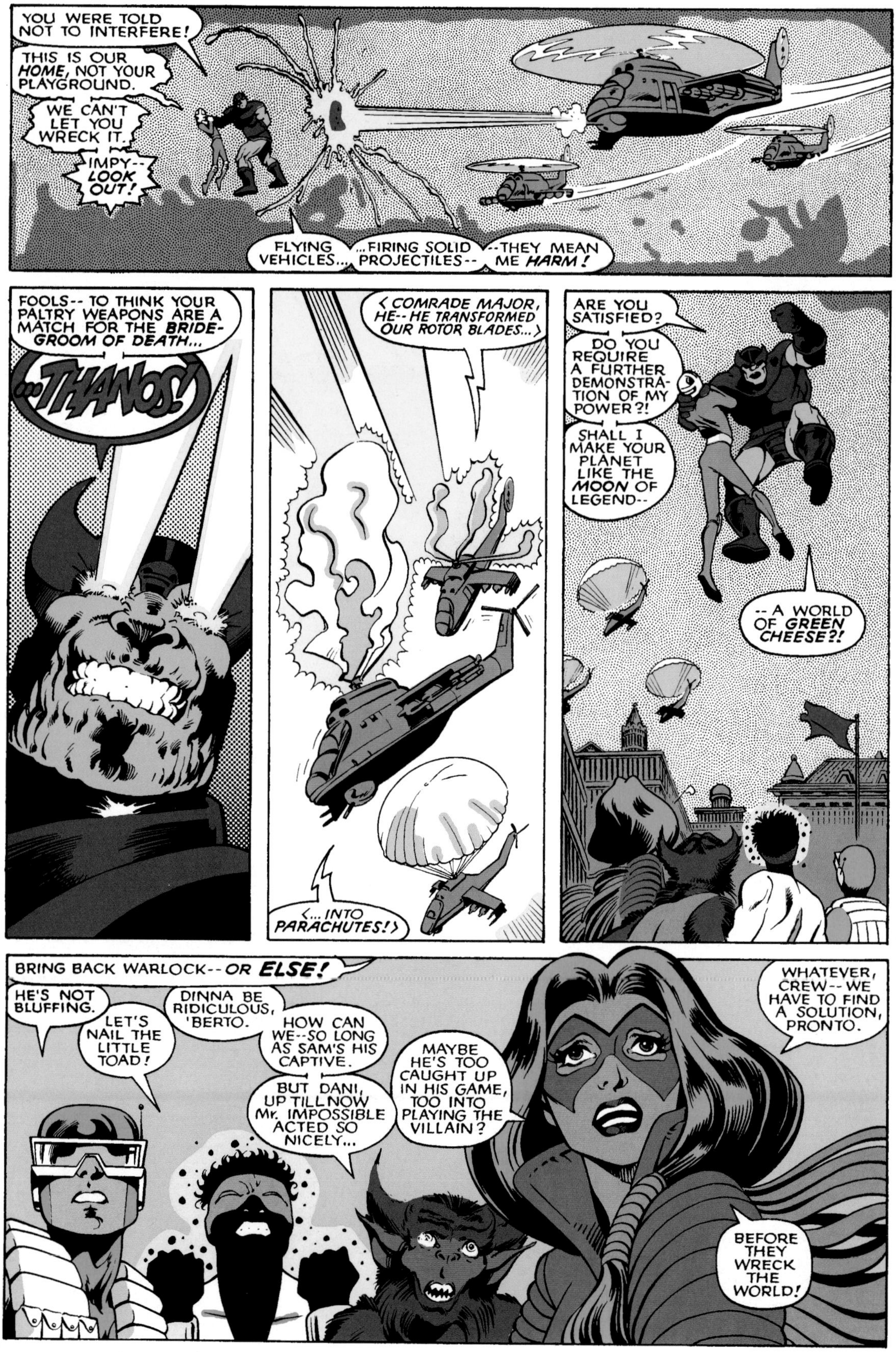
YOU WERE TOLD NOT TO INTERFERE!
THIS IS OUR HOME, NOT YOUR PLAYGROUND.
WE CAN'T LET YOU WRECK IT.
IMPY-- LOOK OUT!
FLYING VEHICLES...
...FIRING SOLID PROJECTILES--
--THEY MEAN ME HARM!
FOOLS-- TO THINK YOUR PALTRY WEAPONS ARE A MATCH FOR THE BRIDE-GROOM OF DEATH...
...THANOS!
<COMRADE MAJOR, HE--HE TRANSFORMED OUR ROTOR BLADES...>
<...INTO PARACHUTES!>
ARE YOU SATISFIED?
DO YOU REQUIRE A FURTHER DEMONSTRATION OF MY POWER?!
SHALL I MAKE YOUR PLANET LIKE THE MOON OF LEGEND--
--A WORLD OF GREEN CHEESE?!
BRING BACK WARLOCK--OR ELSE!
HE'S NOT BLUFFING.
LET'S NAIL THE LITTLE TOAD!
DINNA BE RIDICULOUS, 'BERTO.
HOW CAN WE--SO LONG AS SAM'S HIS CAPTIVE.
BUT DANI, UP TILL NOW Mr. IMPOSSIBLE ACTED SO NICELY...
MAYBE HE'S TOO CAUGHT UP IN HIS GAME, TOO INTO PLAYING THE VILLAIN?
WHATEVER, CREW--WE HAVE TO FIND A SOLUTION, PRONTO.
BEFORE THEY WRECK THE WORLD!

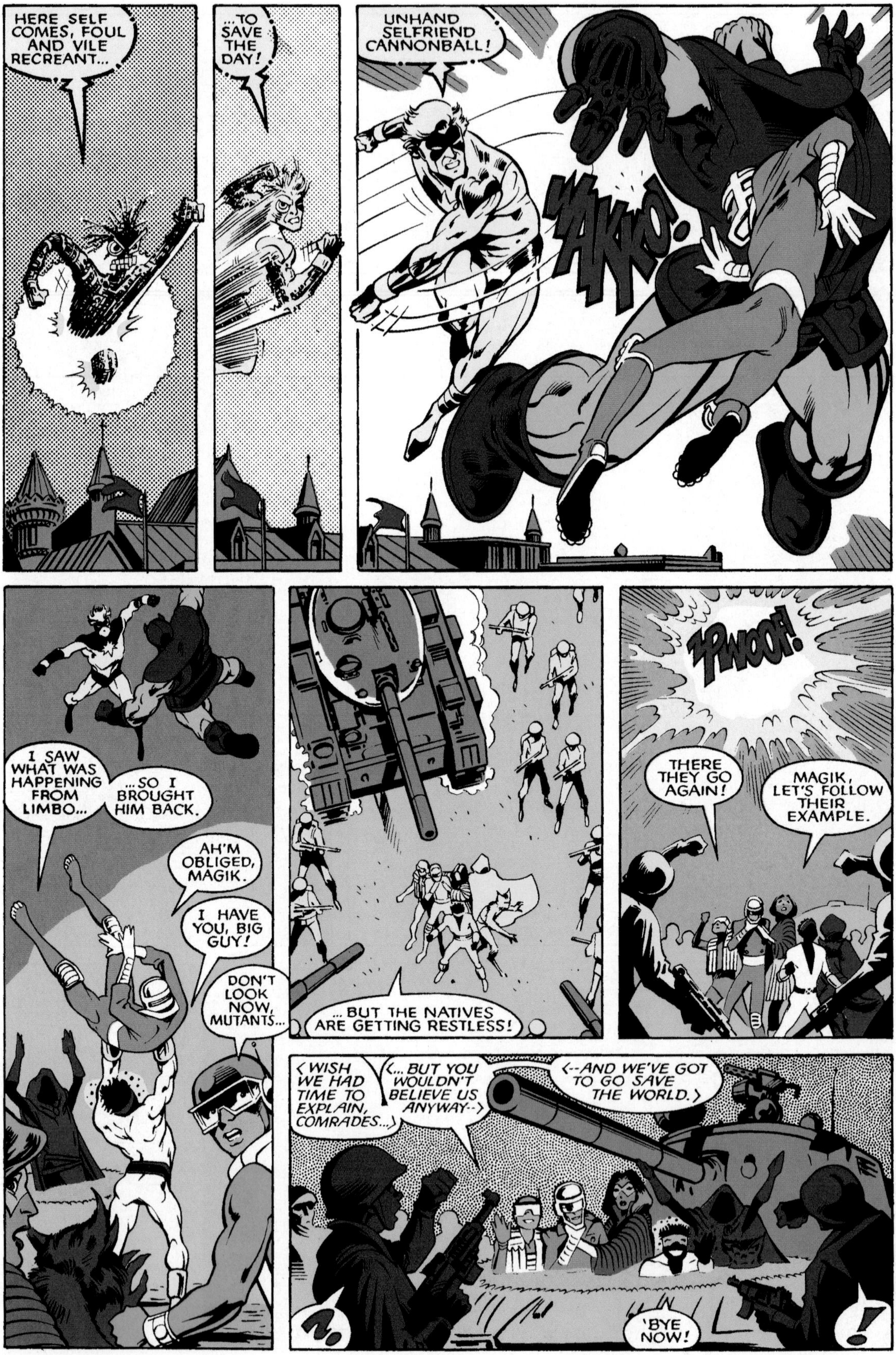
HERE SELF COMES, FOUL AND VILE RECREANT...
...TO SAVE THE DAY!
UNHAND SELFRIEND CANNONBALL!
WAKKO!
I SAW WHAT WAS HAPPENING FROM LIMBO...
...SO I BROUGHT HIM BACK.
AH'M OBLIGED, MAGIK.
I HAVE YOU, BIG GUY!
DON'T LOOK NOW, MUTANTS...
...BUT THE NATIVES ARE GETTING RESTLESS!
PWOOF!
THERE THEY GO AGAIN!
MAGIK, LET'S FOLLOW THEIR EXAMPLE.
<WISH WE HAD TIME TO EXPLAIN, COMRADES...>
<...BUT YOU WOULDN'T BELIEVE US ANYWAY-->
<--AND WE'VE GOT TO GO SAVE THE WORLD.>
'BYE NOW!

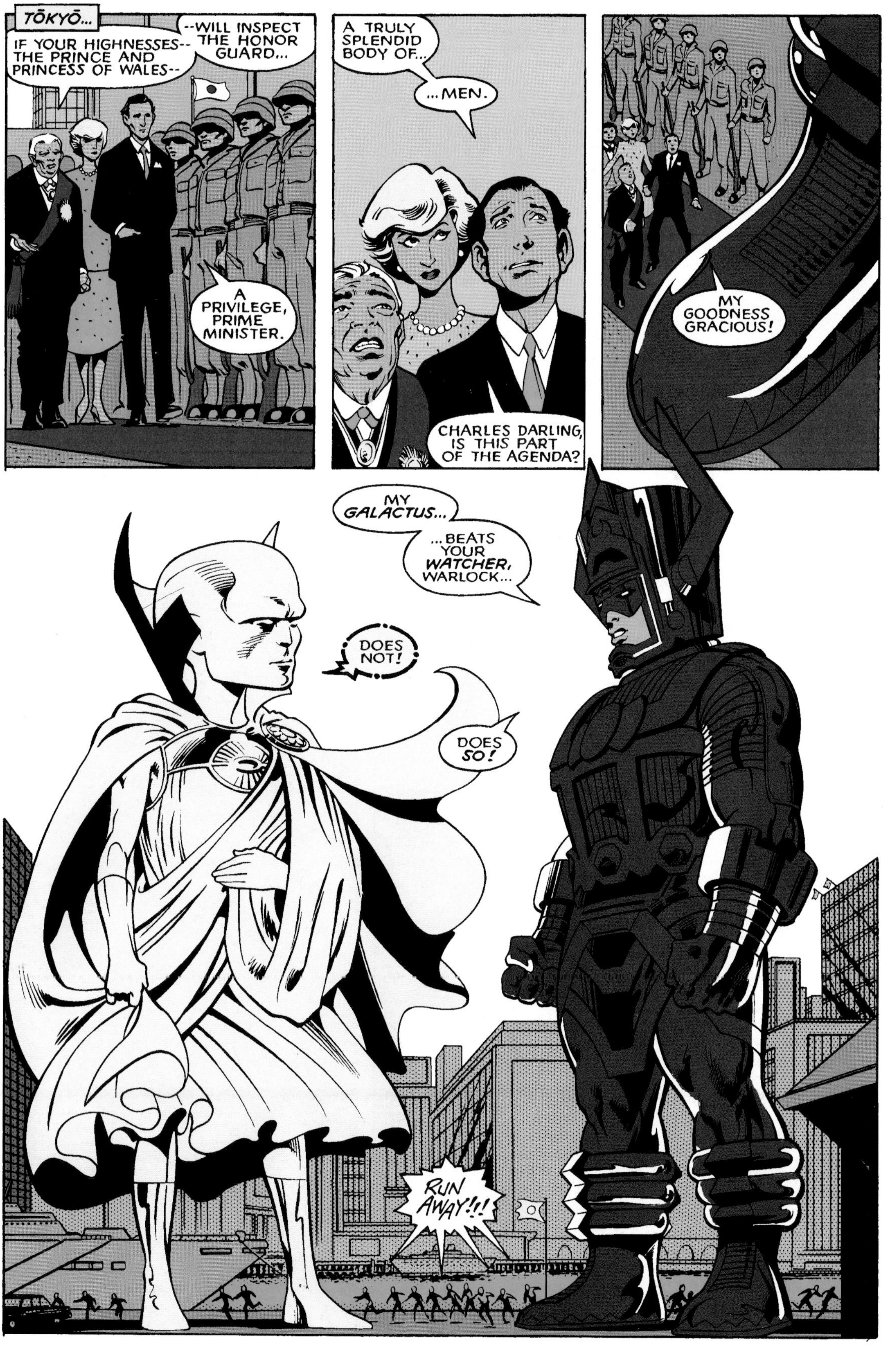
TŌKYŌ...
IF YOUR HIGHNESSES-- THE PRINCE AND PRINCESS OF WALES--
--WILL INSPECT THE HONOR GUARD...
A PRIVILEGE, PRIME MINISTER.
A TRULY SPLENDID BODY OF...
...MEN.
CHARLES DARLING, IS THIS PART OF THE AGENDA?
MY GOODNESS GRACIOUS!
MY GALACTUS...
...BEATS YOUR WATCHER, WARLOCK...
DOES NOT!
DOES SO!
RUN AWAY!!!

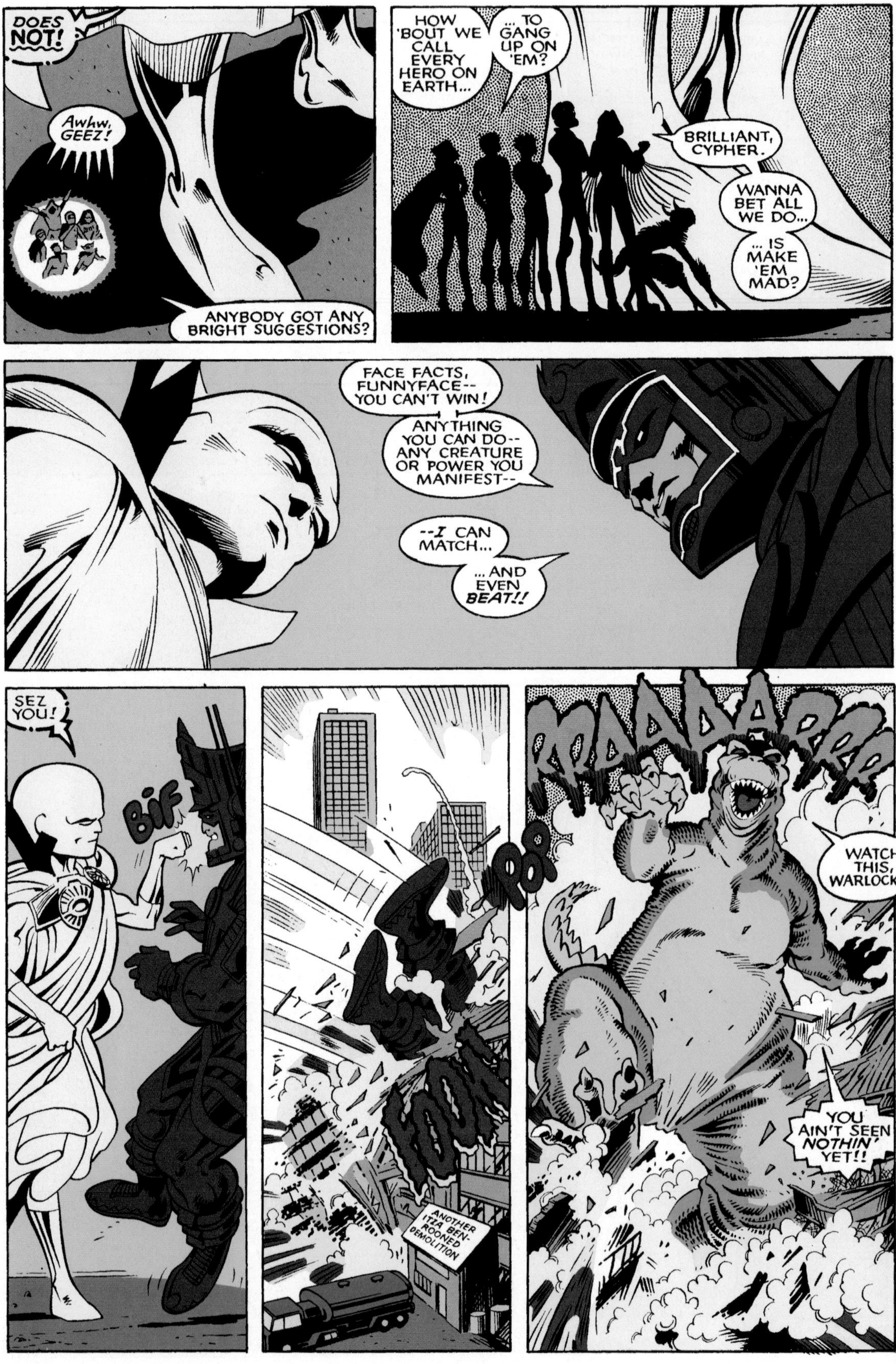
DOES NOT!
Awhw, GEEZ!
ANYBODY GOT ANY BRIGHT SUGGESTIONS?
HOW 'BOUT WE CALL EVERY HERO ON EARTH...
... TO GANG UP ON 'EM?
BRILLIANT, CYPHER.
WANNA BET ALL WE DO...
... IS MAKE 'EM MAD?
FACE FACTS, FUNNYFACE-- YOU CAN'T WIN!
ANYTHING YOU CAN DO-- ANY CREATURE OR POWER YOU MANIFEST--
--I CAN MATCH...
... AND EVEN BEAT!!
SEZ YOU!
BIF
POP
ANOTHER ITZA BEN-ROONED DEMOLITION
WATCH THIS, WARLOCK!
YOU AIN'T SEEN NOTHIN' YET!!

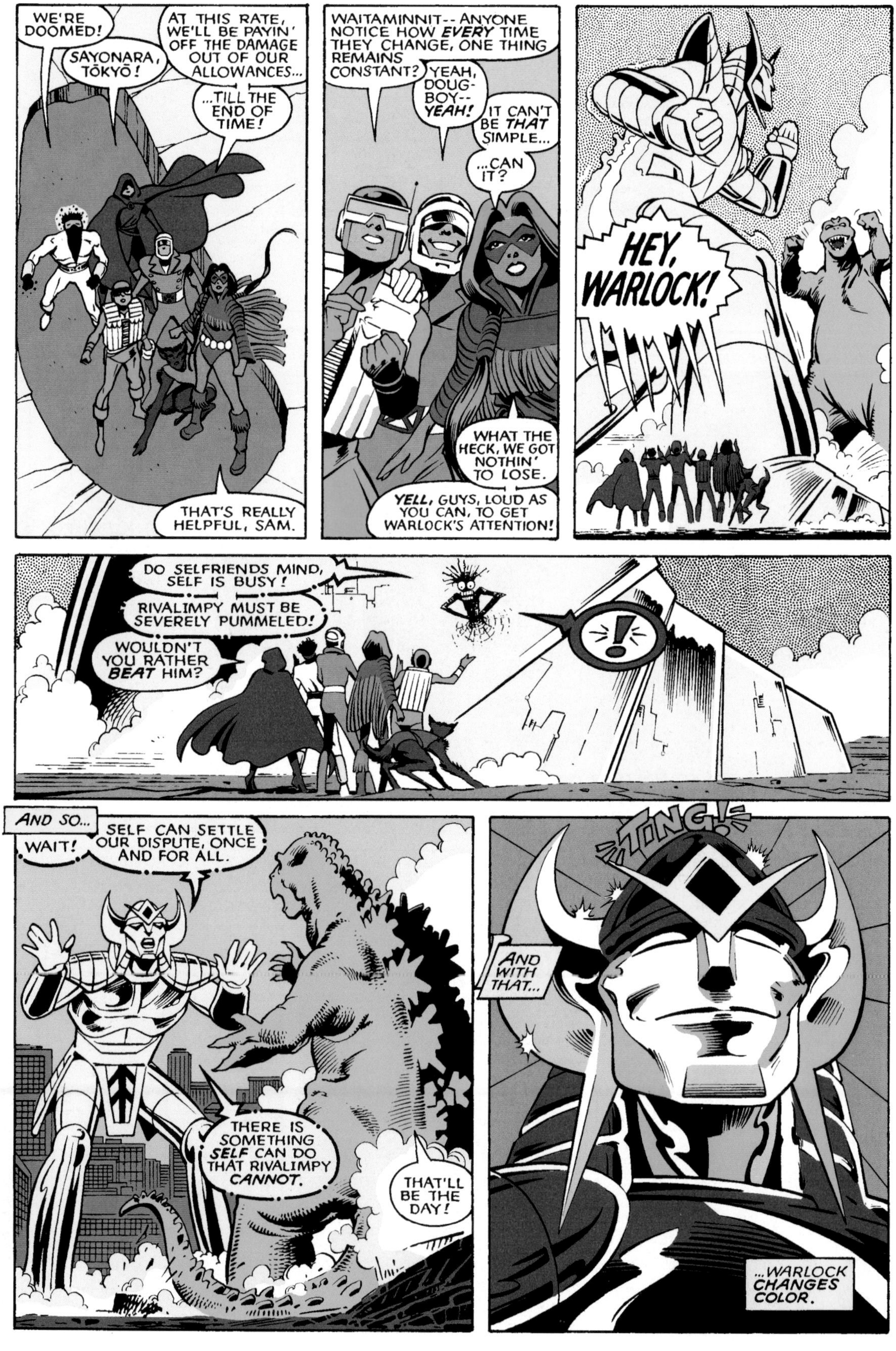
WE'RE DOOMED!
SAYONARA, TŌKYŌ!
AT THIS RATE, WE'LL BE PAYIN' OFF THE DAMAGE OUT OF OUR ALLOWANCES...
...TILL THE END OF TIME!
THAT'S REALLY HELPFUL, SAM.
WAITAMINNIT-- ANYONE NOTICE HOW EVERY TIME THEY CHANGE, ONE THING REMAINS CONSTANT?
YEAH, DOUG-BOY-- YEAH!
IT CAN'T BE THAT SIMPLE...
...CAN IT?
WHAT THE HECK, WE GOT NOTHIN' TO LOSE.
YELL, GUYS, LOUD AS YOU CAN, TO GET WARLOCK'S ATTENTION!
HEY, WARLOCK!
DO SELFRIENDS MIND, SELF IS BUSY!
RIVALIMPY MUST BE SEVERELY PUMMELED!
WOULDN'T YOU RATHER BEAT HIM?
!
AND SO...
WAIT!
SELF CAN SETTLE OUR DISPUTE, ONCE AND FOR ALL.
THERE IS SOMETHING SELF CAN DO THAT RIVALIMPY CANNOT.
THAT'LL BE THE DAY!
TING!
AND WITH THAT...
...WARLOCK CHANGES COLOR.

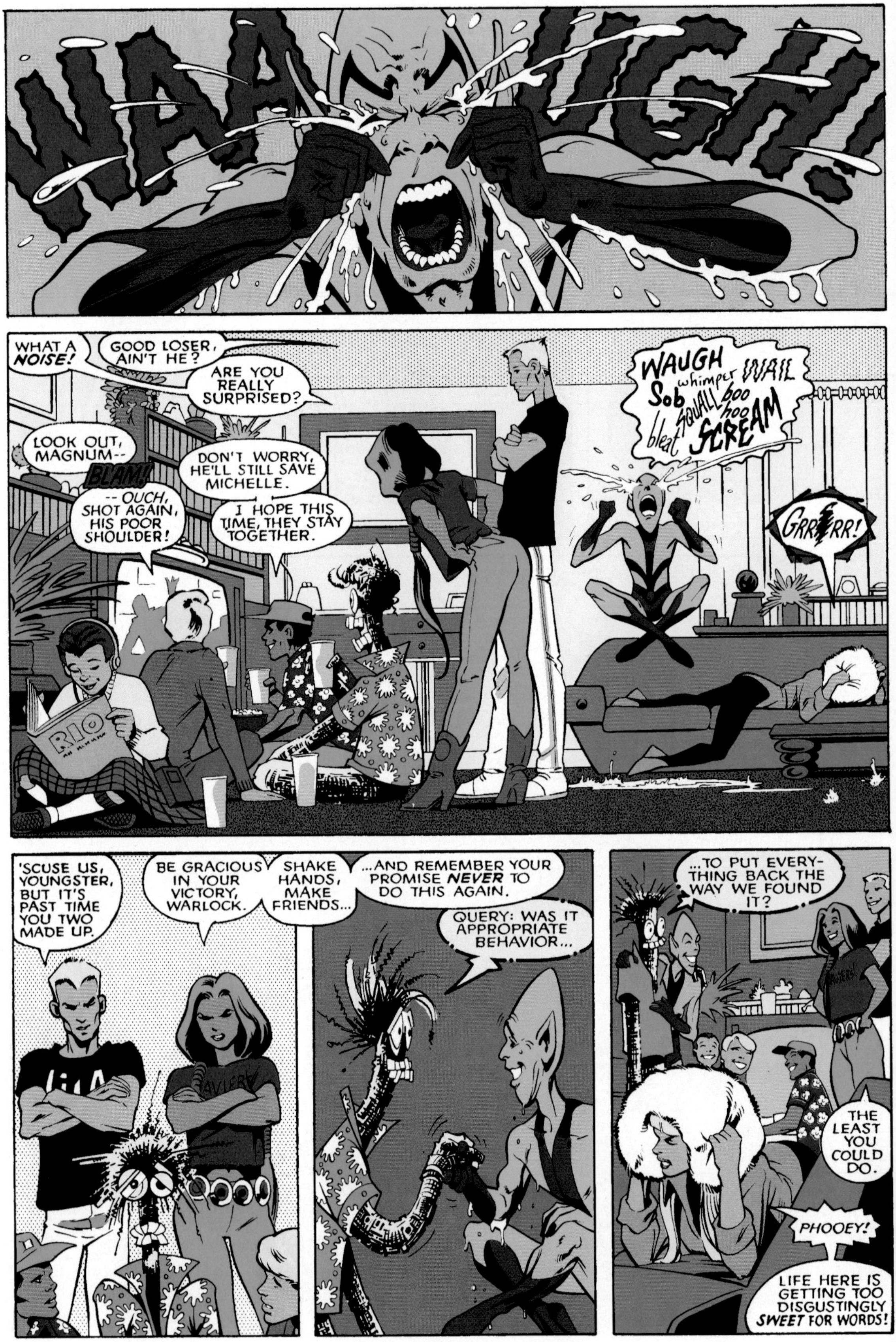
WAAUGH!
WHAT A NOISE!
GOOD LOSER, AIN'T HE?
ARE YOU REALLY SURPRISED?
WAUGH Sob whimper WAIL SQUALL boo hoo bleat SCREAM
LOOK OUT, MAGNUM--
BLAM!
--OUCH, SHOT AGAIN, HIS POOR SHOULDER!
DON'T WORRY, HE'LL STILL SAVE MICHELLE.
I HOPE THIS TIME, THEY STAY TOGETHER.
GRRRRR!
RIO
'SCUSE US, YOUNGSTER, BUT IT'S PAST TIME YOU TWO MADE UP.
BE GRACIOUS IN YOUR VICTORY, WARLOCK.
SHAKE HANDS, MAKE FRIENDS...
...AND REMEMBER YOUR PROMISE NEVER TO DO THIS AGAIN.
QUERY: WAS IT APPROPRIATE BEHAVIOR...
...TO PUT EVERYTHING BACK THE WAY WE FOUND IT?
THE LEAST YOU COULD DO.
PHOOEY!
LIFE HERE IS GETTING TOO DISGUSTINGLY SWEET FOR WORDS!

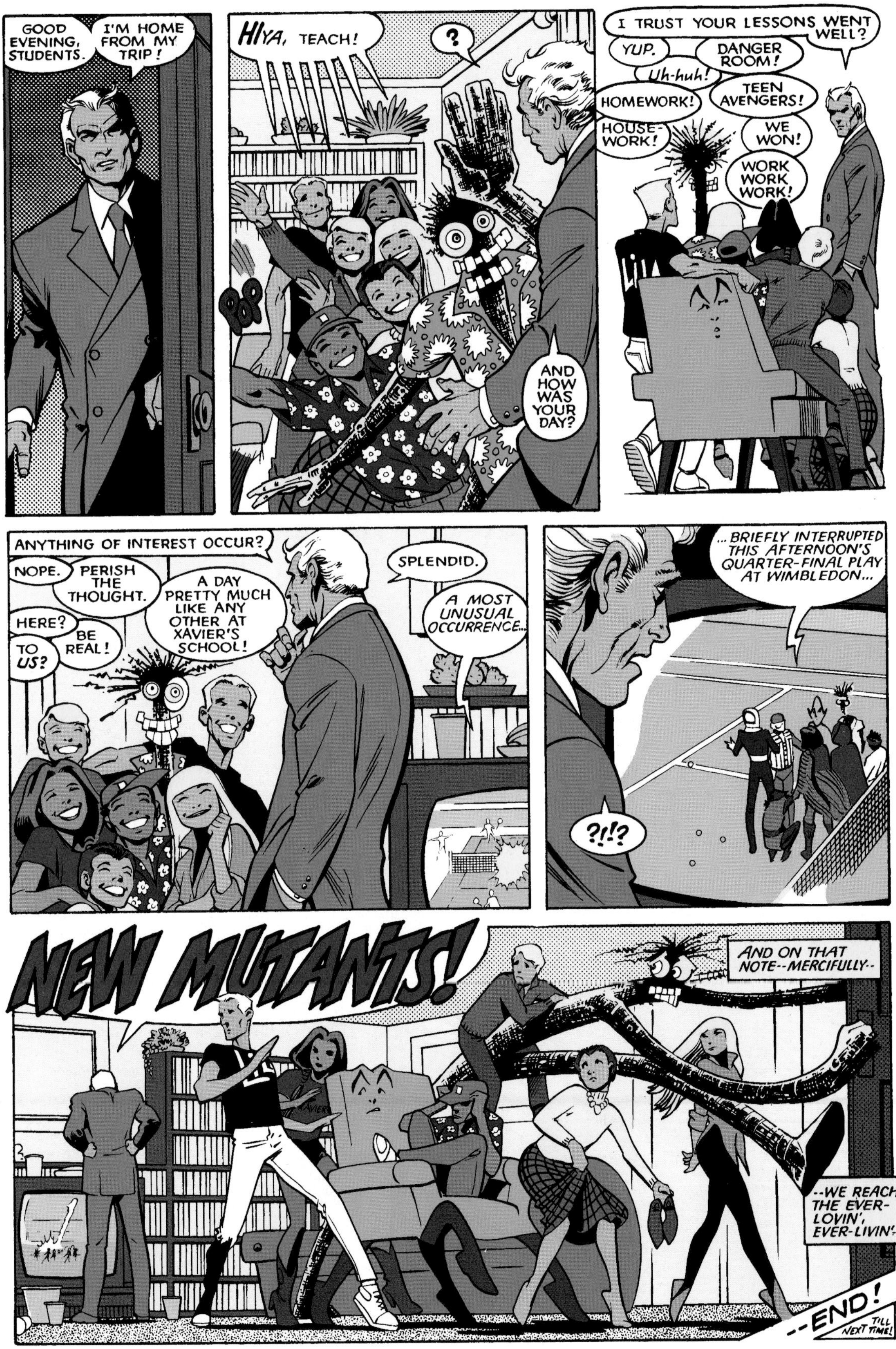
GOOD EVENING, STUDENTS.
I'M HOME FROM MY TRIP!
HIYA, TEACH!
?
AND HOW WAS YOUR DAY?
POP
I TRUST YOUR LESSONS WENT WELL?
YUP.
DANGER ROOM!
Uh-huh!
HOMEWORK!
TEEN AVENGERS!
HOUSE-WORK!
WE WON!
WORK WORK WORK!
ANYTHING OF INTEREST OCCUR?
NOPE.
PERISH THE THOUGHT.
HERE?
BE REAL!
TO US?
A DAY PRETTY MUCH LIKE ANY OTHER AT XAVIER'S SCHOOL!
SPLENDID.
A MOST UNUSUAL OCCURRENCE...
...BRIEFLY INTERRUPTED THIS AFTERNOON'S QUARTER-FINAL PLAY AT WIMBLEDON...
?!!?
NEW MUTANTS!
AND ON THAT NOTE--MERCIFULLY--
--WE REACH THE EVER-LOVIN', EVER-LIVIN'--
--END!
TILL NEXT TIME!

The Uncanny X-Men #213

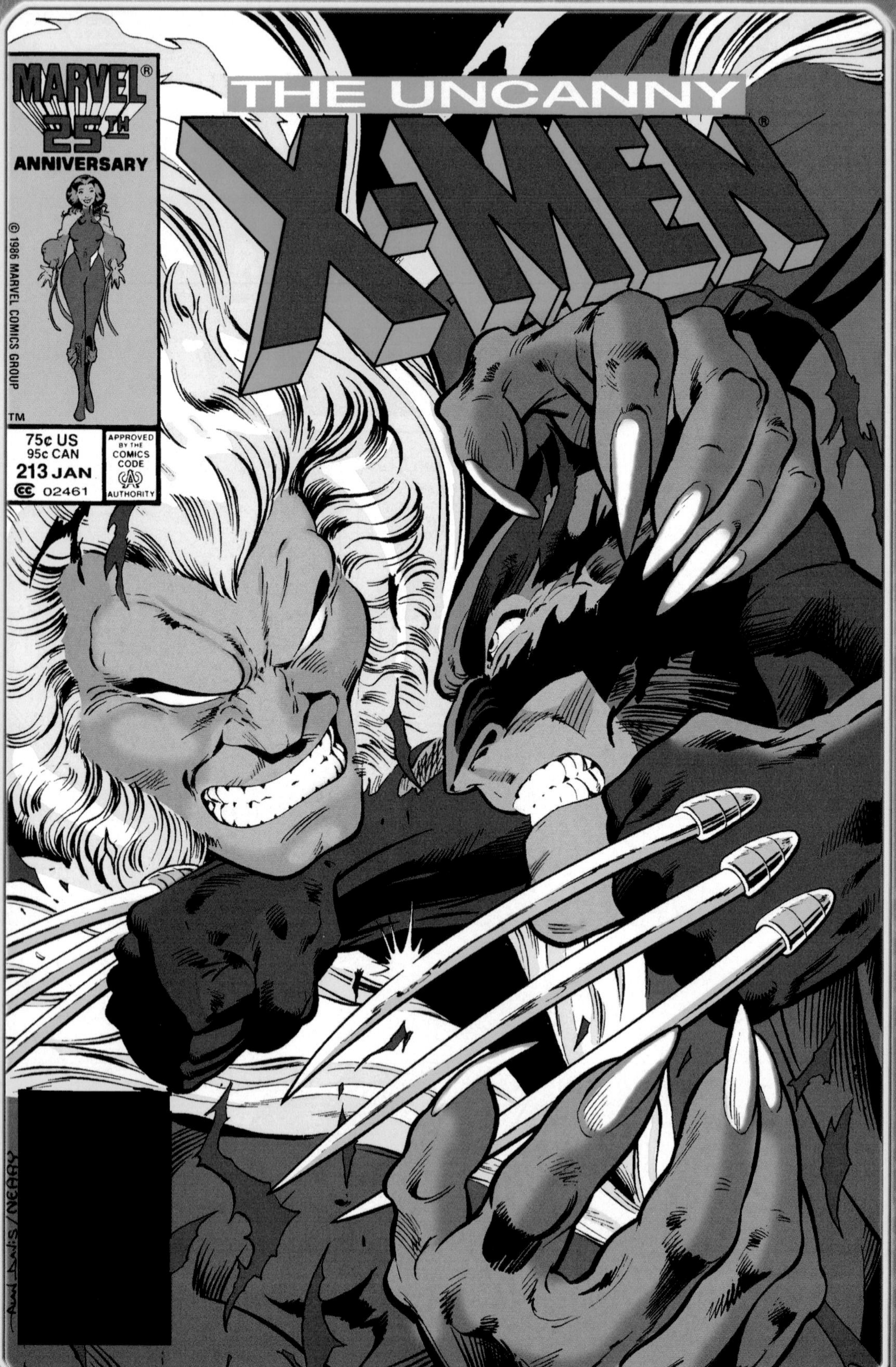
MARVEL
25TH
ANNIVERSARY
© 1986 MARVEL COMICS GROUP
TM
75¢ US
95¢ CAN
213 JAN
02461
APPROVED BY THE COMICS CODE AUTHORITY
THE UNCANNY
X-MEN

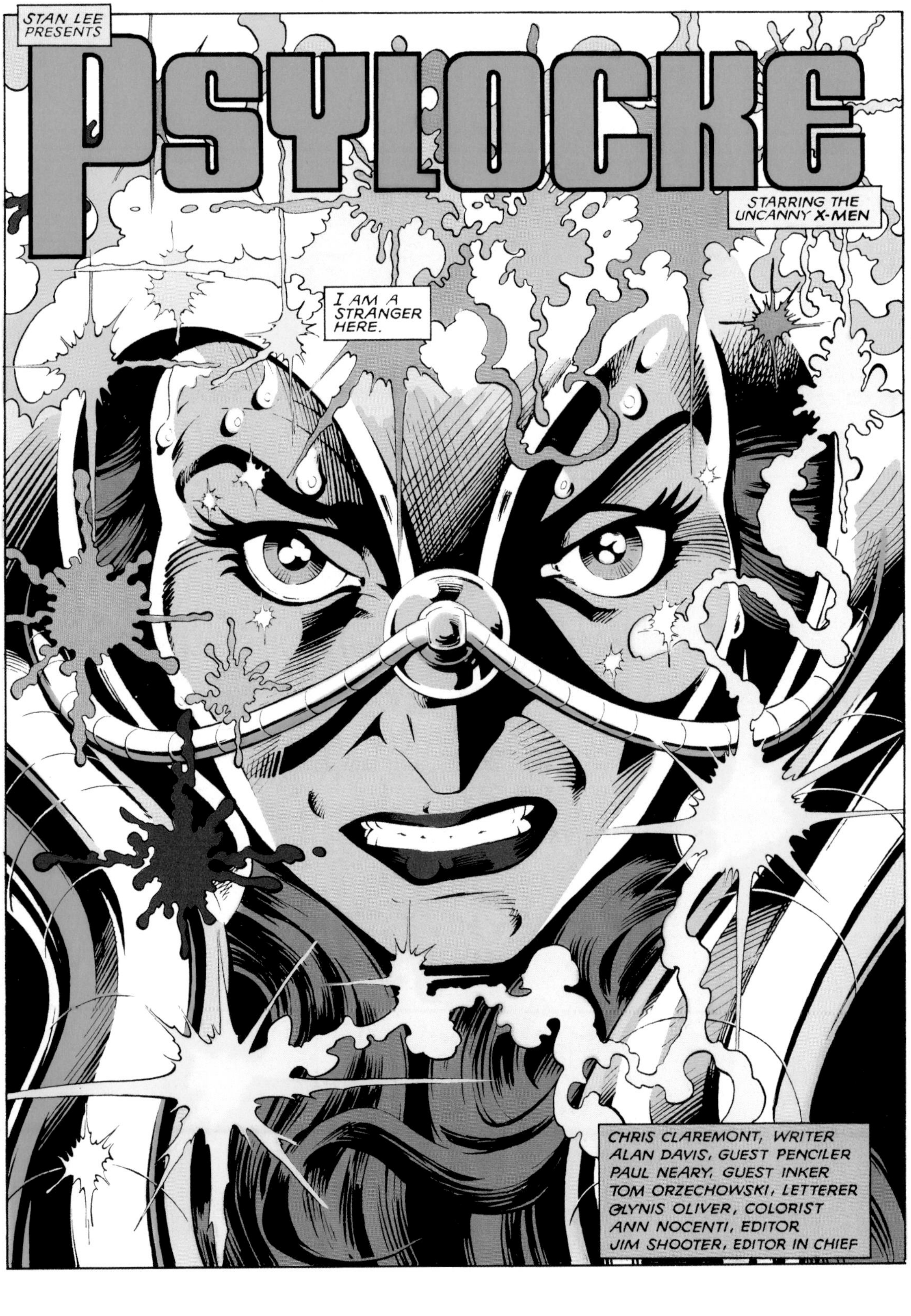
STAN LEE PRESENTS
PSYLOCKE
STARRING THE UNCANNY X-MEN
I AM A STRANGER HERE.
CHRIS CLAREMONT, WRITER
ALAN DAVIS, GUEST PENCILER
PAUL NEARY, GUEST INKER
TOM ORZECHOWSKI, LETTERER
GLYNIS OLIVER, COLORIST
ANN NOCENTI, EDITOR
JIM SHOOTER, EDITOR IN CHIEF

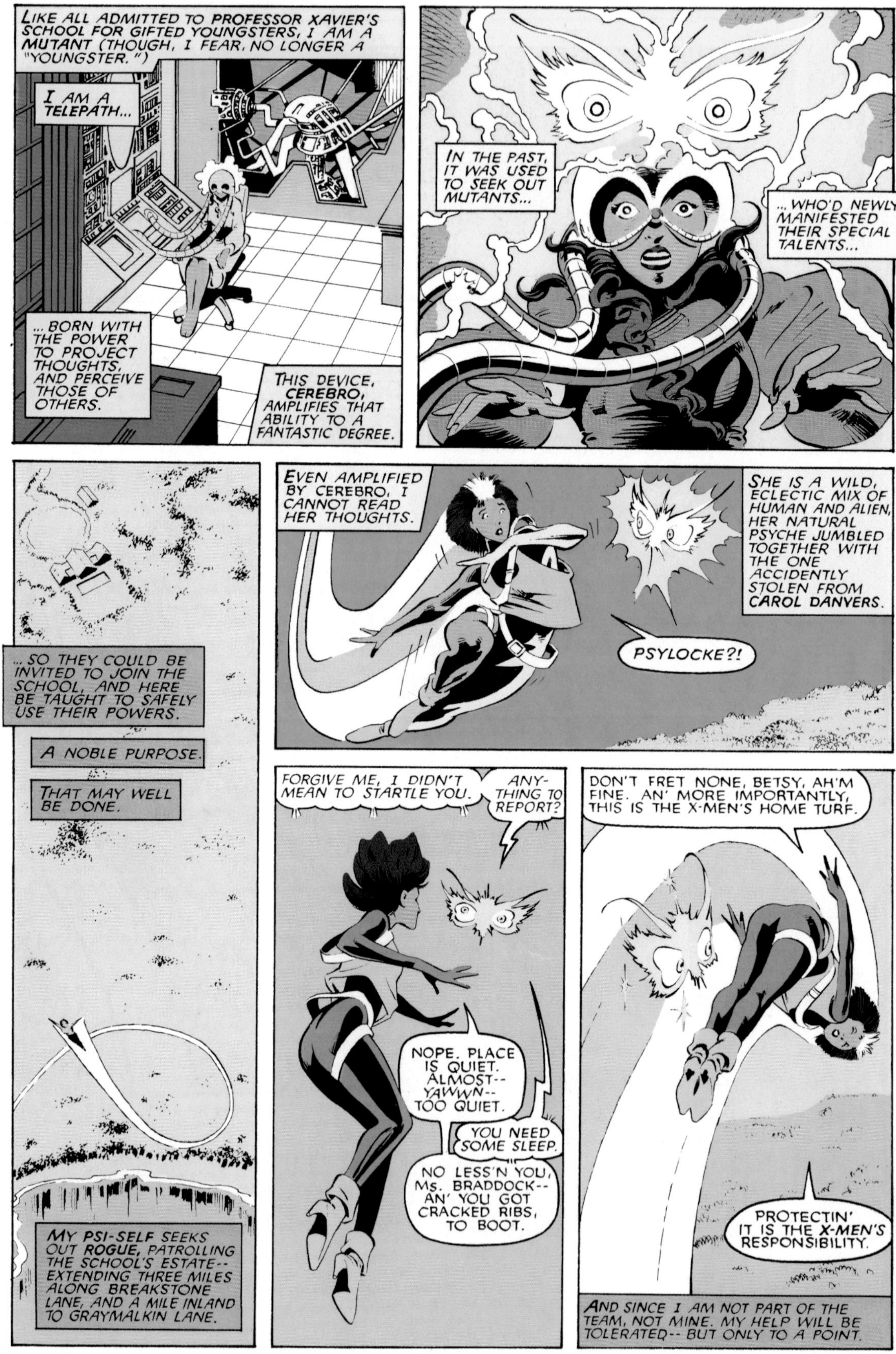
LIKE ALL ADMITTED TO PROFESSOR XAVIER'S SCHOOL FOR GIFTED YOUNGSTERS, I AM A MUTANT (THOUGH, I FEAR, NO LONGER A "YOUNGSTER.")
I AM A TELEPATH...
...BORN WITH THE POWER TO PROJECT THOUGHTS, AND PERCEIVE THOSE OF OTHERS.
THIS DEVICE, CEREBRO, AMPLIFIES THAT ABILITY TO A FANTASTIC DEGREE.
IN THE PAST, IT WAS USED TO SEEK OUT MUTANTS...
...WHO'D NEWLY MANIFESTED THEIR SPECIAL TALENTS...
...SO THEY COULD BE INVITED TO JOIN THE SCHOOL, AND HERE BE TAUGHT TO SAFELY USE THEIR POWERS.
A NOBLE PURPOSE.
THAT MAY WELL BE DONE.
MY PSI-SELF SEEKS OUT ROGUE, PATROLLING THE SCHOOL'S ESTATE-- EXTENDING THREE MILES ALONG BREAKSTONE LANE, AND A MILE INLAND TO GRAYMALKIN LANE.
EVEN AMPLIFIED BY CEREBRO, I CANNOT READ HER THOUGHTS.
SHE IS A WILD, ECLECTIC MIX OF HUMAN AND ALIEN, HER NATURAL PSYCHE JUMBLED TOGETHER WITH THE ONE ACCIDENTLY STOLEN FROM CAROL DANVERS.
PSYLOCKE?!
FORGIVE ME, I DIDN'T MEAN TO STARTLE YOU.
ANYTHING TO REPORT?
NOPE. PLACE IS QUIET. ALMOST-- YAWWN-- TOO QUIET.
YOU NEED SOME SLEEP.
NO LESS'N YOU, Ms. BRADDOCK-- AN' YOU GOT CRACKED RIBS, TO BOOT.
DON'T FRET NONE, BETSY, AH'M FINE. AN' MORE IMPORTANTLY, THIS IS THE X-MEN'S HOME TURF.
PROTECTIN' IT IS THE X-MEN'S RESPONSIBILITY.
AND SINCE I AM NOT PART OF THE TEAM, NOT MINE. MY HELP WILL BE TOLERATED-- BUT ONLY TO A POINT.

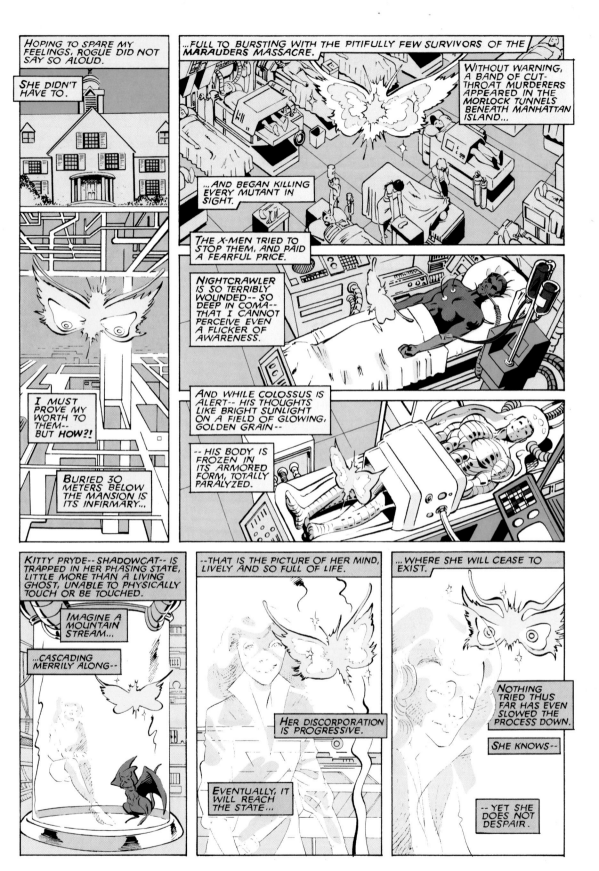

HOPING TO SPARE MY FEELINGS, ROGUE DID NOT SAY SO ALOUD.

SHE DIDN'T HAVE TO.

I MUST PROVE MY WORTH TO THEM-- BUT *HOW?!*

BURIED 30 METERS BELOW THE MANSION IS ITS INFIRMARY...

...FULL TO BURSTING WITH THE PITIFULLY FEW SURVIVORS OF THE MARAUDERS MASSACRE.

WITHOUT WARNING, A BAND OF CUT-THROAT MURDERERS APPEARED IN THE MORLOCK TUNNELS BENEATH MANHATTAN ISLAND...

...AND BEGAN KILLING EVERY MUTANT IN SIGHT.

THE X-MEN TRIED TO STOP THEM, AND PAID A FEARFUL PRICE.

NIGHTCRAWLER IS SO TERRIBLY WOUNDED-- SO DEEP IN COMA-- THAT I CANNOT PERCEIVE EVEN A FLICKER OF AWARENESS.

AND WHILE COLOSSUS IS ALERT-- HIS THOUGHTS LIKE BRIGHT SUNLIGHT ON A FIELD OF GLOWING, GOLDEN GRAIN--

-- HIS BODY IS FROZEN IN ITS ARMORED FORM, TOTALLY PARALYZED.

KITTY PRYDE--SHADOWCAT-- IS TRAPPED IN HER PHASING STATE, LITTLE MORE THAN A LIVING GHOST, UNABLE TO PHYSICALLY TOUCH OR BE TOUCHED.

IMAGINE A MOUNTAIN STREAM...

...CASCADING MERRILY ALONG--

--THAT IS THE PICTURE OF HER MIND, LIVELY AND SO FULL OF LIFE.

HER DISCORPORATION IS PROGRESSIVE.

EVENTUALLY, IT WILL REACH THE STATE...

...WHERE SHE WILL CEASE TO EXIST.

NOTHING TRIED THUS FAR HAS EVEN SLOWED THE PROCESS DOWN.

SHE KNOWS--

-- YET SHE DOES NOT DESPAIR.

HALF MY AGE...

...YET HER COURAGE SHAMES ME.

I WEEP FOR HER...

...AS MY PSI-SELF SOARS THROUGH THE MANSION TO THE RESIDENTIAL WING INHABITED BY THE SCHOOL'S NOVICE CLASS, THE NEW MUTANTS.

THEY ARE ALL GONE.

DISOBEYING ORDERS, THEY ENTERED THE MORLOCK TUNNELS -- NO ONE KNOWS WHY.

THEN, THOSE SAME TUNNELS WERE SWEPT BY A TREMENDOUS WAVE OF HIGH-ENERGY PLASMA.

IF THE MUTANTS WERE IN ITS PATH WHEN THE WAVE STRUCK, THEY ARE SURELY DEAD.

I'VE BEEN SEARCHING FOR THEM WITH CEREBRO. I WILL KEEP ON UNTIL I FIND THEM.

OR UNTIL THEIR DEATHS ARE PROVEN BEYOND ALL DOUBT.

MY LAST STOP IS CYPHER'S ROOM.

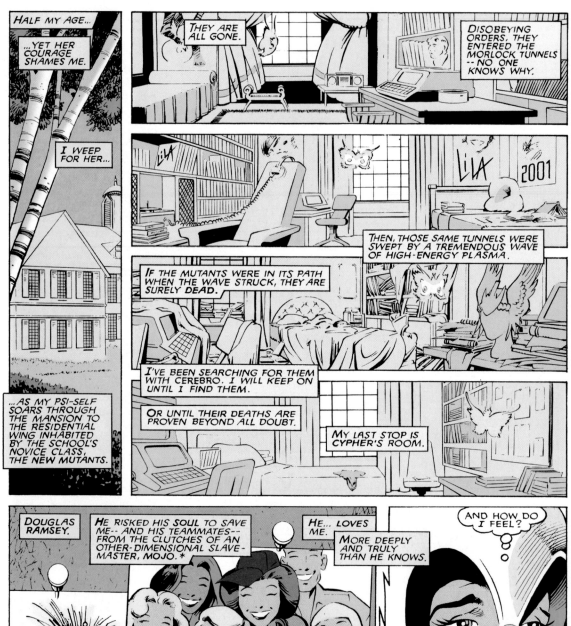

DOUGLAS RAMSEY.

HE RISKED HIS SOUL TO SAVE ME-- AND HIS TEAMMATES-- FROM THE CLUTCHES OF AN OTHER-DIMENSIONAL SLAVE-MASTER, MOJO. *

HE... LOVES ME.

MORE DEEPLY AND TRULY THAN HE KNOWS.

AND HOW DO I FEEL?

*SEE NEW MUTANTS ANNUAL #2. -- AnnN.

98

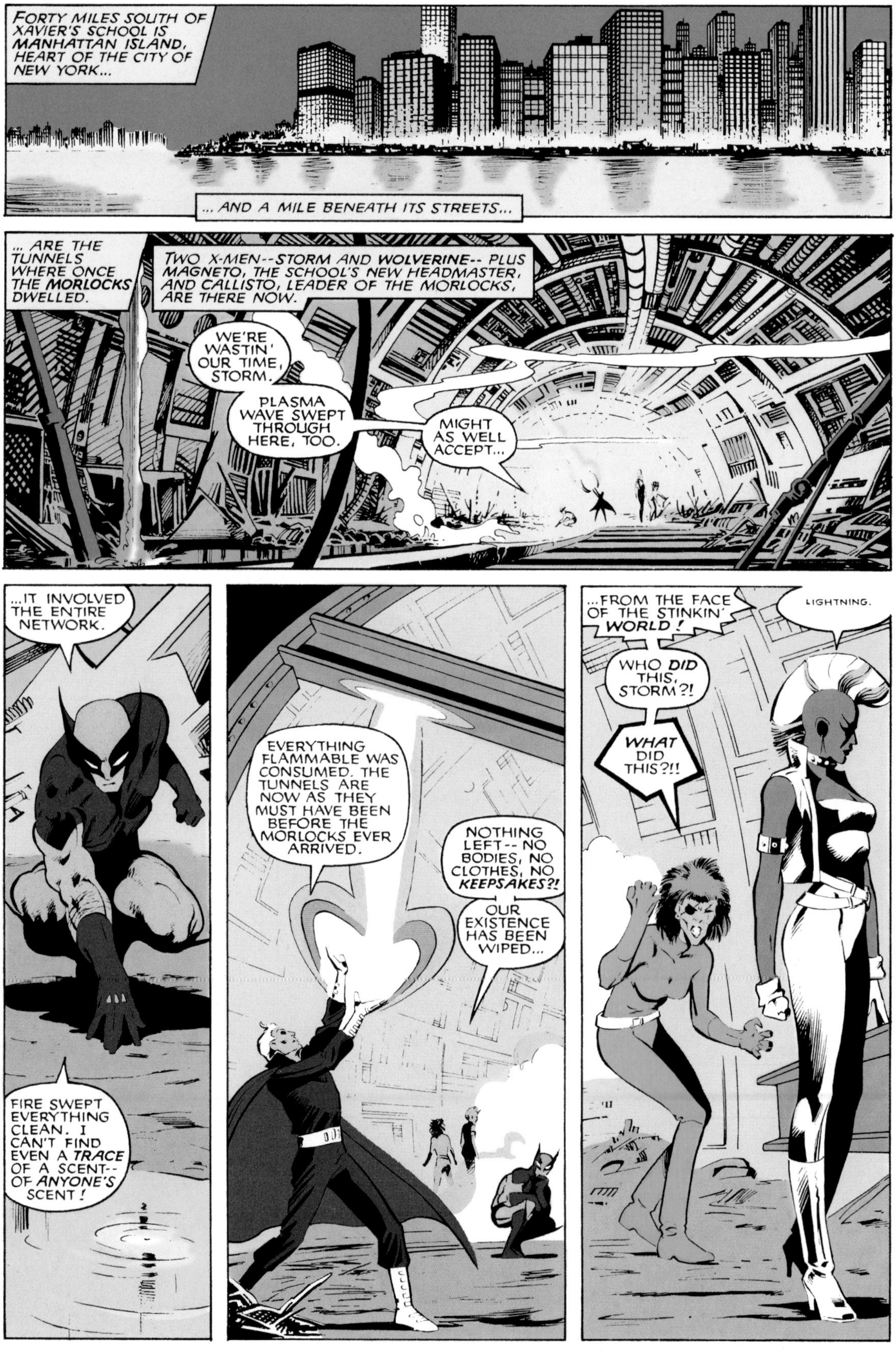
FORTY MILES SOUTH OF XAVIER'S SCHOOL IS MANHATTAN ISLAND, HEART OF THE CITY OF NEW YORK...
... AND A MILE BENEATH ITS STREETS...
... ARE THE TUNNELS WHERE ONCE THE MORLOCKS DWELLED.
TWO X-MEN--STORM AND WOLVERINE-- PLUS MAGNETO, THE SCHOOL'S NEW HEADMASTER, AND CALLISTO, LEADER OF THE MORLOCKS, ARE THERE NOW.
WE'RE WASTIN' OUR TIME, STORM.
PLASMA WAVE SWEPT THROUGH HERE, TOO.
MIGHT AS WELL ACCEPT...
...IT INVOLVED THE ENTIRE NETWORK.
FIRE SWEPT EVERYTHING CLEAN. I CAN'T FIND EVEN A TRACE OF A SCENT-- OF ANYONE'S SCENT!
EVERYTHING FLAMMABLE WAS CONSUMED. THE TUNNELS ARE NOW AS THEY MUST HAVE BEEN BEFORE THE MORLOCKS EVER ARRIVED.
NOTHING LEFT-- NO BODIES, NO CLOTHES, NO KEEPSAKES?!
OUR EXISTENCE HAS BEEN WIPED...
...FROM THE FACE OF THE STINKIN' WORLD!
WHO DID THIS, STORM?!
WHAT DID THIS?!!
LIGHTNING.

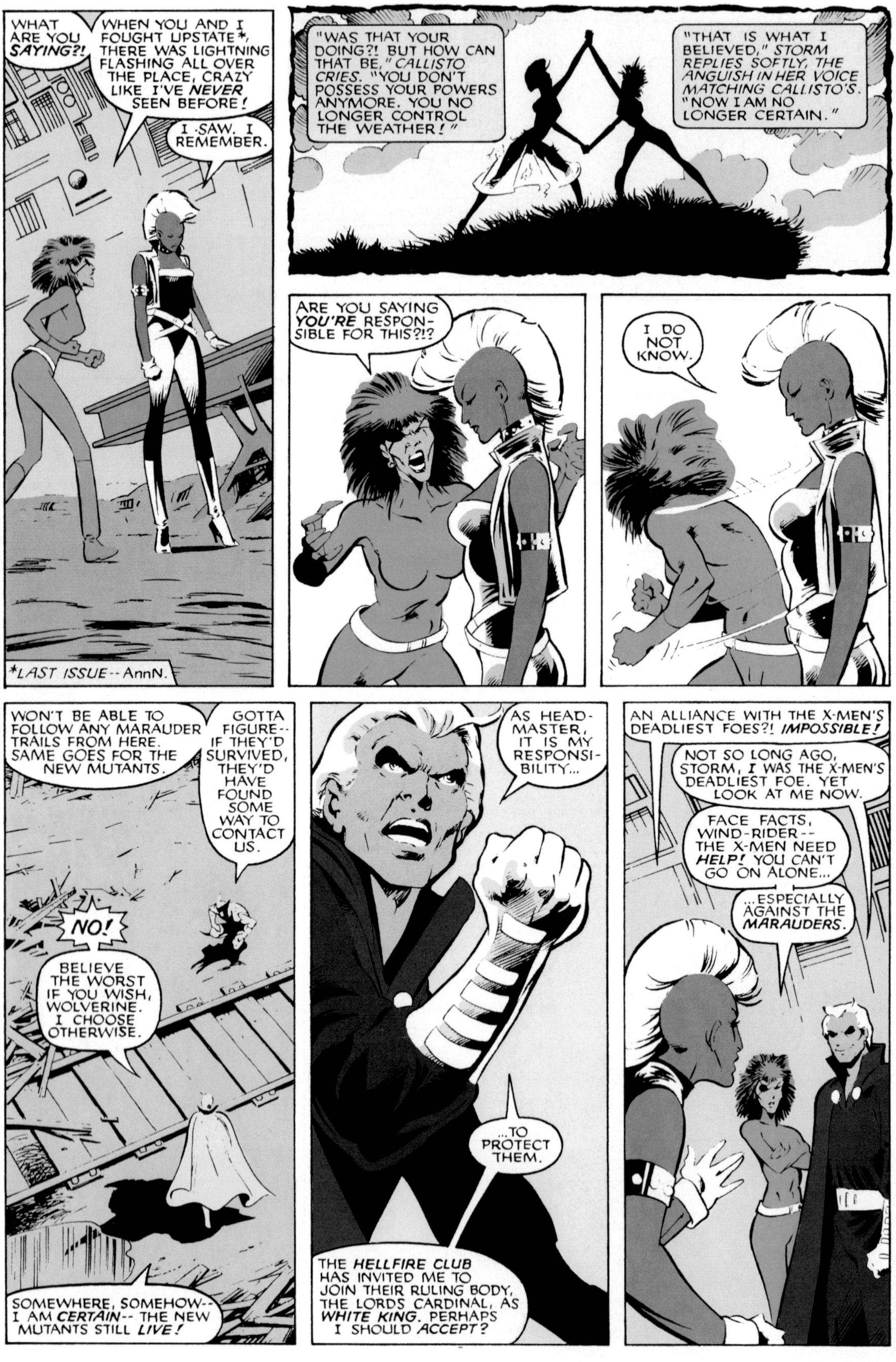
WHAT ARE YOU SAYING?!
WHEN YOU AND I FOUGHT UPSTATE*, THERE WAS LIGHTNING FLASHING ALL OVER THE PLACE, CRAZY LIKE I'VE NEVER SEEN BEFORE!
I SAW. I REMEMBER.
*LAST ISSUE--AnnN.
"WAS THAT YOUR DOING?! BUT HOW CAN THAT BE," CALLISTO CRIES. "YOU DON'T POSSESS YOUR POWERS ANYMORE. YOU NO LONGER CONTROL THE WEATHER!"
"THAT IS WHAT I BELIEVED," STORM REPLIES SOFTLY, THE ANGUISH IN HER VOICE MATCHING CALLISTO'S. "NOW I AM NO LONGER CERTAIN."
ARE YOU SAYING YOU'RE RESPONSIBLE FOR THIS?!?
I DO NOT KNOW.
WON'T BE ABLE TO FOLLOW ANY MARAUDER TRAILS FROM HERE. SAME GOES FOR THE NEW MUTANTS.
GOTTA FIGURE-- IF THEY'D SURVIVED, THEY'D HAVE FOUND SOME WAY TO CONTACT US.
NO!
BELIEVE THE WORST IF YOU WISH, WOLVERINE. I CHOOSE OTHERWISE.
SOMEWHERE, SOMEHOW-- I AM CERTAIN-- THE NEW MUTANTS STILL LIVE!
AS HEADMASTER, IT IS MY RESPONSIBILITY...
...TO PROTECT THEM.
THE HELLFIRE CLUB HAS INVITED ME TO JOIN THEIR RULING BODY, THE LORDS CARDINAL, AS WHITE KING. PERHAPS I SHOULD ACCEPT?
AN ALLIANCE WITH THE X-MEN'S DEADLIEST FOES?! IMPOSSIBLE!
NOT SO LONG AGO, STORM, I WAS THE X-MEN'S DEADLIEST FOE. YET LOOK AT ME NOW.
FACE FACTS, WIND-RIDER-- THE X-MEN NEED HELP! YOU CAN'T GO ON ALONE...
...ESPECIALLY AGAINST THE MARAUDERS.

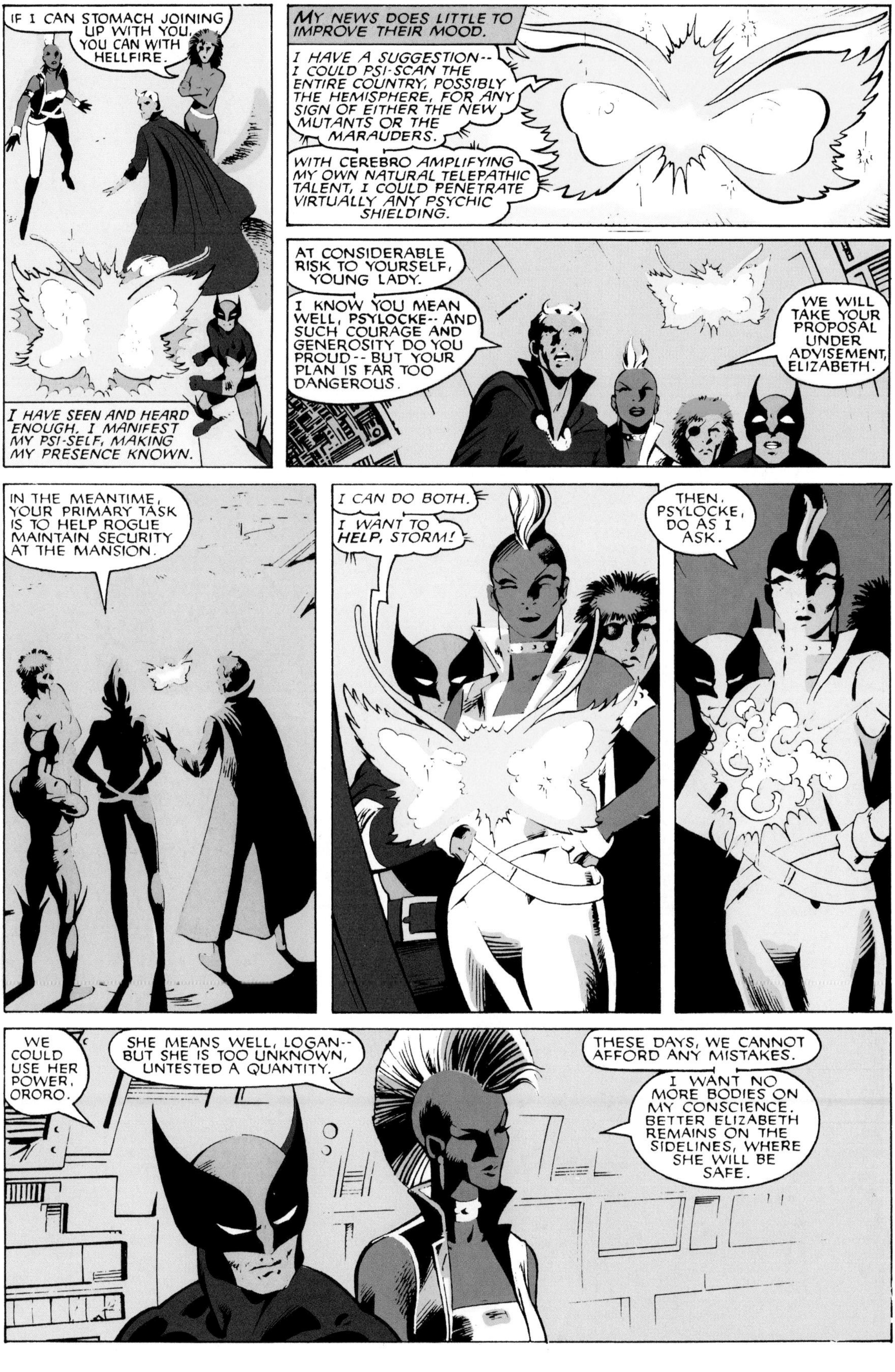
IF I CAN STOMACH JOINING UP WITH YOU, YOU CAN WITH HELLFIRE.
I HAVE SEEN AND HEARD ENOUGH. I MANIFEST MY PSI-SELF, MAKING MY PRESENCE KNOWN.
MY NEWS DOES LITTLE TO IMPROVE THEIR MOOD.
I HAVE A SUGGESTION-- I COULD PSI-SCAN THE ENTIRE COUNTRY, POSSIBLY THE HEMISPHERE, FOR ANY SIGN OF EITHER THE NEW MUTANTS OR THE MARAUDERS.
WITH CEREBRO AMPLIFYING MY OWN NATURAL TELEPATHIC TALENT, I COULD PENETRATE VIRTUALLY ANY PSYCHIC SHIELDING.
AT CONSIDERABLE RISK TO YOURSELF, YOUNG LADY.
I KNOW YOU MEAN WELL, PSYLOCKE-- AND SUCH COURAGE AND GENEROSITY DO YOU PROUD-- BUT YOUR PLAN IS FAR TOO DANGEROUS.
WE WILL TAKE YOUR PROPOSAL UNDER ADVISEMENT, ELIZABETH.
IN THE MEANTIME, YOUR PRIMARY TASK IS TO HELP ROGUE MAINTAIN SECURITY AT THE MANSION.
I CAN DO BOTH.
I WANT TO HELP, STORM!
THEN, PSYLOCKE, DO AS I ASK.
WE COULD USE HER POWER, ORORO.
SHE MEANS WELL, LOGAN-- BUT SHE IS TOO UNKNOWN, UNTESTED A QUANTITY.
THESE DAYS, WE CANNOT AFFORD ANY MISTAKES.
I WANT NO MORE BODIES ON MY CONSCIENCE. BETTER ELIZABETH REMAINS ON THE SIDELINES, WHERE SHE WILL BE SAFE.

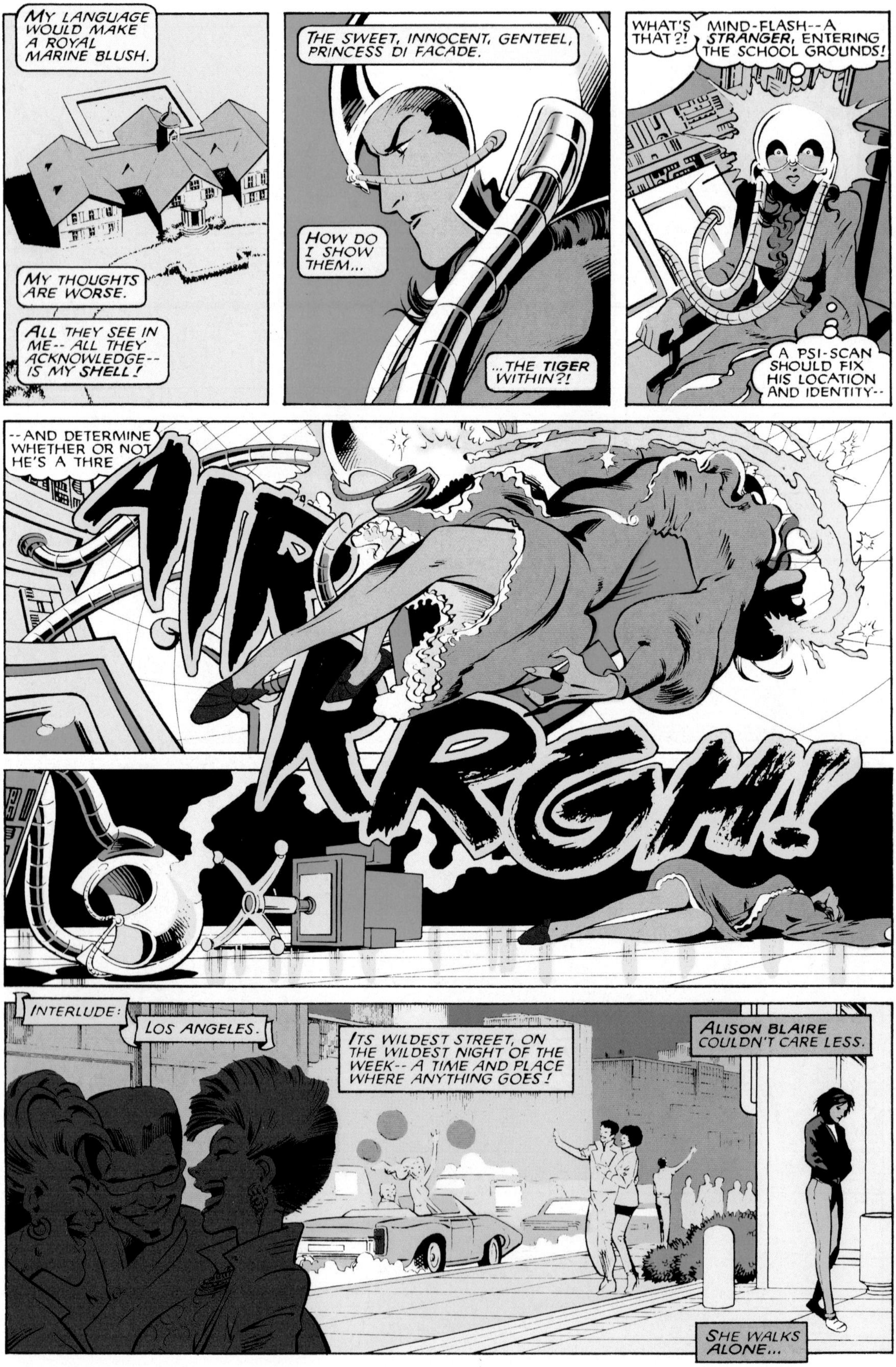
MY LANGUAGE WOULD MAKE A ROYAL MARINE BLUSH.
MY THOUGHTS ARE WORSE.
ALL THEY SEE IN ME-- ALL THEY ACKNOWLEDGE-- IS MY SHELL!
THE SWEET, INNOCENT, GENTEEL, PRINCESS DI FACADE.
HOW DO I SHOW THEM...
...THE TIGER WITHIN?!
WHAT'S THAT?!
MIND-FLASH--A STRANGER, ENTERING THE SCHOOL GROUNDS!
A PSI-SCAN SHOULD FIX HIS LOCATION AND IDENTITY--
--AND DETERMINE WHETHER OR NOT HE'S A THRE
AIIRRRGH!
INTERLUDE:
LOS ANGELES.
ITS WILDEST STREET, ON THE WILDEST NIGHT OF THE WEEK-- A TIME AND PLACE WHERE ANYTHING GOES!
ALISON BLAIRE COULDN'T CARE LESS.
SHE WALKS ALONE...

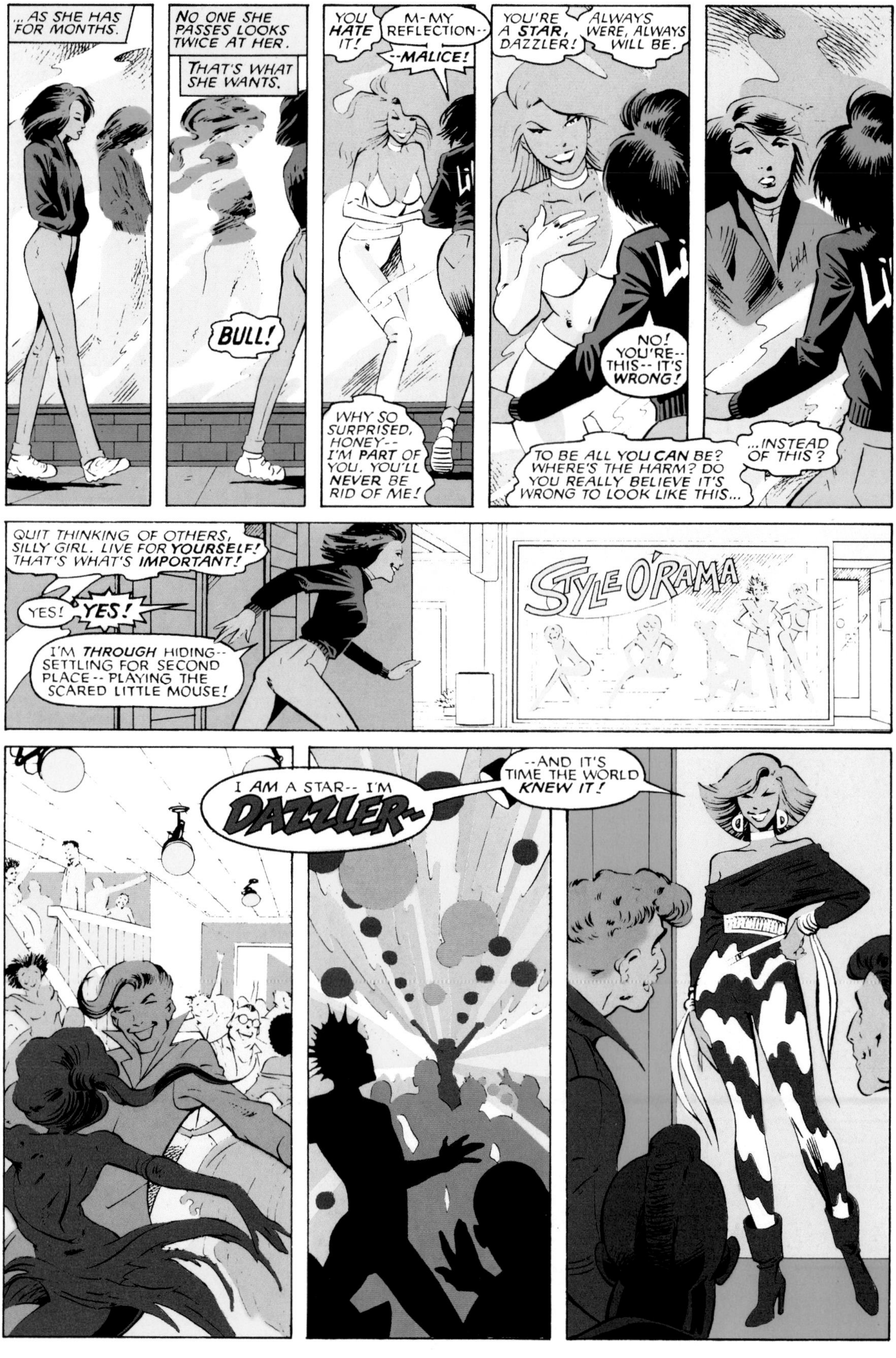
...AS SHE HAS FOR MONTHS.
NO ONE SHE PASSES LOOKS TWICE AT HER.
THAT'S WHAT SHE WANTS.
BULL!
YOU HATE IT!
M-MY REFLECTION--
--MALICE!
WHY SO SURPRISED, HONEY-- I'M PART OF YOU. YOU'LL NEVER BE RID OF ME!
YOU'RE A STAR, DAZZLER!
ALWAYS WERE, ALWAYS WILL BE.
NO! YOU'RE-- THIS-- IT'S WRONG!
TO BE ALL YOU CAN BE? WHERE'S THE HARM? DO YOU REALLY BELIEVE IT'S WRONG TO LOOK LIKE THIS...
...INSTEAD OF THIS?
QUIT THINKING OF OTHERS, SILLY GIRL. LIVE FOR YOURSELF! THAT'S WHAT'S IMPORTANT!
YES!
YES!
I'M THROUGH HIDING-- SETTLING FOR SECOND PLACE-- PLAYING THE SCARED LITTLE MOUSE!
STYLE O'RAMA
I AM A STAR-- I'M DAZZLER-
--AND IT'S TIME THE WORLD KNEW IT!

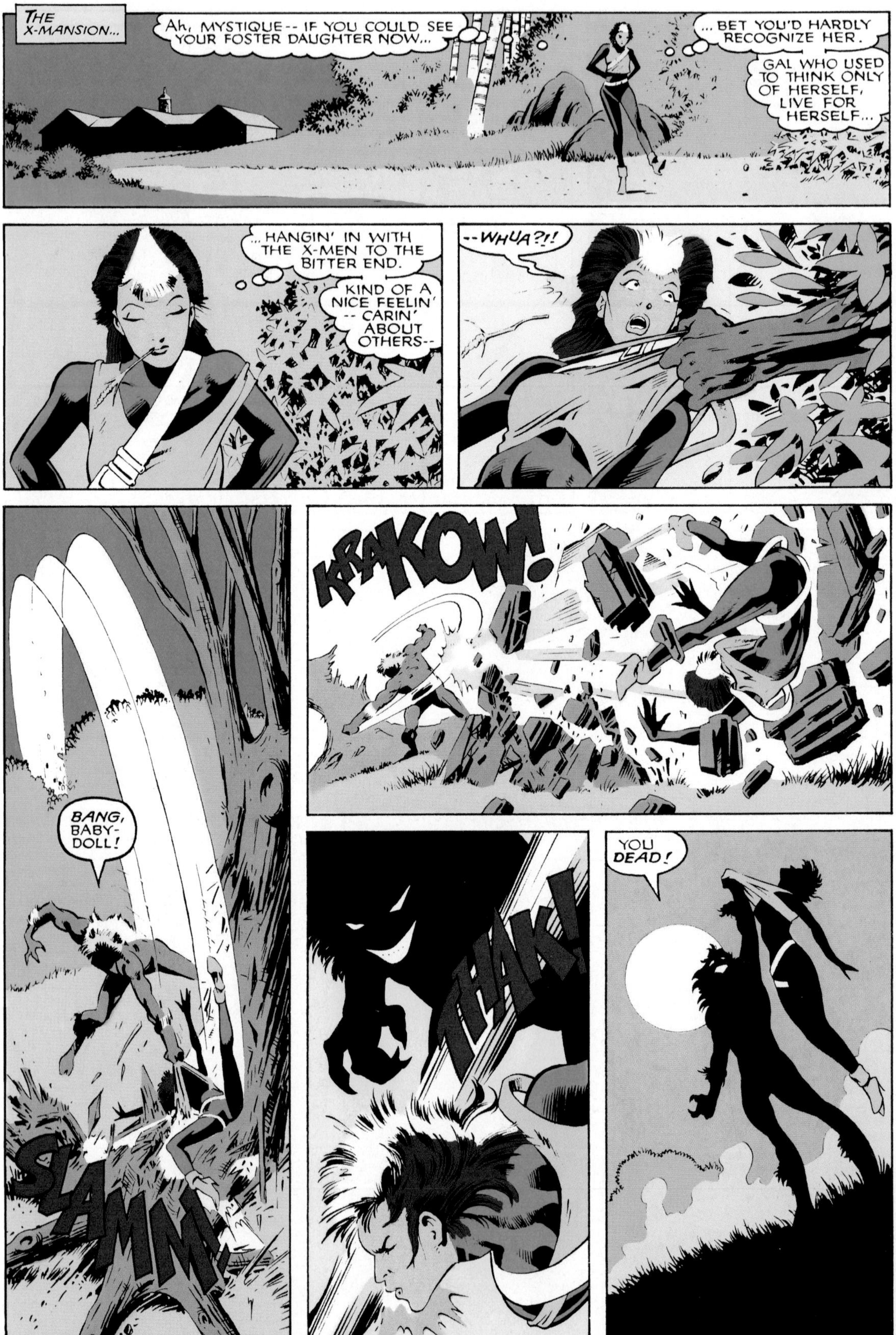
THE X-MANSION...
Ah, MYSTIQUE-- IF YOU COULD SEE YOUR FOSTER DAUGHTER NOW...
...BET YOU'D HARDLY RECOGNIZE HER.
GAL WHO USED TO THINK ONLY OF HERSELF, LIVE FOR HERSELF...
...HANGIN' IN WITH THE X-MEN TO THE BITTER END.
KIND OF A NICE FEELIN' -- CARIN' ABOUT OTHERS--
--WHUA?!!
BANG, BABY-DOLL!
SLAMM!
KRAKOW!
THAK!
YOU DEAD!

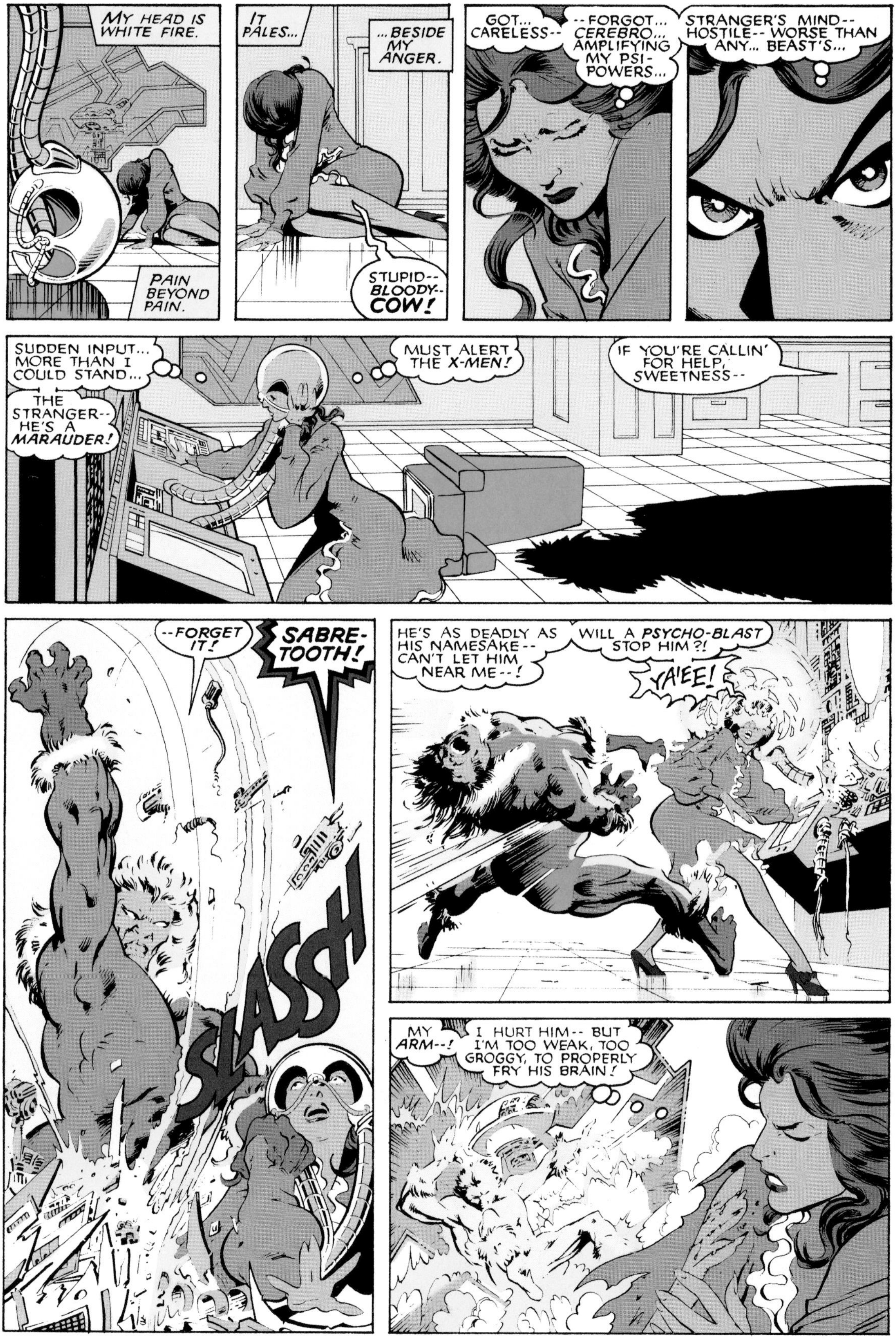
MY HEAD IS WHITE FIRE.
PAIN BEYOND PAIN.
IT PALES...
...BESIDE MY ANGER.
STUPID-- BLOODY-- COW!
GOT... CARELESS--
--FORGOT... CEREBRO... AMPLIFYING MY PSI-POWERS...
STRANGER'S MIND-- HOSTILE-- WORSE THAN ANY... BEAST'S...
SUDDEN INPUT... MORE THAN I COULD STAND...
THE STRANGER-- HE'S A MARAUDER!
MUST ALERT THE X-MEN!
IF YOU'RE CALLIN' FOR HELP, SWEETNESS--
--FORGET IT!
SABRE-TOOTH!
SLASSH
HE'S AS DEADLY AS HIS NAMESAKE-- CAN'T LET HIM NEAR ME--!
WILL A PSYCHO-BLAST STOP HIM?!
YA'EE!
MY ARM--!
I HURT HIM-- BUT I'M TOO WEAK, TOO GROGGY, TO PROPERLY FRY HIS BRAIN!

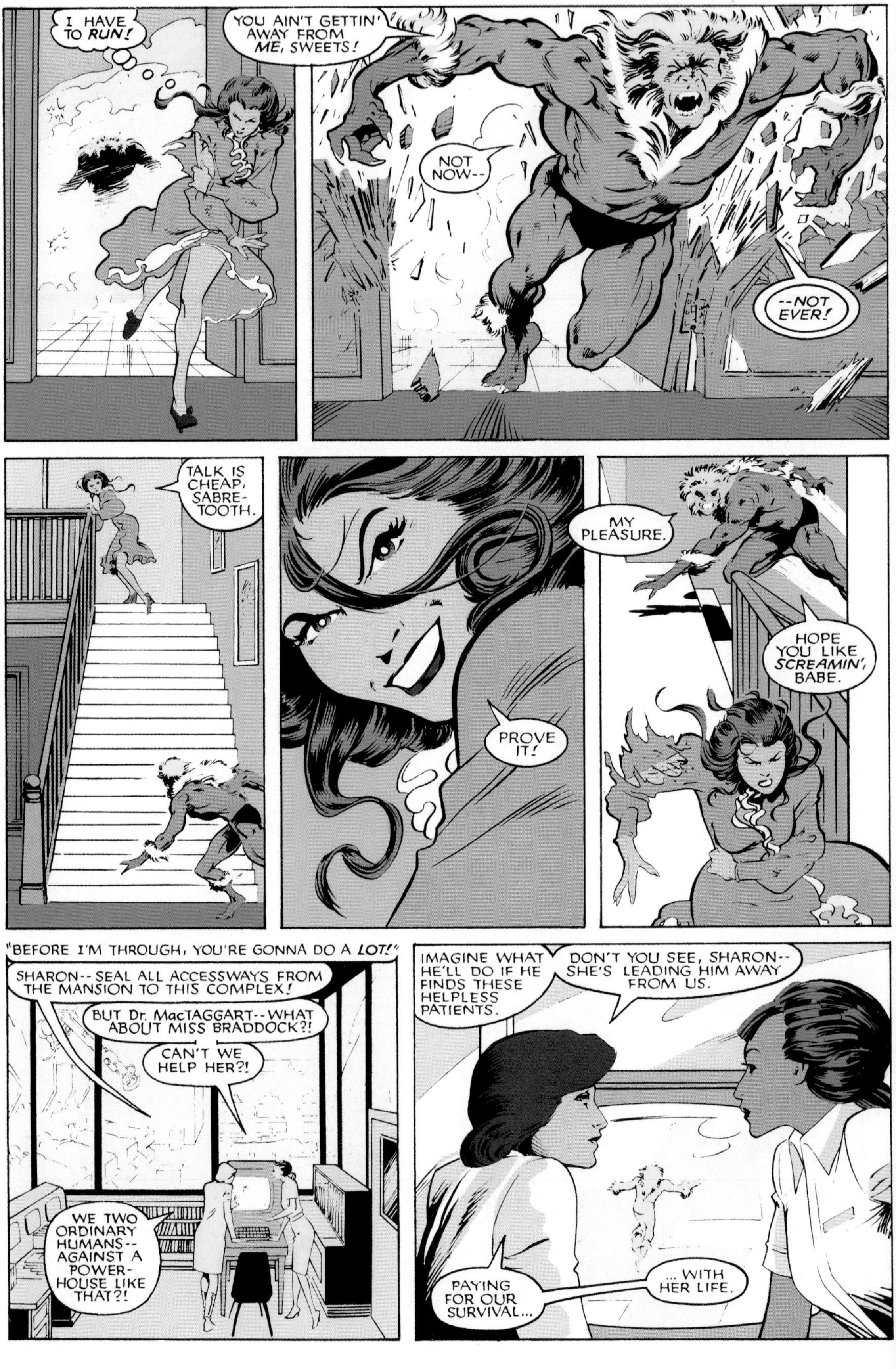
I HAVE TO RUN!
YOU AIN'T GETTIN' AWAY FROM ME, SWEETS!
NOT NOW--
--NOT EVER!
TALK IS CHEAP, SABRE-TOOTH.
PROVE IT!
MY PLEASURE.
HOPE YOU LIKE SCREAMIN', BABE.
"BEFORE I'M THROUGH, YOU'RE GONNA DO A LOT!"
SHARON--SEAL ALL ACCESSWAYS FROM THE MANSION TO THIS COMPLEX!
BUT Dr. MacTAGGART--WHAT ABOUT MISS BRADDOCK?!
CAN'T WE HELP HER?!
WE TWO ORDINARY HUMANS--AGAINST A POWER-HOUSE LIKE THAT?!
IMAGINE WHAT HE'LL DO IF HE FINDS THESE HELPLESS PATIENTS.
DON'T YOU SEE, SHARON--SHE'S LEADING HIM AWAY FROM US.
PAYING FOR OUR SURVIVAL...
...WITH HER LIFE.

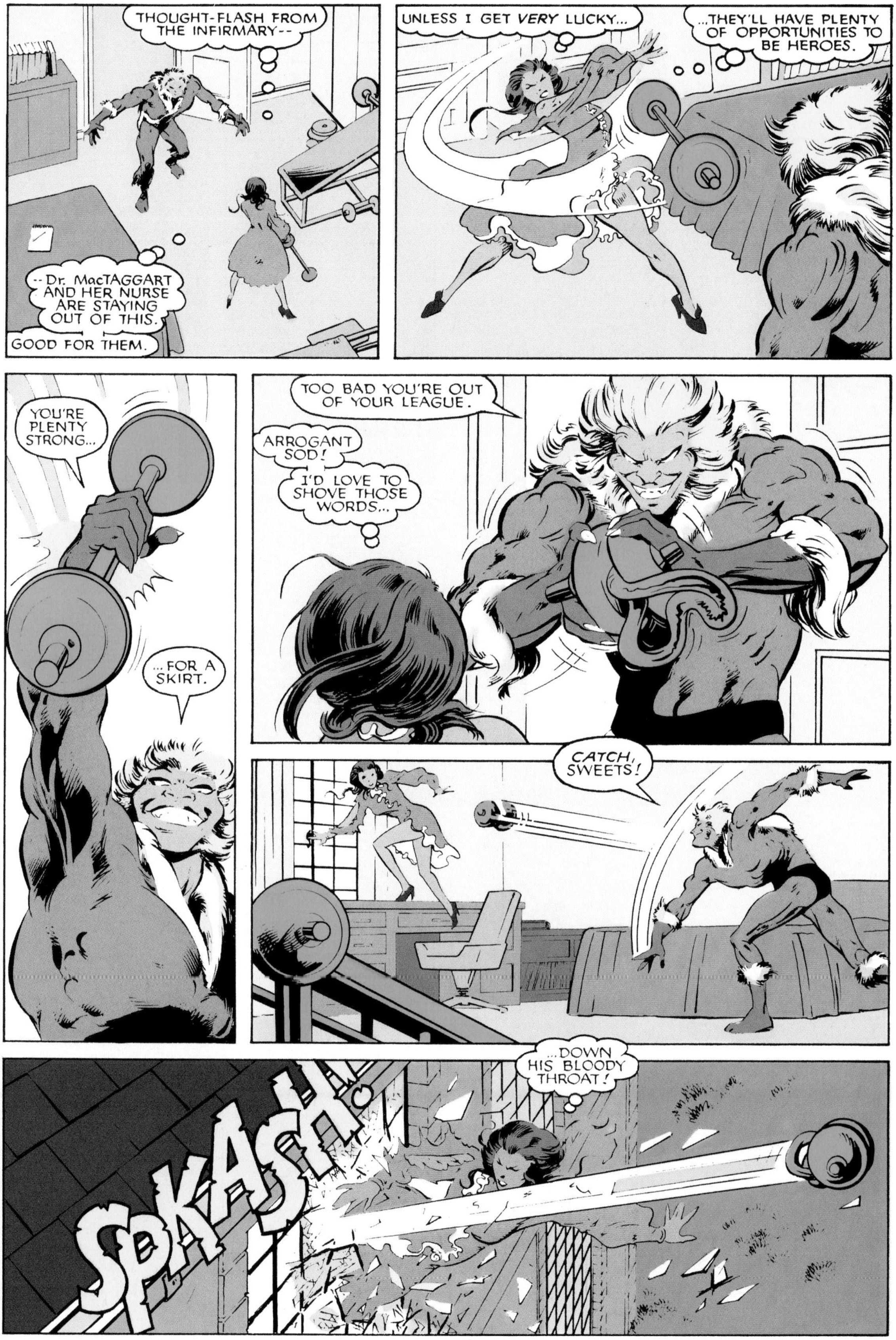
THOUGHT-FLASH FROM THE INFIRMARY--
--Dr. MacTAGGART AND HER NURSE ARE STAYING OUT OF THIS.
GOOD FOR THEM.
UNLESS I GET VERY LUCKY...
...THEY'LL HAVE PLENTY OF OPPORTUNITIES TO BE HEROES.
YOU'RE PLENTY STRONG...
...FOR A SKIRT.
TOO BAD YOU'RE OUT OF YOUR LEAGUE.
ARROGANT SOD!
I'D LOVE TO SHOVE THOSE WORDS...
CATCH, SWEETS!
...DOWN HIS BLOODY THROAT!
SPKASH!

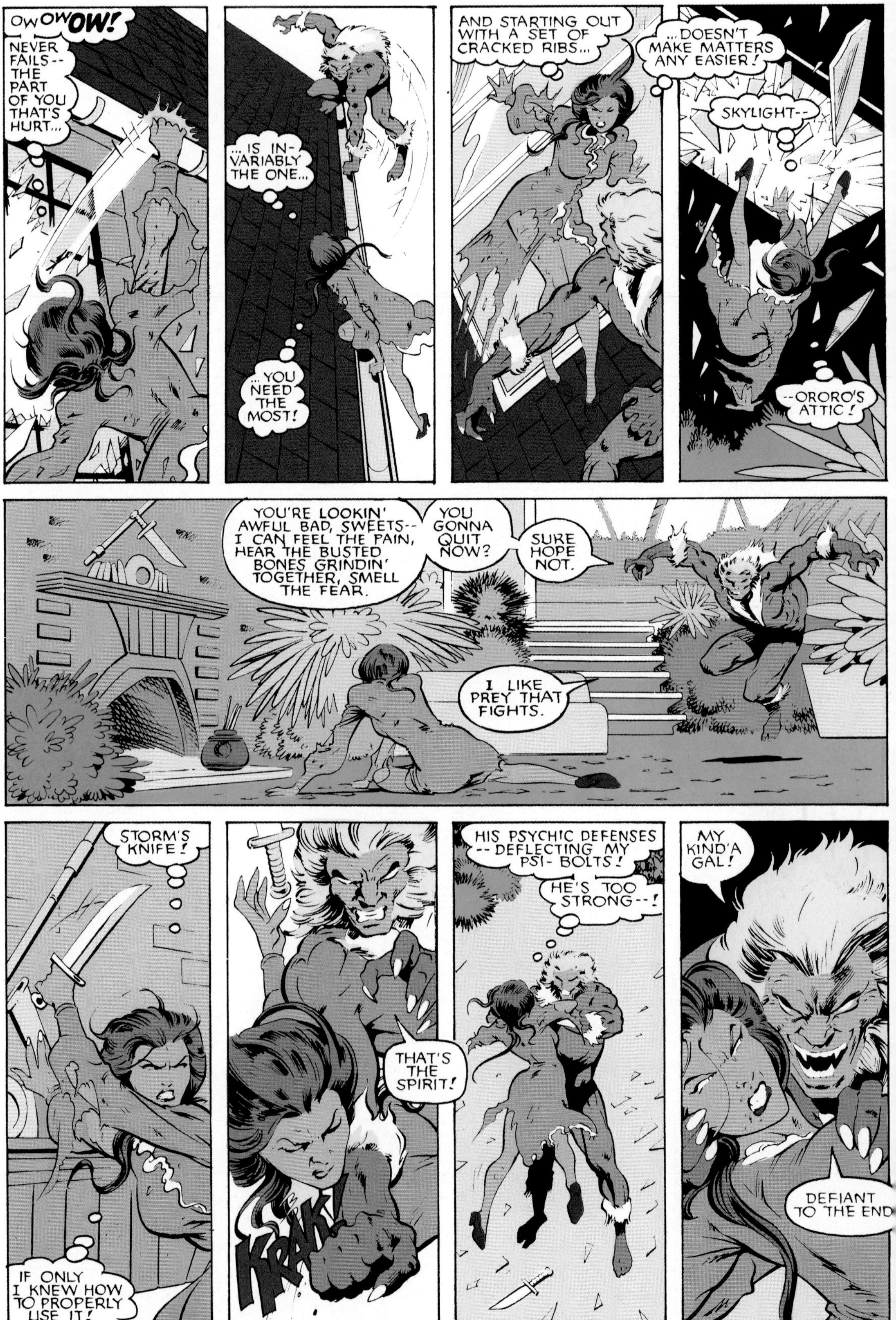

OW OW OW!
NEVER FAILS-- THE PART OF YOU THAT'S HURT...
...IS INVARIABLY THE ONE...
...YOU NEED THE MOST!
AND STARTING OUT WITH A SET OF CRACKED RIBS...
...DOESN'T MAKE MATTERS ANY EASIER!
SKYLIGHT--
--ORORO'S ATTIC!
YOU'RE LOOKIN' AWFUL BAD, SWEETS-- I CAN FEEL THE PAIN, HEAR THE BUSTED BONES GRINDIN' TOGETHER, SMELL THE FEAR.
YOU GONNA QUIT NOW?
SURE HOPE NOT.
I LIKE PREY THAT FIGHTS.
STORM'S KNIFE!
IF ONLY I KNEW HOW TO PROPERLY USE IT!
THAT'S THE SPIRIT!
KRAK
HIS PSYCHIC DEFENSES --DEFLECTING MY PSI-BOLTS!
HE'S TOO STRONG--!
MY KIND'A GAL!
DEFIANT TO THE END

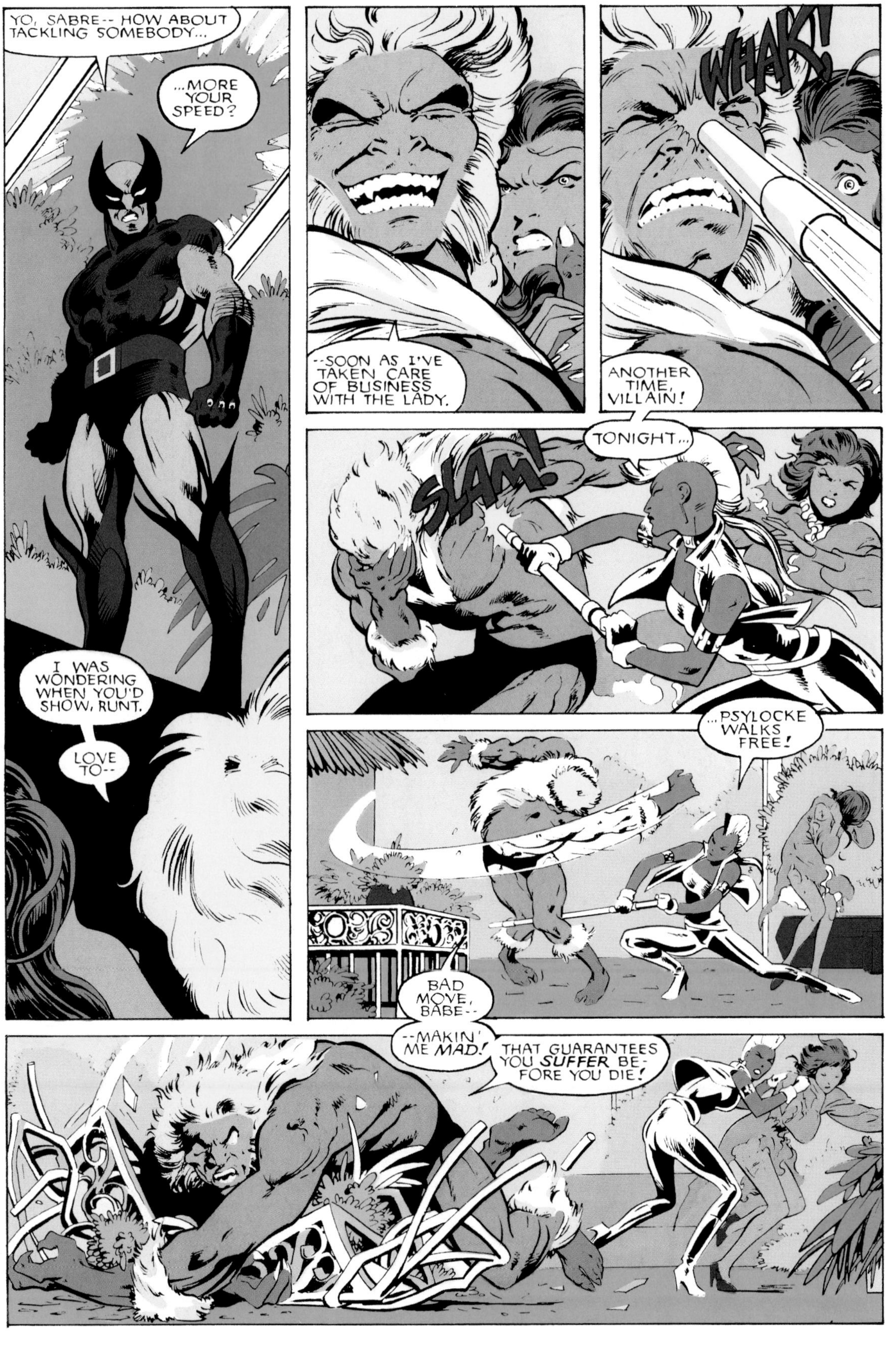
YO, SABRE-- HOW ABOUT TACKLING SOMEBODY...
...MORE YOUR SPEED?
--SOON AS I'VE TAKEN CARE OF BUSINESS WITH THE LADY.
WHAK!
ANOTHER TIME, VILLAIN!
TONIGHT...
SLAM!
...PSYLOCKE WALKS FREE!
I WAS WONDERING WHEN YOU'D SHOW, RUNT.
LOVE TO--
BAD MOVE, BABE--
--MAKIN' ME MAD!
THAT GUARANTEES YOU SUFFER BEFORE YOU DIE!

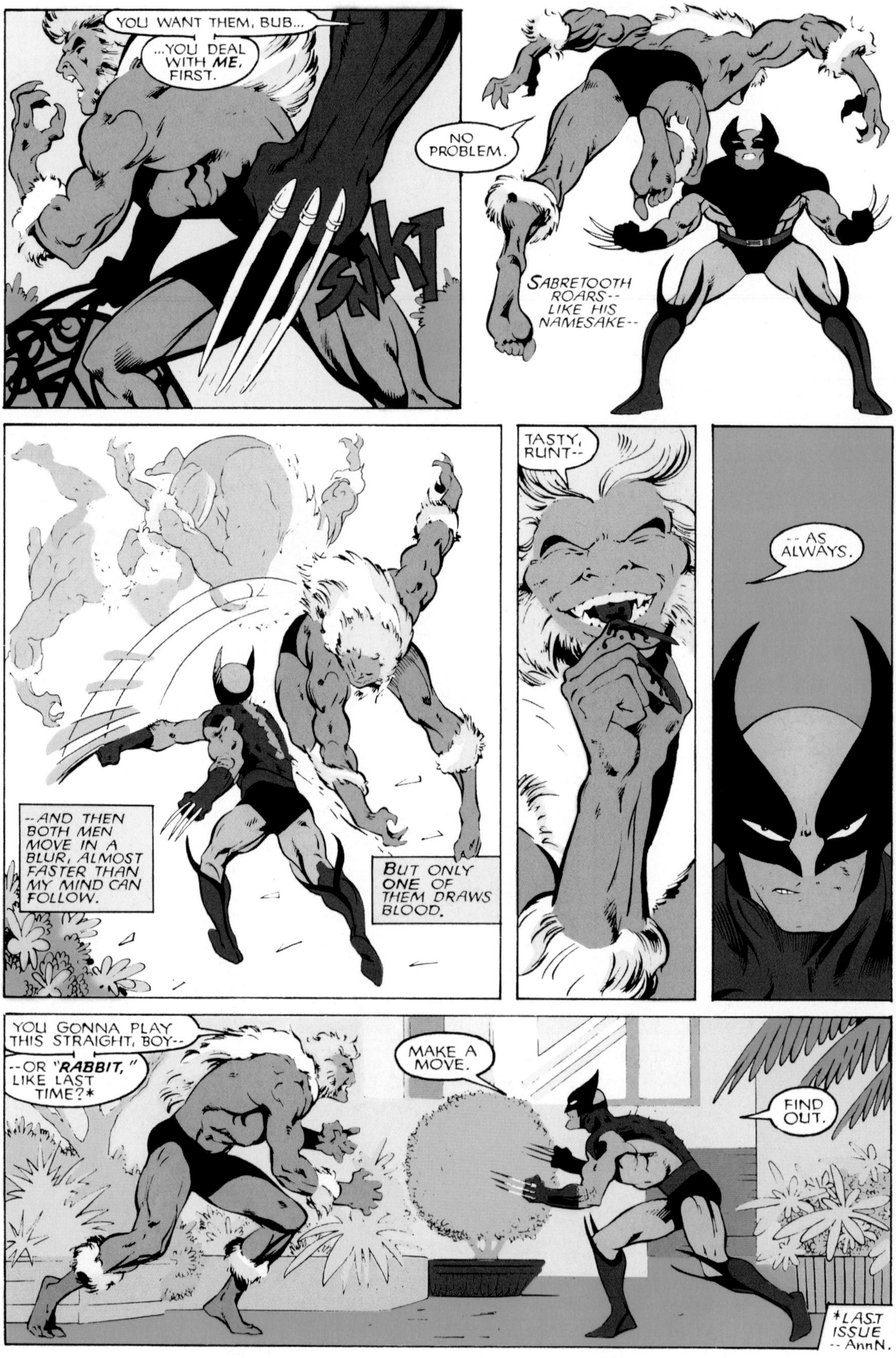
YOU WANT THEM, BUB...
...YOU DEAL WITH ME, FIRST.
SNIKT
NO PROBLEM.
SABRETOOTH ROARS-- LIKE HIS NAMESAKE--
--AND THEN BOTH MEN MOVE IN A BLUR, ALMOST FASTER THAN MY MIND CAN FOLLOW.
BUT ONLY ONE OF THEM DRAWS BLOOD.
TASTY, RUNT--
--AS ALWAYS.
YOU GONNA PLAY THIS STRAIGHT, BOY--
--OR "RABBIT," LIKE LAST TIME?*
MAKE A MOVE.
FIND OUT.
*LAST ISSUE --AnnN.

THIS TIME, NEITHER TRIES ANYTHING FANCY.

THEIR HATRED IS A PALPABLE PRESENCE IN THE ROOM.

THEY ARE THE PERSONIFICATION OF VIOLENCE--

--THE DARKEST SIDE OF MAN'S PRIMEVAL NATURE BROUGHT TO LIFE.

QUARTER WILL NOT BE ASKED BETWEEN THEM...

...NOR GIVEN.

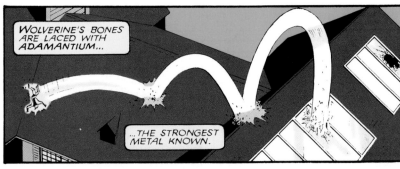

WOLVERINE'S BONES ARE LACED WITH ADAMANTIUM...

...THE STRONGEST METAL KNOWN.

BUT SABRETOOTH IS LARGER, FASTER, STRONGER.

HIS CLAWS ARE NATURAL--

--WHERE WOLVERINE'S ARE MAN-MADE--

--BUT THAT MAKES THEM...

...NO LESS DEADLY.

111

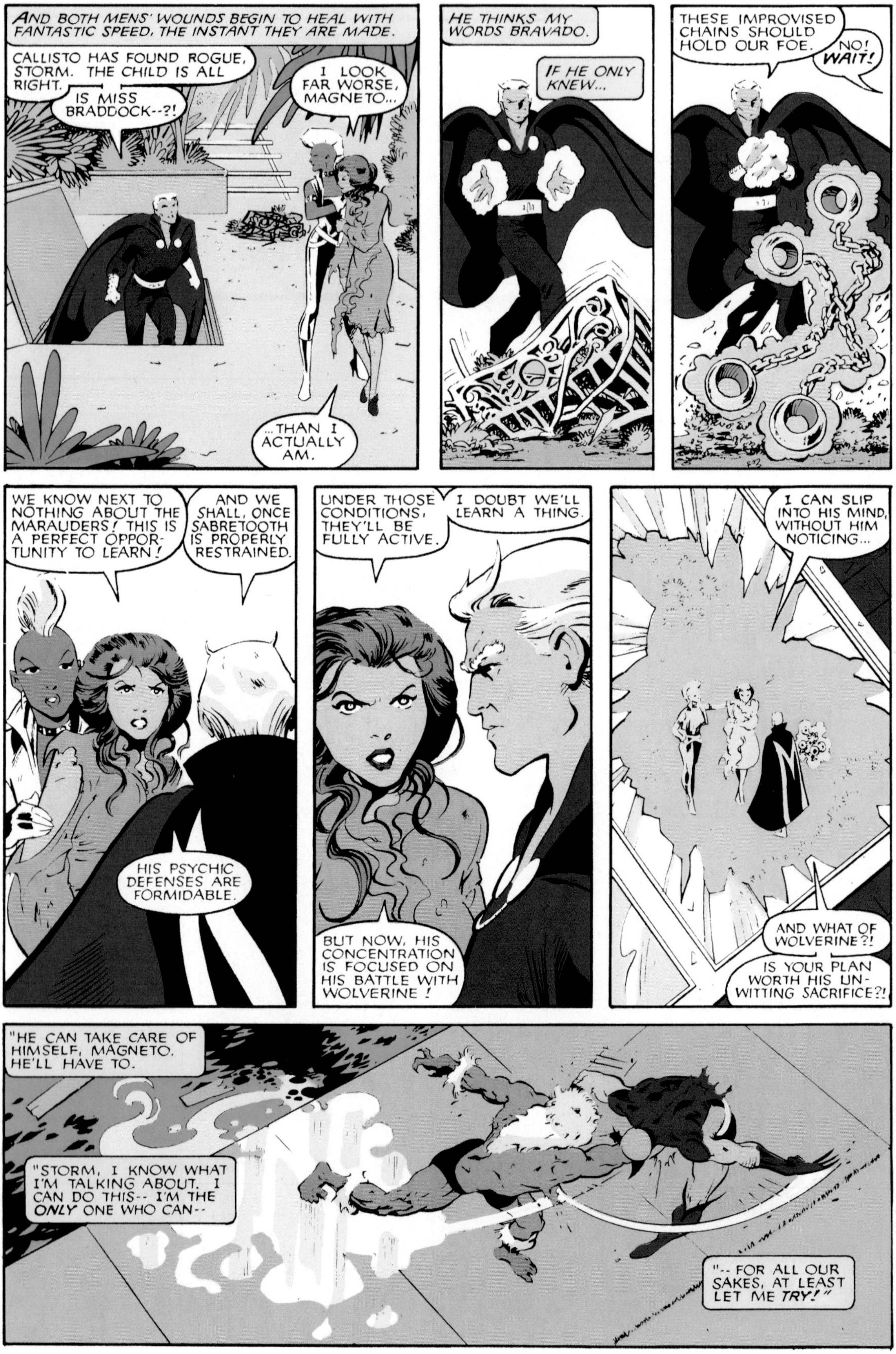
AND BOTH MENS' WOUNDS BEGIN TO HEAL WITH FANTASTIC SPEED, THE INSTANT THEY ARE MADE.
CALLISTO HAS FOUND ROGUE, STORM. THE CHILD IS ALL RIGHT.
IS MISS BRADDOCK--?!
I LOOK FAR WORSE, MAGNETO...
...THAN I ACTUALLY AM.
HE THINKS MY WORDS BRAVADO.
IF HE ONLY KNEW...
THESE IMPROVISED CHAINS SHOULD HOLD OUR FOE.
NO! WAIT!
WE KNOW NEXT TO NOTHING ABOUT THE MARAUDERS! THIS IS A PERFECT OPPORTUNITY TO LEARN!
AND WE SHALL, ONCE SABRETOOTH IS PROPERLY RESTRAINED.
HIS PSYCHIC DEFENSES ARE FORMIDABLE.
UNDER THOSE CONDITIONS, THEY'LL BE FULLY ACTIVE.
I DOUBT WE'LL LEARN A THING.
BUT NOW, HIS CONCENTRATION IS FOCUSED ON HIS BATTLE WITH WOLVERINE!
I CAN SLIP INTO HIS MIND, WITHOUT HIM NOTICING...
AND WHAT OF WOLVERINE?!
IS YOUR PLAN WORTH HIS UNWITTING SACRIFICE?!
"HE CAN TAKE CARE OF HIMSELF, MAGNETO. HE'LL HAVE TO.
"STORM, I KNOW WHAT I'M TALKING ABOUT. I CAN DO THIS-- I'M THE ONLY ONE WHO CAN--
"-- FOR ALL OUR SAKES, AT LEAST LET ME TRY!"

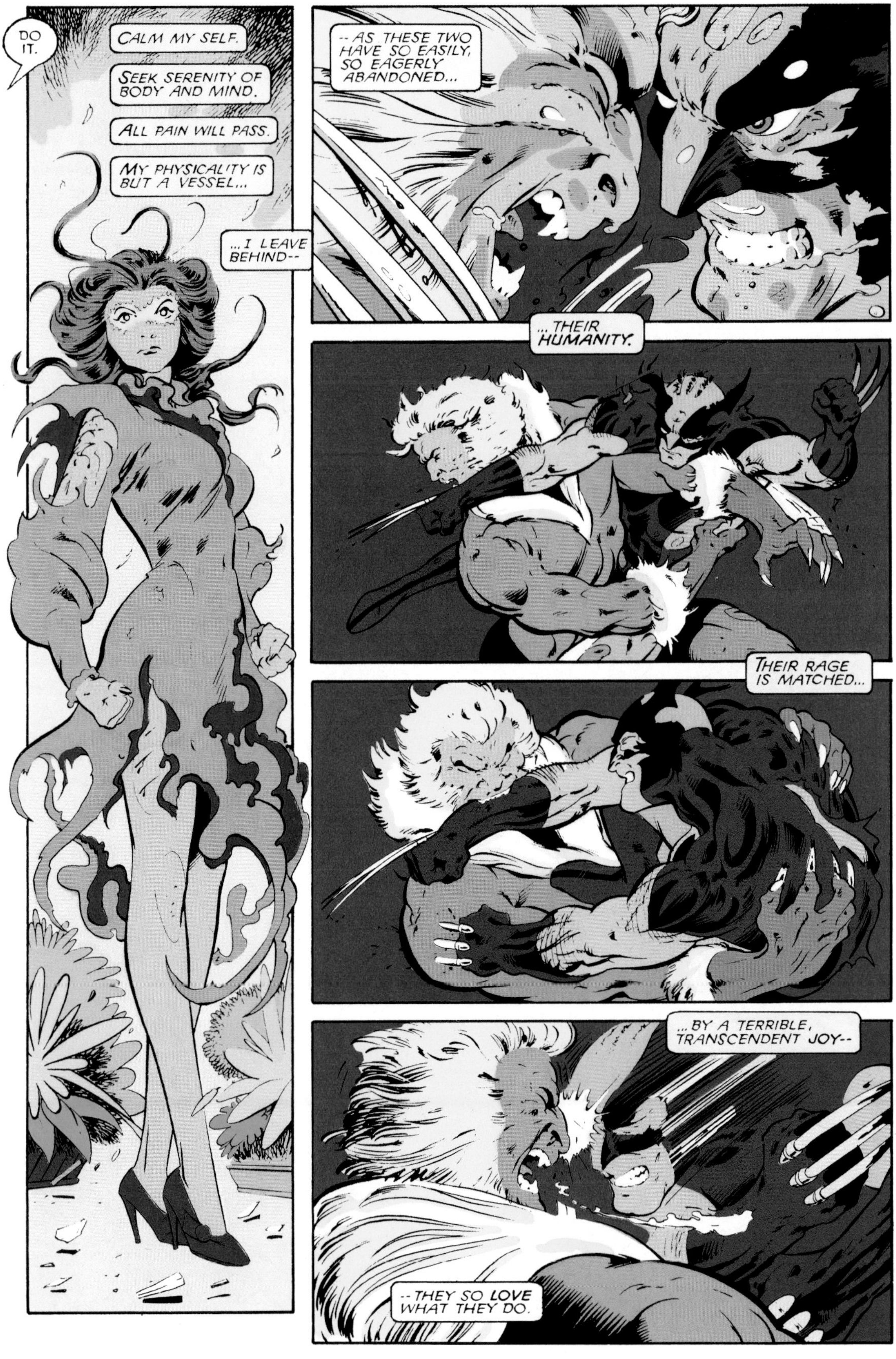
DO IT.
CALM MY SELF.
SEEK SERENITY OF BODY AND MIND.
ALL PAIN WILL PASS.
MY PHYSICALITY IS BUT A VESSEL...
...I LEAVE BEHIND--
--AS THESE TWO HAVE SO EASILY, SO EAGERLY ABANDONED...
...THEIR HUMANITY.
THEIR RAGE IS MATCHED...
...BY A TERRIBLE, TRANSCENDENT JOY--
--THEY SO LOVE WHAT THEY DO.

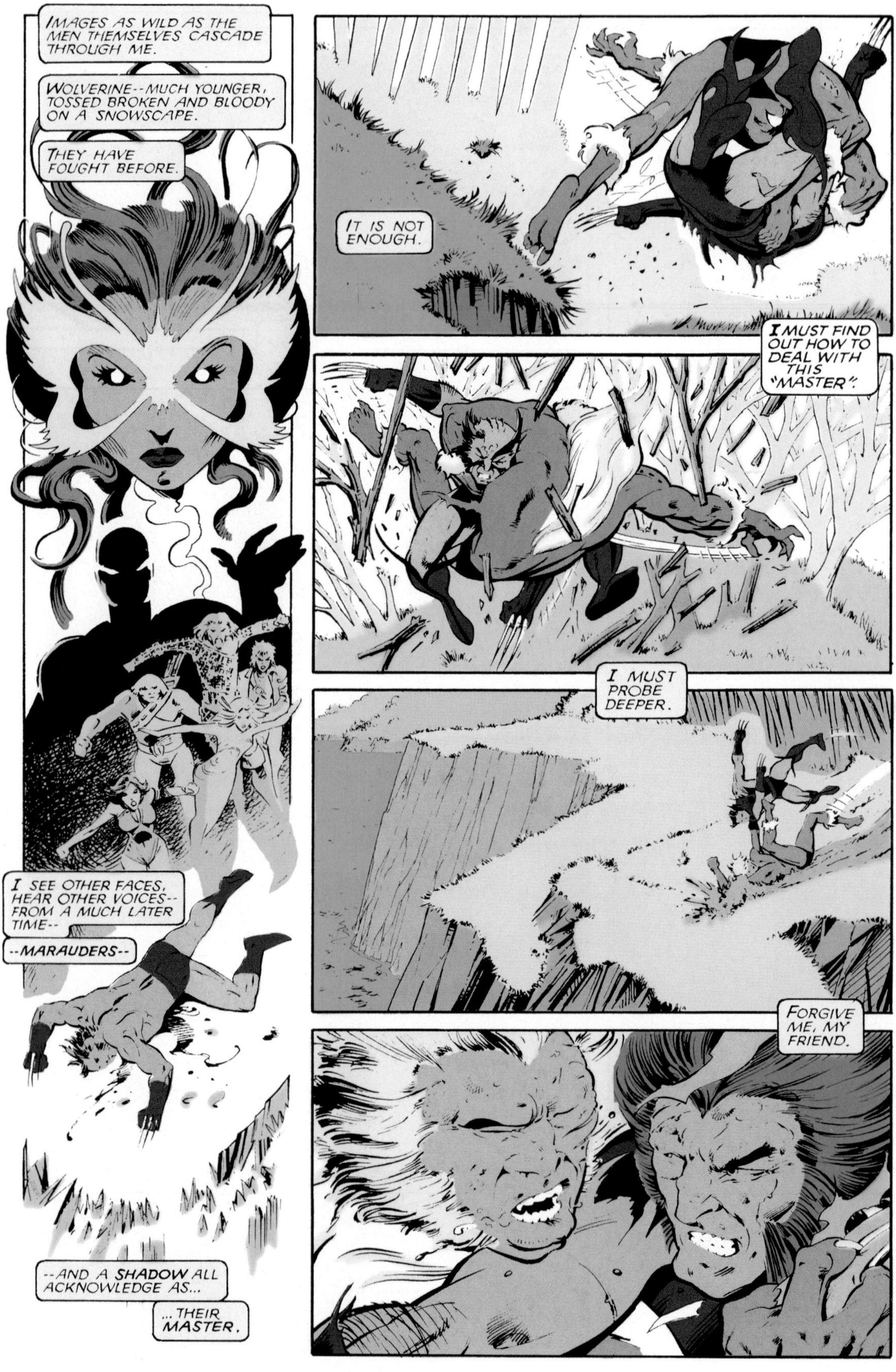
IMAGES AS WILD AS THE MEN THEMSELVES CASCADE THROUGH ME.
WOLVERINE--MUCH YOUNGER, TOSSED BROKEN AND BLOODY ON A SNOWSCAPE.
THEY HAVE FOUGHT BEFORE.
I SEE OTHER FACES, HEAR OTHER VOICES--FROM A MUCH LATER TIME--
--MARAUDERS--
--AND A SHADOW ALL ACKNOWLEDGE AS...
...THEIR MASTER.
IT IS NOT ENOUGH.
I MUST FIND OUT HOW TO DEAL WITH THIS "MASTER".
I MUST PROBE DEEPER.
FORGIVE ME, MY FRIEND.

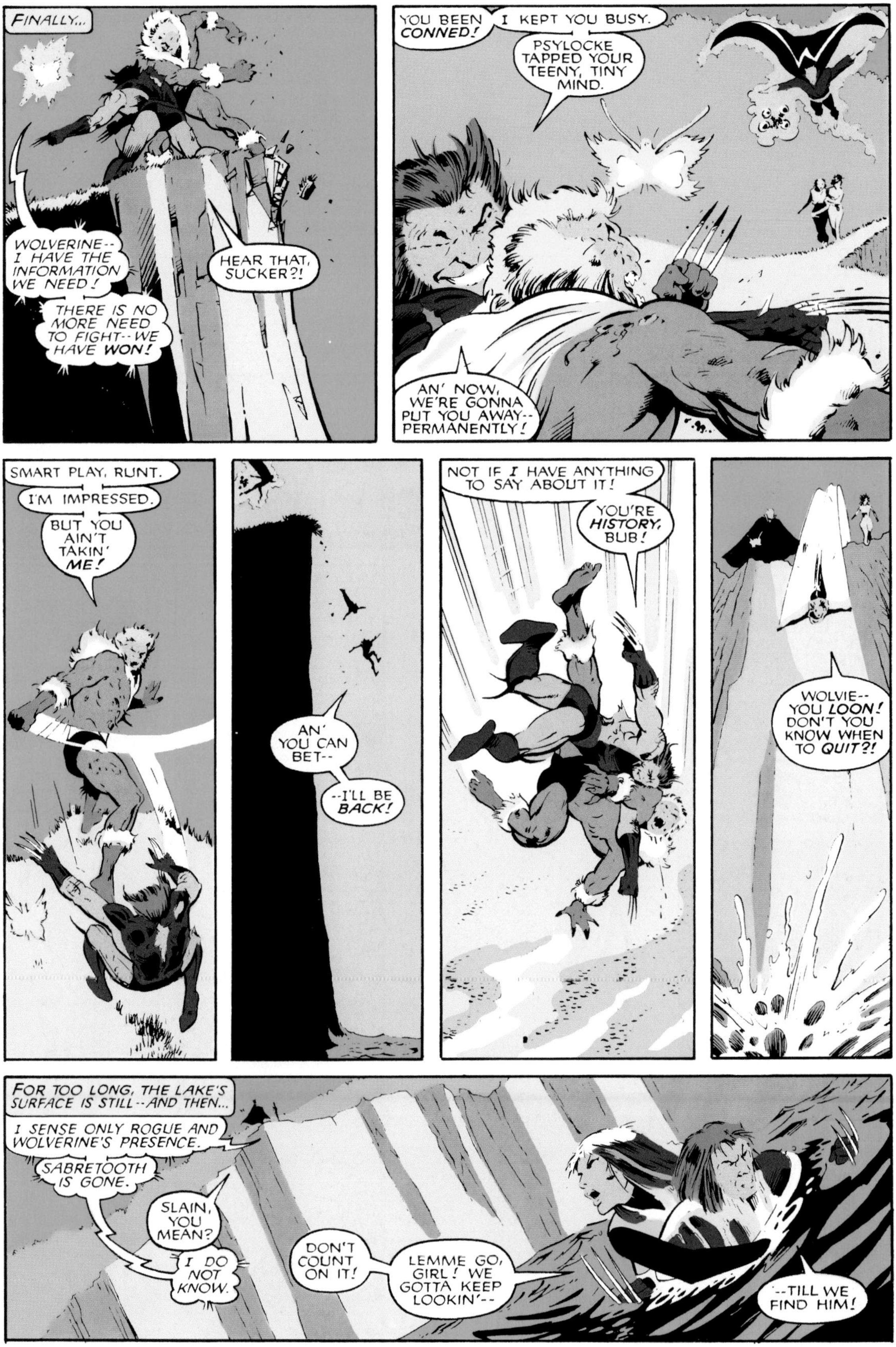

FINALLY...
WOLVERINE-- I HAVE THE INFORMATION WE NEED!
THERE IS NO MORE NEED TO FIGHT--WE HAVE WON!
HEAR THAT, SUCKER?!
YOU BEEN CONNED!
I KEPT YOU BUSY.
PSYLOCKE TAPPED YOUR TEENY, TINY MIND.
AN' NOW, WE'RE GONNA PUT YOU AWAY-- PERMANENTLY!
SMART PLAY, RUNT.
I'M IMPRESSED.
BUT YOU AIN'T TAKIN' ME!
AN' YOU CAN BET--
--I'LL BE BACK!
NOT IF I HAVE ANYTHING TO SAY ABOUT IT!
YOU'RE HISTORY, BUB!
WOLVIE-- YOU LOON! DON'T YOU KNOW WHEN TO QUIT?!
FOR TOO LONG, THE LAKE'S SURFACE IS STILL--AND THEN...
I SENSE ONLY ROGUE AND WOLVERINE'S PRESENCE.
SABRETOOTH IS GONE.
SLAIN, YOU MEAN?
I DO NOT KNOW.
DON'T COUNT ON IT!
LEMME GO, GIRL! WE GOTTA KEEP LOOKIN'--
--TILL WE FIND HIM!

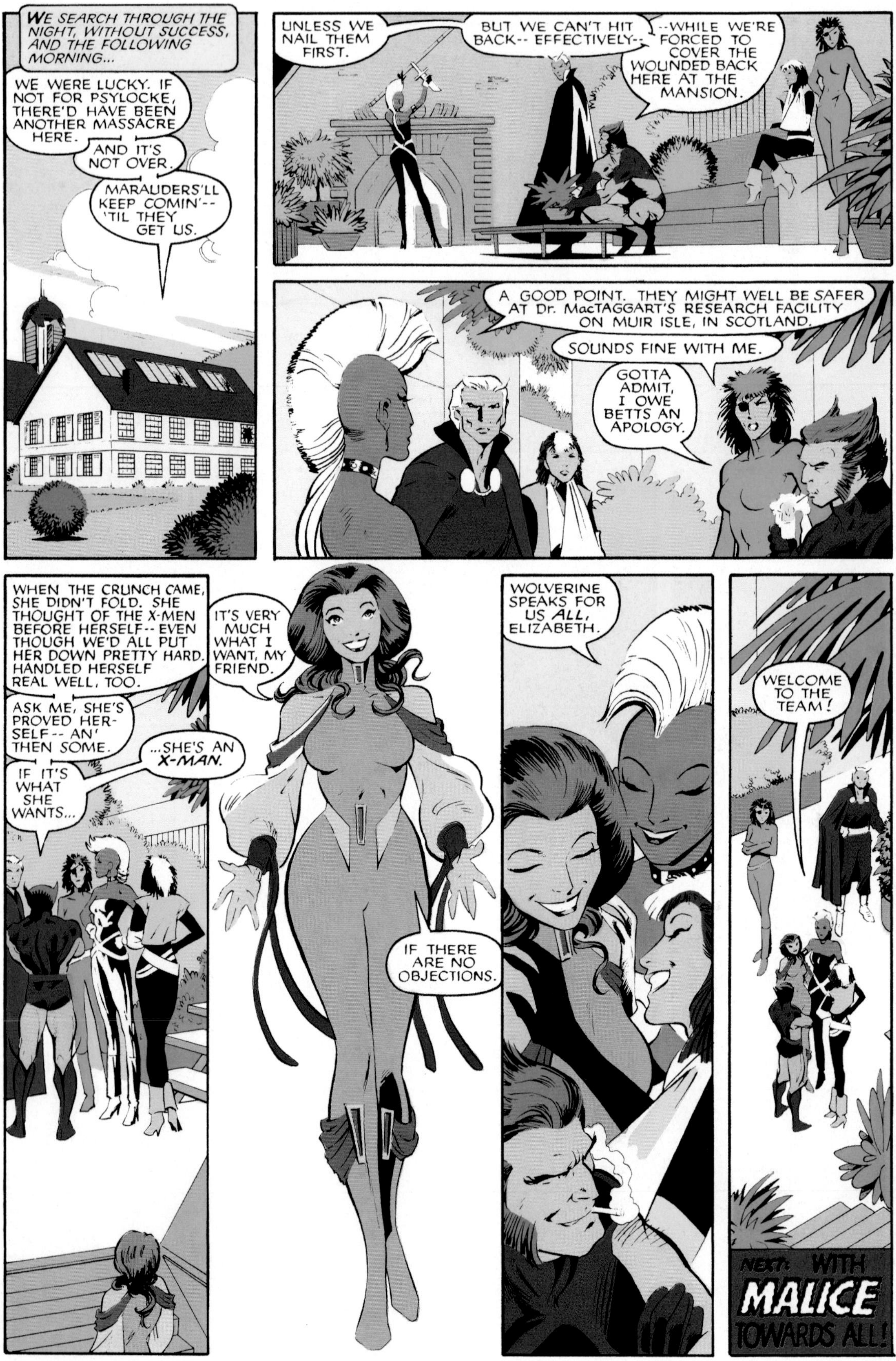
WE SEARCH THROUGH THE NIGHT, WITHOUT SUCCESS, AND THE FOLLOWING MORNING...
WE WERE LUCKY. IF NOT FOR PSYLOCKE, THERE'D HAVE BEEN ANOTHER MASSACRE HERE.
AND IT'S NOT OVER.
MARAUDERS'LL KEEP COMIN'-- 'TIL THEY GET US.
UNLESS WE NAIL THEM FIRST.
BUT WE CAN'T HIT BACK-- EFFECTIVELY--
--WHILE WE'RE FORCED TO COVER THE WOUNDED BACK HERE AT THE MANSION.
A GOOD POINT. THEY MIGHT WELL BE SAFER AT Dr. MacTAGGART'S RESEARCH FACILITY ON MUIR ISLE, IN SCOTLAND.
SOUNDS FINE WITH ME.
GOTTA ADMIT, I OWE BETTS AN APOLOGY.
WHEN THE CRUNCH CAME, SHE DIDN'T FOLD. SHE THOUGHT OF THE X-MEN BEFORE HERSELF-- EVEN THOUGH WE'D ALL PUT HER DOWN PRETTY HARD. HANDLED HERSELF REAL WELL, TOO.
ASK ME, SHE'S PROVED HERSELF-- AN' THEN SOME.
...SHE'S AN X-MAN.
IF IT'S WHAT SHE WANTS...
IT'S VERY MUCH WHAT I WANT, MY FRIEND.
IF THERE ARE NO OBJECTIONS.
WOLVERINE SPEAKS FOR US ALL, ELIZABETH.
WELCOME TO THE TEAM!
NEXT: WITH MALICE TOWARDS ALL!

The Uncanny X-Men #215

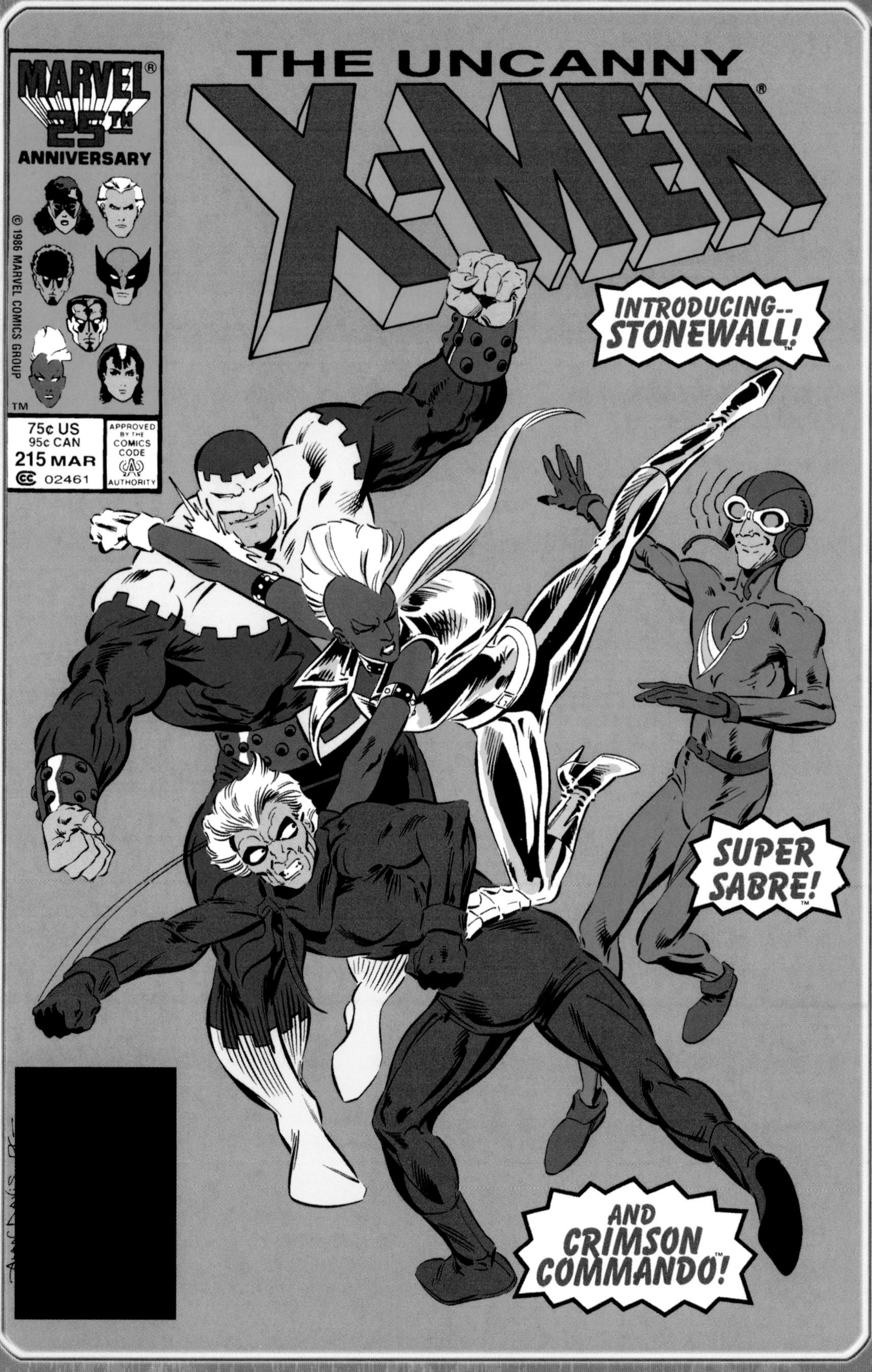
MARVEL 25TH ANNIVERSARY
© 1986 MARVEL COMICS GROUP
TM
75¢ US
95¢ CAN
215 MAR
02461
APPROVED BY THE COMICS CODE AUTHORITY
THE UNCANNY
X-MEN
INTRODUCING-- STONEWALL!
SUPER SABRE!
AND CRIMSON COMMANDO!

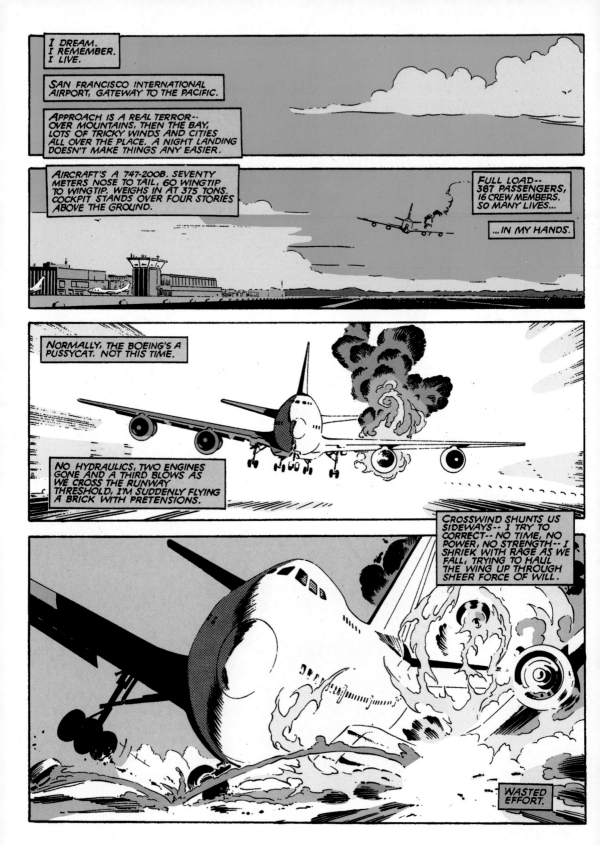

I DREAM.
I REMEMBER.
I LIVE.

SAN FRANCISCO INTERNATIONAL AIRPORT, GATEWAY TO THE PACIFIC.

APPROACH IS A REAL TERROR-- OVER MOUNTAINS, THEN THE BAY, LOTS OF TRICKY WINDS AND CITIES ALL OVER THE PLACE. A NIGHT LANDING DOESN'T MAKE THINGS ANY EASIER.

AIRCRAFT'S A 747-200B. SEVENTY METERS NOSE TO TAIL, 60 WINGTIP TO WINGTIP. WEIGHS IN AT 375 TONS. COCKPIT STANDS OVER FOUR STORIES ABOVE THE GROUND.

FULL LOAD-- 387 PASSENGERS, 16 CREW MEMBERS, SO MANY LIVES...

...IN MY HANDS.

NORMALLY, THE BOEING'S A PUSSYCAT. NOT THIS TIME.

NO HYDRAULICS, TWO ENGINES GONE AND A THIRD BLOWS AS WE CROSS THE RUNWAY THRESHOLD, I'M SUDDENLY FLYING A BRICK WITH PRETENSIONS.

CROSSWIND SHUNTS US SIDEWAYS-- I TRY TO CORRECT-- NO TIME, NO POWER, NO STRENGTH-- I SHRIEK WITH RAGE AS WE FALL, TRYING TO HAUL THE WING UP THROUGH SHEER FORCE OF WILL.

WASTED EFFORT.

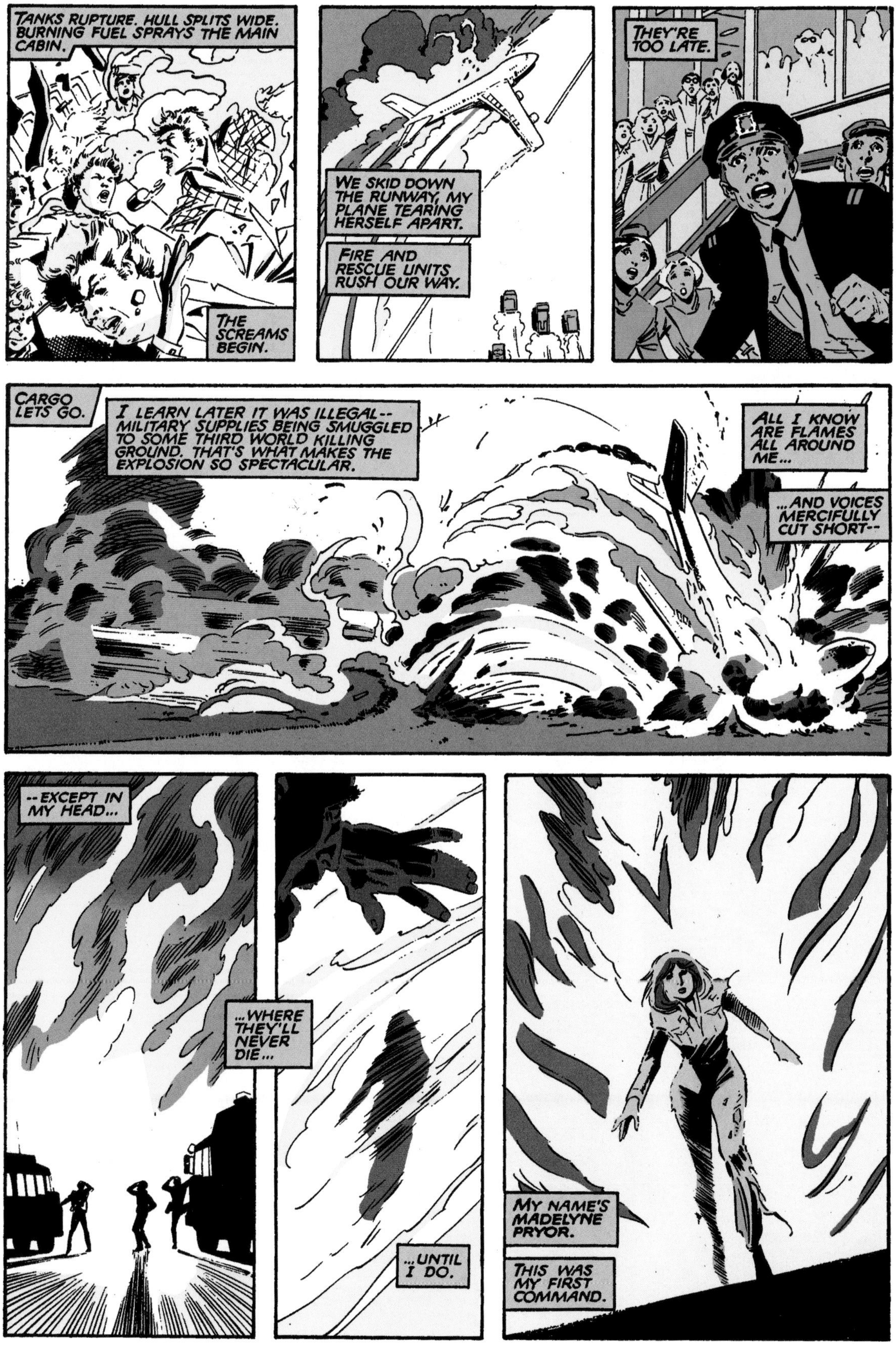
TANKS RUPTURE. HULL SPLITS WIDE. BURNING FUEL SPRAYS THE MAIN CABIN.
THE SCREAMS BEGIN.
WE SKID DOWN THE RUNWAY, MY PLANE TEARING HERSELF APART.
FIRE AND RESCUE UNITS RUSH OUR WAY.
THEY'RE TOO LATE.
CARGO LETS GO.
I LEARN LATER IT WAS ILLEGAL-- MILITARY SUPPLIES BEING SMUGGLED TO SOME THIRD WORLD KILLING GROUND. THAT'S WHAT MAKES THE EXPLOSION SO SPECTACULAR.
ALL I KNOW ARE FLAMES ALL AROUND ME...
...AND VOICES MERCIFULLY CUT SHORT--
--EXCEPT IN MY HEAD...
...WHERE THEY'LL NEVER DIE...
...UNTIL I DO.
MY NAME'S MADELYNE PRYOR.
THIS WAS MY FIRST COMMAND.

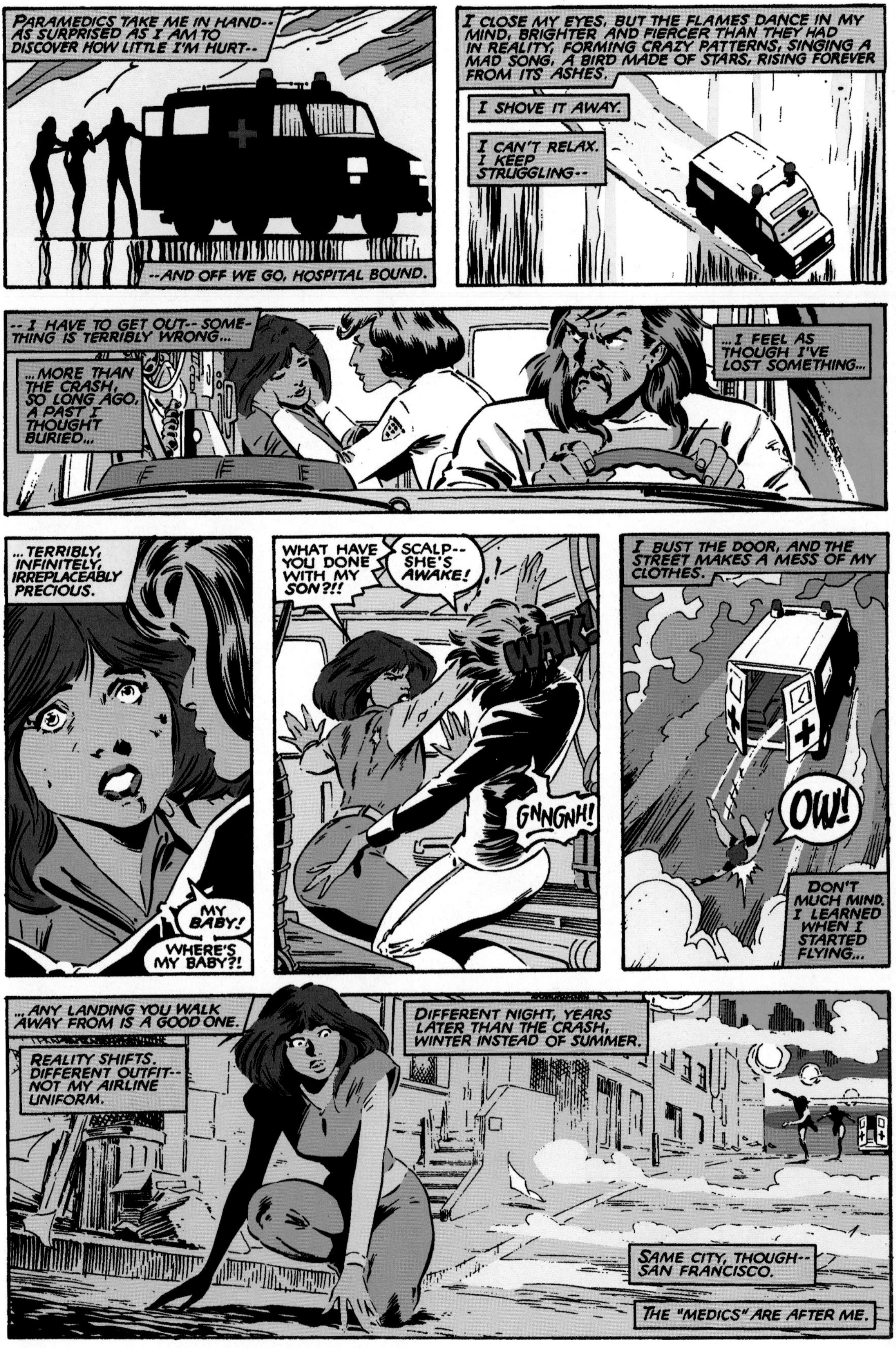

PARAMEDICS TAKE ME IN HAND-- AS SURPRISED AS I AM TO DISCOVER HOW LITTLE I'M HURT--
--AND OFF WE GO, HOSPITAL BOUND.
I CLOSE MY EYES, BUT THE FLAMES DANCE IN MY MIND, BRIGHTER AND FIERCER THAN THEY HAD IN REALITY, FORMING CRAZY PATTERNS, SINGING A MAD SONG, A BIRD MADE OF STARS, RISING FOREVER FROM ITS ASHES.
I SHOVE IT AWAY.
I CAN'T RELAX. I KEEP STRUGGLING--
-- I HAVE TO GET OUT-- SOMETHING IS TERRIBLY WRONG...
...MORE THAN THE CRASH, SO LONG AGO, A PAST I THOUGHT BURIED...
...I FEEL AS THOUGH I'VE LOST SOMETHING...
...TERRIBLY, INFINITELY, IRREPLACEABLY PRECIOUS.
MY BABY!
WHERE'S MY BABY?!
WHAT HAVE YOU DONE WITH MY SON?!!
SCALP-- SHE'S AWAKE!
WAK!
GNNGNH!
I BUST THE DOOR, AND THE STREET MAKES A MESS OF MY CLOTHES.
OW!
DON'T MUCH MIND. I LEARNED WHEN I STARTED FLYING...
...ANY LANDING YOU WALK AWAY FROM IS A GOOD ONE.
REALITY SHIFTS. DIFFERENT OUTFIT-- NOT MY AIRLINE UNIFORM.
DIFFERENT NIGHT, YEARS LATER THAN THE CRASH, WINTER INSTEAD OF SUMMER.
SAME CITY, THOUGH-- SAN FRANCISCO.
THE "MEDICS" ARE AFTER ME.

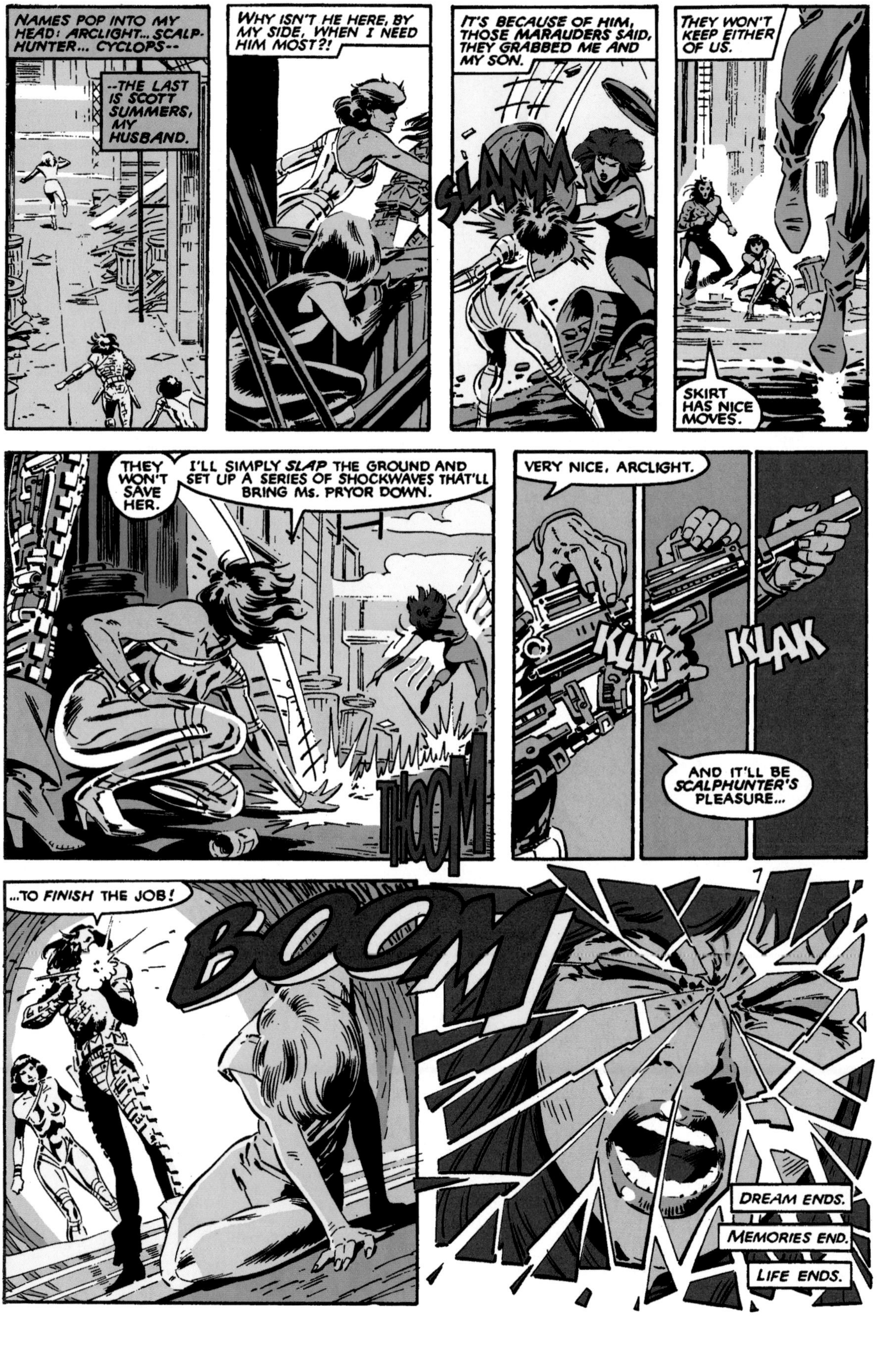
NAMES POP INTO MY HEAD: ARCLIGHT... SCALPHUNTER... CYCLOPS--
--THE LAST IS SCOTT SUMMERS, MY HUSBAND.
WHY ISN'T HE HERE, BY MY SIDE, WHEN I NEED HIM MOST?!
IT'S BECAUSE OF HIM, THOSE MARAUDERS SAID, THEY GRABBED ME AND MY SON.
SLAMM
THEY WON'T KEEP EITHER OF US.
SKIRT HAS NICE MOVES.
THEY WON'T SAVE HER.
I'LL SIMPLY SLAP THE GROUND AND SET UP A SERIES OF SHOCKWAVES THAT'LL BRING Ms. PRYOR DOWN.
THOOM
VERY NICE, ARCLIGHT.
KLIK
KLAK
AND IT'LL BE SCALPHUNTER'S PLEASURE...
...TO FINISH THE JOB!
BOOM
DREAM ENDS.
MEMORIES END.
LIFE ENDS.

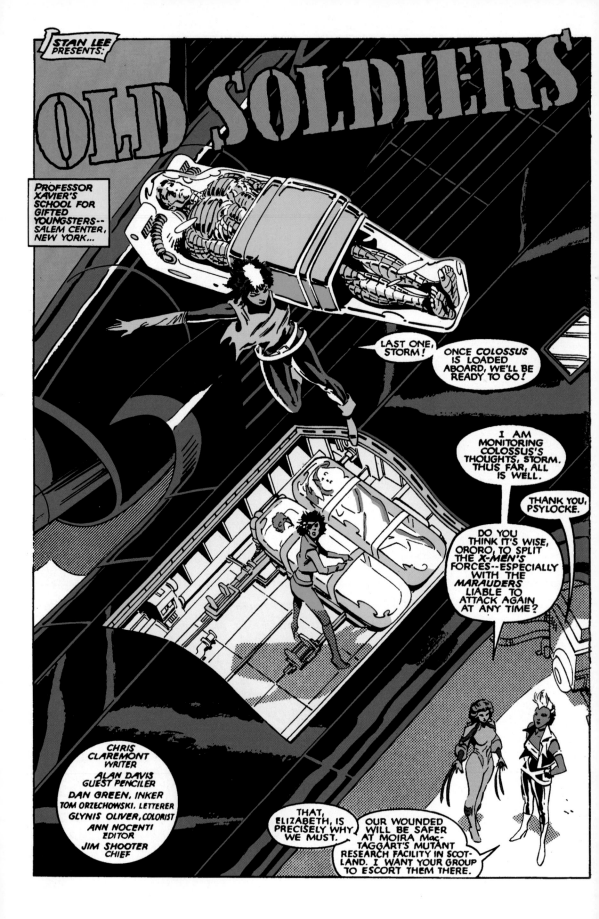

STAN LEE PRESENTS:

OLD SOLDIERS

PROFESSOR XAVIER'S SCHOOL FOR GIFTED YOUNGSTERS-- SALEM CENTER, NEW YORK...

LAST ONE, STORM! ONCE *COLOSSUS* IS LOADED ABOARD, WE'LL BE READY TO GO!

I AM MONITORING *COLOSSUS'S* THOUGHTS, STORM. THUS FAR, ALL IS WELL.

THANK YOU, PSYLOCKE.

DO YOU THINK IT'S WISE, ORORO, TO SPLIT THE *X-MEN'S* FORCES--ESPECIALLY WITH THE *MARAUDERS* LIABLE TO ATTACK AGAIN AT ANY TIME?

CHRIS CLAREMONT WRITER

ALAN DAVIS GUEST PENCILER

DAN GREEN, INKER

TOM ORZECHOWSKI, LETTERER

GLYNIS OLIVER, COLORIST

ANN NOCENTI EDITOR

JIM SHOOTER CHIEF

THAT, ELIZABETH, IS PRECISELY WHY WE MUST.

OUR WOUNDED WILL BE SAFER AT MOIRA Mac- TAGGART'S MUTANT RESEARCH FACILITY IN SCOT- LAND. I WANT YOUR GROUP TO ESCORT THEM THERE.

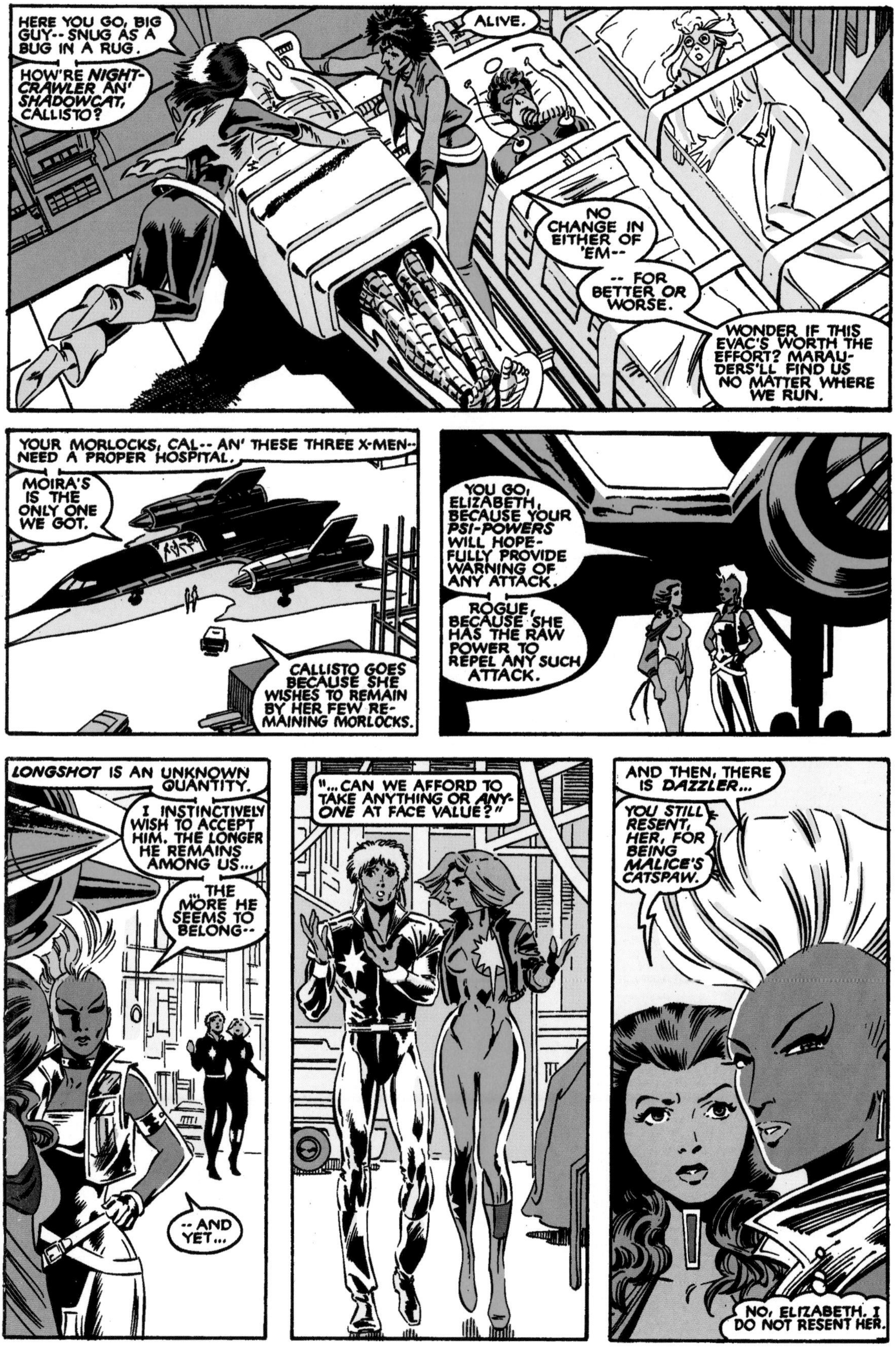

HERE YOU GO, BIG GUY-- SNUG AS A BUG IN A RUG.
HOW'RE NIGHTCRAWLER AN' SHADOWCAT, CALLISTO?
ALIVE.
NO CHANGE IN EITHER OF 'EM--
-- FOR BETTER OR WORSE.
WONDER IF THIS EVAC'S WORTH THE EFFORT? MARAUDERS'LL FIND US NO MATTER WHERE WE RUN.
YOUR MORLOCKS, CAL-- AN' THESE THREE X-MEN-- NEED A PROPER HOSPITAL.
MOIRA'S IS THE ONLY ONE WE GOT.
CALLISTO GOES BECAUSE SHE WISHES TO REMAIN BY HER FEW REMAINING MORLOCKS.
YOU GO, ELIZABETH, BECAUSE YOUR PSI-POWERS WILL HOPEFULLY PROVIDE WARNING OF ANY ATTACK.
ROGUE, BECAUSE SHE HAS THE RAW POWER TO REPEL ANY SUCH ATTACK.
LONGSHOT IS AN UNKNOWN QUANTITY.
I INSTINCTIVELY WISH TO ACCEPT HIM. THE LONGER HE REMAINS AMONG US...
...THE MORE HE SEEMS TO BELONG--
--AND YET...
"...CAN WE AFFORD TO TAKE ANYTHING OR ANYONE AT FACE VALUE?"
AND THEN, THERE IS DAZZLER...
YOU STILL RESENT, HER, FOR BEING MALICE'S CATSPAW.
NO, ELIZABETH. I DO NOT RESENT HER.

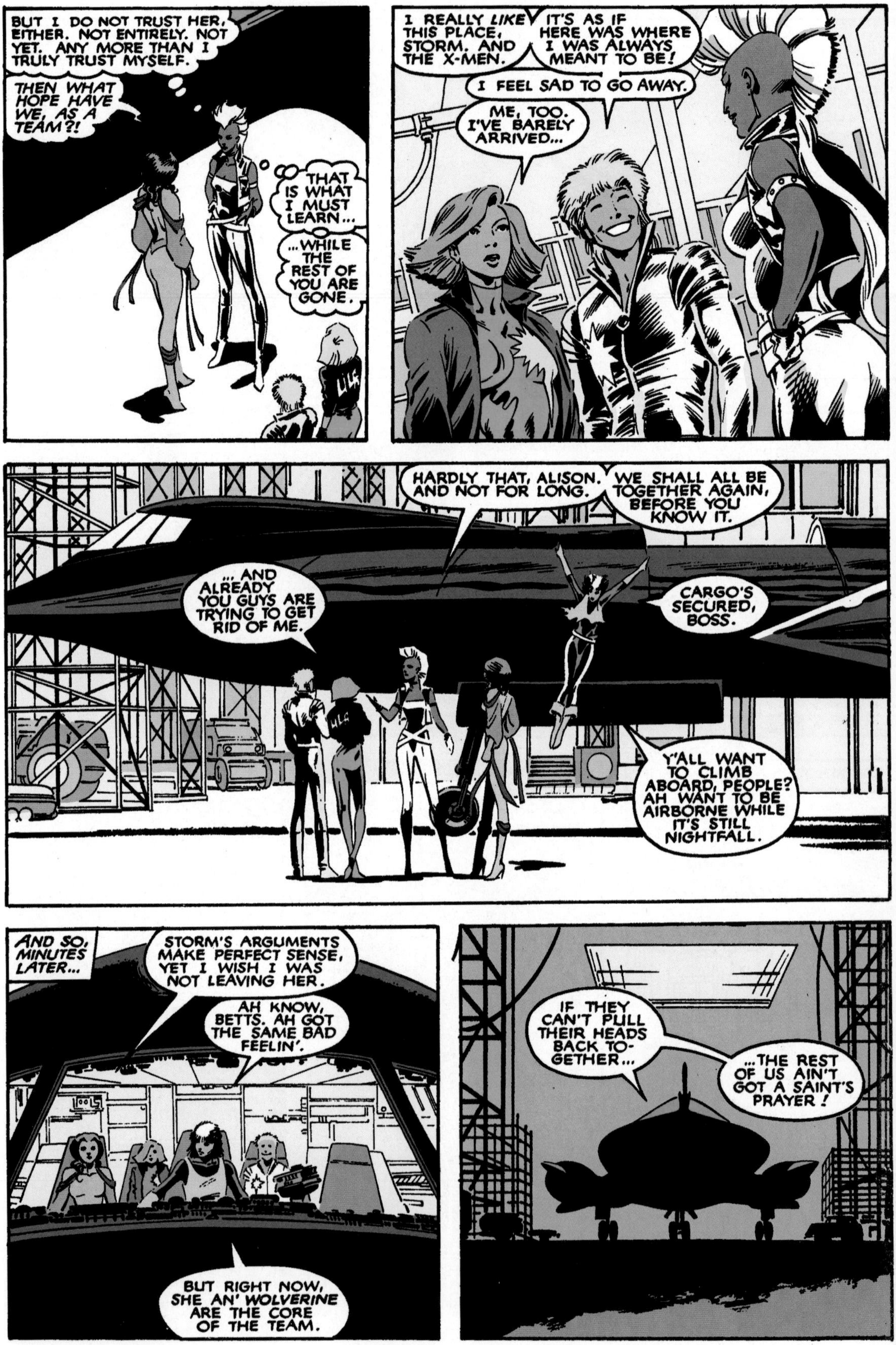
BUT I DO NOT TRUST HER, EITHER. NOT ENTIRELY. NOT YET. ANY MORE THAN I TRULY TRUST MYSELF.
THEN WHAT HOPE HAVE WE, AS A TEAM?!
THAT IS WHAT I MUST LEARN...
...WHILE THE REST OF YOU ARE GONE.
I REALLY LIKE THIS PLACE, STORM. AND THE X-MEN.
IT'S AS IF HERE WAS WHERE I WAS ALWAYS MEANT TO BE!
I FEEL SAD TO GO AWAY.
ME, TOO. I'VE BARELY ARRIVED...
...AND ALREADY YOU GUYS ARE TRYING TO GET RID OF ME.
HARDLY THAT, ALISON. AND NOT FOR LONG.
WE SHALL ALL BE TOGETHER AGAIN, BEFORE YOU KNOW IT.
CARGO'S SECURED, BOSS.
Y'ALL WANT TO CLIMB ABOARD, PEOPLE? AH WANT TO BE AIRBORNE WHILE IT'S STILL NIGHTFALL.
AND SO, MINUTES LATER...
STORM'S ARGUMENTS MAKE PERFECT SENSE, YET I WISH I WAS NOT LEAVING HER.
AH KNOW, BETTS. AH GOT THE SAME BAD FEELIN'.
BUT RIGHT NOW, SHE AN' WOLVERINE ARE THE CORE OF THE TEAM.
IF THEY CAN'T PULL THEIR HEADS BACK TO-GETHER...
...THE REST OF US AIN'T GOT A SAINT'S PRAYER!

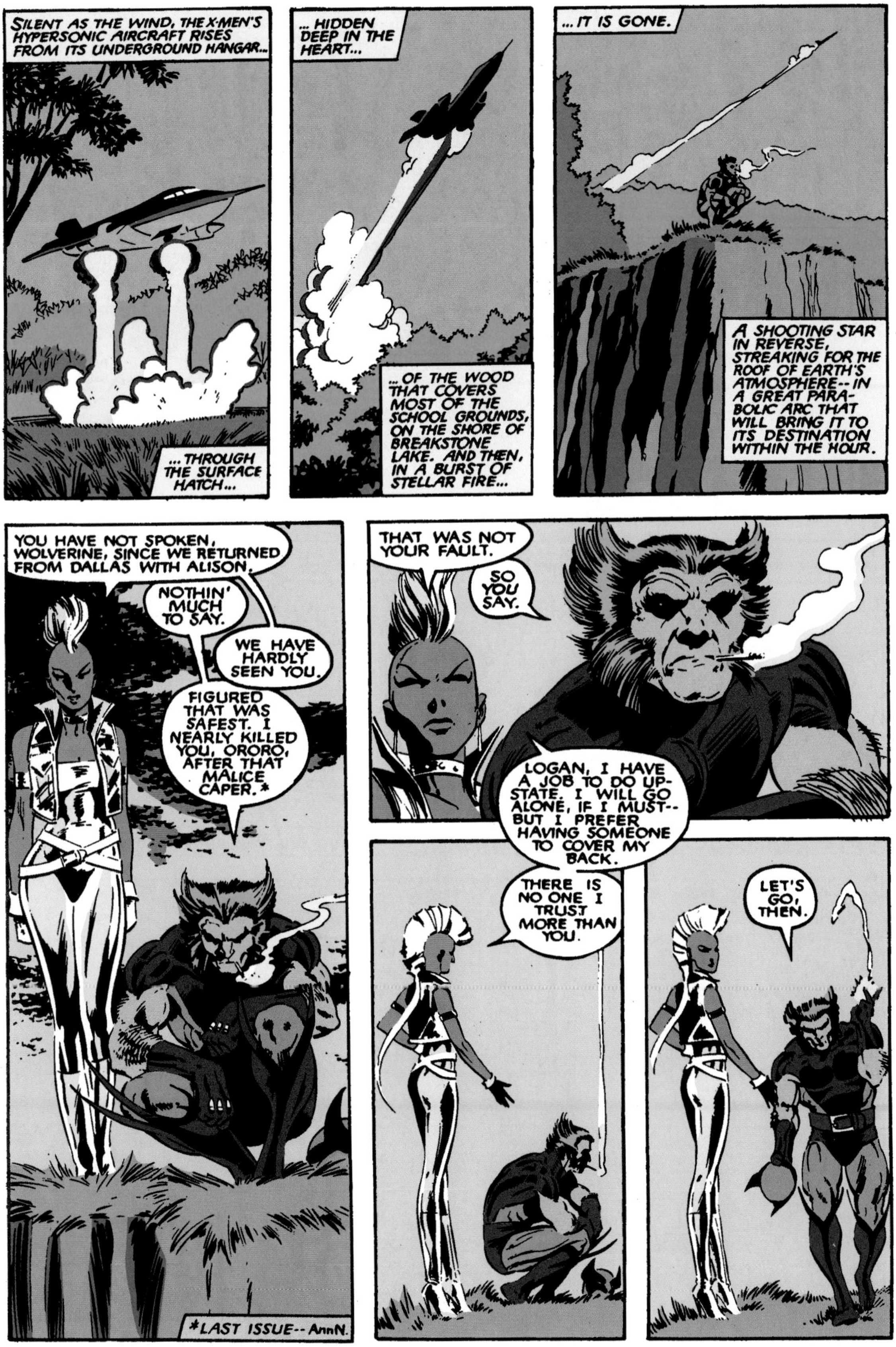
SILENT AS THE WIND, THE X-MEN'S HYPERSONIC AIRCRAFT RISES FROM ITS UNDERGROUND HANGAR...
...THROUGH THE SURFACE HATCH...
...HIDDEN DEEP IN THE HEART...
...OF THE WOOD THAT COVERS MOST OF THE SCHOOL GROUNDS, ON THE SHORE OF BREAKSTONE LAKE. AND THEN, IN A BURST OF STELLAR FIRE...
...IT IS GONE.
A SHOOTING STAR IN REVERSE, STREAKING FOR THE ROOF OF EARTH'S ATMOSPHERE-- IN A GREAT PARABOLIC ARC THAT WILL BRING IT TO ITS DESTINATION WITHIN THE HOUR.
YOU HAVE NOT SPOKEN, WOLVERINE, SINCE WE RETURNED FROM DALLAS WITH ALISON.
NOTHIN' MUCH TO SAY.
WE HAVE HARDLY SEEN YOU.
FIGURED THAT WAS SAFEST. I NEARLY KILLED YOU, ORORO, AFTER THAT MALICE CAPER.*
*LAST ISSUE-- AnnN.
THAT WAS NOT YOUR FAULT.
SO YOU SAY.
LOGAN, I HAVE A JOB TO DO UPSTATE. I WILL GO ALONE, IF I MUST-- BUT I PREFER HAVING SOMEONE TO COVER MY BACK.
THERE IS NO ONE I TRUST MORE THAN YOU.
LET'S GO, THEN.

SAME MOMENT, THREE TIME ZONES DISTANT ACROSS THE CONTINENT...

I NEVER WORKED WITH A LIVING LEGEND BEFORE, DOCTOR.

SAN FRANCISCO GENERAL HOSPITAL

EMERGENCY   EMERGENCY

FLATTERER. I LOVE IT! PATIENT WAS ADMITTED AS A *JANE DOE*-- WE HAVEN'T IDENTIFIED HER SINCE--

--SUFFERING FROM MULTIPLE GUNSHOT WOUNDS.

INITIAL PROGNOSIS WAS PRETTY BLEAK-- SEVERE TRAUMA, MASSIVE BLOOD LOSS, NOBODY THOUGHT SHE'D LAST THE NIGHT-- BUT SHE SURPRISED US.

IN FACT, PHYSICALLY, SHE'S WELL ON THE WAY TO RECOVERY.

UNFORTUNATELY, SHE'S MAINTAINED THIS DEEP COMATOSE STATE, RESISTING ALL EFFORTS TO BRING HER OUT OF IT.

WE'VE DONE ALL WE CAN FOR HER-- AND WE NEED THE BED SPACE, ESPECIALLY SINCE, AS A "JANE DOE," THE STATE PICKS UP THE TAB--

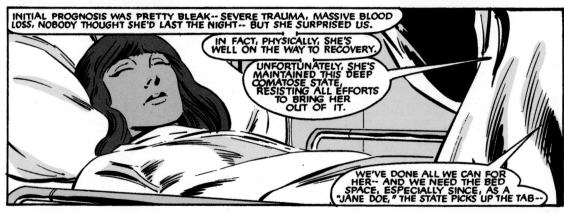

-- SO, NEXT WEEK, WE'LL BE TRANSFERRING HER TO A CUSTODIAL FACILITY.

Uhnh!

YOU SAY SOMETHING, DIANE?

Uhnnh!

JULIE-- IT'S YOUR "JANE DOE!"

GLORY BE, SHE'S *WAKING UP!!*

AM... AM I ALIVE?

VERY MUCH SO. AND QUITE WELL, TOO. I'M Dr. SCHWARTZ, THIS IS Dr. DUANE, AND WE'RE VERY GLAD TO MEET YOU, Ms...?

PRYOR. MY NAME IS MADELYNE PRYOR.

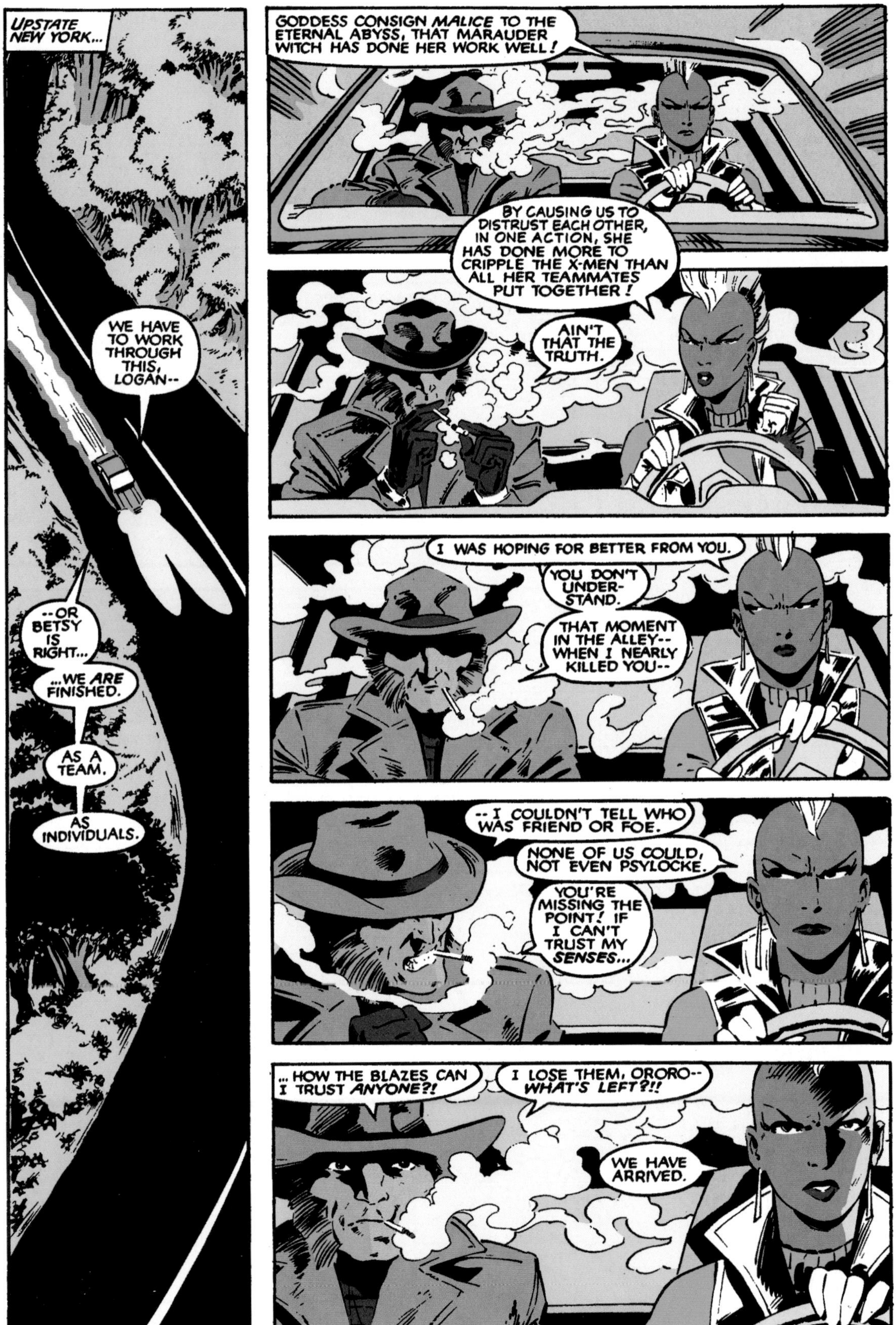
UPSTATE NEW YORK...
GODDESS CONSIGN MALICE TO THE ETERNAL ABYSS, THAT MARAUDER WITCH HAS DONE HER WORK WELL!
BY CAUSING US TO DISTRUST EACH OTHER, IN ONE ACTION, SHE HAS DONE MORE TO CRIPPLE THE X-MEN THAN ALL HER TEAMMATES PUT TOGETHER!
AIN'T THAT THE TRUTH.
WE HAVE TO WORK THROUGH THIS, LOGAN--
--OR BETSY IS RIGHT...
...WE ARE FINISHED.
AS A TEAM.
AS INDIVIDUALS.
I WAS HOPING FOR BETTER FROM YOU.
YOU DON'T UNDER-STAND.
THAT MOMENT IN THE ALLEY-- WHEN I NEARLY KILLED YOU--
--I COULDN'T TELL WHO WAS FRIEND OR FOE.
NONE OF US COULD, NOT EVEN PSYLOCKE.
YOU'RE MISSING THE POINT! IF I CAN'T TRUST MY SENSES...
...HOW THE BLAZES CAN I TRUST ANYONE?!
I LOSE THEM, ORORO-- WHAT'S LEFT?!!
WE HAVE ARRIVED.

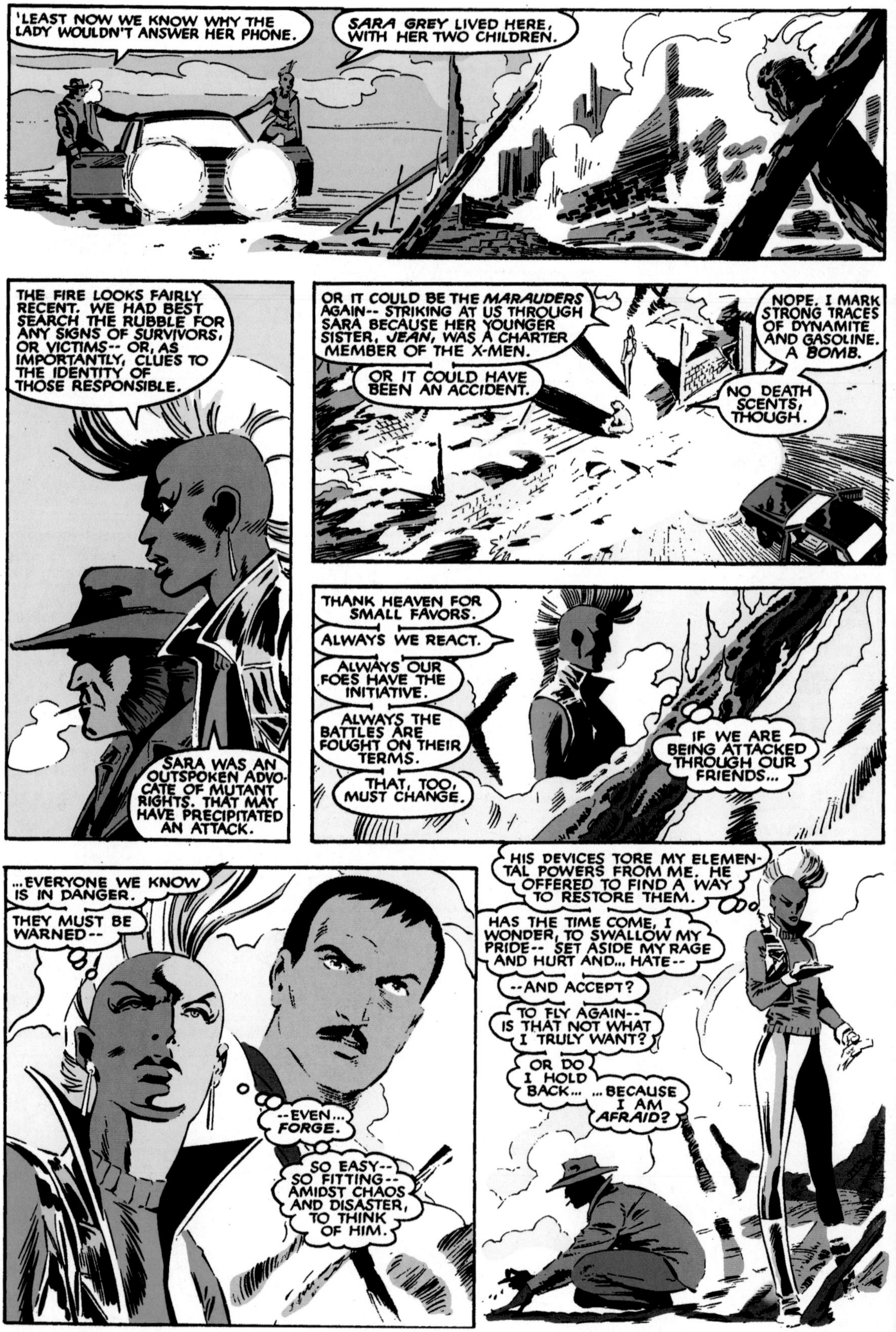
'LEAST NOW WE KNOW WHY THE LADY WOULDN'T ANSWER HER PHONE.
SARA GREY LIVED HERE, WITH HER TWO CHILDREN.
THE FIRE LOOKS FAIRLY RECENT. WE HAD BEST SEARCH THE RUBBLE FOR ANY SIGNS OF SURVIVORS, OR VICTIMS-- OR, AS IMPORTANTLY, CLUES TO THE IDENTITY OF THOSE RESPONSIBLE.
SARA WAS AN OUTSPOKEN ADVOCATE OF MUTANT RIGHTS. THAT MAY HAVE PRECIPITATED AN ATTACK.
OR IT COULD HAVE BEEN AN ACCIDENT.
OR IT COULD BE THE MARAUDERS AGAIN-- STRIKING AT US THROUGH SARA BECAUSE HER YOUNGER SISTER, JEAN, WAS A CHARTER MEMBER OF THE X-MEN.
NOPE. I MARK STRONG TRACES OF DYNAMITE AND GASOLINE. A BOMB.
NO DEATH SCENTS, THOUGH.
THANK HEAVEN FOR SMALL FAVORS.
ALWAYS WE REACT.
ALWAYS OUR FOES HAVE THE INITIATIVE.
ALWAYS THE BATTLES ARE FOUGHT ON THEIR TERMS.
THAT, TOO, MUST CHANGE.
IF WE ARE BEING ATTACKED THROUGH OUR FRIENDS...
...EVERYONE WE KNOW IS IN DANGER.
THEY MUST BE WARNED--
--EVEN... FORGE.
SO EASY-- SO FITTING-- AMIDST CHAOS AND DISASTER, TO THINK OF HIM.
HIS DEVICES TORE MY ELEMENTAL POWERS FROM ME. HE OFFERED TO FIND A WAY TO RESTORE THEM.
HAS THE TIME COME, I WONDER, TO SWALLOW MY PRIDE-- SET ASIDE MY RAGE AND HURT AND... HATE--
--AND ACCEPT?
TO FLY AGAIN-- IS THAT NOT WHAT I TRULY WANT?
OR DO I HOLD BACK...
...BECAUSE I AM AFRAID?

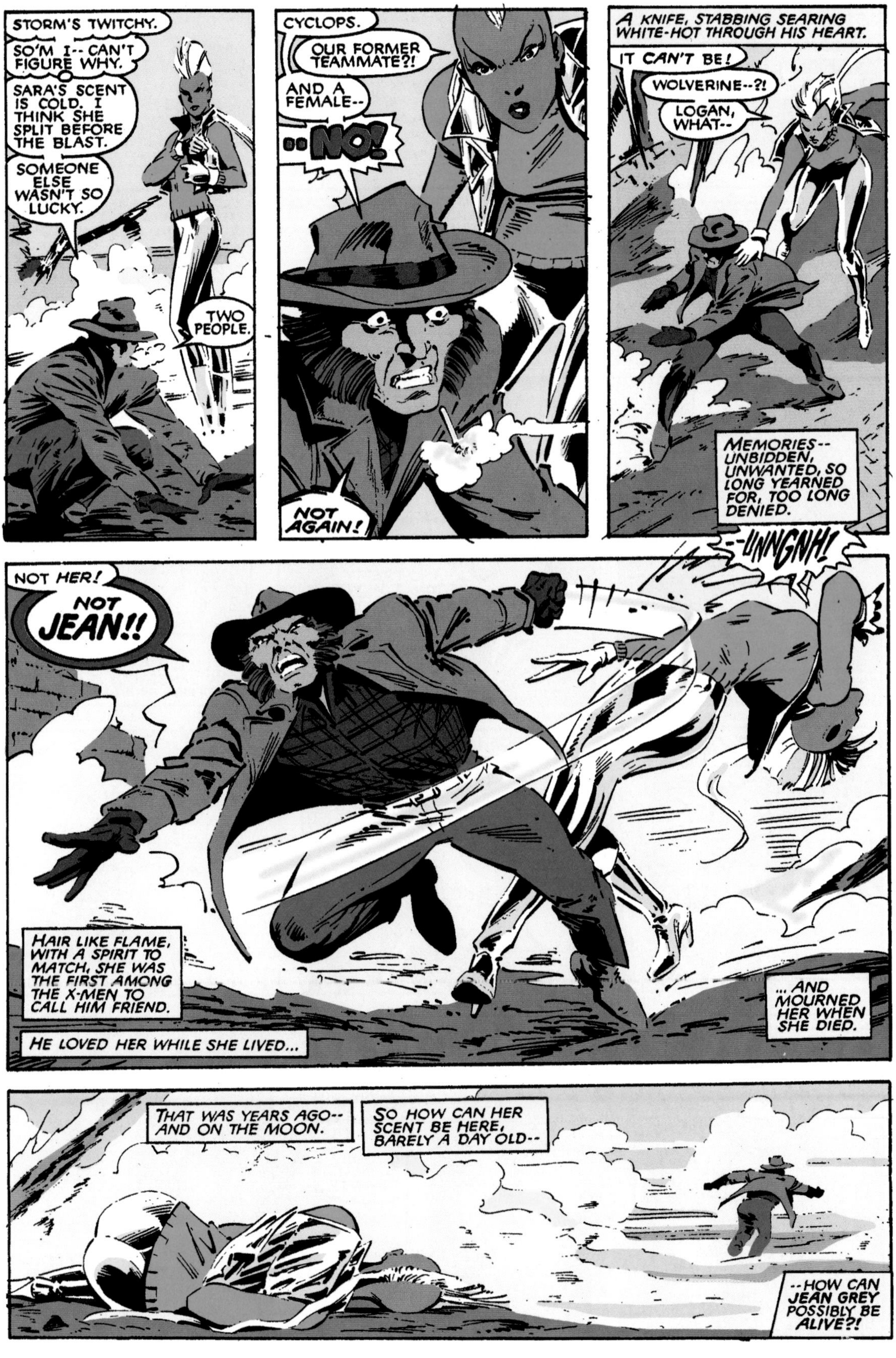

STORM'S TWITCHY.
SO'M I-- CAN'T FIGURE WHY.
SARA'S SCENT IS COLD. I THINK SHE SPLIT BEFORE THE BLAST.
SOMEONE ELSE WASN'T SO LUCKY.
TWO PEOPLE.
CYCLOPS.
OUR FORMER TEAMMATE?!
AND A FEMALE--
--NO!
NOT AGAIN!
A KNIFE, STABBING SEARING WHITE-HOT THROUGH HIS HEART.
IT CAN'T BE!
WOLVERINE--?!
LOGAN, WHAT--
MEMORIES-- UNBIDDEN, UNWANTED, SO LONG YEARNED FOR, TOO LONG DENIED.
NOT HER!
NOT JEAN!!
--UNNGNH!
HAIR LIKE FLAME, WITH A SPIRIT TO MATCH, SHE WAS THE FIRST AMONG THE X-MEN TO CALL HIM FRIEND.
HE LOVED HER WHILE SHE LIVED...
...AND MOURNED HER WHEN SHE DIED.
THAT WAS YEARS AGO-- AND ON THE MOON.
SO HOW CAN HER SCENT BE HERE, BARELY A DAY OLD--
--HOW CAN JEAN GREY POSSIBLY BE ALIVE?!

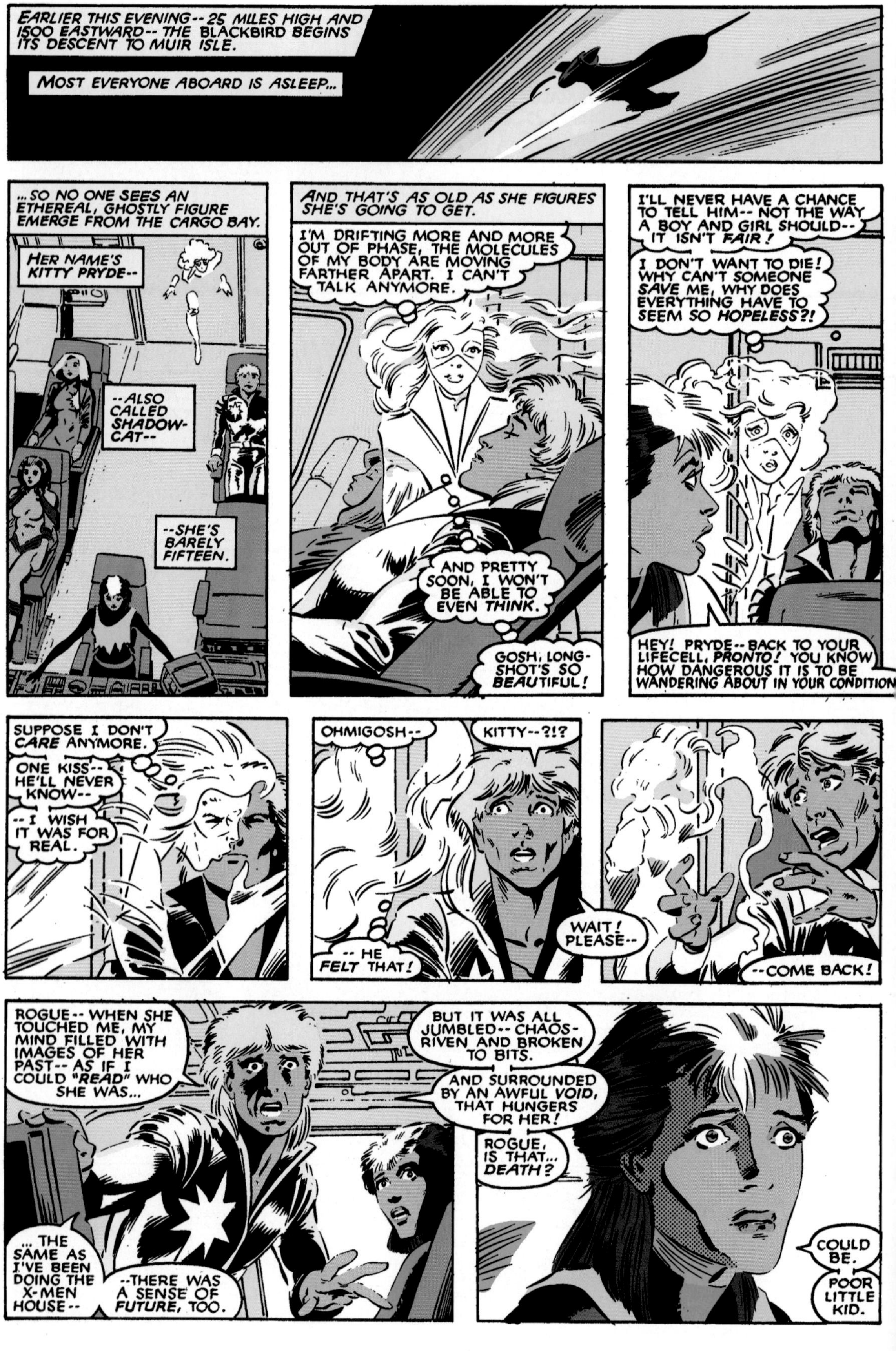
EARLIER THIS EVENING-- 25 MILES HIGH AND 1500 EASTWARD-- THE BLACKBIRD BEGINS ITS DESCENT TO MUIR ISLE.
MOST EVERYONE ABOARD IS ASLEEP...
...SO NO ONE SEES AN ETHEREAL, GHOSTLY FIGURE EMERGE FROM THE CARGO BAY.
HER NAME'S KITTY PRYDE--
--ALSO CALLED SHADOW-CAT--
--SHE'S BARELY FIFTEEN.
AND THAT'S AS OLD AS SHE FIGURES SHE'S GOING TO GET.
I'M DRIFTING MORE AND MORE OUT OF PHASE, THE MOLECULES OF MY BODY ARE MOVING FARTHER APART. I CAN'T TALK ANYMORE.
AND PRETTY SOON, I WON'T BE ABLE TO EVEN THINK.
GOSH, LONG-SHOT'S SO BEAUTIFUL!
I'LL NEVER HAVE A CHANCE TO TELL HIM-- NOT THE WAY A BOY AND GIRL SHOULD-- IT ISN'T FAIR!
I DON'T WANT TO DIE! WHY CAN'T SOMEONE SAVE ME, WHY DOES EVERYTHING HAVE TO SEEM SO HOPELESS?!
HEY! PRYDE-- BACK TO YOUR LIFECELL, PRONTO! YOU KNOW HOW DANGEROUS IT IS TO BE WANDERING ABOUT IN YOUR CONDITION
SUPPOSE I DON'T CARE ANYMORE.
ONE KISS-- HE'LL NEVER KNOW--
-- I WISH IT WAS FOR REAL.
OHMIGOSH--
KITTY--?!?
-- HE FELT THAT!
WAIT! PLEASE--
--COME BACK!
ROGUE-- WHEN SHE TOUCHED ME, MY MIND FILLED WITH IMAGES OF HER PAST-- AS IF I COULD "READ" WHO SHE WAS...
BUT IT WAS ALL JUMBLED-- CHAOS-RIVEN AND BROKEN TO BITS.
AND SURROUNDED BY AN AWFUL VOID, THAT HUNGERS FOR HER!
... THE SAME AS I'VE BEEN DOING THE X-MEN HOUSE--
--THERE WAS A SENSE OF FUTURE, TOO.
ROGUE, IS THAT... DEATH?
COULD BE.
POOR LITTLE KID.

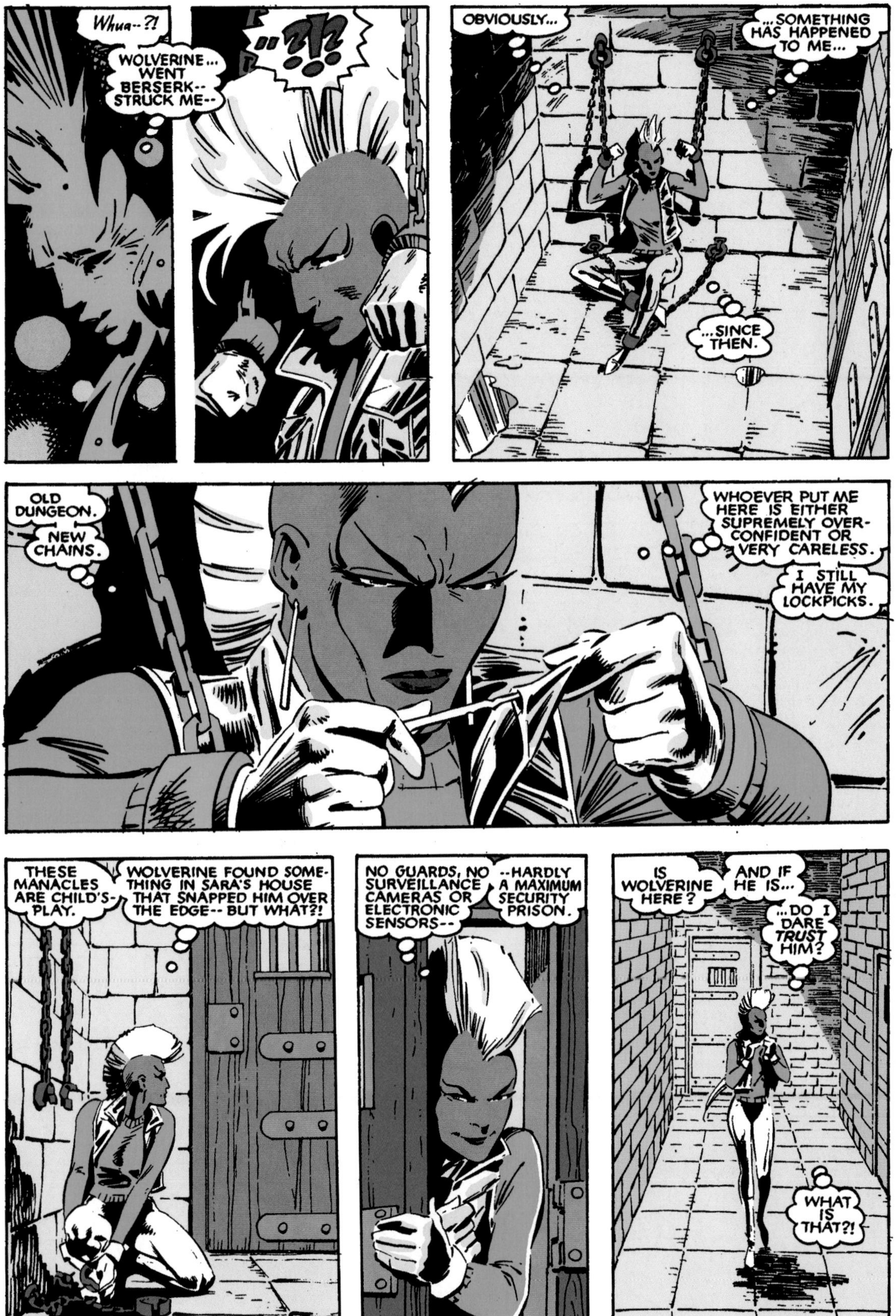
Whua--?!
WOLVERINE... WENT BERSERK-- STRUCK ME--
--?!?
OBVIOUSLY...
...SOMETHING HAS HAPPENED TO ME...
...SINCE THEN.
OLD DUNGEON.
NEW CHAINS.
WHOEVER PUT ME HERE IS EITHER SUPREMELY OVER-CONFIDENT OR VERY CARELESS.
I STILL HAVE MY LOCKPICKS.
THESE MANACLES ARE CHILD'S-PLAY.
WOLVERINE FOUND SOME-THING IN SARA'S HOUSE THAT SNAPPED HIM OVER THE EDGE-- BUT WHAT?!
NO GUARDS, NO SURVEILLANCE CAMERAS OR ELECTRONIC SENSORS--
--HARDLY A MAXIMUM SECURITY PRISON.
IS WOLVERINE HERE?
AND IF HE IS...
...DO I DARE TRUST HIM?
WHAT IS THAT?!

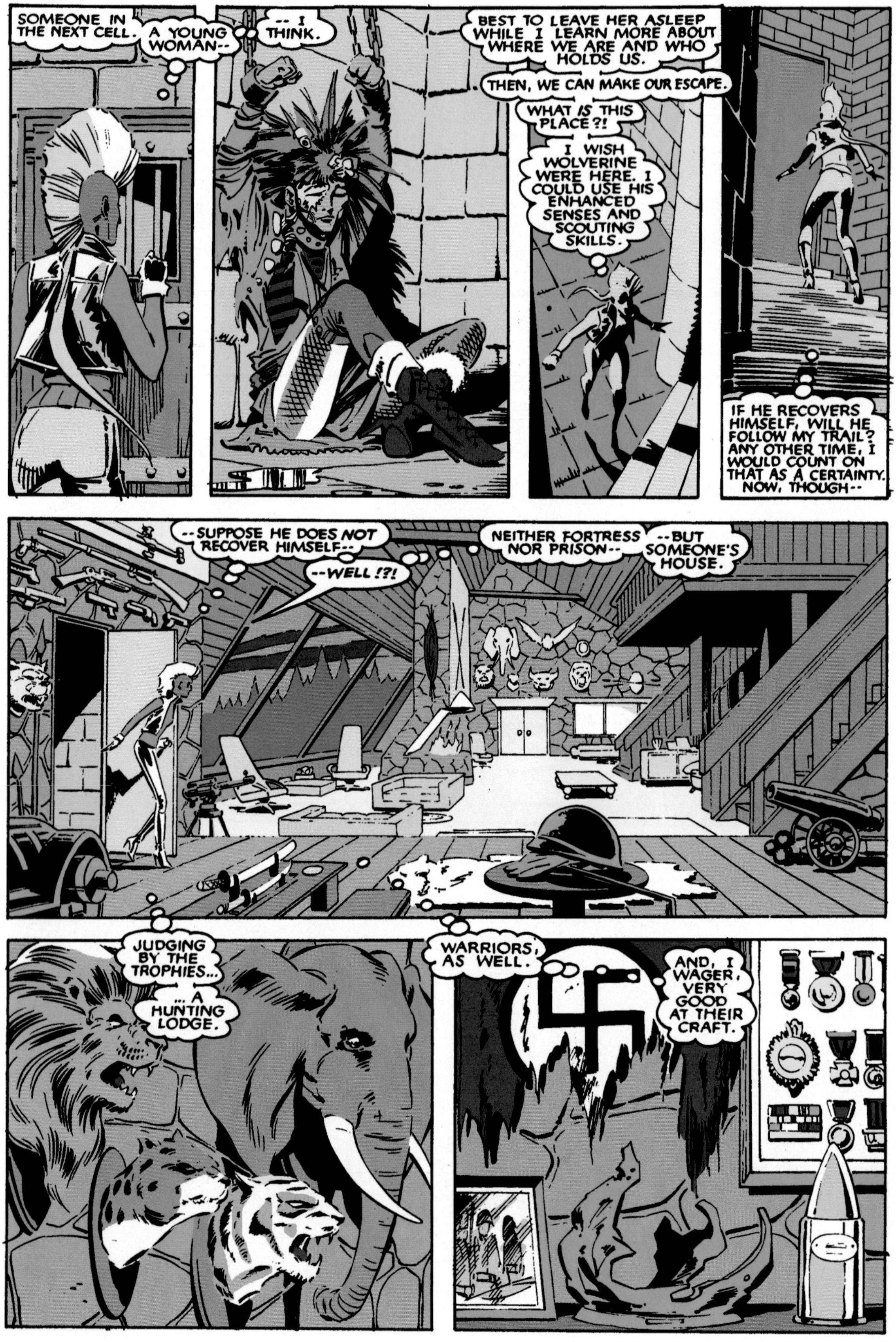
SOMEONE IN THE NEXT CELL.
A YOUNG WOMAN--
-- I THINK.
BEST TO LEAVE HER ASLEEP WHILE I LEARN MORE ABOUT WHERE WE ARE AND WHO HOLDS US.
THEN, WE CAN MAKE OUR ESCAPE.
WHAT *IS* THIS PLACE?!
I WISH WOLVERINE WERE HERE. I COULD USE HIS ENHANCED SENSES AND SCOUTING SKILLS.
IF HE RECOVERS HIMSELF, WILL HE FOLLOW MY TRAIL? ANY OTHER TIME, I WOULD COUNT ON THAT AS A CERTAINTY. NOW, THOUGH--
--SUPPOSE HE DOES *NOT* RECOVER HIMSELF--
--*WELL!?!*
NEITHER FORTRESS NOR PRISON--
--BUT SOMEONE'S HOUSE.
JUDGING BY THE TROPHIES...
... A HUNTING LODGE.
WARRIORS, AS WELL.
AND, I WAGER, VERY GOOD AT THEIR CRAFT.

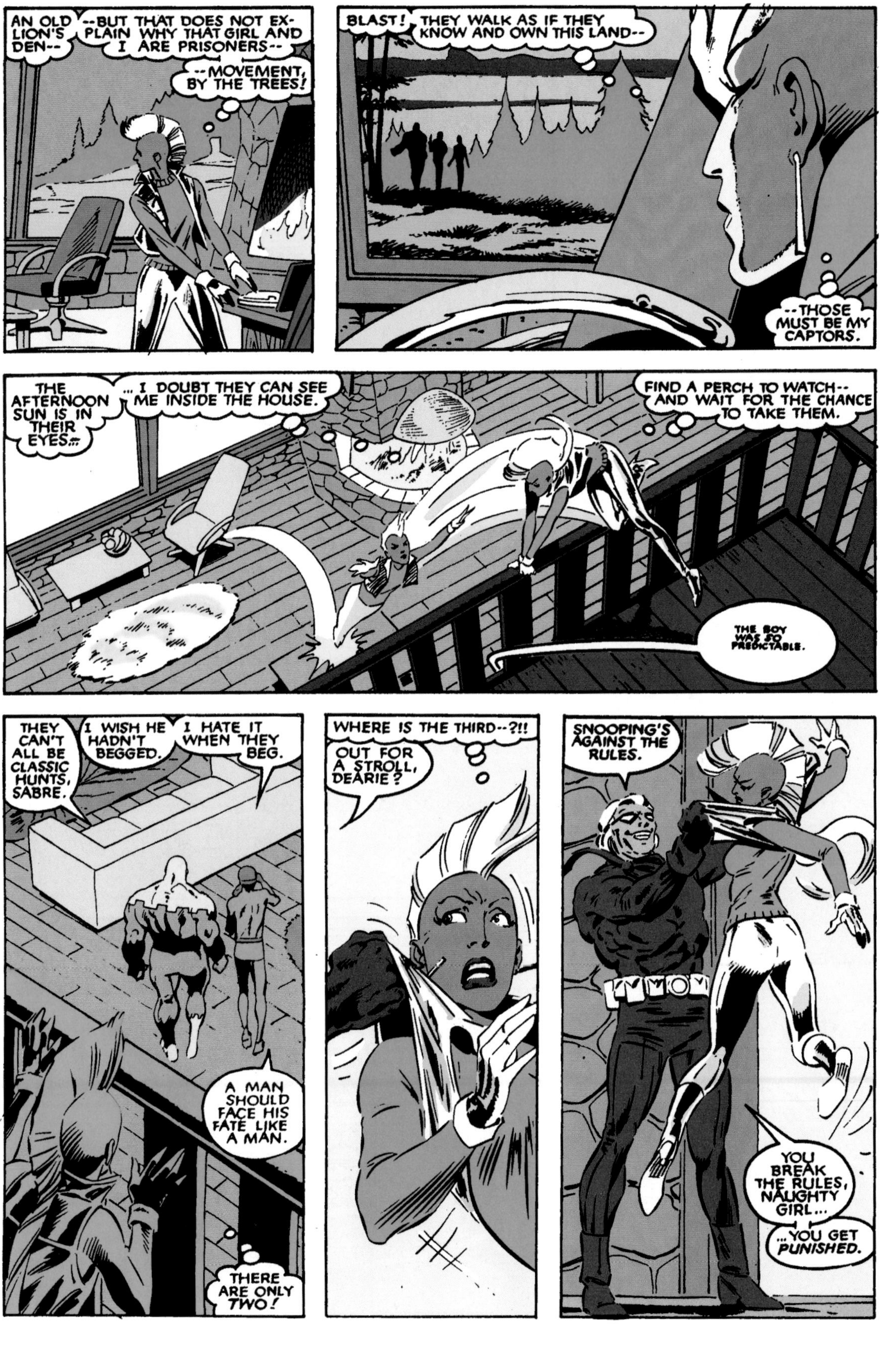
AN OLD LION'S DEN--
--BUT THAT DOES NOT EXPLAIN WHY THAT GIRL AND I ARE PRISONERS--
--MOVEMENT, BY THE TREES!
BLAST! THEY WALK AS IF THEY KNOW AND OWN THIS LAND--
--THOSE MUST BE MY CAPTORS.
THE AFTERNOON SUN IS IN THEIR EYES...
...I DOUBT THEY CAN SEE ME INSIDE THE HOUSE.
FIND A PERCH TO WATCH-- AND WAIT FOR THE CHANCE TO TAKE THEM.
THE BOY WAS SO PREDICTABLE.
THEY CAN'T ALL BE CLASSIC HUNTS, SABRE.
I WISH HE HADN'T BEGGED.
I HATE IT WHEN THEY BEG.
A MAN SHOULD FACE HIS FATE LIKE A MAN.
THERE ARE ONLY TWO!
WHERE IS THE THIRD--?!!
OUT FOR A STROLL, DEARIE?
SNOOPING'S AGAINST THE RULES.
YOU BREAK THE RULES, NAUGHTY GIRL...
...YOU GET PUNISHED.

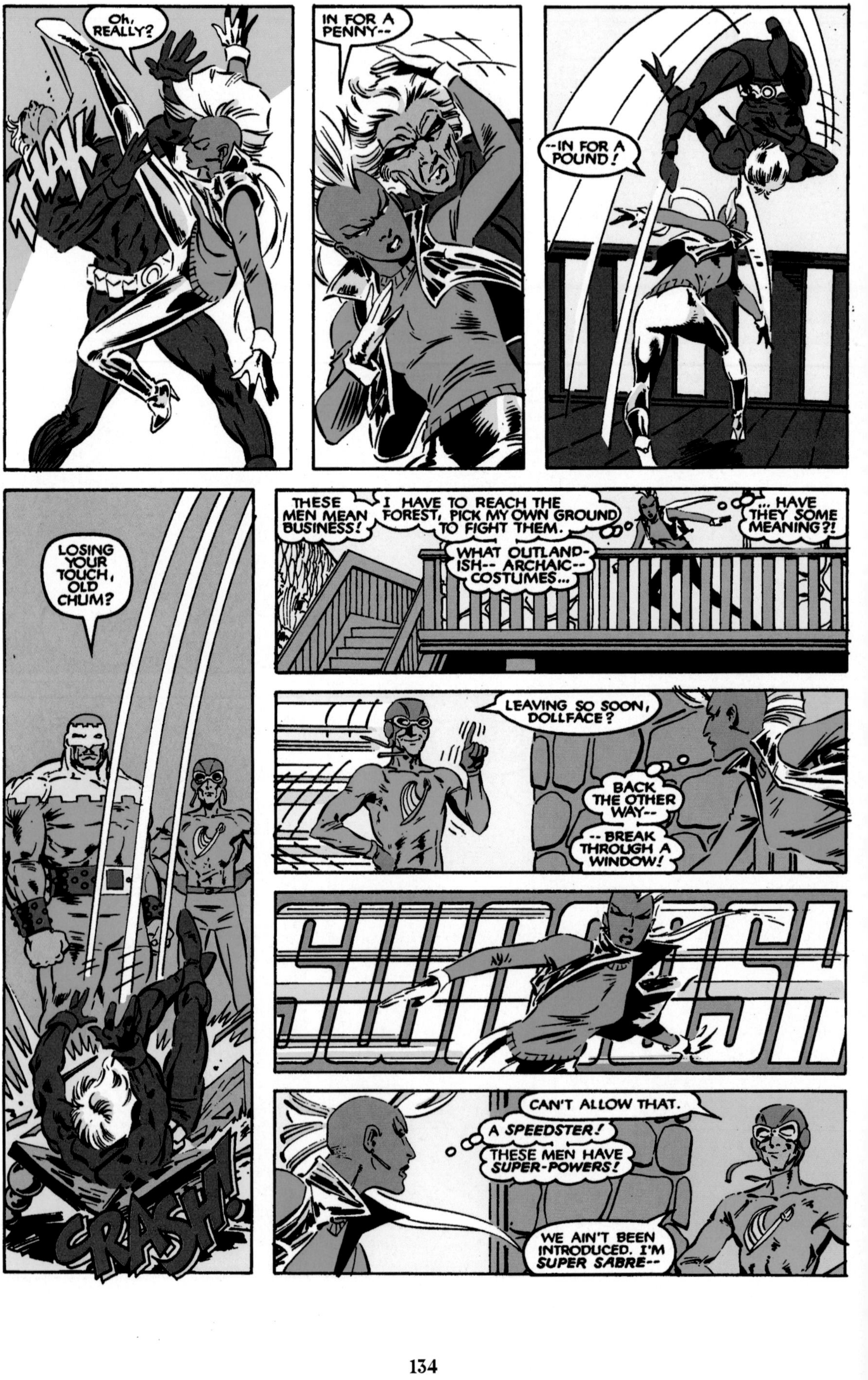

Oh, REALLY?
THAK
IN FOR A PENNY--
--IN FOR A POUND!
LOSING YOUR TOUCH, OLD CHUM?
CRASH!
THESE MEN MEAN BUSINESS!
I HAVE TO REACH THE FOREST, PICK MY OWN GROUND TO FIGHT THEM.
WHAT OUTLAND-ISH-- ARCHAIC-- COSTUMES...
... HAVE THEY SOME MEANING?!
LEAVING SO SOON, DOLLFACE?
BACK THE OTHER WAY--
-- BREAK THROUGH A WINDOW!
SWOOSH
CAN'T ALLOW THAT.
A SPEEDSTER!
THESE MEN HAVE SUPER-POWERS!
WE AIN'T BEEN INTRODUCED. I'M SUPER SABRE--

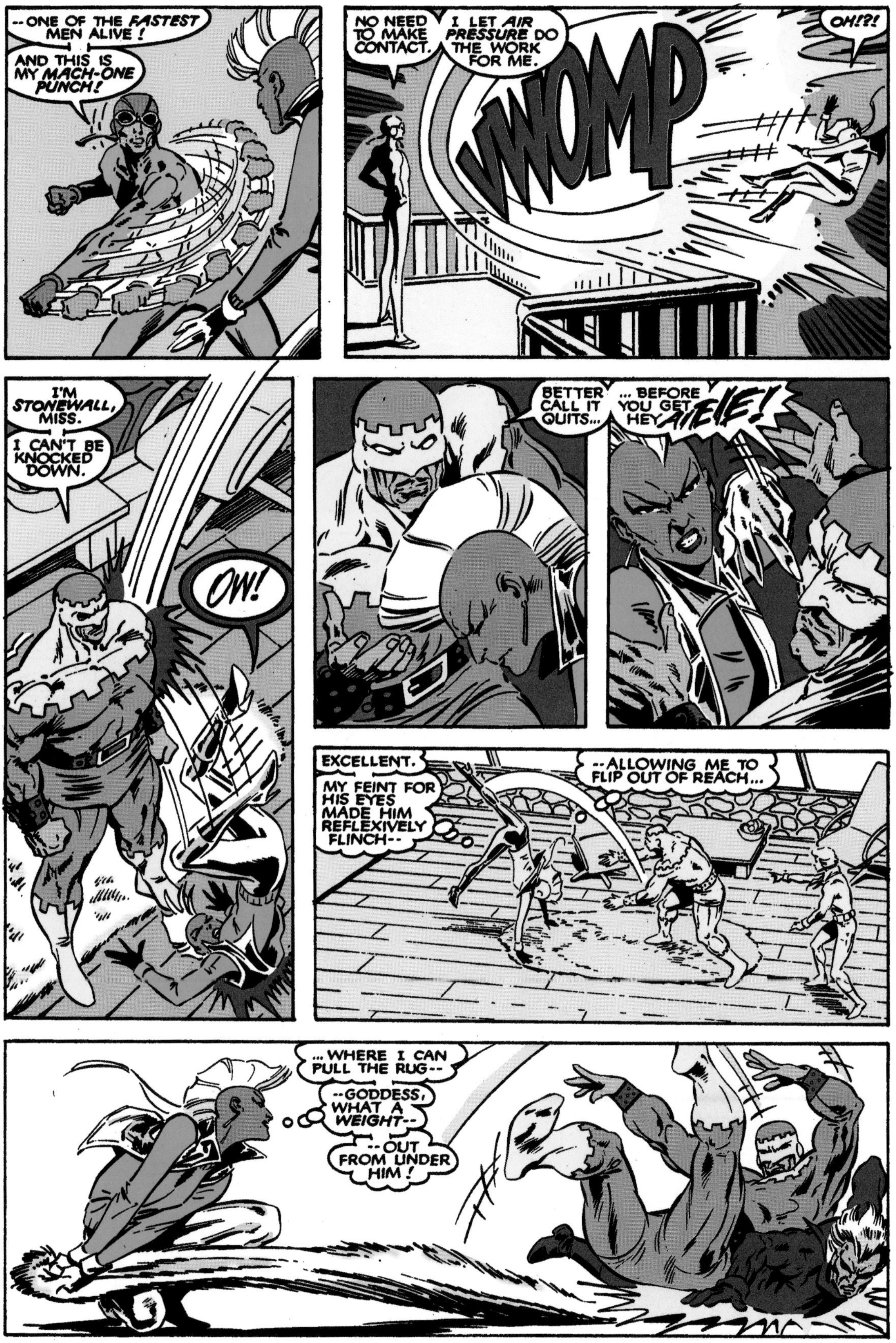
--ONE OF THE FASTEST MEN ALIVE!
AND THIS IS MY MACH-ONE PUNCH!
NO NEED TO MAKE CONTACT.
I LET AIR PRESSURE DO THE WORK FOR ME.
VWOMP
OH!?!
I'M STONEWALL, MISS.
I CAN'T BE KNOCKED DOWN.
OW!
BETTER CALL IT QUITS...
... BEFORE YOU GET HEY
AIEIE!
EXCELLENT.
MY FEINT FOR HIS EYES MADE HIM REFLEXIVELY FLINCH--
--ALLOWING ME TO FLIP OUT OF REACH...
... WHERE I CAN PULL THE RUG--
--GODDESS, WHAT A WEIGHT--
--OUT FROM UNDER HIM!

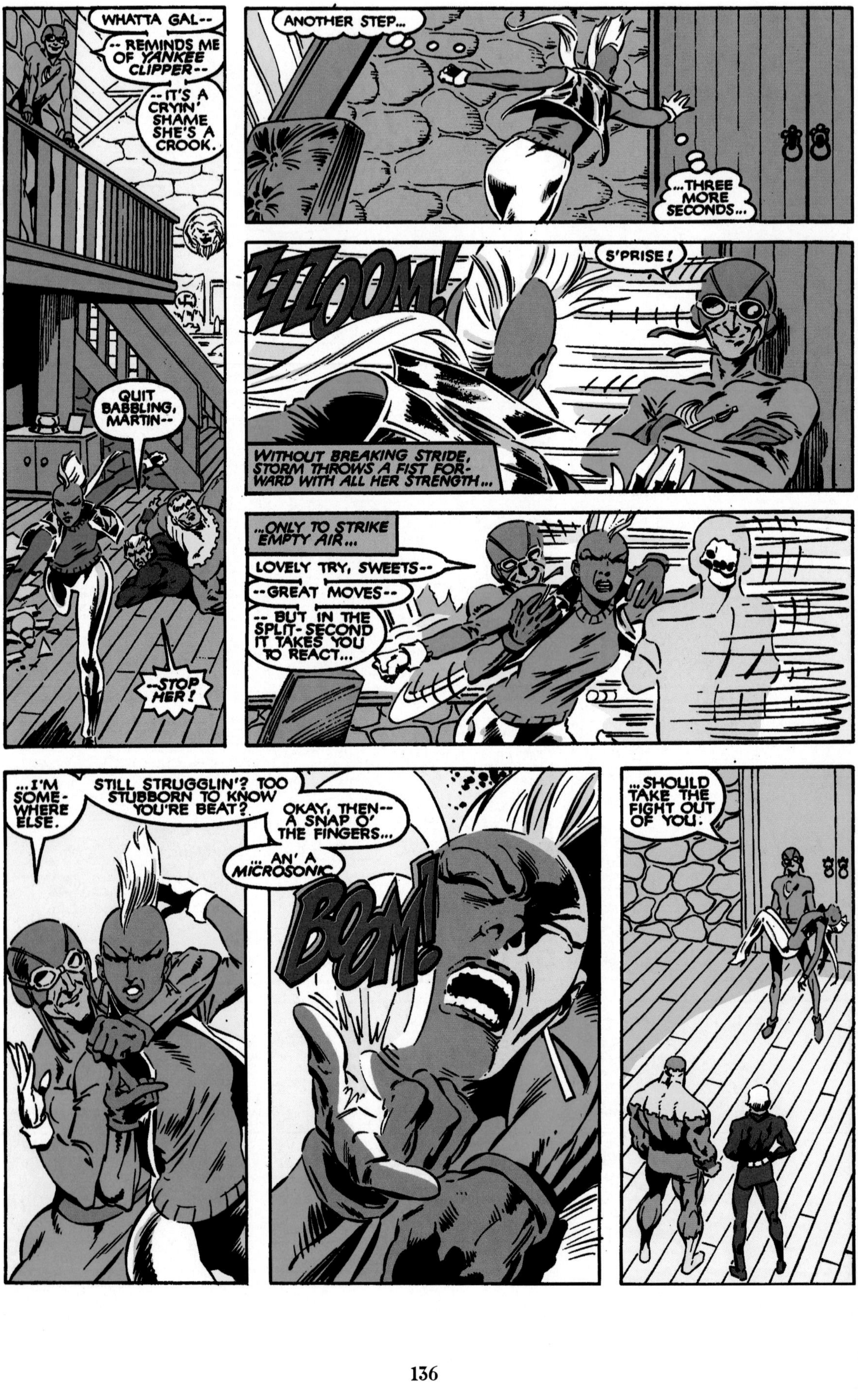

WHATTA GAL--
--REMINDS ME OF YANKEE CLIPPER--
--IT'S A CRYIN' SHAME SHE'S A CROOK.
QUIT BABBLING, MARTIN--
--STOP HER!
ANOTHER STEP...
...THREE MORE SECONDS...
ZZZOOM!
S'PRISE!
WITHOUT BREAKING STRIDE, STORM THROWS A FIST FORWARD WITH ALL HER STRENGTH...
...ONLY TO STRIKE EMPTY AIR...
LOVELY TRY, SWEETS--
--GREAT MOVES--
-- BUT IN THE SPLIT-SECOND IT TAKES YOU TO REACT...
...I'M SOMEWHERE ELSE.
STILL STRUGGLIN'? TOO STUBBORN TO KNOW YOU'RE BEAT?
OKAY, THEN-- A SNAP O' THE FINGERS...
...AN' A MICROSONIC
BOOM!
...SHOULD TAKE THE FIGHT OUT OF YOU.

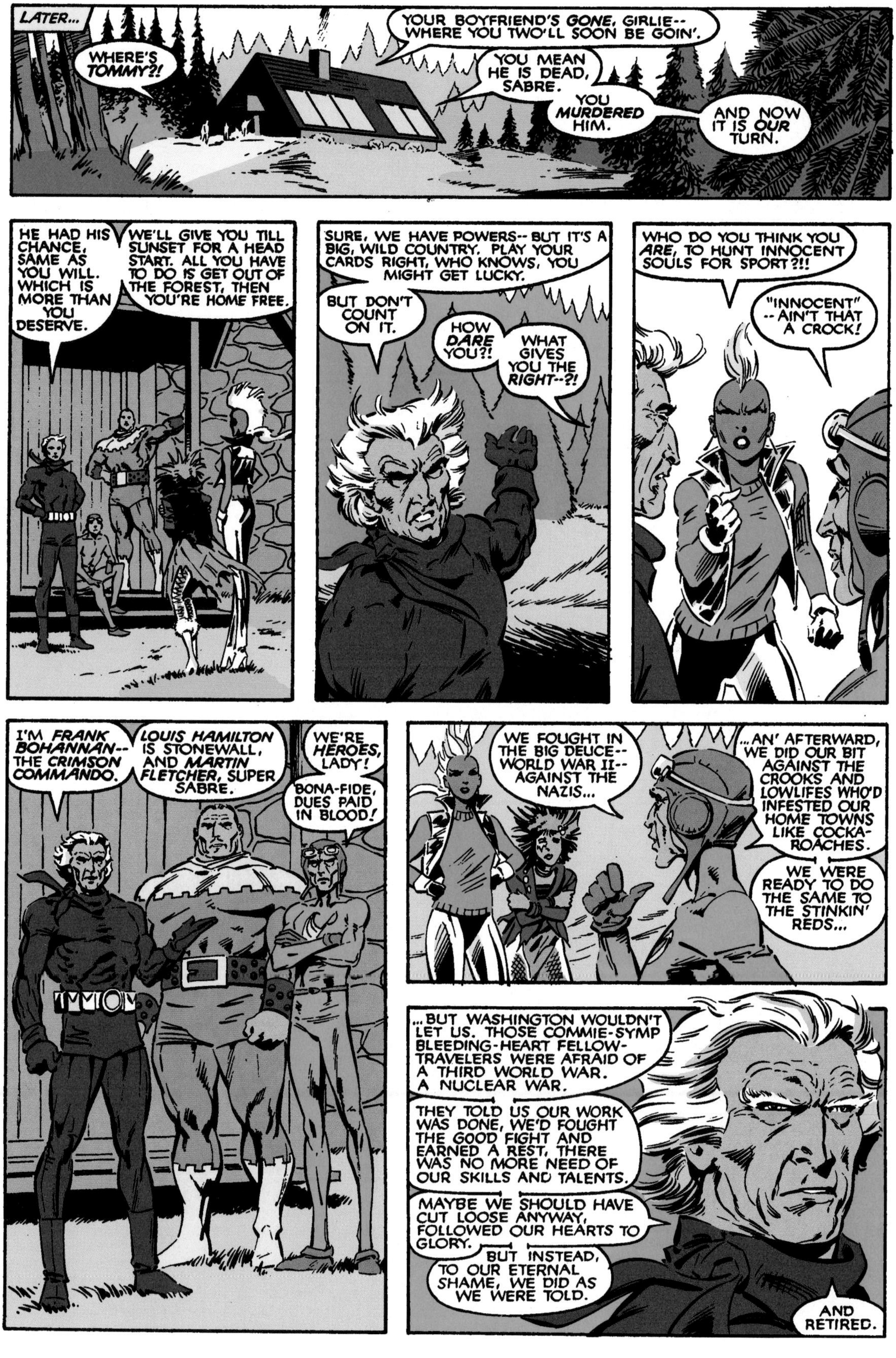
LATER...
WHERE'S TOMMY?!
YOUR BOYFRIEND'S GONE, GIRLIE-- WHERE YOU TWO'LL SOON BE GOIN'.
YOU MEAN HE IS DEAD, SABRE.
YOU MURDERED HIM.
AND NOW IT IS OUR TURN.
HE HAD HIS CHANCE, SAME AS YOU WILL. WHICH IS MORE THAN YOU DESERVE.
WE'LL GIVE YOU TILL SUNSET FOR A HEAD START. ALL YOU HAVE TO DO IS GET OUT OF THE FOREST, THEN YOU'RE HOME FREE.
SURE, WE HAVE POWERS-- BUT IT'S A BIG, WILD COUNTRY. PLAY YOUR CARDS RIGHT, WHO KNOWS, YOU MIGHT GET LUCKY.
BUT DON'T COUNT ON IT.
HOW DARE YOU?!
WHAT GIVES YOU THE RIGHT--?!
WHO DO YOU THINK YOU ARE, TO HUNT INNOCENT SOULS FOR SPORT?!!
"INNOCENT" --AIN'T THAT A CROCK!
I'M FRANK BOHANNAN-- THE CRIMSON COMMANDO.
LOUIS HAMILTON IS STONEWALL, AND MARTIN FLETCHER, SUPER SABRE.
WE'RE HEROES, LADY!
BONA-FIDE, DUES PAID IN BLOOD!
WE FOUGHT IN THE BIG DEUCE-- WORLD WAR II-- AGAINST THE NAZIS...
...AN' AFTERWARD, WE DID OUR BIT AGAINST THE CROOKS AND LOWLIFES WHO'D INFESTED OUR HOME TOWNS LIKE COCKA-ROACHES.
WE WERE READY TO DO THE SAME TO THE STINKIN' REDS...
...BUT WASHINGTON WOULDN'T LET US. THOSE COMMIE-SYMP BLEEDING-HEART FELLOW-TRAVELERS WERE AFRAID OF A THIRD WORLD WAR. A NUCLEAR WAR.
THEY TOLD US OUR WORK WAS DONE, WE'D FOUGHT THE GOOD FIGHT AND EARNED A REST. THERE WAS NO MORE NEED OF OUR SKILLS AND TALENTS.
MAYBE WE SHOULD HAVE CUT LOOSE ANYWAY, FOLLOWED OUR HEARTS TO GLORY.
BUT INSTEAD, TO OUR ETERNAL SHAME, WE DID AS WE WERE TOLD.
AND RETIRED.

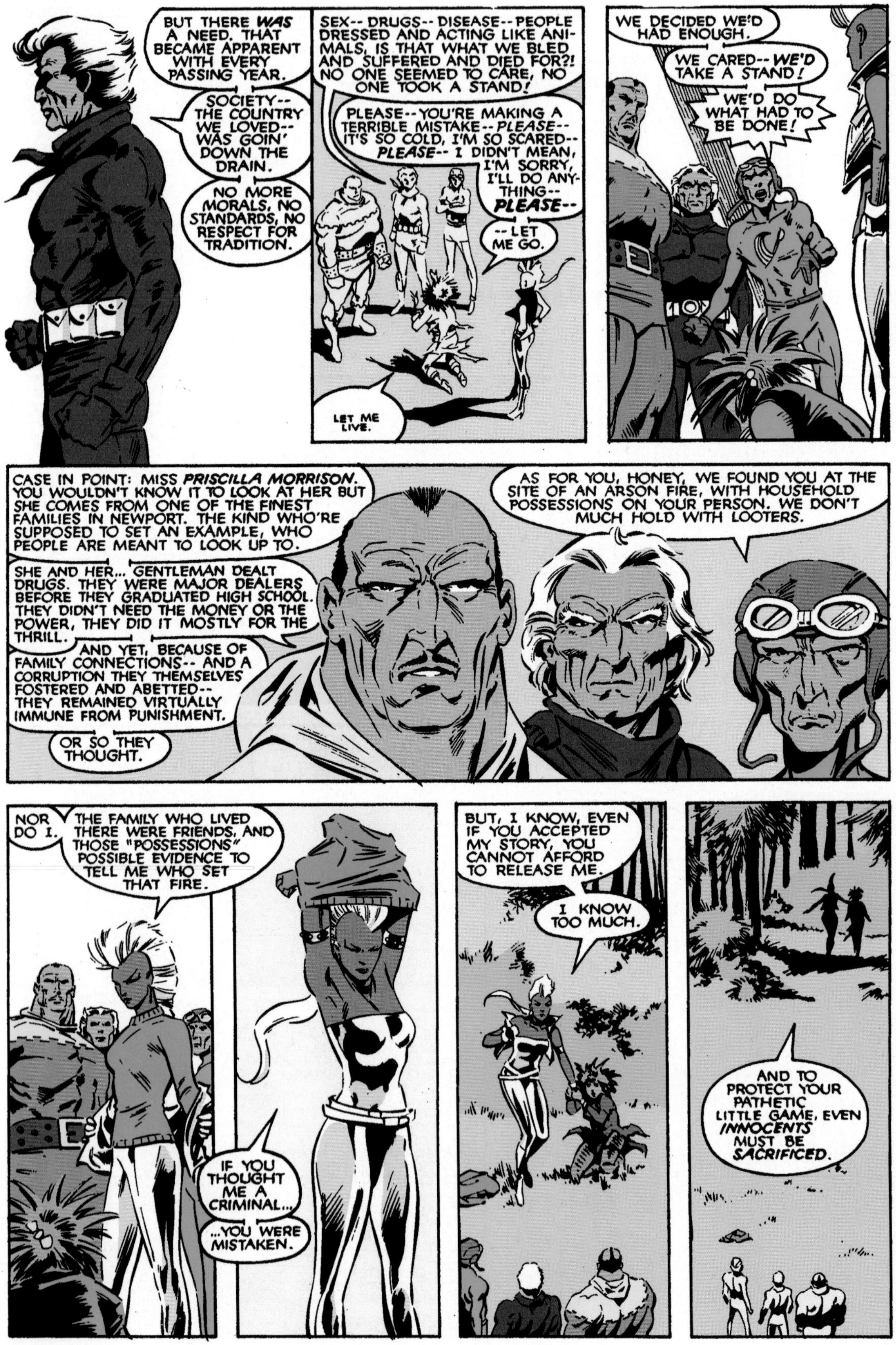
BUT THERE WAS A NEED. THAT BECAME APPARENT WITH EVERY PASSING YEAR.
SOCIETY-- THE COUNTRY WE LOVED-- WAS GOIN' DOWN THE DRAIN.
NO MORE MORALS, NO STANDARDS, NO RESPECT FOR TRADITION.
SEX-- DRUGS-- DISEASE-- PEOPLE DRESSED AND ACTING LIKE ANIMALS, IS THAT WHAT WE BLED AND SUFFERED AND DIED FOR?! NO ONE SEEMED TO CARE, NO ONE TOOK A STAND!
PLEASE-- YOU'RE MAKING A TERRIBLE MISTAKE-- PLEASE-- IT'S SO COLD, I'M SO SCARED-- PLEASE-- I DIDN'T MEAN, I'M SORRY, I'LL DO ANYTHING-- PLEASE--
--LET ME GO.
LET ME LIVE.
WE DECIDED WE'D HAD ENOUGH.
WE CARED-- WE'D TAKE A STAND!
WE'D DO WHAT HAD TO BE DONE!
CASE IN POINT: MISS PRISCILLA MORRISON. YOU WOULDN'T KNOW IT TO LOOK AT HER BUT SHE COMES FROM ONE OF THE FINEST FAMILIES IN NEWPORT. THE KIND WHO'RE SUPPOSED TO SET AN EXAMPLE, WHO PEOPLE ARE MEANT TO LOOK UP TO.
SHE AND HER... GENTLEMAN DEALT DRUGS. THEY WERE MAJOR DEALERS BEFORE THEY GRADUATED HIGH SCHOOL. THEY DIDN'T NEED THE MONEY OR THE POWER, THEY DID IT MOSTLY FOR THE THRILL.
AND YET, BECAUSE OF FAMILY CONNECTIONS-- AND A CORRUPTION THEY THEMSELVES FOSTERED AND ABETTED-- THEY REMAINED VIRTUALLY IMMUNE FROM PUNISHMENT.
OR SO THEY THOUGHT.
AS FOR YOU, HONEY, WE FOUND YOU AT THE SITE OF AN ARSON FIRE, WITH HOUSEHOLD POSSESSIONS ON YOUR PERSON. WE DON'T MUCH HOLD WITH LOOTERS.
NOR DO I.
THE FAMILY WHO LIVED THERE WERE FRIENDS, AND THOSE "POSSESSIONS" POSSIBLE EVIDENCE TO TELL ME WHO SET THAT FIRE.
IF YOU THOUGHT ME A CRIMINAL...
...YOU WERE MISTAKEN.
BUT, I KNOW, EVEN IF YOU ACCEPTED MY STORY, YOU CANNOT AFFORD TO RELEASE ME.
I KNOW TOO MUCH.
AND TO PROTECT YOUR PATHETIC LITTLE GAME, EVEN INNOCENTS MUST BE SACRIFICED.

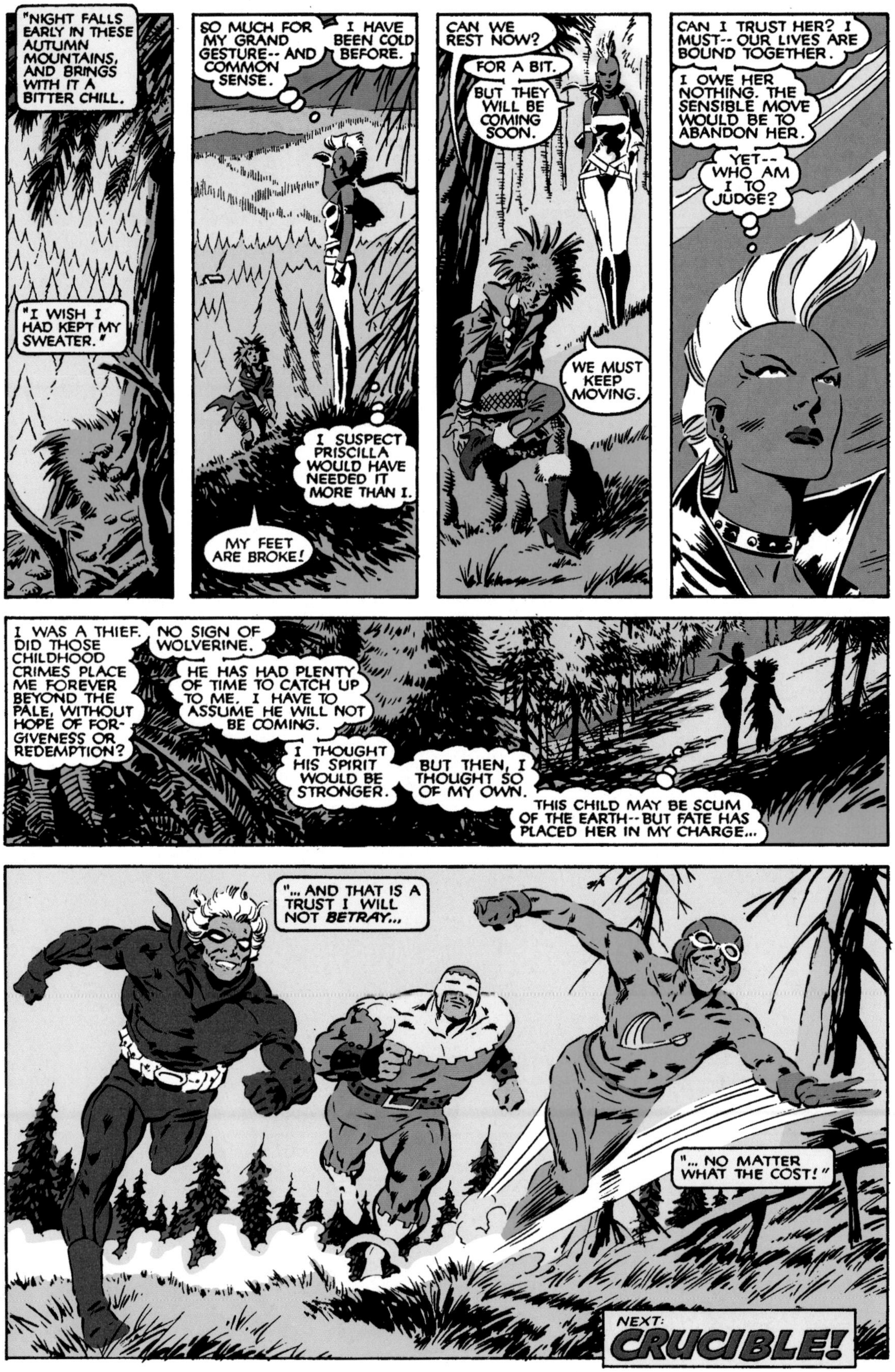
"NIGHT FALLS EARLY IN THESE AUTUMN MOUNTAINS, AND BRINGS WITH IT A BITTER CHILL.
"I WISH I HAD KEPT MY SWEATER."
SO MUCH FOR MY GRAND GESTURE-- AND COMMON SENSE.
I HAVE BEEN COLD BEFORE.
I SUSPECT PRISCILLA WOULD HAVE NEEDED IT MORE THAN I.
MY FEET ARE BROKE!
CAN WE REST NOW?
FOR A BIT.
BUT THEY WILL BE COMING SOON.
WE MUST KEEP MOVING.
CAN I TRUST HER? I MUST-- OUR LIVES ARE BOUND TOGETHER.
I OWE HER NOTHING. THE SENSIBLE MOVE WOULD BE TO ABANDON HER.
YET-- WHO AM I TO JUDGE?
I WAS A THIEF. DID THOSE CHILDHOOD CRIMES PLACE ME FOREVER BEYOND THE PALE, WITHOUT HOPE OF FORGIVENESS OR REDEMPTION?
NO SIGN OF WOLVERINE.
HE HAS HAD PLENTY OF TIME TO CATCH UP TO ME. I HAVE TO ASSUME HE WILL NOT BE COMING.
I THOUGHT HIS SPIRIT WOULD BE STRONGER.
BUT THEN, I THOUGHT SO OF MY OWN.
THIS CHILD MAY BE SCUM OF THE EARTH--BUT FATE HAS PLACED HER IN MY CHARGE...
"... AND THAT IS A TRUST I WILL NOT *BETRAY*...
"... NO MATTER WHAT THE COST!"
NEXT: CRUCIBLE!

X-Men Annual #11

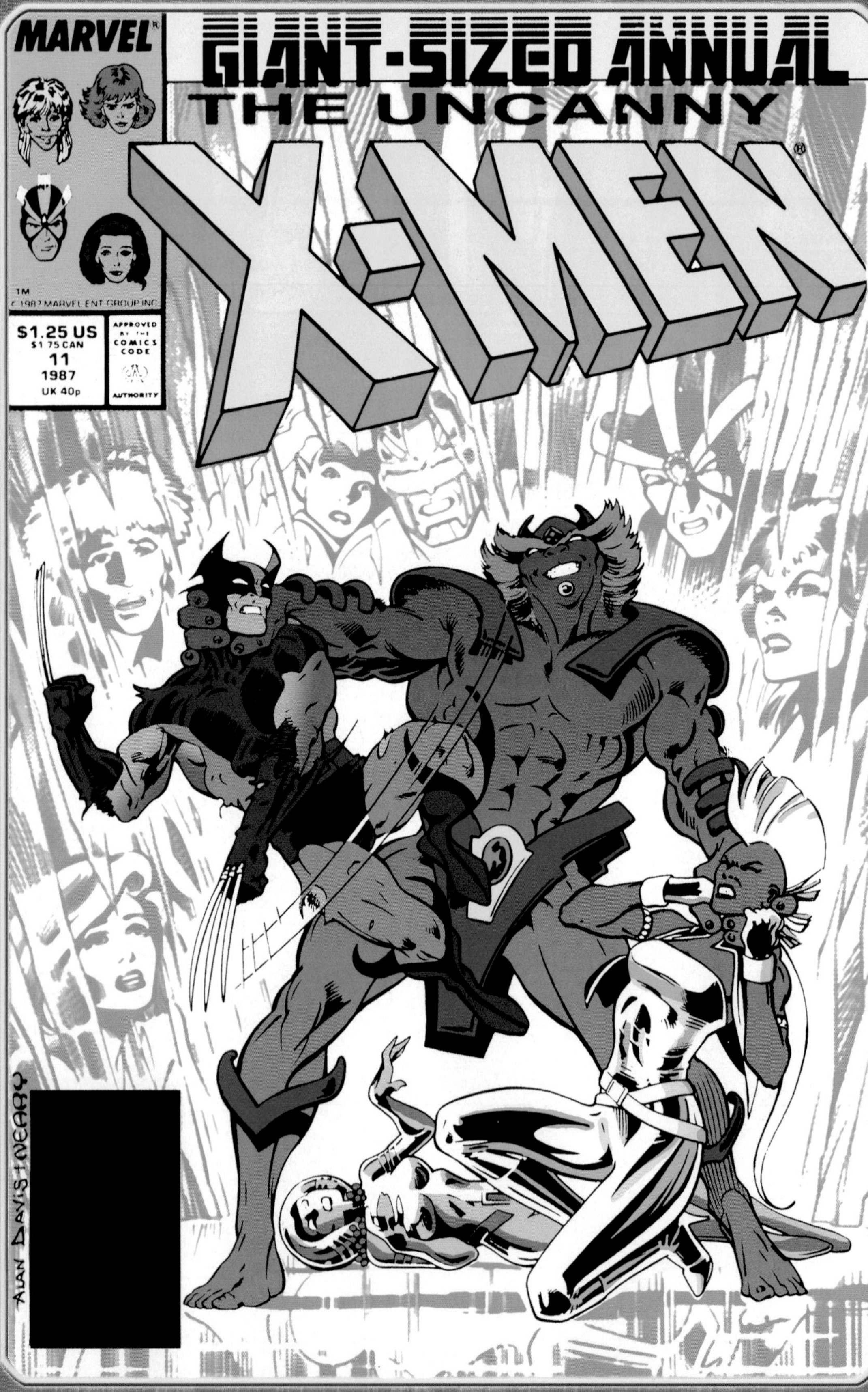
MARVEL
GIANT-SIZED ANNUAL
THE UNCANNY
X-MEN
TM
© 1987 MARVEL ENT GROUP INC
$1.25 US
$1.75 CAN
11
1987
UK 40p
APPROVED BY THE COMICS CODE AUTHORITY
ALAN DAVIS + NEARY

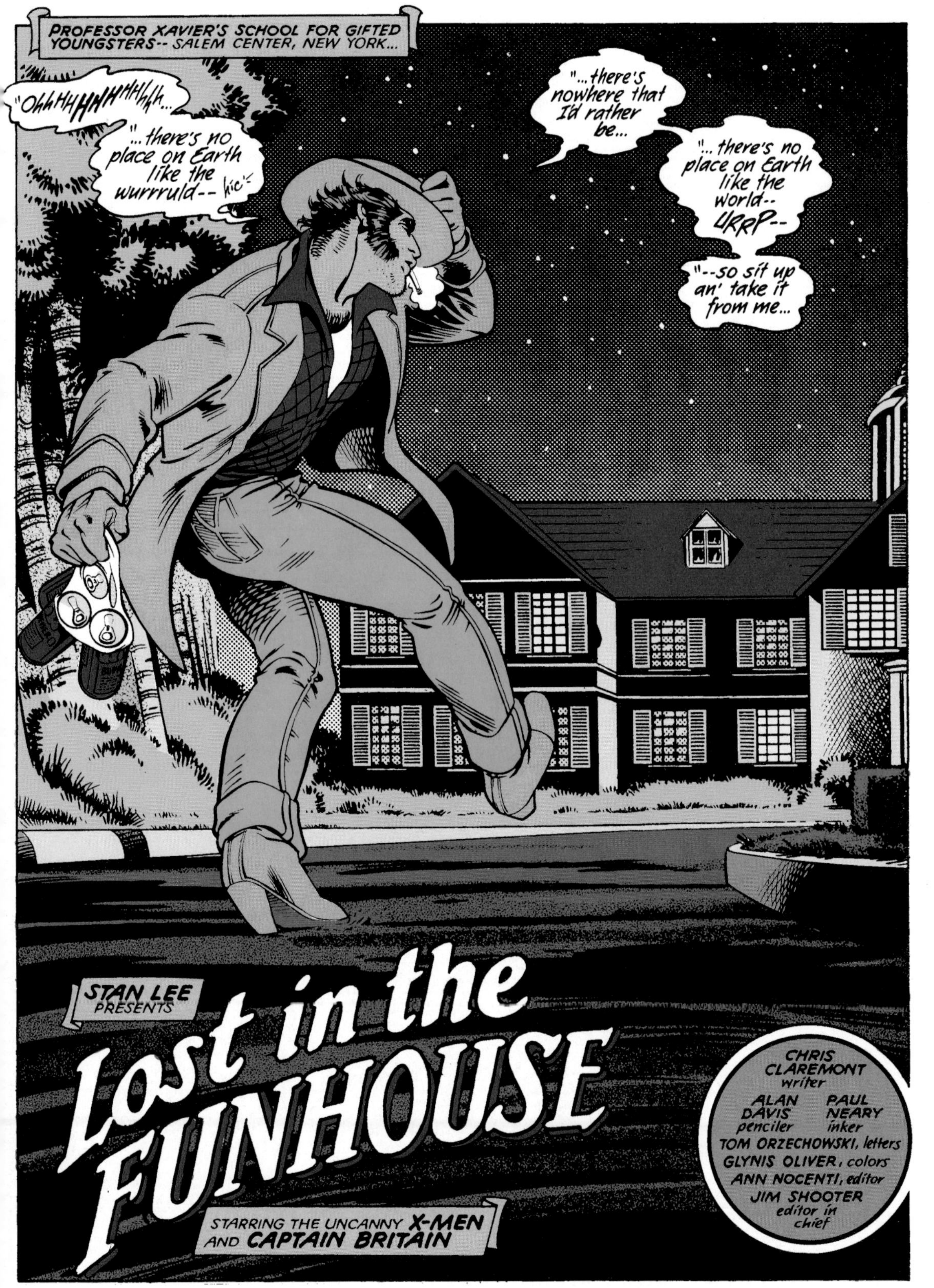
PROFESSOR XAVIER'S SCHOOL FOR GIFTED YOUNGSTERS-- SALEM CENTER, NEW YORK...
"OhhHHHHHHHhhhh...
"...there's no place on Earth like the wurrruld-- hic!-
"...there's nowhere that I'd rather be...
"...there's no place on Earth like the world-- URRP--
"--so sit up an' take it from me...
STAN LEE PRESENTS
Lost in the FUNHOUSE
STARRING THE UNCANNY X-MEN AND CAPTAIN BRITAIN
CHRIS CLAREMONT writer
ALAN DAVIS penciler
PAUL NEARY inker
TOM ORZECHOWSKI, letters
GLYNIS OLIVER, colors
ANN NOCENTI, editor
JIM SHOOTER editor in chief

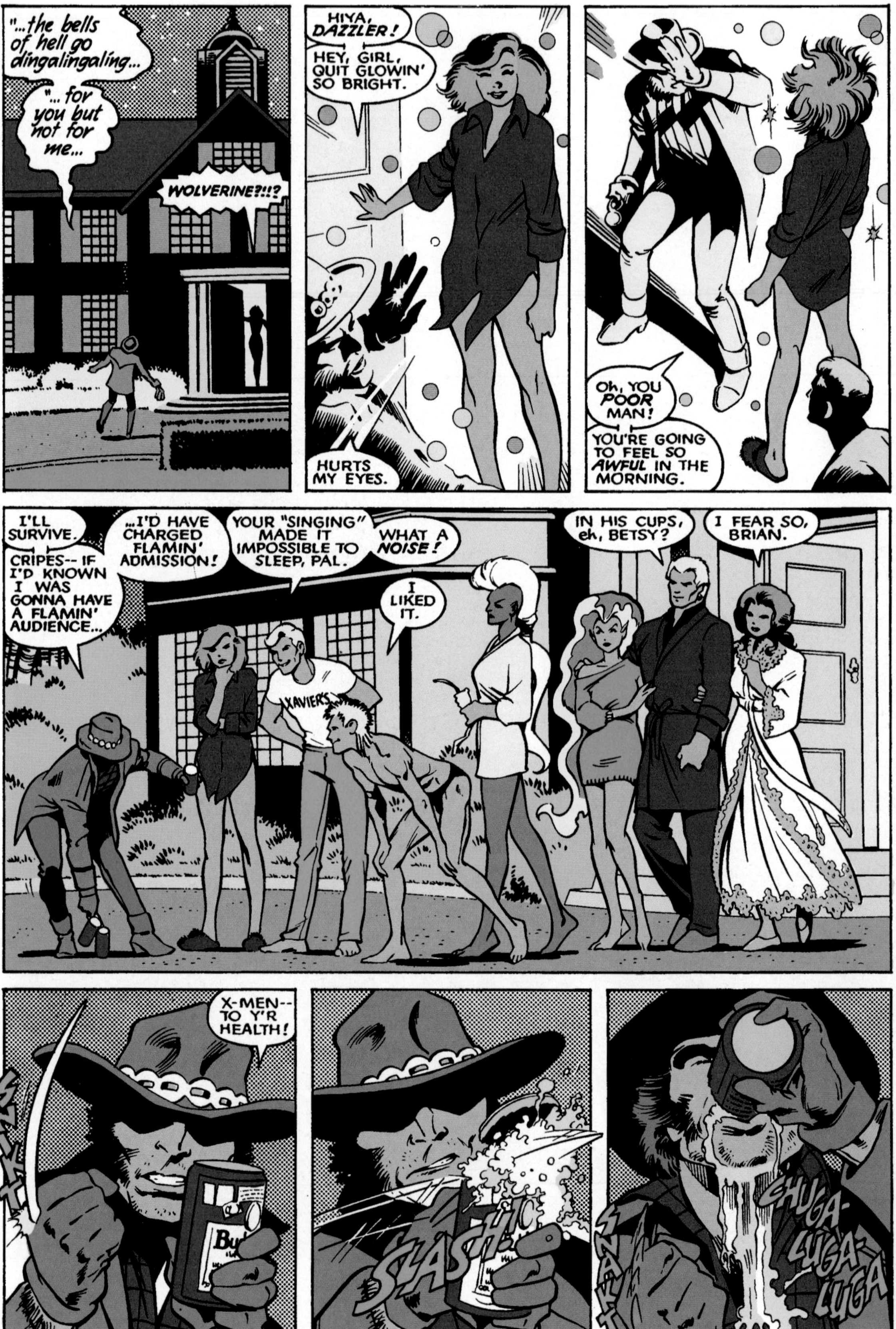
"...the bells of hell go dingalingaling...
"...for you but not for me...
WOLVERINE?!!?
HIYA, DAZZLER!
HEY, GIRL, QUIT GLOWIN' SO BRIGHT.
HURTS MY EYES.
Oh, YOU POOR MAN!
YOU'RE GOING TO FEEL SO AWFUL IN THE MORNING.
I'LL SURVIVE.
CRIPES-- IF I'D KNOWN I WAS GONNA HAVE A FLAMIN' AUDIENCE...
...I'D HAVE CHARGED FLAMIN' ADMISSION!
YOUR "SINGING" MADE IT IMPOSSIBLE TO SLEEP, PAL.
WHAT A NOISE!
I LIKED IT.
IN HIS CUPS, eh, BETSY?
I FEAR SO, BRIAN.
XAVIER'S
X-MEN-- TO Y'R HEALTH!
SNIKT
SLASH
SNIKT
CHUGA-LUGA-LUGA

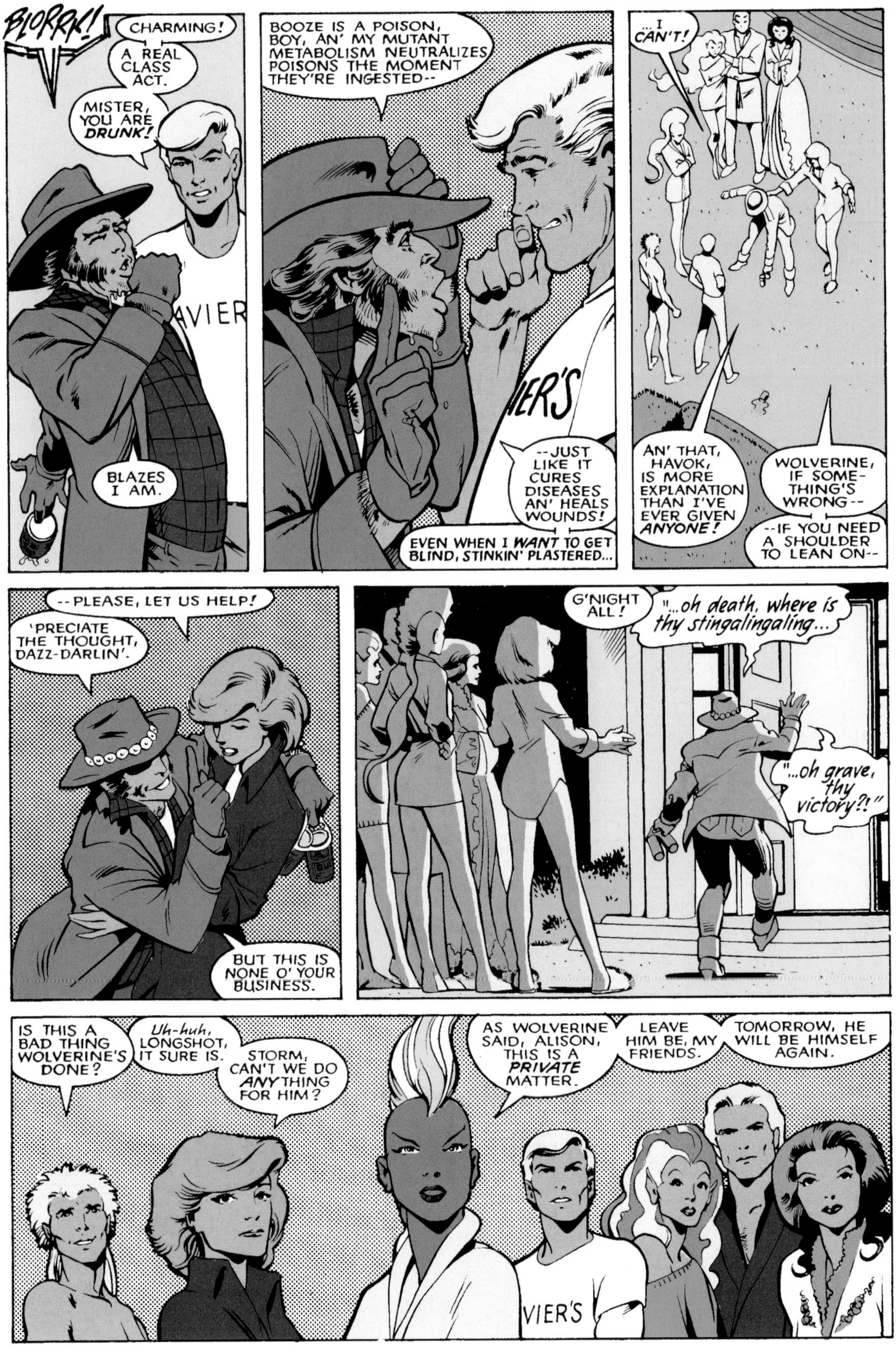
BLORRK!
CHARMING!
A REAL CLASS ACT.
MISTER, YOU ARE *DRUNK!*
BLAZES I AM.
AVIER
BOOZE IS A POISON, BOY, AN' MY MUTANT METABOLISM NEUTRALIZES POISONS THE MOMENT THEY'RE INGESTED--
--JUST LIKE IT CURES DISEASES AN' HEALS WOUNDS!
EVEN WHEN I *WANT* TO GET BLIND, STINKIN' PLASTERED...
IER'S
...I *CAN'T!*
AN' THAT, HAVOK, IS MORE EXPLANATION THAN I'VE EVER GIVEN *ANYONE!*
WOLVERINE, IF SOME-THING'S WRONG--
--IF YOU NEED A SHOULDER TO LEAN ON--
--PLEASE, LET US HELP!
'PRECIATE THE THOUGHT, DAZZ-DARLIN'.
BUT THIS IS NONE O' YOUR BUSINESS.
G'NIGHT ALL!
"...oh death, where is thy stingalingaling...
"...oh grave, thy victory?!"
IS THIS A BAD THING WOLVERINE'S DONE?
Uh-huh, LONGSHOT, IT SURE IS.
STORM, CAN'T WE DO *ANY*THING FOR HIM?
AS WOLVERINE SAID, ALISON, THIS IS A *PRIVATE* MATTER.
LEAVE HIM BE, MY FRIENDS.
TOMORROW, HE WILL BE HIMSELF AGAIN.
VIER'S

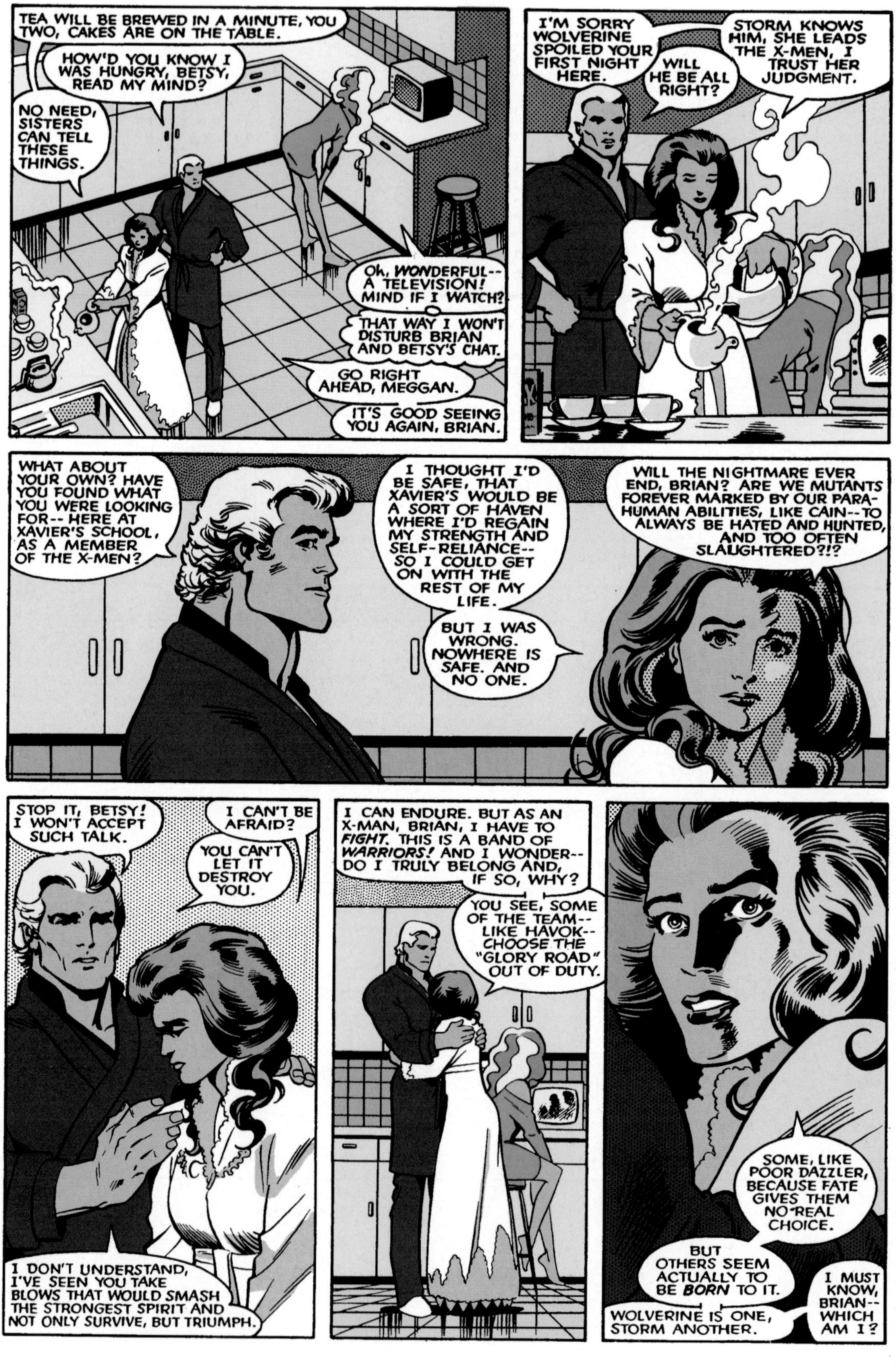

TEA WILL BE BREWED IN A MINUTE, YOU TWO, CAKES ARE ON THE TABLE.
HOW'D YOU KNOW I WAS HUNGRY, BETSY, READ MY MIND?
NO NEED, SISTERS CAN TELL THESE THINGS.
Oh, WONDERFUL-- A TELEVISION! MIND IF I WATCH?
THAT WAY I WON'T DISTURB BRIAN AND BETSY'S CHAT.
GO RIGHT AHEAD, MEGGAN.
IT'S GOOD SEEING YOU AGAIN, BRIAN.
I'M SORRY WOLVERINE SPOILED YOUR FIRST NIGHT HERE.
WILL HE BE ALL RIGHT?
STORM KNOWS HIM, SHE LEADS THE X-MEN, I TRUST HER JUDGMENT.
WHAT ABOUT YOUR OWN? HAVE YOU FOUND WHAT YOU WERE LOOKING FOR-- HERE AT XAVIER'S SCHOOL, AS A MEMBER OF THE X-MEN?
I THOUGHT I'D BE SAFE, THAT XAVIER'S WOULD BE A SORT OF HAVEN WHERE I'D REGAIN MY STRENGTH AND SELF-RELIANCE-- SO I COULD GET ON WITH THE REST OF MY LIFE.
BUT I WAS WRONG. NOWHERE IS SAFE. AND NO ONE.
WILL THE NIGHTMARE EVER END, BRIAN? ARE WE MUTANTS FOREVER MARKED BY OUR PARA-HUMAN ABILITIES, LIKE CAIN--TO ALWAYS BE HATED AND HUNTED, AND TOO OFTEN SLAUGHTERED?!?
STOP IT, BETSY! I WON'T ACCEPT SUCH TALK.
I CAN'T BE AFRAID?
YOU CAN'T LET IT DESTROY YOU.
I DON'T UNDERSTAND, I'VE SEEN YOU TAKE BLOWS THAT WOULD SMASH THE STRONGEST SPIRIT AND NOT ONLY SURVIVE, BUT TRIUMPH.
I CAN ENDURE. BUT AS AN X-MAN, BRIAN, I HAVE TO FIGHT. THIS IS A BAND OF WARRIORS! AND I WONDER-- DO I TRULY BELONG AND, IF SO, WHY?
YOU SEE, SOME OF THE TEAM-- LIKE HAVOK-- CHOOSE THE "GLORY ROAD" OUT OF DUTY.
SOME, LIKE POOR DAZZLER, BECAUSE FATE GIVES THEM NO REAL CHOICE.
BUT OTHERS SEEM ACTUALLY TO BE BORN TO IT.
WOLVERINE IS ONE, STORM ANOTHER.
I MUST KNOW, BRIAN-- WHICH AM I?

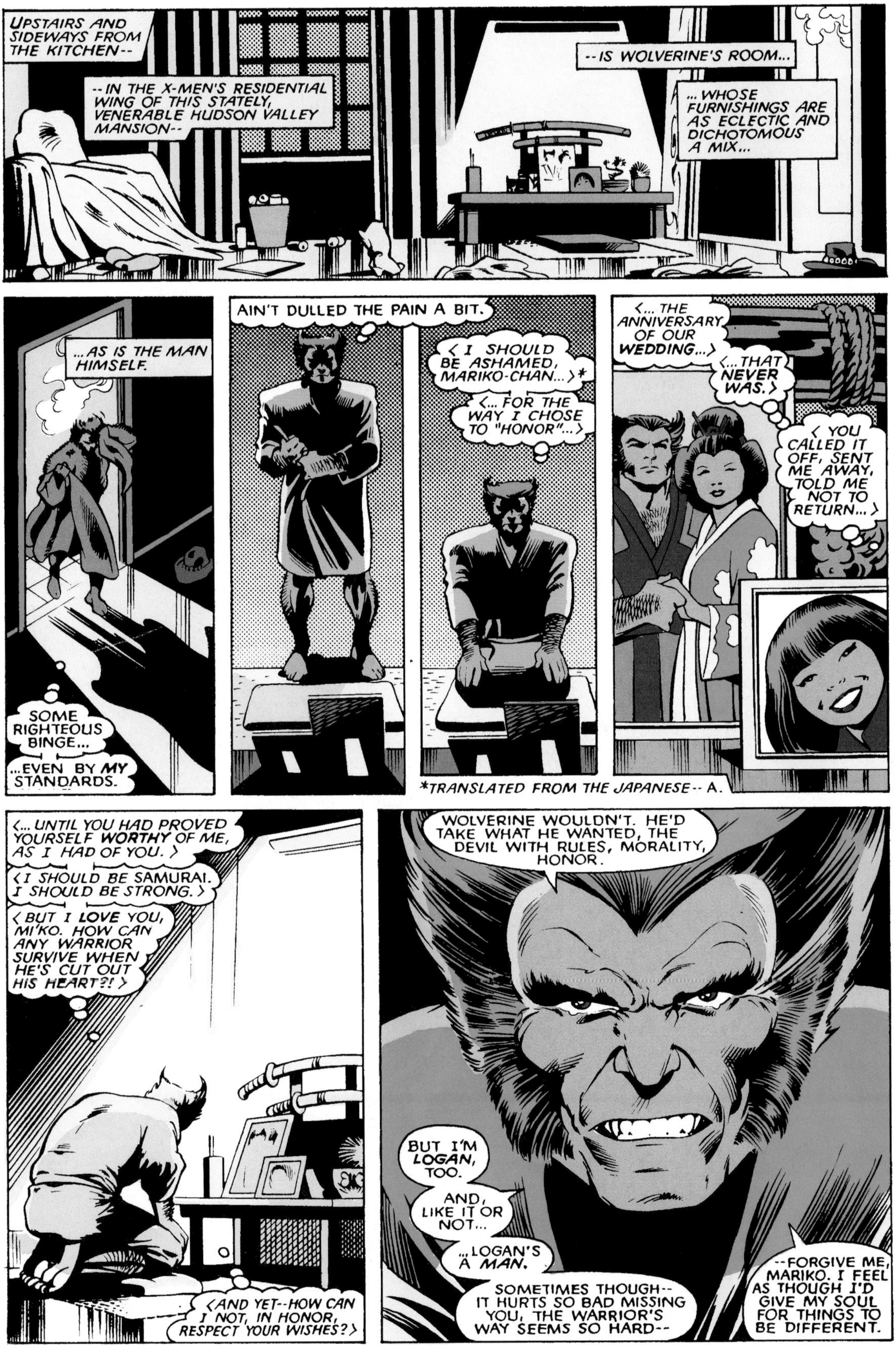
UPSTAIRS AND SIDEWAYS FROM THE KITCHEN--
--IN THE X-MEN'S RESIDENTIAL WING OF THIS STATELY, VENERABLE HUDSON VALLEY MANSION--
--IS WOLVERINE'S ROOM...
...WHOSE FURNISHINGS ARE AS ECLECTIC AND DICHOTOMOUS A MIX...
...AS IS THE MAN HIMSELF.
SOME RIGHTEOUS BINGE...
...EVEN BY MY STANDARDS.
AIN'T DULLED THE PAIN A BIT.
<I SHOULD BE ASHAMED, MARIKO-CHAN...>*
<...FOR THE WAY I CHOSE TO "HONOR"...>
<...THE ANNIVERSARY OF OUR WEDDING...>
<...THAT NEVER WAS.>
<YOU CALLED IT OFF, SENT ME AWAY, TOLD ME NOT TO RETURN...>
*TRANSLATED FROM THE JAPANESE-- A.
<...UNTIL YOU HAD PROVED YOURSELF WORTHY OF ME, AS I HAD OF YOU.>
<I SHOULD BE SAMURAI. I SHOULD BE STRONG.>
<BUT I LOVE YOU, MI'KO. HOW CAN ANY WARRIOR SURVIVE WHEN HE'S CUT OUT HIS HEART?!>
<AND YET--HOW CAN I NOT, IN HONOR, RESPECT YOUR WISHES?>
WOLVERINE WOULDN'T. HE'D TAKE WHAT HE WANTED, THE DEVIL WITH RULES, MORALITY, HONOR.
BUT I'M LOGAN, TOO.
AND, LIKE IT OR NOT...
...LOGAN'S A MAN.
SOMETIMES THOUGH-- IT HURTS SO BAD MISSING YOU, THE WARRIOR'S WAY SEEMS SO HARD--
--FORGIVE ME, MARIKO. I FEEL AS THOUGH I'D GIVE MY SOUL FOR THINGS TO BE DIFFERENT.

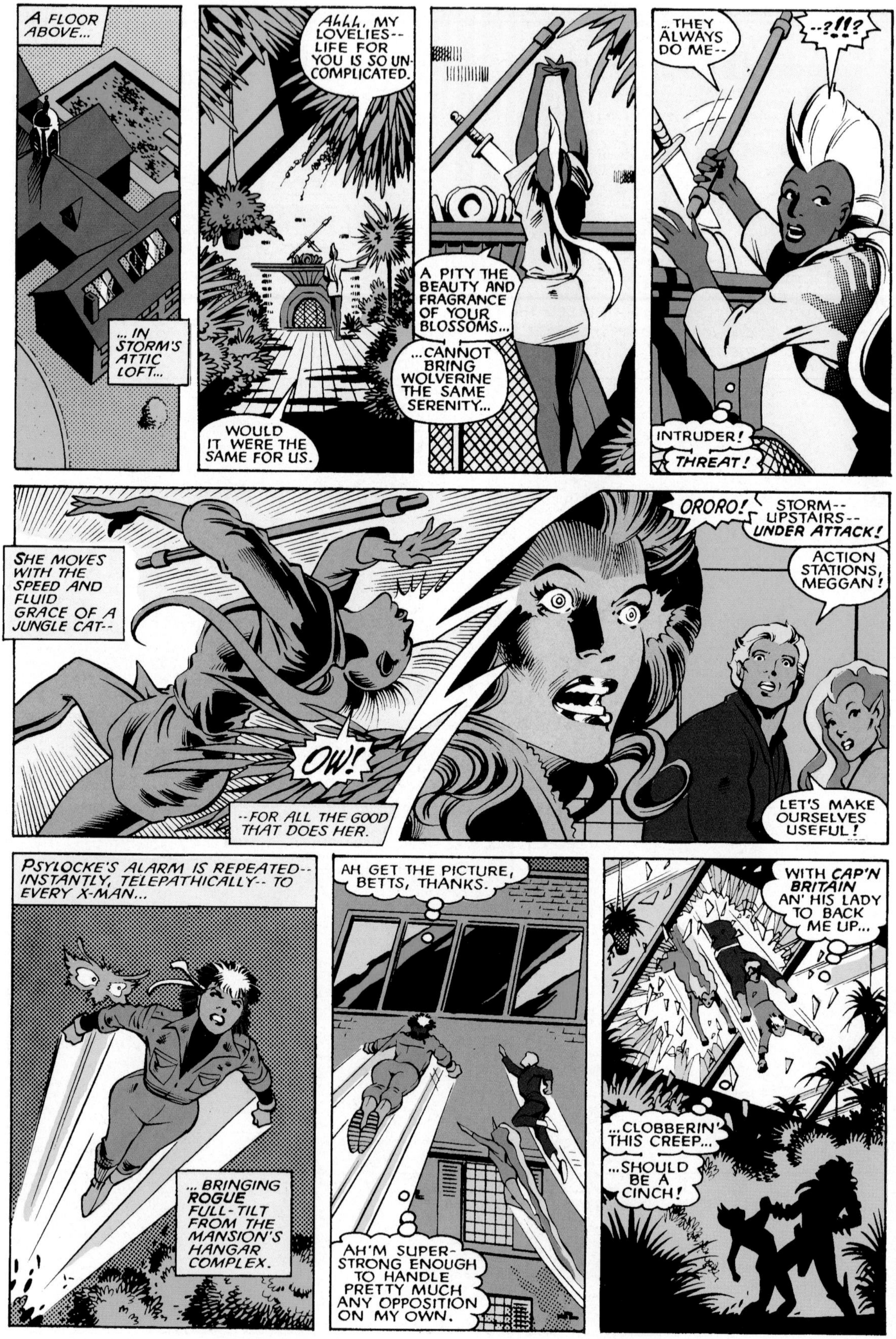
A FLOOR ABOVE...
...IN STORM'S ATTIC LOFT...
Ahhh, MY LOVELIES-- LIFE FOR YOU IS SO UNCOMPLICATED.
WOULD IT WERE THE SAME FOR US.
A PITY THE BEAUTY AND FRAGRANCE OF YOUR BLOSSOMS...
...CANNOT BRING WOLVERINE THE SAME SERENITY...
...THEY ALWAYS DO ME--
--?!!?
INTRUDER!
THREAT!
SHE MOVES WITH THE SPEED AND FLUID GRACE OF A JUNGLE CAT--
OW!
--FOR ALL THE GOOD THAT DOES HER.
ORORO!
STORM-- UPSTAIRS-- UNDER ATTACK!
ACTION STATIONS, MEGGAN!
LET'S MAKE OURSELVES USEFUL!
PSYLOCKE'S ALARM IS REPEATED-- INSTANTLY, TELEPATHICALLY-- TO EVERY X-MAN...
...BRINGING ROGUE FULL-TILT FROM THE MANSION'S HANGAR COMPLEX.
AH GET THE PICTURE, BETTS, THANKS.
AH'M SUPER-STRONG ENOUGH TO HANDLE PRETTY MUCH ANY OPPOSITION ON MY OWN.
WITH CAP'N BRITAIN AN' HIS LADY TO BACK ME UP...
...CLOBBERIN' THIS CREEP...
...SHOULD BE A CINCH!

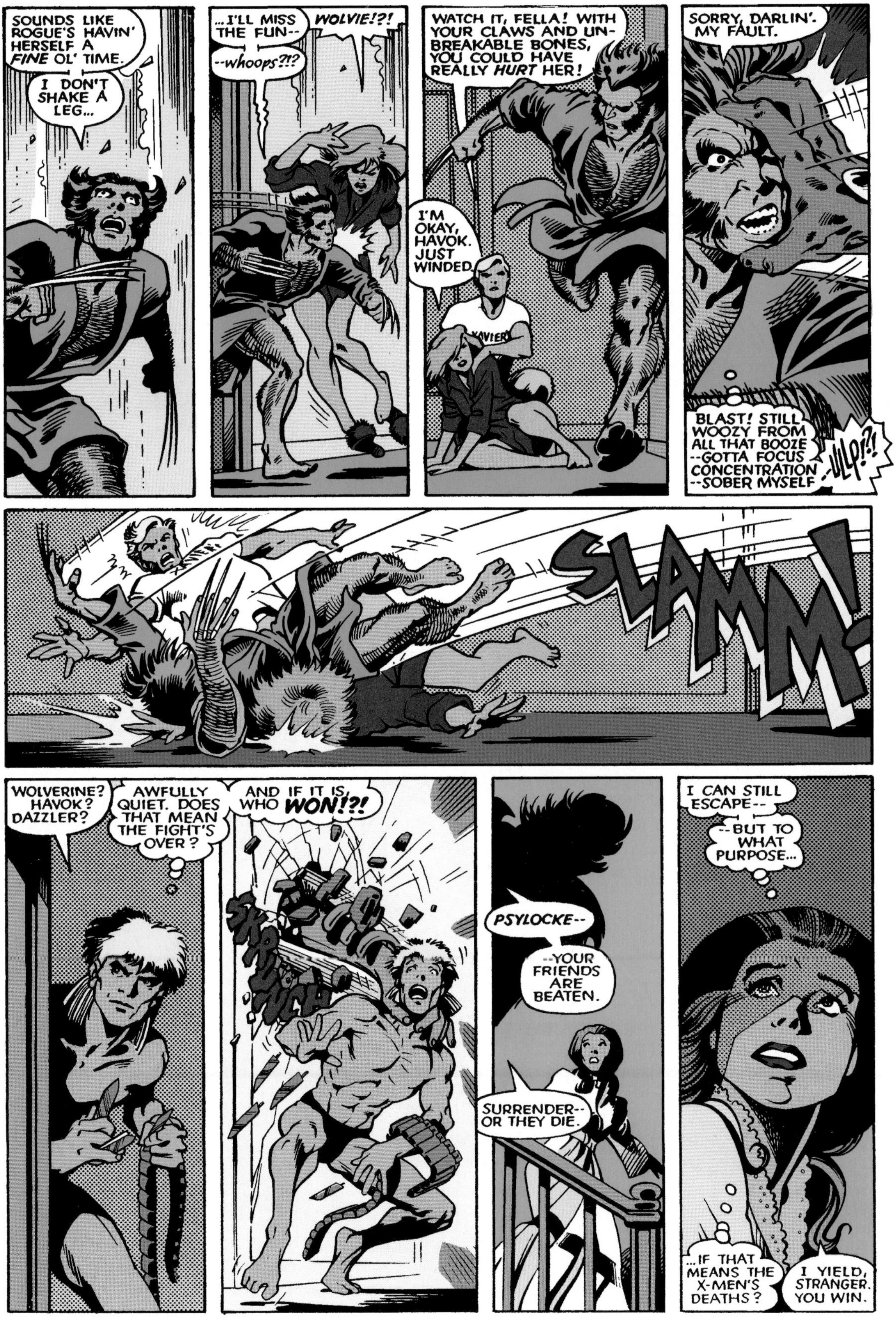
SOUNDS LIKE ROGUE'S HAVIN' HERSELF A FINE OL' TIME.
I DON'T SHAKE A LEG...
...I'LL MISS THE FUN--
WOLVIE!?!
--whoops?!?
WATCH IT, FELLA! WITH YOUR CLAWS AND UN-BREAKABLE BONES, YOU COULD HAVE REALLY HURT HER!
I'M OKAY, HAVOK. JUST WINDED.
XAVIER
SORRY, DARLIN'. MY FAULT.
BLAST! STILL WOOZY FROM ALL THAT BOOZE --GOTTA FOCUS CONCENTRATION --SOBER MYSELF
ULLP!?!
SLAMM!
WOLVERINE? HAVOK? DAZZLER?
AWFULLY QUIET. DOES THAT MEAN THE FIGHT'S OVER?
AND IF IT IS, WHO WON!?!
SKRUNCH
PSYLOCKE--
--YOUR FRIENDS ARE BEATEN.
SURRENDER--OR THEY DIE.
I CAN STILL ESCAPE--
--BUT TO WHAT PURPOSE...
...IF THAT MEANS THE X-MEN'S DEATHS?
I YIELD, STRANGER. YOU WIN.

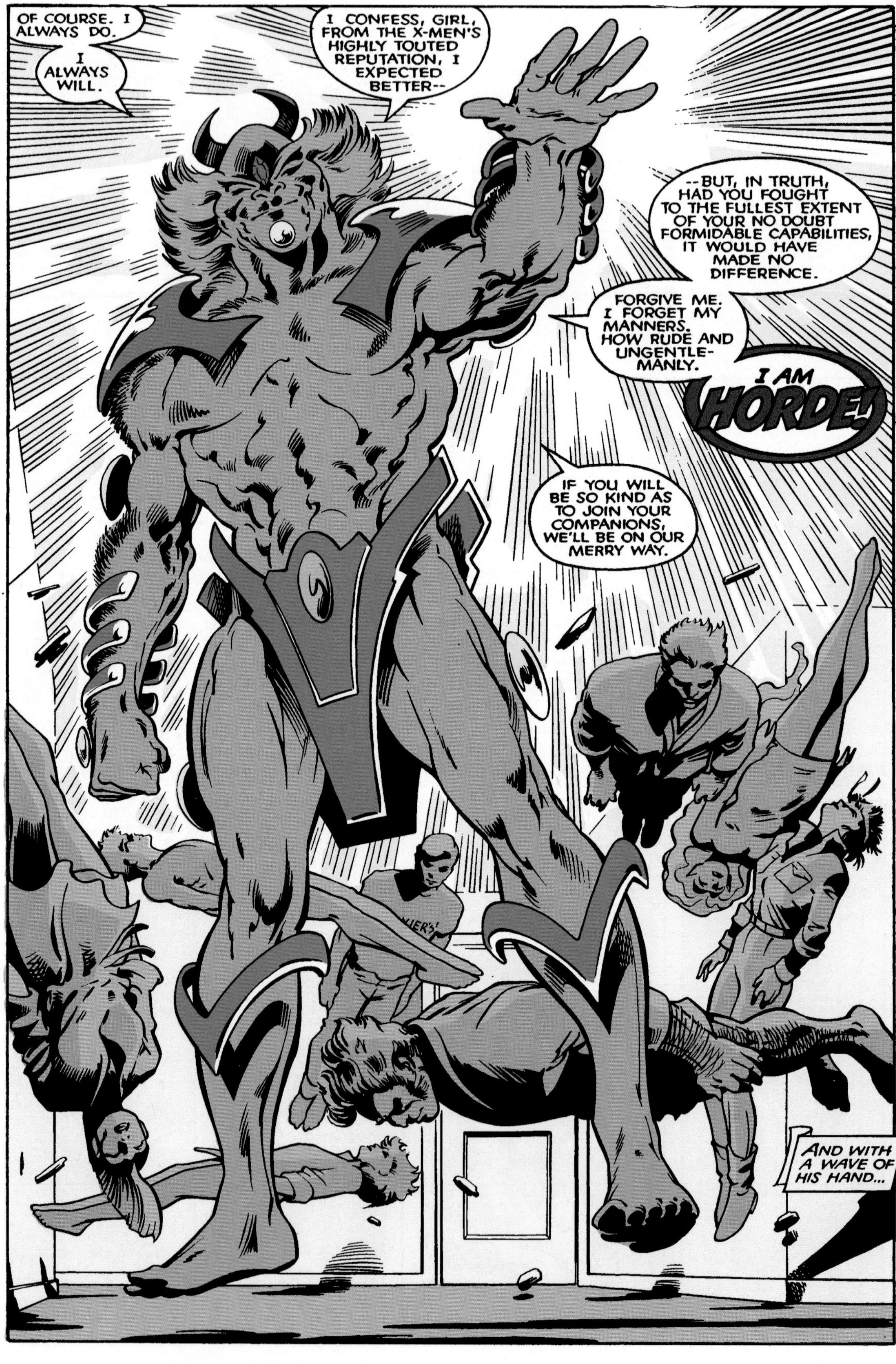

OF COURSE. I ALWAYS DO.
I ALWAYS WILL.
I CONFESS, GIRL, FROM THE X-MEN'S HIGHLY TOUTED REPUTATION, I EXPECTED BETTER--
--BUT, IN TRUTH, HAD YOU FOUGHT TO THE FULLEST EXTENT OF YOUR NO DOUBT FORMIDABLE CAPABILITIES, IT WOULD HAVE MADE NO DIFFERENCE.
FORGIVE ME. I FORGET MY MANNERS. HOW RUDE AND UNGENTLE-MANLY.
I AM HORDE!
IF YOU WILL BE SO KIND AS TO JOIN YOUR COMPANIONS, WE'LL BE ON OUR MERRY WAY.
AND WITH A WAVE OF HIS HAND...

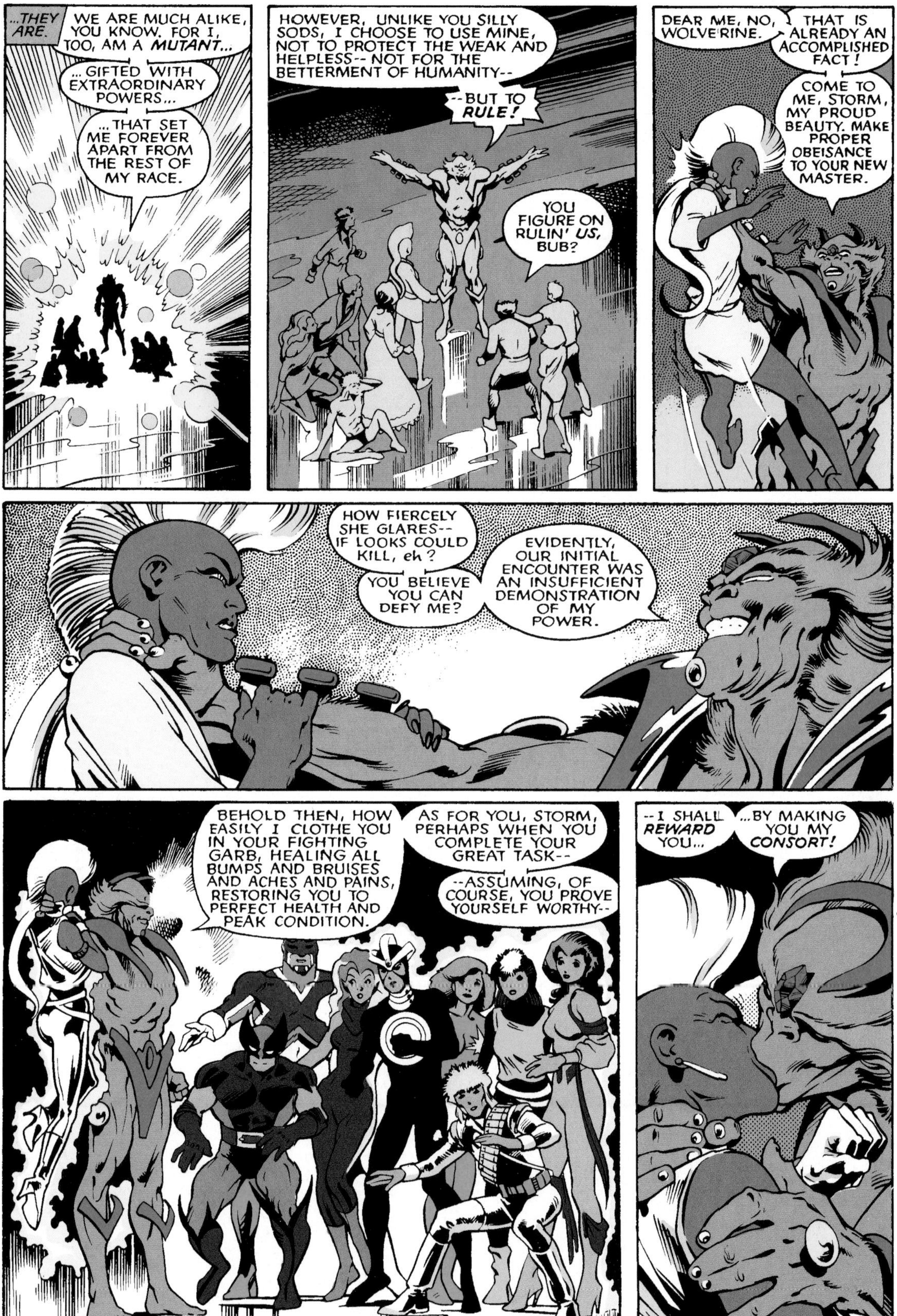
...THEY ARE.
WE ARE MUCH ALIKE, YOU KNOW. FOR I, TOO, AM A MUTANT...
...GIFTED WITH EXTRAORDINARY POWERS...
...THAT SET ME FOREVER APART FROM THE REST OF MY RACE.
HOWEVER, UNLIKE YOU SILLY SODS, I CHOOSE TO USE MINE, NOT TO PROTECT THE WEAK AND HELPLESS-- NOT FOR THE BETTERMENT OF HUMANITY--
--BUT TO RULE!
YOU FIGURE ON RULIN' US, BUB?
DEAR ME, NO, WOLVERINE.
THAT IS ALREADY AN ACCOMPLISHED FACT!
COME TO ME, STORM, MY PROUD BEAUTY. MAKE PROPER OBEISANCE TO YOUR NEW MASTER.
HOW FIERCELY SHE GLARES-- IF LOOKS COULD KILL, eh?
YOU BELIEVE YOU CAN DEFY ME?
EVIDENTLY, OUR INITIAL ENCOUNTER WAS AN INSUFFICIENT DEMONSTRATION OF MY POWER.
BEHOLD THEN, HOW EASILY I CLOTHE YOU IN YOUR FIGHTING GARB, HEALING ALL BUMPS AND BRUISES AND ACHES AND PAINS, RESTORING YOU TO PERFECT HEALTH AND PEAK CONDITION.
AS FOR YOU, STORM, PERHAPS WHEN YOU COMPLETE YOUR GREAT TASK--
--ASSUMING, OF COURSE, YOU PROVE YOURSELF WORTHY--
--I SHALL REWARD YOU...
...BY MAKING YOU MY CONSORT!

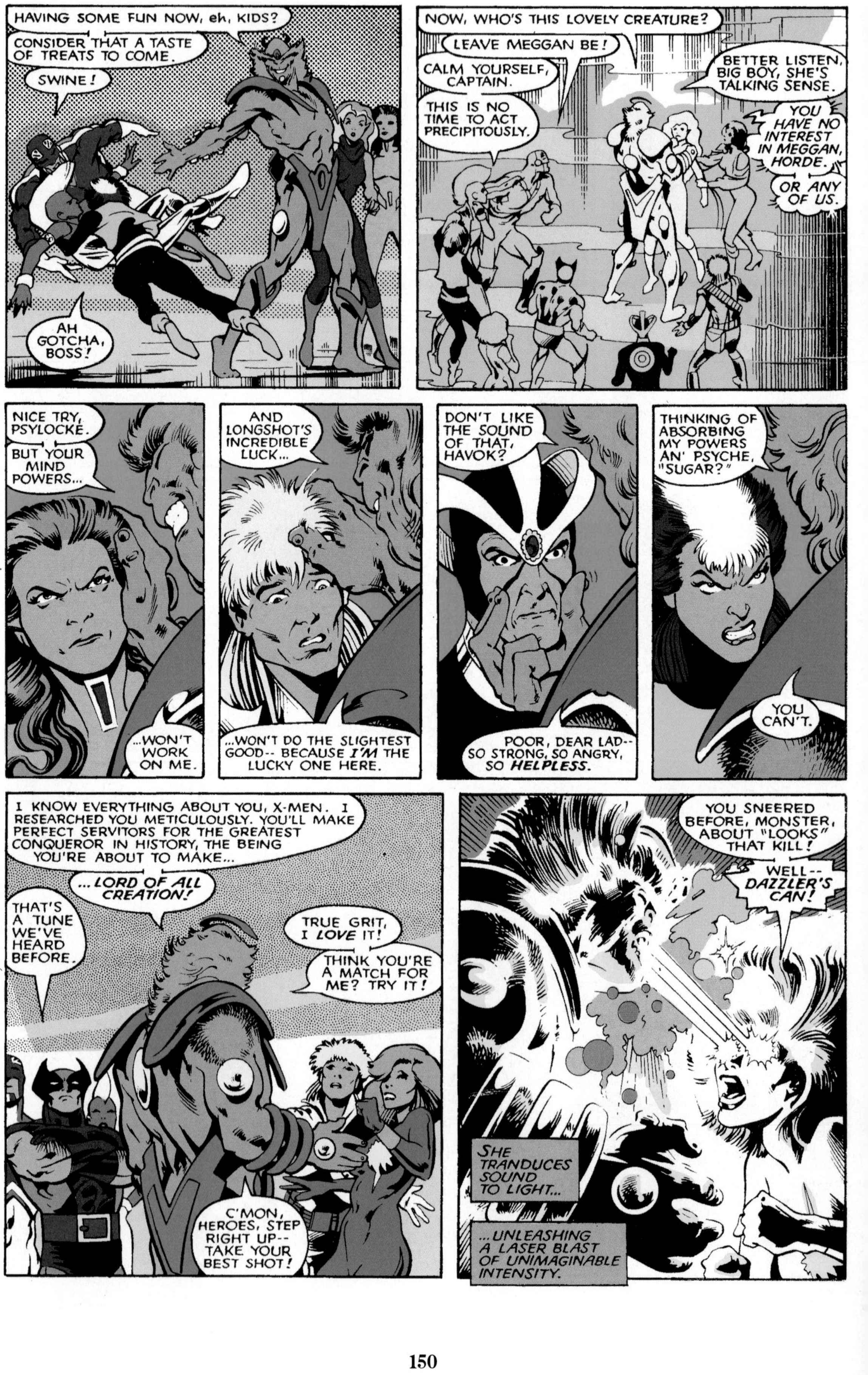

HAVING SOME FUN NOW, eh, KIDS?
CONSIDER THAT A TASTE OF TREATS TO COME.
SWINE!
AH GOTCHA, BOSS!
NOW, WHO'S THIS LOVELY CREATURE?
LEAVE MEGGAN BE!
CALM YOURSELF, CAPTAIN.
THIS IS NO TIME TO ACT PRECIPITOUSLY.
BETTER LISTEN, BIG BOY, SHE'S TALKING SENSE.
YOU HAVE NO INTEREST IN MEGGAN, HORDE.
OR ANY OF US.
NICE TRY, PSYLOCKE.
BUT YOUR MIND POWERS...
...WON'T WORK ON ME.
AND LONGSHOT'S INCREDIBLE LUCK...
...WON'T DO THE SLIGHTEST GOOD-- BECAUSE I'M THE LUCKY ONE HERE.
DON'T LIKE THE SOUND OF THAT, HAVOK?
POOR, DEAR LAD-- SO STRONG, SO ANGRY, SO HELPLESS.
THINKING OF ABSORBING MY POWERS AN' PSYCHE, "SUGAR?"
YOU CAN'T.
I KNOW EVERYTHING ABOUT YOU, X-MEN. I RESEARCHED YOU METICULOUSLY. YOU'LL MAKE PERFECT SERVITORS FOR THE GREATEST CONQUEROR IN HISTORY, THE BEING YOU'RE ABOUT TO MAKE...
...LORD OF ALL CREATION!
THAT'S A TUNE WE'VE HEARD BEFORE.
TRUE GRIT, I LOVE IT!
THINK YOU'RE A MATCH FOR ME? TRY IT!
C'MON, HEROES, STEP RIGHT UP-- TAKE YOUR BEST SHOT!
YOU SNEERED BEFORE, MONSTER, ABOUT "LOOKS" THAT KILL!
WELL-- DAZZLER'S CAN!
SHE TRANDUCES SOUND TO LIGHT...
...UNLEASHING A LASER BLAST OF UNIMAGINABLE INTENSITY.

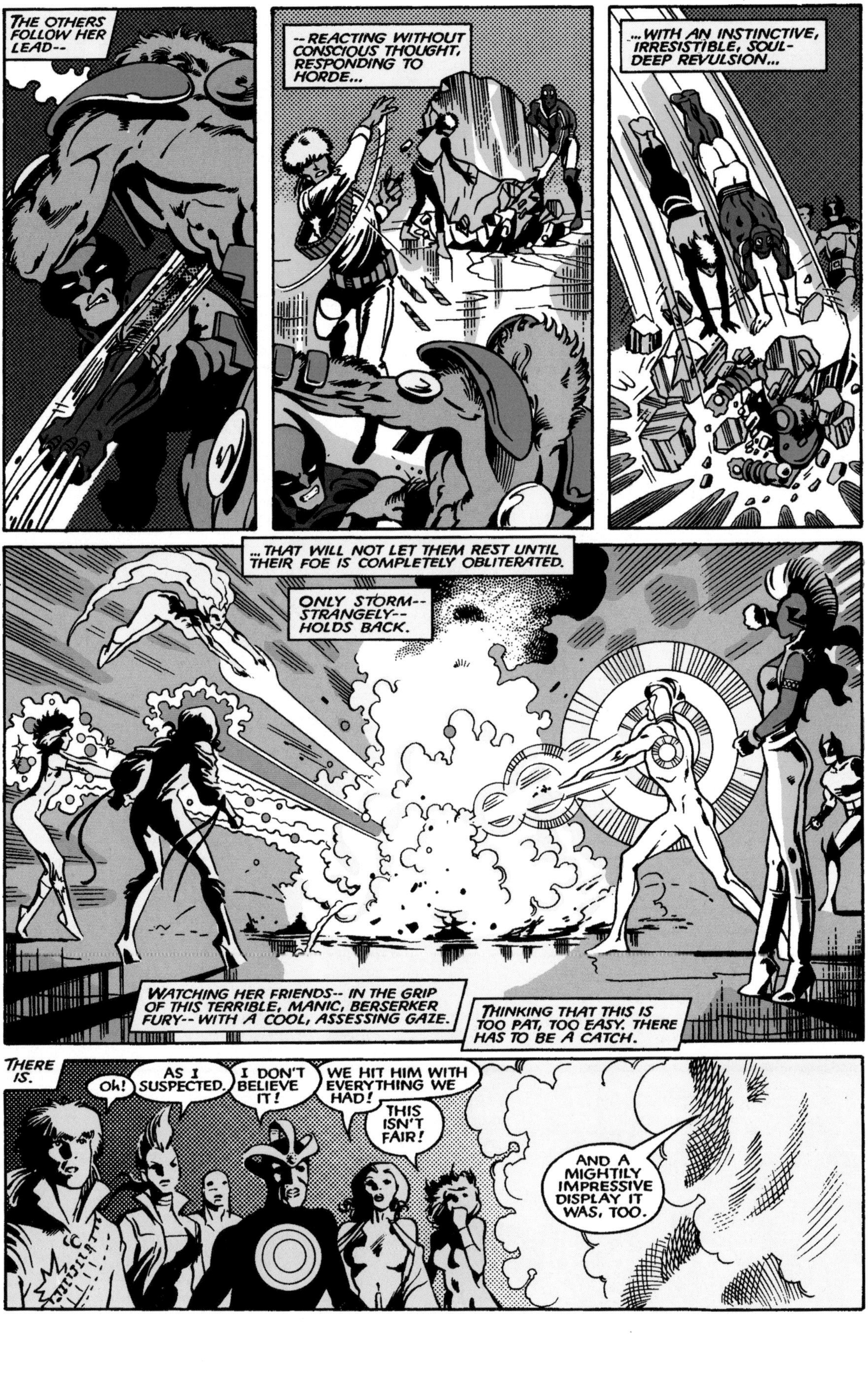
THE OTHERS FOLLOW HER LEAD--
--REACTING WITHOUT CONSCIOUS THOUGHT, RESPONDING TO HORDE...
...WITH AN INSTINCTIVE, IRRESISTIBLE, SOUL-DEEP REVULSION...
...THAT WILL NOT LET THEM REST UNTIL THEIR FOE IS COMPLETELY OBLITERATED.
ONLY STORM--STRANGELY--HOLDS BACK.
WATCHING HER FRIENDS-- IN THE GRIP OF THIS TERRIBLE, MANIC, BERSERKER FURY-- WITH A COOL, ASSESSING GAZE.
THINKING THAT THIS IS TOO PAT, TOO EASY. THERE HAS TO BE A CATCH.
THERE IS.
Oh!
AS I SUSPECTED.
I DON'T BELIEVE IT!
WE HIT HIM WITH EVERYTHING WE HAD!
THIS ISN'T FAIR!
AND A MIGHTILY IMPRESSIVE DISPLAY IT WAS, TOO.

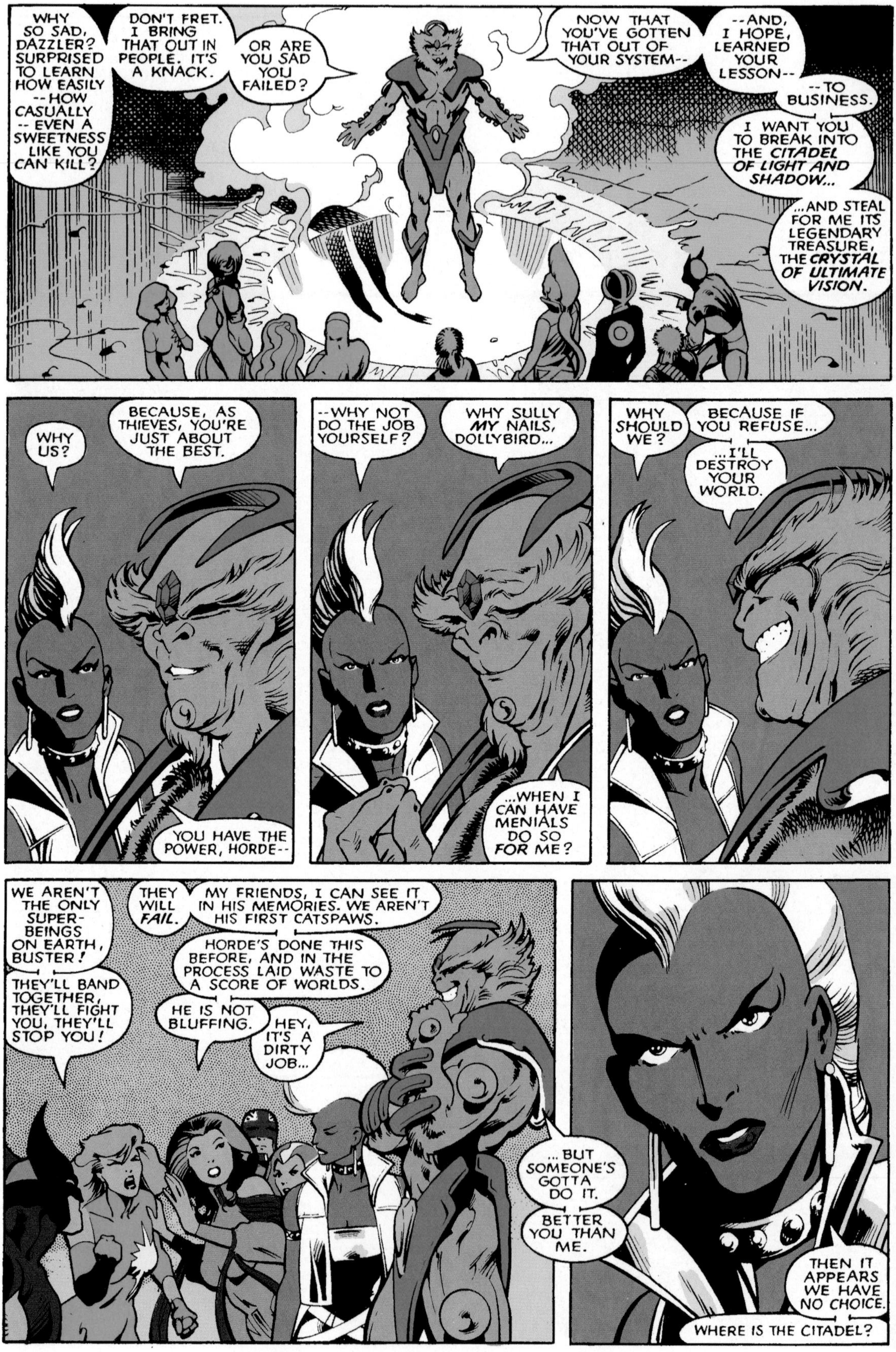

WHY SO SAD, DAZZLER? SURPRISED TO LEARN HOW EASILY --HOW CASUALLY -- EVEN A SWEETNESS LIKE YOU CAN KILL?
DON'T FRET. I BRING THAT OUT IN PEOPLE. IT'S A KNACK.
OR ARE YOU SAD YOU FAILED?
NOW THAT YOU'VE GOTTEN THAT OUT OF YOUR SYSTEM--
--AND, I HOPE, LEARNED YOUR LESSON--
--TO BUSINESS.
I WANT YOU TO BREAK INTO THE CITADEL OF LIGHT AND SHADOW...
...AND STEAL FOR ME ITS LEGENDARY TREASURE, THE CRYSTAL OF ULTIMATE VISION.
WHY US?
BECAUSE, AS THIEVES, YOU'RE JUST ABOUT THE BEST.
YOU HAVE THE POWER, HORDE--
--WHY NOT DO THE JOB YOURSELF?
WHY SULLY MY NAILS, DOLLYBIRD...
...WHEN I CAN HAVE MENIALS DO SO FOR ME?
WHY SHOULD WE?
BECAUSE IF YOU REFUSE...
...I'LL DESTROY YOUR WORLD.
WE AREN'T THE ONLY SUPER-BEINGS ON EARTH, BUSTER!
THEY'LL BAND TOGETHER, THEY'LL FIGHT YOU, THEY'LL STOP YOU!
THEY WILL FAIL.
MY FRIENDS, I CAN SEE IT IN HIS MEMORIES. WE AREN'T HIS FIRST CATSPAWS.
HORDE'S DONE THIS BEFORE, AND IN THE PROCESS LAID WASTE TO A SCORE OF WORLDS.
HE IS NOT BLUFFING.
HEY, IT'S A DIRTY JOB...
...BUT SOMEONE'S GOTTA DO IT.
BETTER YOU THAN ME.
THEN IT APPEARS WE HAVE NO CHOICE.
WHERE IS THE CITADEL?

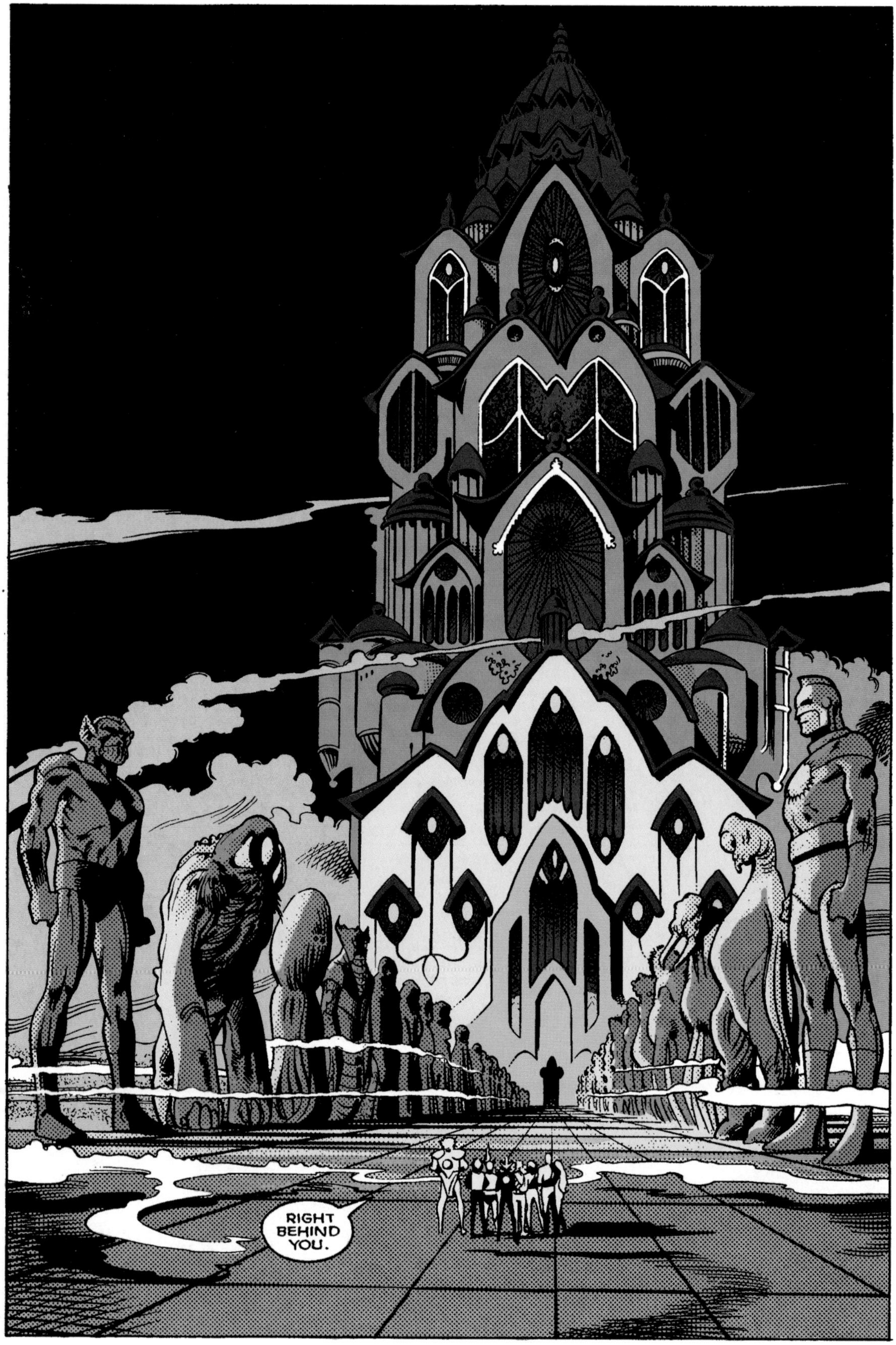
RIGHT BEHIND YOU.

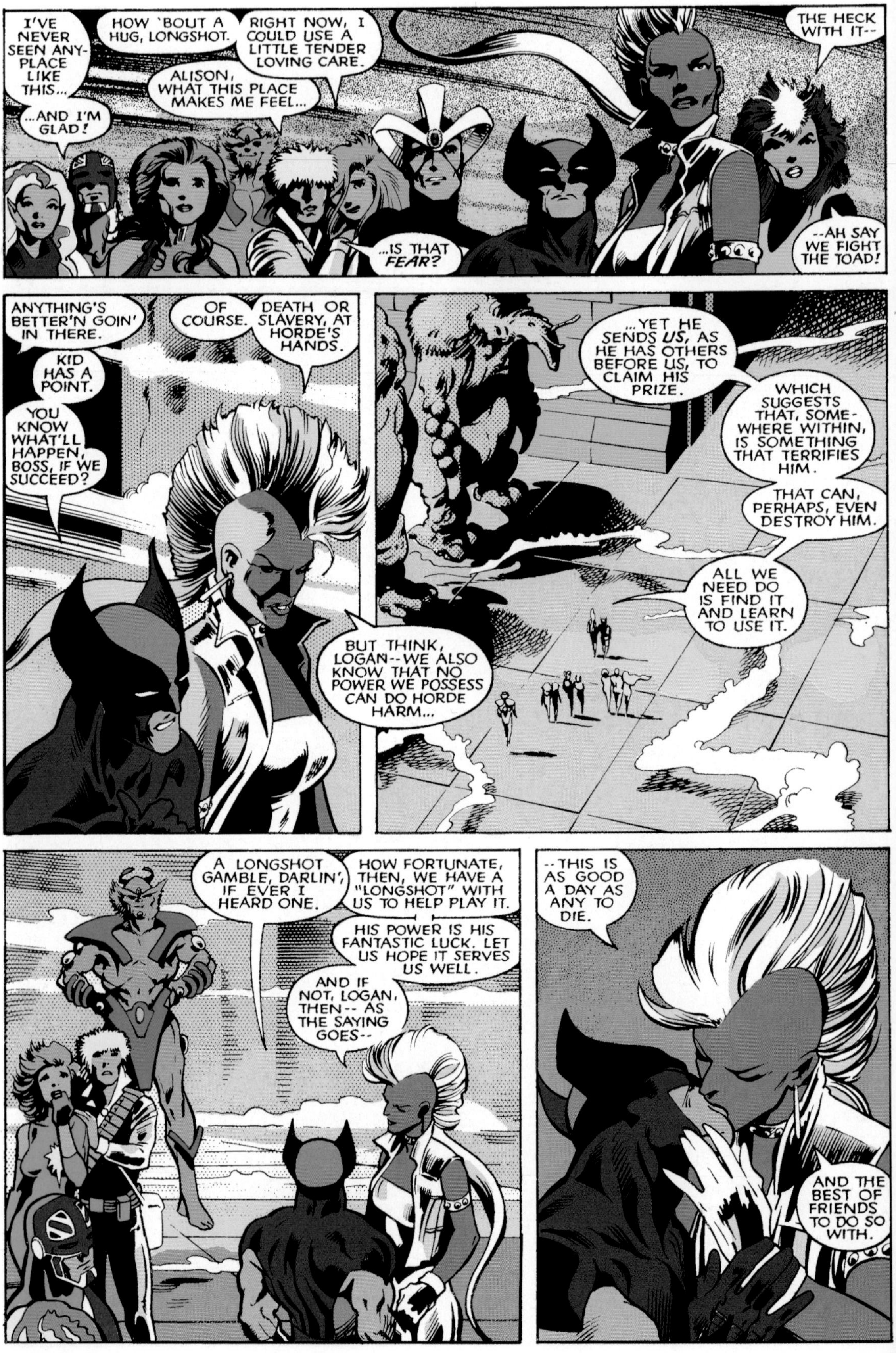
I'VE NEVER SEEN ANY-PLACE LIKE THIS...
...AND I'M GLAD!
HOW 'BOUT A HUG, LONGSHOT.
ALISON, WHAT THIS PLACE MAKES ME FEEL...
RIGHT NOW, I COULD USE A LITTLE TENDER LOVING CARE.
...IS THAT FEAR?
THE HECK WITH IT--
--AH SAY WE FIGHT THE TOAD!
ANYTHING'S BETTER'N GOIN' IN THERE.
KID HAS A POINT.
YOU KNOW WHAT'LL HAPPEN, BOSS, IF WE SUCCEED?
OF COURSE.
DEATH OR SLAVERY, AT HORDE'S HANDS.
BUT THINK, LOGAN--WE ALSO KNOW THAT NO POWER WE POSSESS CAN DO HORDE HARM...
...YET HE SENDS US, AS HE HAS OTHERS BEFORE US, TO CLAIM HIS PRIZE.
WHICH SUGGESTS THAT, SOME-WHERE WITHIN, IS SOMETHING THAT TERRIFIES HIM.
THAT CAN, PERHAPS, EVEN DESTROY HIM.
ALL WE NEED DO IS FIND IT AND LEARN TO USE IT.
A LONGSHOT GAMBLE, DARLIN', IF EVER I HEARD ONE.
HOW FORTUNATE, THEN, WE HAVE A "LONGSHOT" WITH US TO HELP PLAY IT.
HIS POWER IS HIS FANTASTIC LUCK. LET US HOPE IT SERVES US WELL.
AND IF NOT, LOGAN, THEN-- AS THE SAYING GOES--
--THIS IS AS GOOD A DAY AS ANY TO DIE.
AND THE BEST OF FRIENDS TO DO SO WITH.

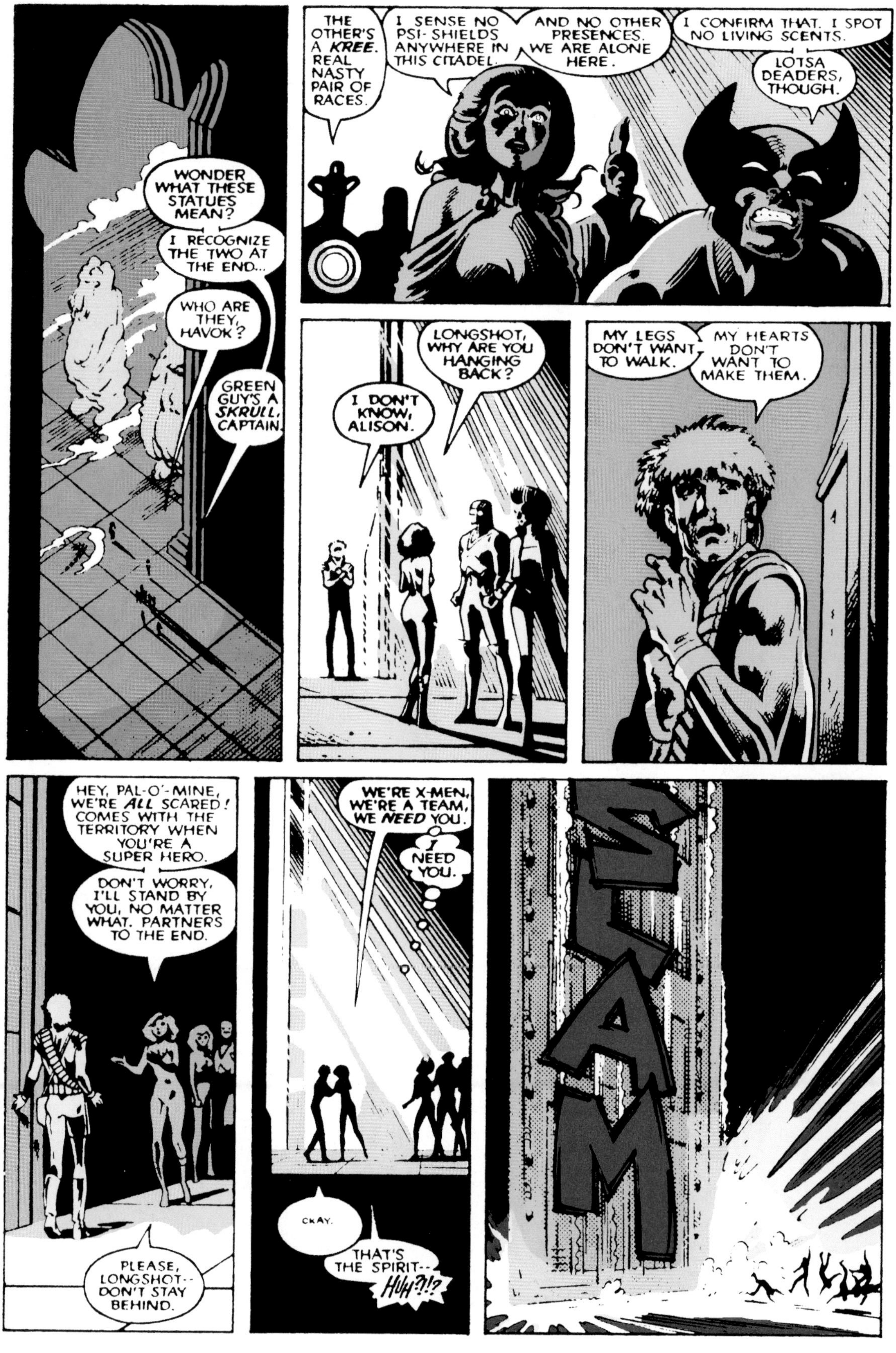
WONDER WHAT THESE STATUES MEAN?
I RECOGNIZE THE TWO AT THE END...
WHO ARE THEY, HAVOK?
GREEN GUY'S A *SKRULL*, CAPTAIN.
THE OTHER'S A *KREE*. REAL NASTY PAIR OF RACES.
I SENSE NO PSI-SHIELDS ANYWHERE IN THIS CITADEL.
AND NO OTHER PRESENCES. WE ARE ALONE HERE.
I CONFIRM THAT. I SPOT NO LIVING SCENTS.
LOTSA DEADERS, THOUGH.
LONGSHOT, WHY ARE YOU HANGING BACK?
I DON'T KNOW, ALISON.
MY LEGS DON'T WANT TO WALK.
MY HEARTS DON'T WANT TO MAKE THEM.
HEY, PAL-O'-MINE, WE'RE *ALL* SCARED! COMES WITH THE TERRITORY WHEN YOU'RE A SUPER HERO.
DON'T WORRY, I'LL STAND BY YOU, NO MATTER WHAT. PARTNERS TO THE END.
PLEASE, LONGSHOT-- DON'T STAY BEHIND.
WE'RE X-MEN, WE'RE A TEAM, WE *NEED* YOU.
I NEED YOU.
CKAY.
THAT'S THE SPIRIT-- *HUH?!?*
SLAM

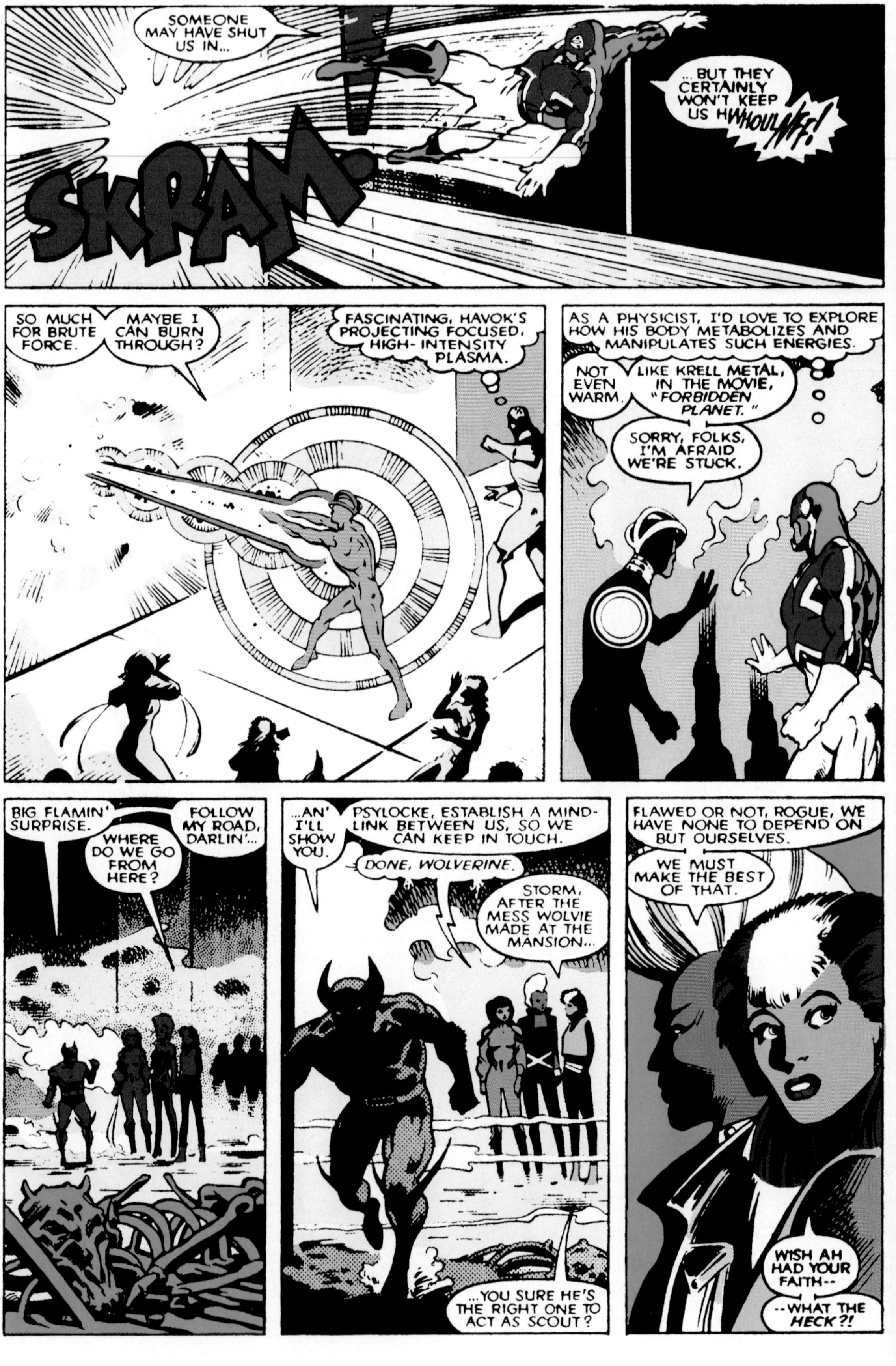

SOMEONE MAY HAVE SHUT US IN...
...BUT THEY CERTAINLY WON'T KEEP US H
WHOUUMFF!
SKRAM!
SO MUCH FOR BRUTE FORCE.
MAYBE I CAN BURN THROUGH?
FASCINATING. HAVOK'S PROJECTING FOCUSED, HIGH-INTENSITY PLASMA.
AS A PHYSICIST, I'D LOVE TO EXPLORE HOW HIS BODY METABOLIZES AND MANIPULATES SUCH ENERGIES.
NOT EVEN WARM.
LIKE KRELL METAL, IN THE MOVIE, "FORBIDDEN PLANET."
SORRY, FOLKS, I'M AFRAID WE'RE STUCK.
BIG FLAMIN' SURPRISE.
WHERE DO WE GO FROM HERE?
FOLLOW MY ROAD, DARLIN'...
...AN' I'LL SHOW YOU.
PSYLOCKE, ESTABLISH A MIND-LINK BETWEEN US, SO WE CAN KEEP IN TOUCH.
DONE, WOLVERINE.
STORM, AFTER THE MESS WOLVIE MADE AT THE MANSION...
...YOU SURE HE'S THE RIGHT ONE TO ACT AS SCOUT?
FLAWED OR NOT, ROGUE, WE HAVE NONE TO DEPEND ON BUT OURSELVES.
WE MUST MAKE THE BEST OF THAT.
WISH AH HAD YOUR FAITH--
--WHAT THE HECK?!

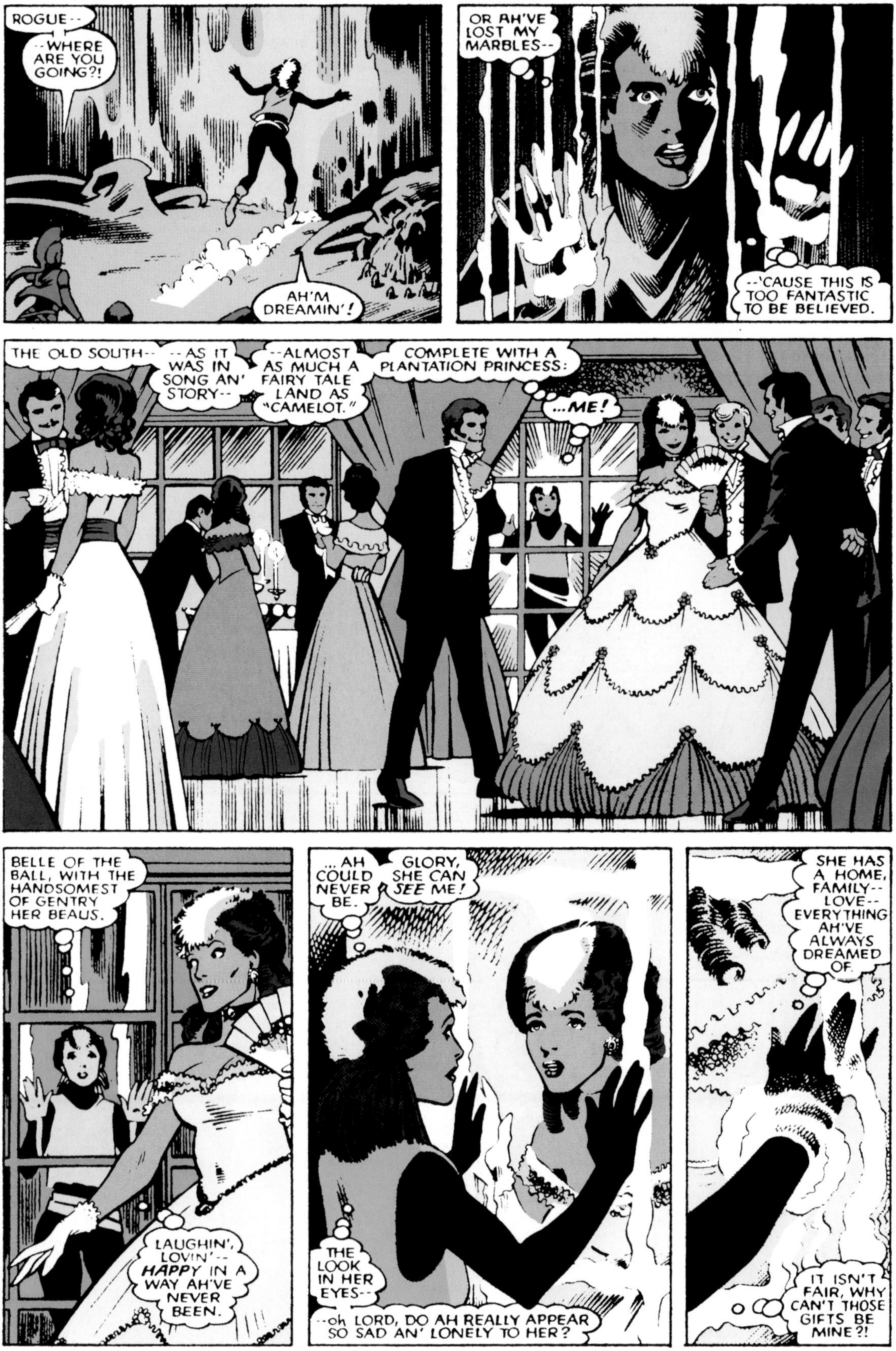

ROGUE--
--WHERE ARE YOU GOING?!
AH'M DREAMIN'!
OR AH'VE LOST MY MARBLES--
--'CAUSE THIS IS TOO FANTASTIC TO BE BELIEVED.
THE OLD SOUTH--
--AS IT WAS IN SONG AN' STORY--
--ALMOST AS MUCH A FAIRY TALE LAND AS "CAMELOT."
COMPLETE WITH A PLANTATION PRINCESS:
...ME!
BELLE OF THE BALL, WITH THE HANDSOMEST OF GENTRY HER BEAUS.
LAUGHIN', LOVIN'-- HAPPY IN A WAY AH'VE NEVER BEEN.
...AH COULD NEVER BE.
GLORY, SHE CAN SEE ME!
THE LOOK IN HER EYES--
--oh LORD, DO AH REALLY APPEAR SO SAD AN' LONELY TO HER?
SHE HAS A HOME, FAMILY-- LOVE-- EVERYTHING AH'VE ALWAYS DREAMED OF.
IT ISN'T FAIR, WHY CAN'T THOSE GIFTS BE MINE?!

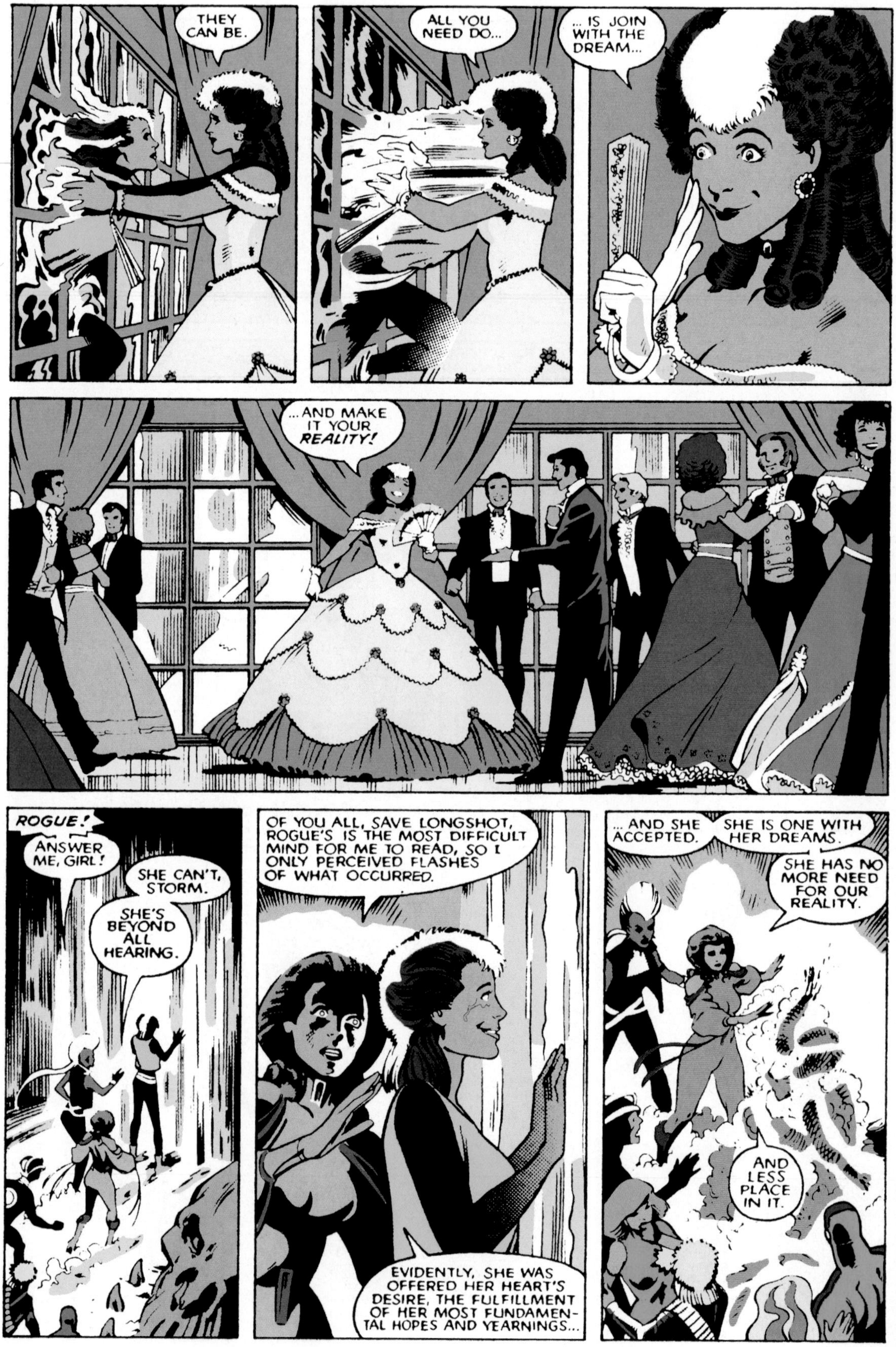

THEY CAN BE.
ALL YOU NEED DO...
... IS JOIN WITH THE DREAM...
... AND MAKE IT YOUR *REALITY!*
ROGUE!
ANSWER ME, GIRL!
SHE CAN'T, STORM.
SHE'S BEYOND ALL HEARING.
OF YOU ALL, SAVE LONGSHOT, ROGUE'S IS THE MOST DIFFICULT MIND FOR ME TO READ, SO I ONLY PERCEIVED FLASHES OF WHAT OCCURRED.
EVIDENTLY, SHE WAS OFFERED HER HEART'S DESIRE, THE FULFILLMENT OF HER MOST FUNDAMENTAL HOPES AND YEARNINGS...
... AND SHE ACCEPTED.
SHE IS ONE WITH HER DREAMS.
SHE HAS NO MORE NEED FOR OUR REALITY.
AND LESS PLACE IN IT.

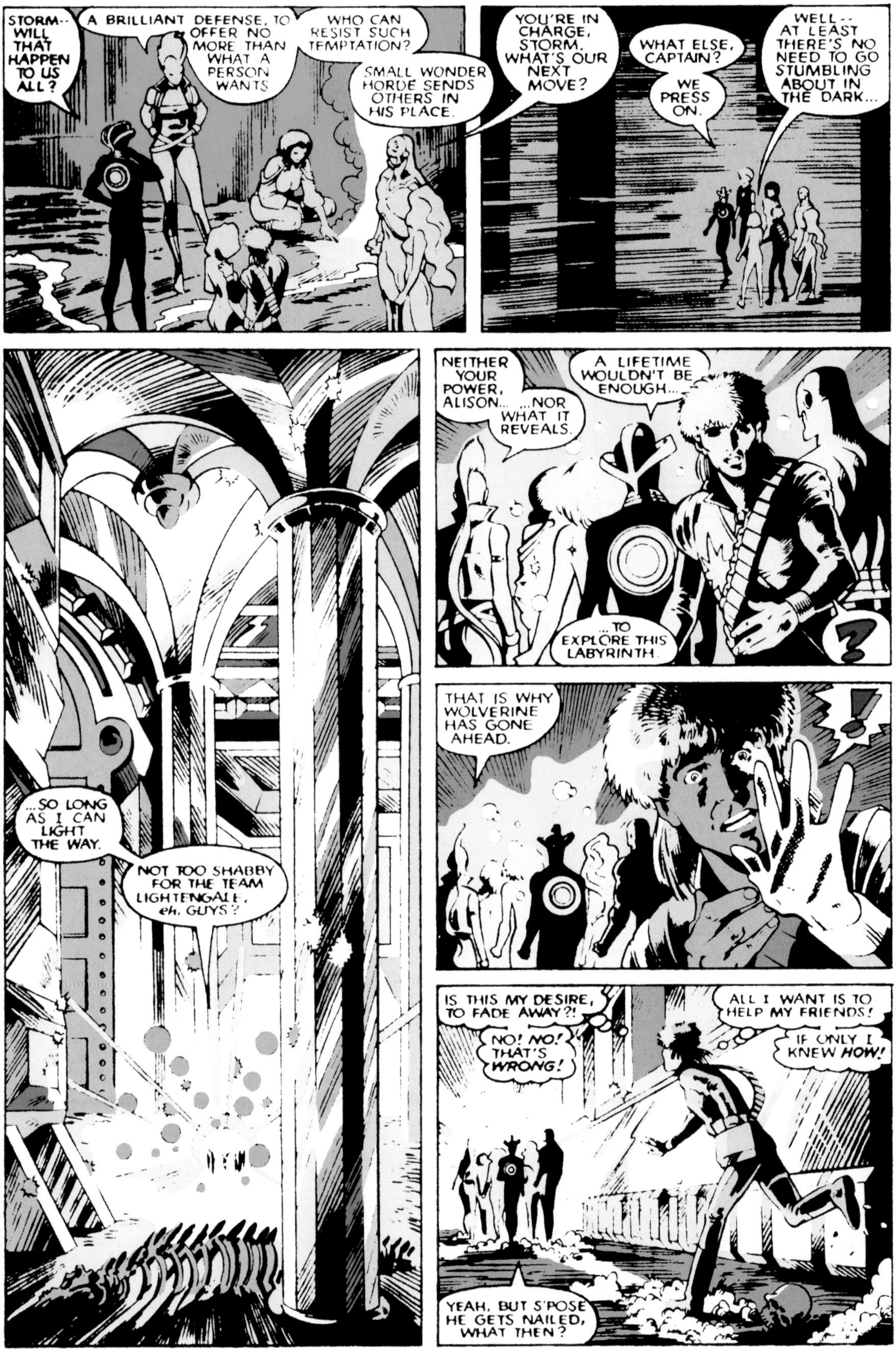
STORM-- WILL THAT HAPPEN TO US ALL?
A BRILLIANT DEFENSE, TO OFFER NO MORE THAN WHAT A PERSON WANTS
WHO CAN RESIST SUCH TEMPTATION?
SMALL WONDER HORDE SENDS OTHERS IN HIS PLACE.
YOU'RE IN CHARGE, STORM. WHAT'S OUR NEXT MOVE?
WHAT ELSE, CAPTAIN?
WE PRESS ON.
WELL-- AT LEAST THERE'S NO NEED TO GO STUMBLING ABOUT IN THE DARK...
...SO LONG AS I CAN LIGHT THE WAY.
NOT TOO SHABBY FOR THE TEAM LIGHTENGALE, eh, GUYS?
NEITHER YOUR POWER, ALISON...
...NOR WHAT IT REVEALS.
A LIFETIME WOULDN'T BE ENOUGH...
...TO EXPLORE THIS LABYRINTH.
?
THAT IS WHY WOLVERINE HAS GONE AHEAD.
!
IS THIS MY DESIRE, TO FADE AWAY?!
NO! NO! THAT'S WRONG!
ALL I WANT IS TO HELP MY FRIENDS!
IF ONLY I KNEW HOW!
YEAH, BUT S'POSE HE GETS NAILED, WHAT THEN?

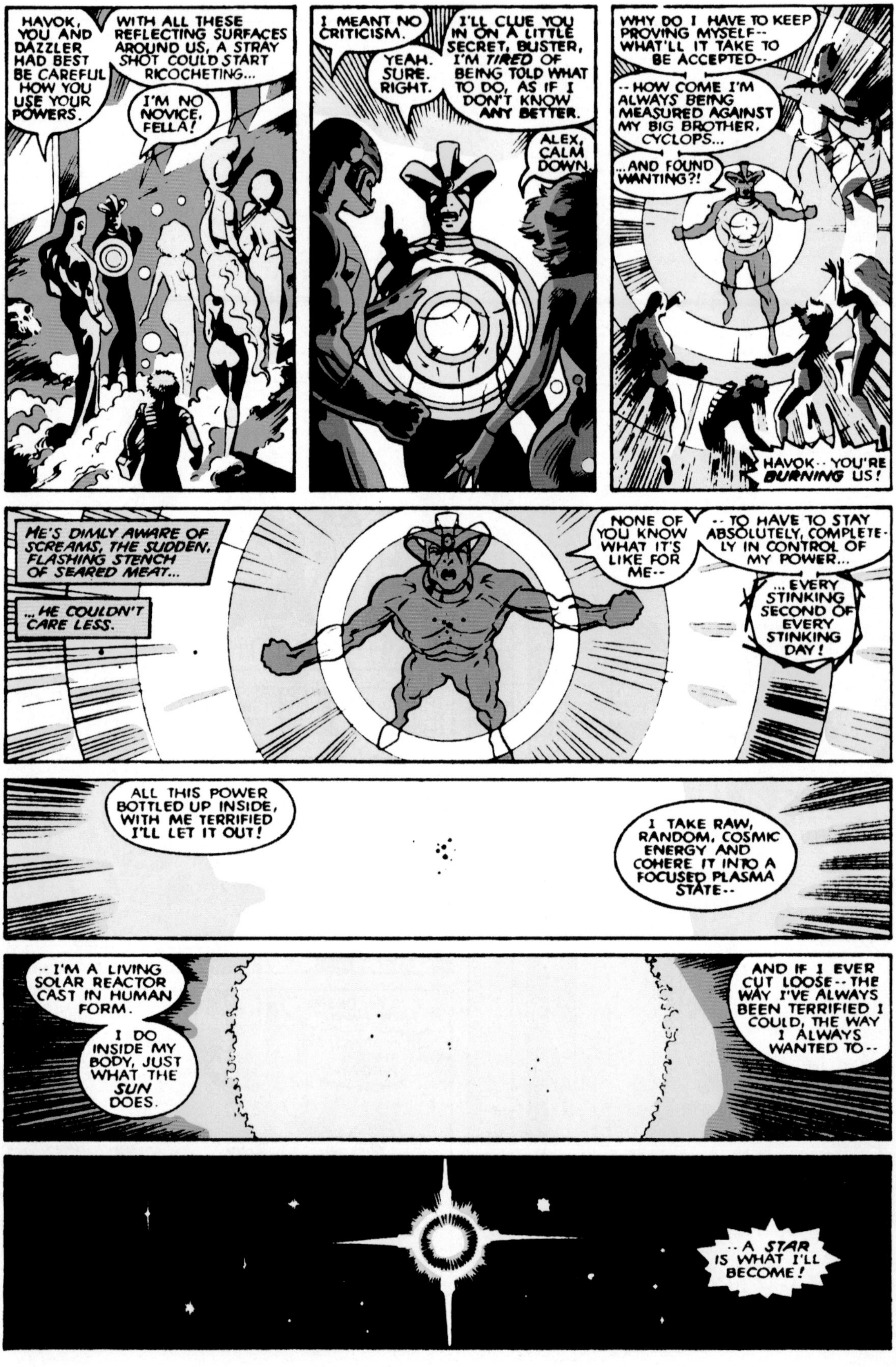
HAVOK, YOU AND DAZZLER HAD BEST BE CAREFUL HOW YOU USE YOUR POWERS.
WITH ALL THESE REFLECTING SURFACES AROUND US, A STRAY SHOT COULD START RICOCHETING...
I'M NO NOVICE, FELLA!
I MEANT NO CRITICISM.
YEAH. SURE. RIGHT.
I'LL CLUE YOU IN ON A LITTLE SECRET, BUSTER. I'M TIRED OF BEING TOLD WHAT TO DO, AS IF I DON'T KNOW ANY BETTER.
ALEX, CALM DOWN.
WHY DO I HAVE TO KEEP PROVING MYSELF-- WHAT'LL IT TAKE TO BE ACCEPTED--
--HOW COME I'M ALWAYS BEING MEASURED AGAINST MY BIG BROTHER, CYCLOPS...
...AND FOUND WANTING?!
HAVOK-- YOU'RE BURNING US!
HE'S DIMLY AWARE OF SCREAMS, THE SUDDEN, FLASHING STENCH OF SEARED MEAT...
...HE COULDN'T CARE LESS.
NONE OF YOU KNOW WHAT IT'S LIKE FOR ME--
--TO HAVE TO STAY ABSOLUTELY, COMPLETE-LY IN CONTROL OF MY POWER...
...EVERY STINKING SECOND OF EVERY STINKING DAY!
ALL THIS POWER BOTTLED UP INSIDE, WITH ME TERRIFIED I'LL LET IT OUT!
I TAKE RAW, RANDOM, COSMIC ENERGY AND COHERE IT INTO A FOCUSED PLASMA STATE--
--I'M A LIVING SOLAR REACTOR CAST IN HUMAN FORM.
I DO INSIDE MY BODY, JUST WHAT THE SUN DOES.
AND IF I EVER CUT LOOSE-- THE WAY I'VE ALWAYS BEEN TERRIFIED I COULD, THE WAY I ALWAYS WANTED TO--
--A STAR IS WHAT I'LL BECOME!

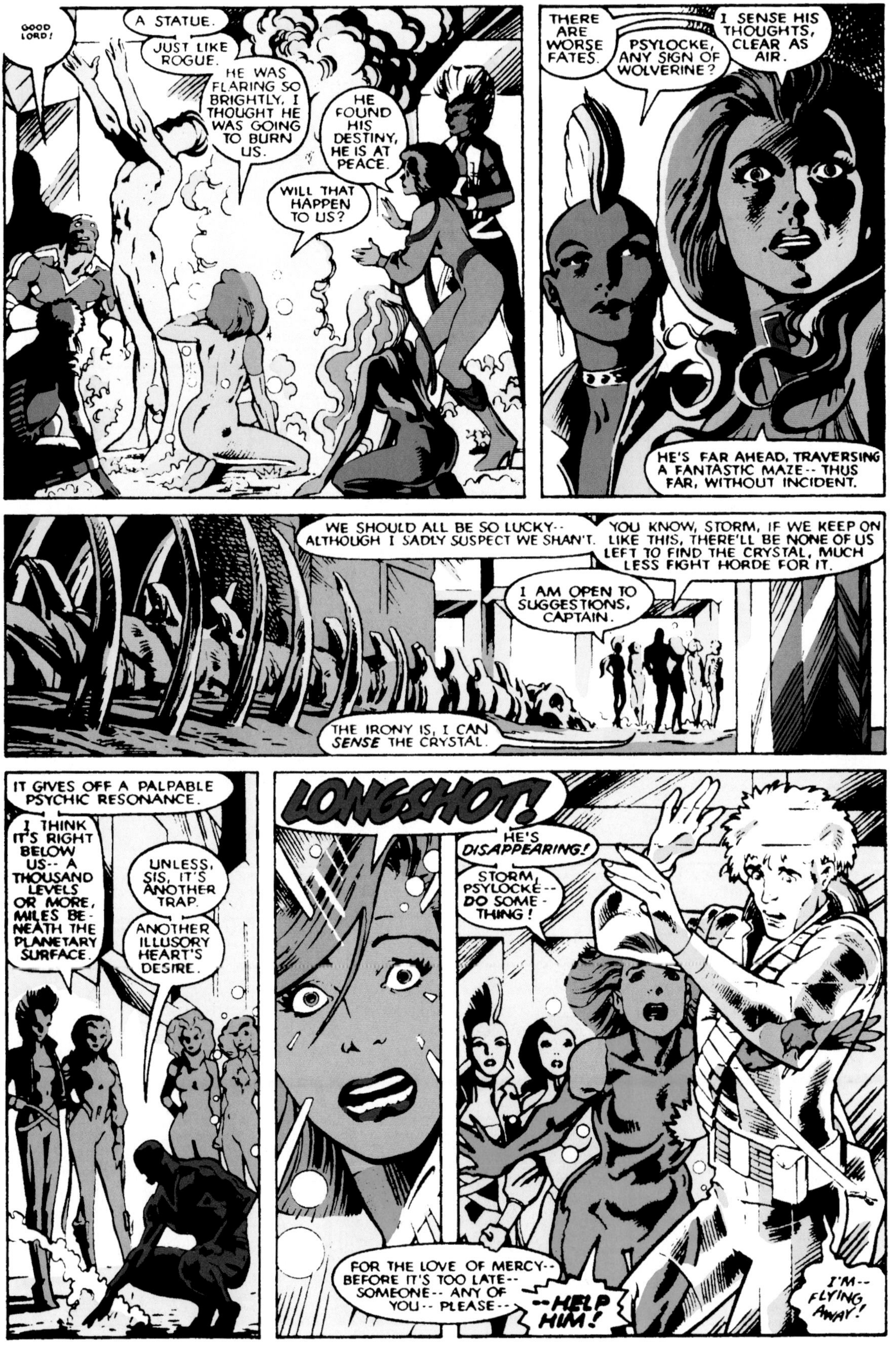
GOOD LORD!
A STATUE.
JUST LIKE ROGUE.
HE WAS FLARING SO BRIGHTLY, I THOUGHT HE WAS GOING TO BURN US.
HE FOUND HIS DESTINY, HE IS AT PEACE.
WILL THAT HAPPEN TO US?
THERE ARE WORSE FATES.
PSYLOCKE, ANY SIGN OF WOLVERINE?
I SENSE HIS THOUGHTS, CLEAR AS AIR.
HE'S FAR AHEAD, TRAVERSING A FANTASTIC MAZE-- THUS FAR, WITHOUT INCIDENT.
WE SHOULD ALL BE SO LUCKY-- ALTHOUGH I SADLY SUSPECT WE SHAN'T.
YOU KNOW, STORM, IF WE KEEP ON LIKE THIS, THERE'LL BE NONE OF US LEFT TO FIND THE CRYSTAL, MUCH LESS FIGHT HORDE FOR IT.
I AM OPEN TO SUGGESTIONS, CAPTAIN.
THE IRONY IS, I CAN *SENSE* THE CRYSTAL.
IT GIVES OFF A PALPABLE PSYCHIC RESONANCE.
I THINK IT'S RIGHT BELOW US-- A THOUSAND LEVELS OR MORE, MILES BENEATH THE PLANETARY SURFACE.
UNLESS, SIS, IT'S ANOTHER TRAP.
ANOTHER ILLUSORY HEART'S DESIRE.
LONGSHOT!
HE'S *DISAPPEARING!*
STORM, PSYLOCKE-- *DO* SOMETHING!
FOR THE LOVE OF MERCY-- BEFORE IT'S TOO LATE-- SOMEONE-- ANY OF YOU-- PLEASE--
--HELP HIM!
I'M-- FLYING AWAY!

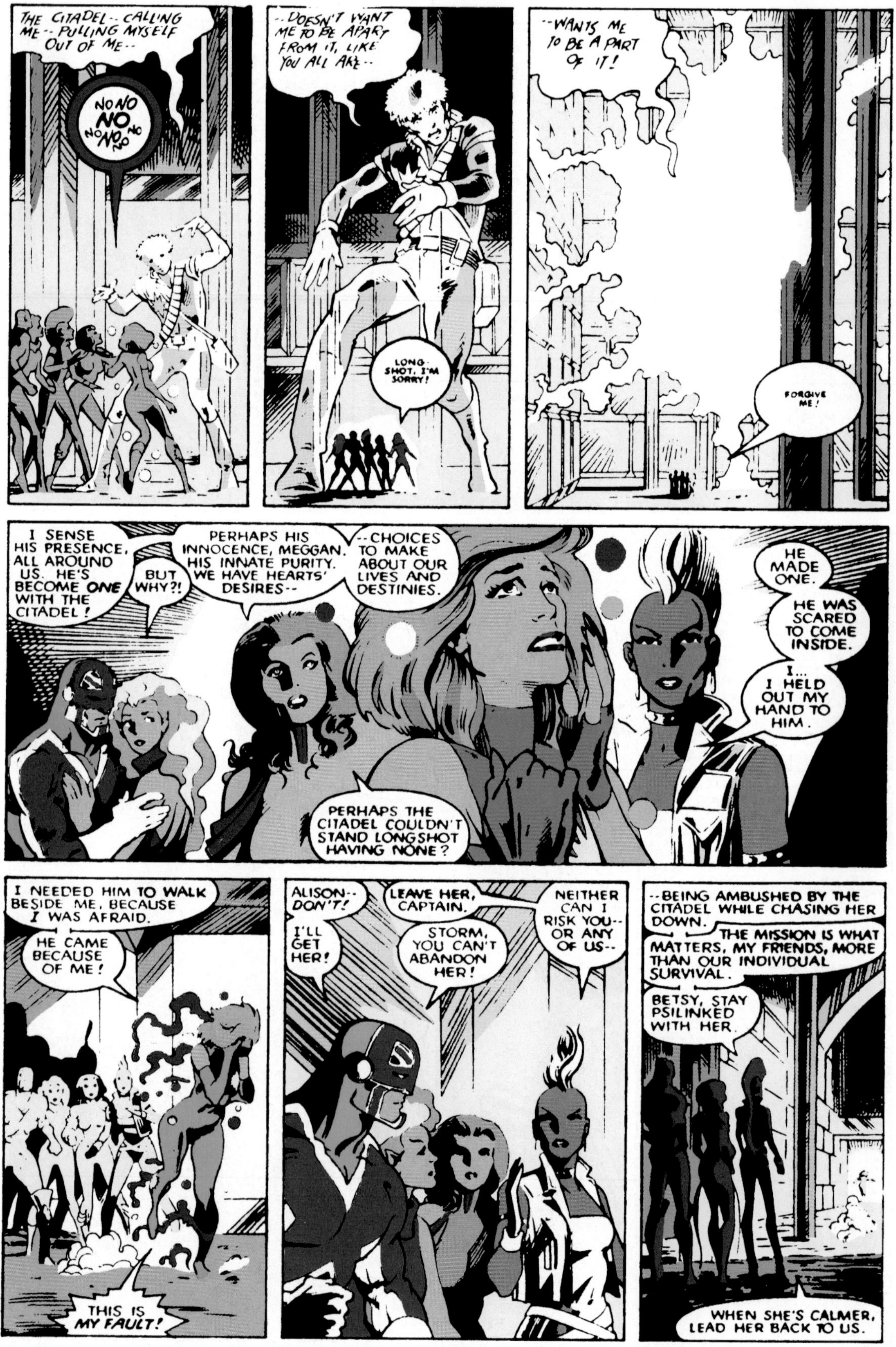
THE CITADEL-- CALLING ME-- PULLING MYSELF OUT OF ME--
NO NO NO NO NO NO NO
--DOESN'T WANT ME TO BE APART FROM IT, LIKE YOU ALL ARE--
LONG-SHOT, I'M SORRY!
--WANTS ME TO BE A PART OF IT!
FORGIVE ME!
I SENSE HIS PRESENCE, ALL AROUND US. HE'S BECOME ONE WITH THE CITADEL!
BUT WHY?!
PERHAPS HIS INNOCENCE, MEGGAN. HIS INNATE PURITY. WE HAVE HEARTS' DESIRES--
--CHOICES TO MAKE ABOUT OUR LIVES AND DESTINIES.
PERHAPS THE CITADEL COULDN'T STAND LONGSHOT HAVING NONE?
HE MADE ONE.
HE WAS SCARED TO COME INSIDE.
I... I HELD OUT MY HAND TO HIM.
I NEEDED HIM TO WALK BESIDE ME, BECAUSE I WAS AFRAID.
HE CAME BECAUSE OF ME!
THIS IS MY FAULT!
ALISON-- DON'T!
I'LL GET HER!
LEAVE HER, CAPTAIN.
STORM, YOU CAN'T ABANDON HER!
NEITHER CAN I RISK YOU-- OR ANY OF US--
--BEING AMBUSHED BY THE CITADEL WHILE CHASING HER DOWN.
THE MISSION IS WHAT MATTERS, MY FRIENDS, MORE THAN OUR INDIVIDUAL SURVIVAL.
BETSY, STAY PSILINKED WITH HER.
WHEN SHE'S CALMER, LEAD HER BACK TO US.

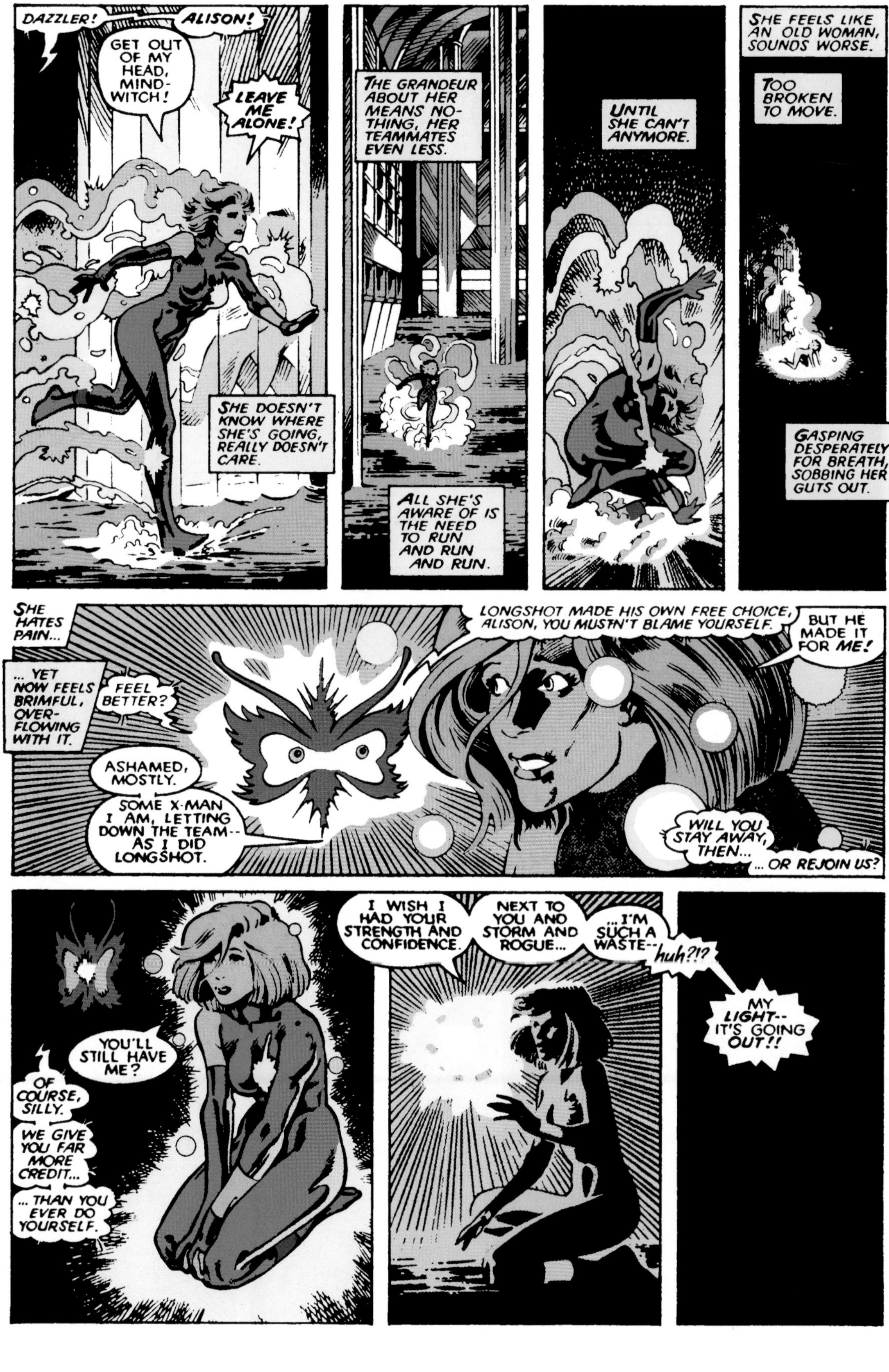

DAZZLER!
ALISON!
GET OUT OF MY HEAD, MIND-WITCH!
LEAVE ME ALONE!
SHE DOESN'T KNOW WHERE SHE'S GOING, REALLY DOESN'T CARE.
THE GRANDEUR ABOUT HER MEANS NOTHING, HER TEAMMATES EVEN LESS.
ALL SHE'S AWARE OF IS THE NEED TO RUN AND RUN AND RUN.
UNTIL SHE CAN'T ANYMORE.
SHE FEELS LIKE AN OLD WOMAN, SOUNDS WORSE.
TOO BROKEN TO MOVE.
GASPING DESPERATELY FOR BREATH, SOBBING HER GUTS OUT.
SHE HATES PAIN...
... YET NOW FEELS BRIMFUL, OVERFLOWING WITH IT.
FEEL BETTER?
ASHAMED, MOSTLY.
SOME X-MAN I AM, LETTING DOWN THE TEAM-- AS I DID LONGSHOT.
LONGSHOT MADE HIS OWN FREE CHOICE, ALISON, YOU MUSTN'T BLAME YOURSELF.
BUT HE MADE IT FOR ME!
WILL YOU STAY AWAY, THEN...
... OR REJOIN US?
YOU'LL STILL HAVE ME?
OF COURSE, SILLY.
WE GIVE YOU FAR MORE CREDIT...
... THAN YOU EVER DO YOURSELF.
I WISH I HAD YOUR STRENGTH AND CONFIDENCE.
NEXT TO YOU AND STORM AND ROGUE...
... I'M SUCH A WASTE--
huh?!?
MY LIGHT-- IT'S GOING OUT!!

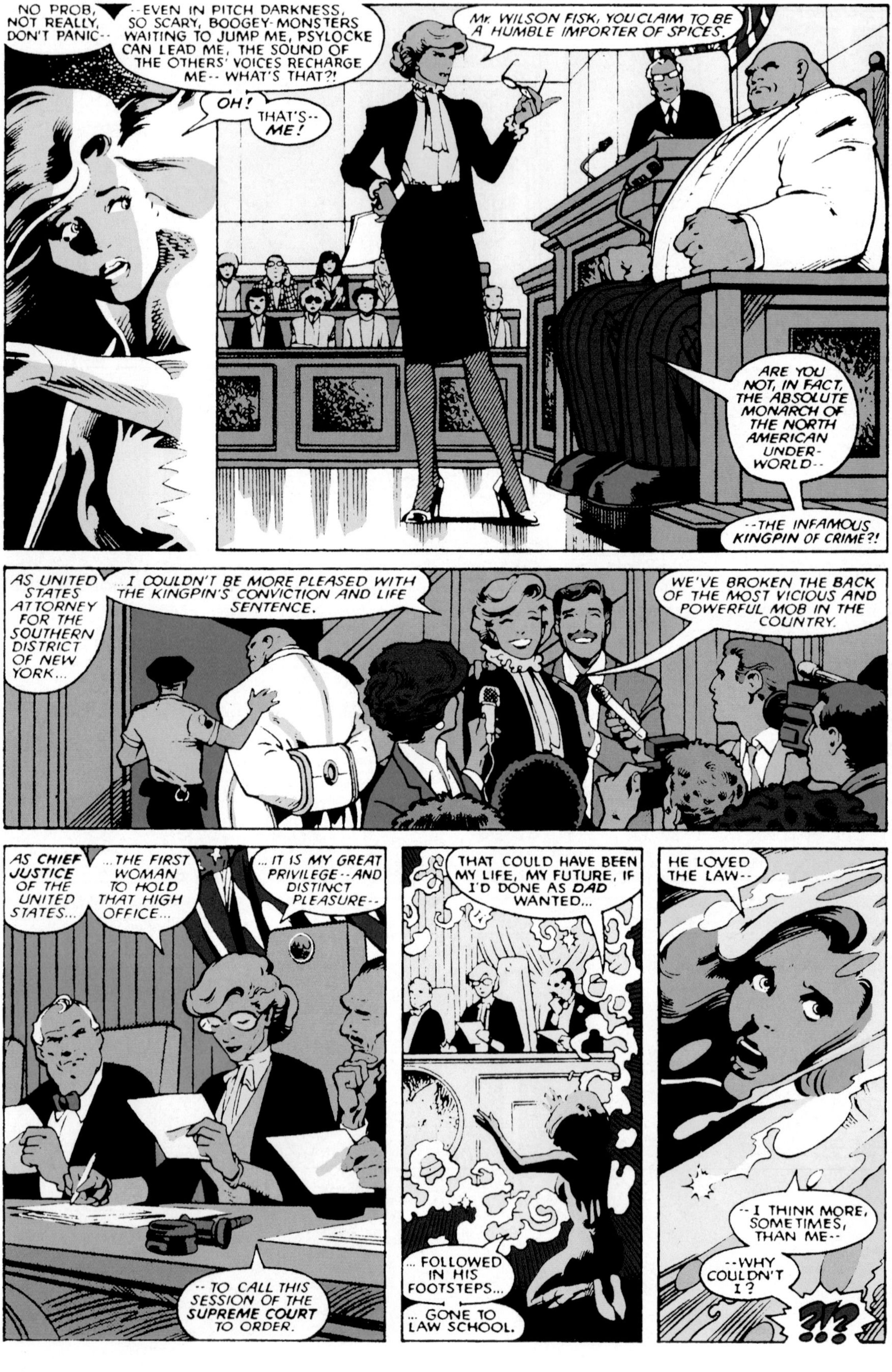
NO PROB, NOT REALLY, DON'T PANIC--
--EVEN IN PITCH DARKNESS, SO SCARY, BOOGEY-MONSTERS WAITING TO JUMP ME, PSYLOCKE CAN LEAD ME, THE SOUND OF THE OTHERS' VOICES RECHARGE ME-- WHAT'S THAT?!
OH!
THAT'S-- ME!
MR. WILSON FISK, YOU CLAIM TO BE A HUMBLE IMPORTER OF SPICES.
ARE YOU NOT, IN FACT, THE ABSOLUTE MONARCH OF THE NORTH AMERICAN UNDER-WORLD--
--THE INFAMOUS KINGPIN OF CRIME?!
AS UNITED STATES ATTORNEY FOR THE SOUTHERN DISTRICT OF NEW YORK...
...I COULDN'T BE MORE PLEASED WITH THE KINGPIN'S CONVICTION AND LIFE SENTENCE.
WE'VE BROKEN THE BACK OF THE MOST VICIOUS AND POWERFUL MOB IN THE COUNTRY.
AS CHIEF JUSTICE OF THE UNITED STATES...
...THE FIRST WOMAN TO HOLD THAT HIGH OFFICE...
...IT IS MY GREAT PRIVILEGE--AND DISTINCT PLEASURE--
--TO CALL THIS SESSION OF THE SUPREME COURT TO ORDER.
THAT COULD HAVE BEEN MY LIFE, MY FUTURE, IF I'D DONE AS DAD WANTED...
...FOLLOWED IN HIS FOOTSTEPS...
...GONE TO LAW SCHOOL.
HE LOVED THE LAW--
--I THINK MORE, SOMETIMES, THAN ME--
--WHY COULDN'T I?
?!?

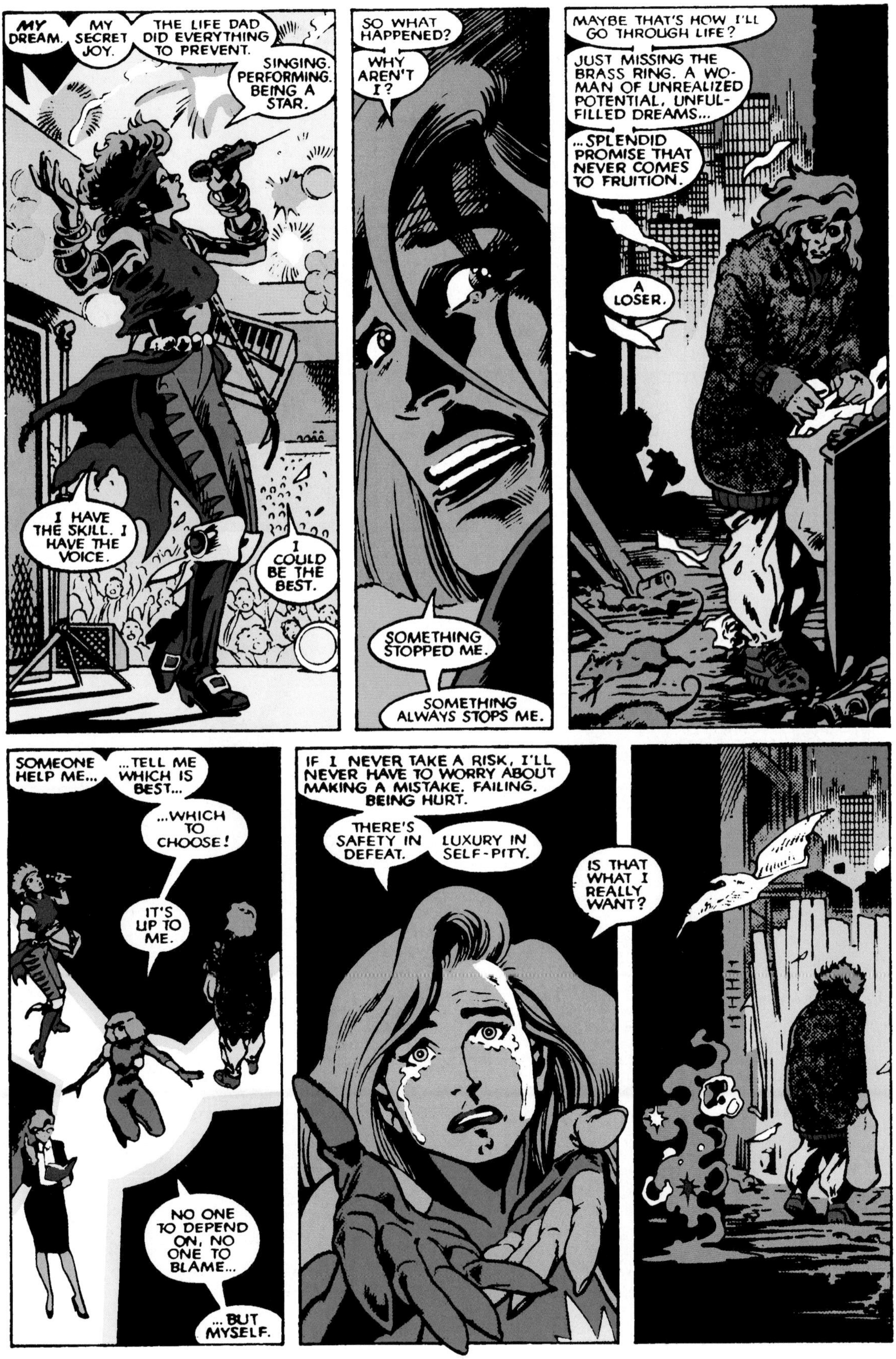
MY DREAM.
MY SECRET JOY.
THE LIFE DAD DID EVERYTHING TO PREVENT.
SINGING. PERFORMING. BEING A STAR.
I HAVE THE SKILL. I HAVE THE VOICE.
I COULD BE THE BEST.
SO WHAT HAPPENED?
WHY AREN'T I?
SOMETHING STOPPED ME.
SOMETHING ALWAYS STOPS ME.
MAYBE THAT'S HOW I'LL GO THROUGH LIFE?
JUST MISSING THE BRASS RING. A WOMAN OF UNREALIZED POTENTIAL, UNFULFILLED DREAMS...
...SPLENDID PROMISE THAT NEVER COMES TO FRUITION.
A LOSER.
SOMEONE HELP ME...
...TELL ME WHICH IS BEST...
...WHICH TO CHOOSE!
IT'S UP TO ME.
NO ONE TO DEPEND ON, NO ONE TO BLAME...
...BUT MYSELF.
IF I NEVER TAKE A RISK, I'LL NEVER HAVE TO WORRY ABOUT MAKING A MISTAKE. FAILING. BEING HURT.
THERE'S SAFETY IN DEFEAT.
LUXURY IN SELF-PITY.
IS THAT WHAT I REALLY WANT?

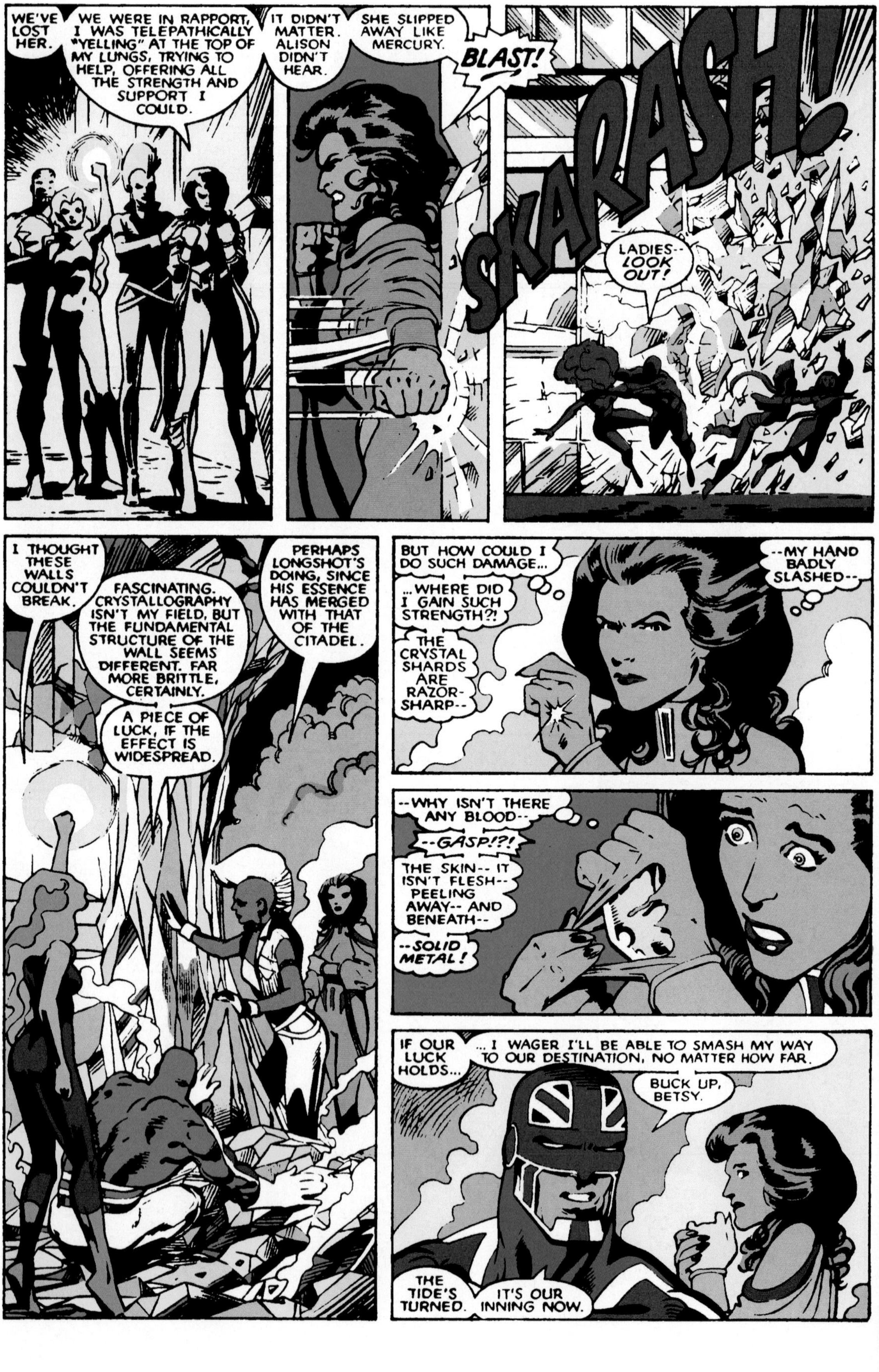
WE'VE LOST HER.
WE WERE IN RAPPORT, I WAS TELEPATHICALLY "YELLING" AT THE TOP OF MY LUNGS, TRYING TO HELP, OFFERING ALL THE STRENGTH AND SUPPORT I COULD.
IT DIDN'T MATTER. ALISON DIDN'T HEAR.
SHE SLIPPED AWAY LIKE MERCURY.
BLAST!
SKARASH!
LADIES-- LOOK OUT!
I THOUGHT THESE WALLS COULDN'T BREAK.
FASCINATING. CRYSTALLOGRAPHY ISN'T MY FIELD, BUT THE FUNDAMENTAL STRUCTURE OF THE WALL SEEMS DIFFERENT. FAR MORE BRITTLE, CERTAINLY.
A PIECE OF LUCK, IF THE EFFECT IS WIDESPREAD.
PERHAPS LONGSHOT'S DOING, SINCE HIS ESSENCE HAS MERGED WITH THAT OF THE CITADEL.
BUT HOW COULD I DO SUCH DAMAGE...
...WHERE DID I GAIN SUCH STRENGTH?!
THE CRYSTAL SHARDS ARE RAZOR-SHARP--
--MY HAND BADLY SLASHED--
--WHY ISN'T THERE ANY BLOOD--
--GASP!?!
THE SKIN-- IT ISN'T FLESH-- PEELING AWAY-- AND BENEATH--
--SOLID METAL!
IF OUR LUCK HOLDS...
... I WAGER I'LL BE ABLE TO SMASH MY WAY TO OUR DESTINATION, NO MATTER HOW FAR.
BUCK UP, BETSY.
THE TIDE'S TURNED.
IT'S OUR INNING NOW.

YOU LOOK AFTER STORM AND BETSY, MEGGAN. I'LL LEAD THE WAY.

HE DIDN'T ASK TO BE A HERO.

HIS WERE NORMAL DREAMS.

UNTIL FATE HELD OUT THE MANTLE OF CAPTAIN BRITAIN.

HE STILL WONDERS, IF THE OFFER WERE MADE AGAIN-- WITH HIM KNOWING THE COST...

SKOOM

...THE NEVER-ENDING, ALL-CONSUMING SACRIFICE--

...WOULD HE ACCEPT?

BOOM

BOOM

BOOM

GLORY!

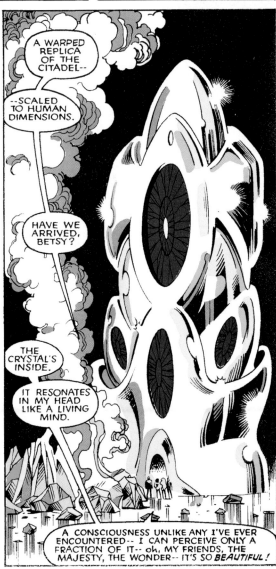

A WARPED REPLICA OF THE CITADEL--

--SCALED TO HUMAN DIMENSIONS.

HAVE WE ARRIVED, BETSY?

THE CRYSTAL'S INSIDE.

IT RESONATES IN MY HEAD LIKE A LIVING MIND.

A CONSCIOUSNESS UNLIKE ANY I'VE EVER ENCOUNTERED-- I CAN PERCEIVE ONLY A FRACTION OF IT-- oh, MY FRIENDS, THE MAJESTY, THE WONDER-- IT'S SO *BEAUTIFUL!*

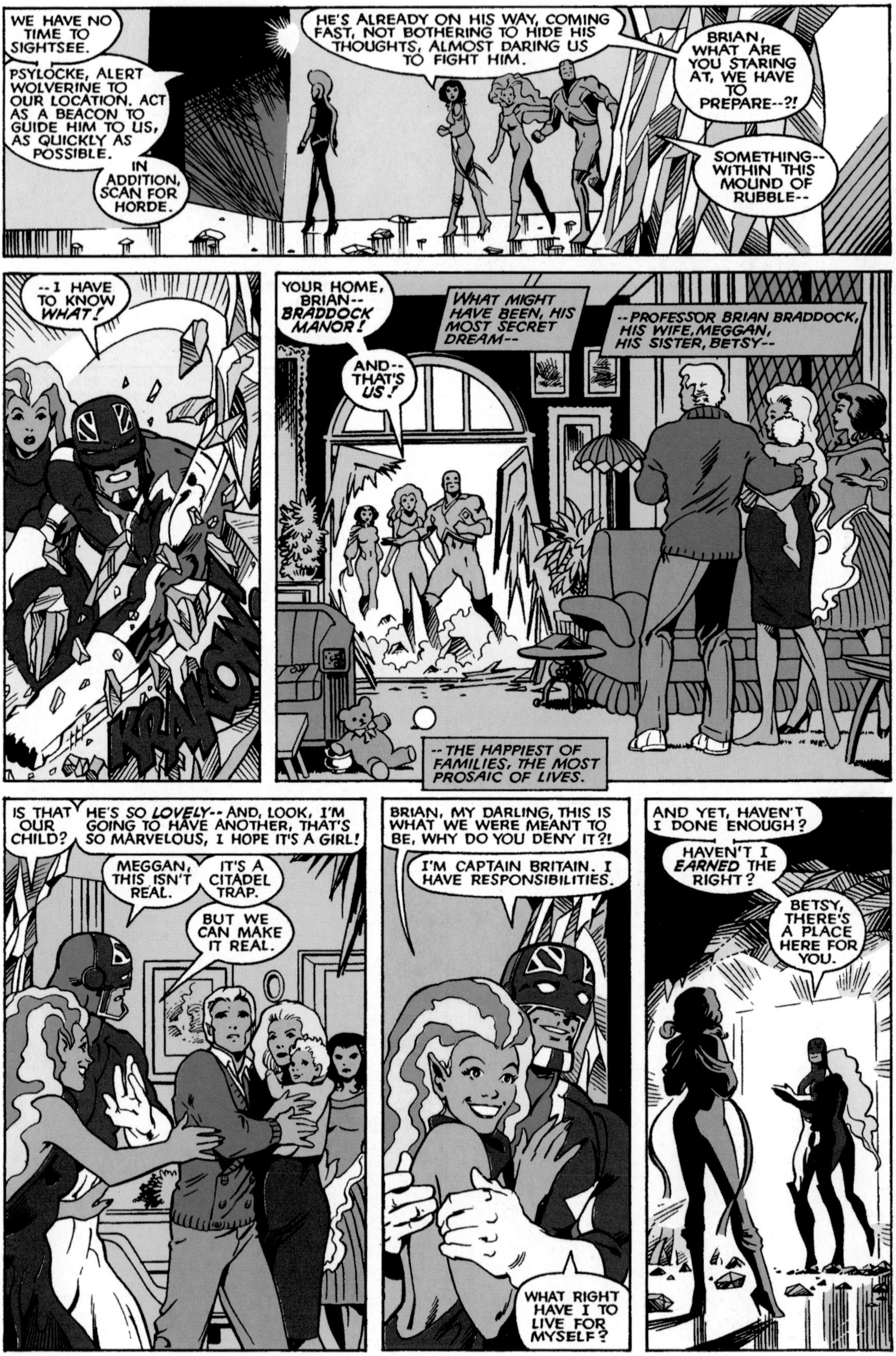
WE HAVE NO TIME TO SIGHTSEE.
PSYLOCKE, ALERT WOLVERINE TO OUR LOCATION. ACT AS A BEACON TO GUIDE HIM TO US, AS QUICKLY AS POSSIBLE.
IN ADDITION, SCAN FOR HORDE.
HE'S ALREADY ON HIS WAY, COMING FAST, NOT BOTHERING TO HIDE HIS THOUGHTS, ALMOST DARING US TO FIGHT HIM.
BRIAN, WHAT ARE YOU STARING AT, WE HAVE TO PREPARE--?!
SOMETHING--WITHIN THIS MOUND OF RUBBLE--
--I HAVE TO KNOW WHAT!
KRAKOW
YOUR HOME, BRIAN--BRADDOCK MANOR!
AND--THAT'S US!
WHAT MIGHT HAVE BEEN, HIS MOST SECRET DREAM--
--PROFESSOR BRIAN BRADDOCK, HIS WIFE, MEGGAN, HIS SISTER, BETSY--
--THE HAPPIEST OF FAMILIES, THE MOST PROSAIC OF LIVES.
IS THAT OUR CHILD?
HE'S SO LOVELY-- AND, LOOK, I'M GOING TO HAVE ANOTHER, THAT'S SO MARVELOUS, I HOPE IT'S A GIRL!
MEGGAN, THIS ISN'T REAL.
IT'S A CITADEL TRAP.
BUT WE CAN MAKE IT REAL.
BRIAN, MY DARLING, THIS IS WHAT WE WERE MEANT TO BE, WHY DO YOU DENY IT?!
I'M CAPTAIN BRITAIN. I HAVE RESPONSIBILITIES.
WHAT RIGHT HAVE I TO LIVE FOR MYSELF?
AND YET, HAVEN'T I DONE ENOUGH?
HAVEN'T I EARNED THE RIGHT?
BETSY, THERE'S A PLACE HERE FOR YOU.

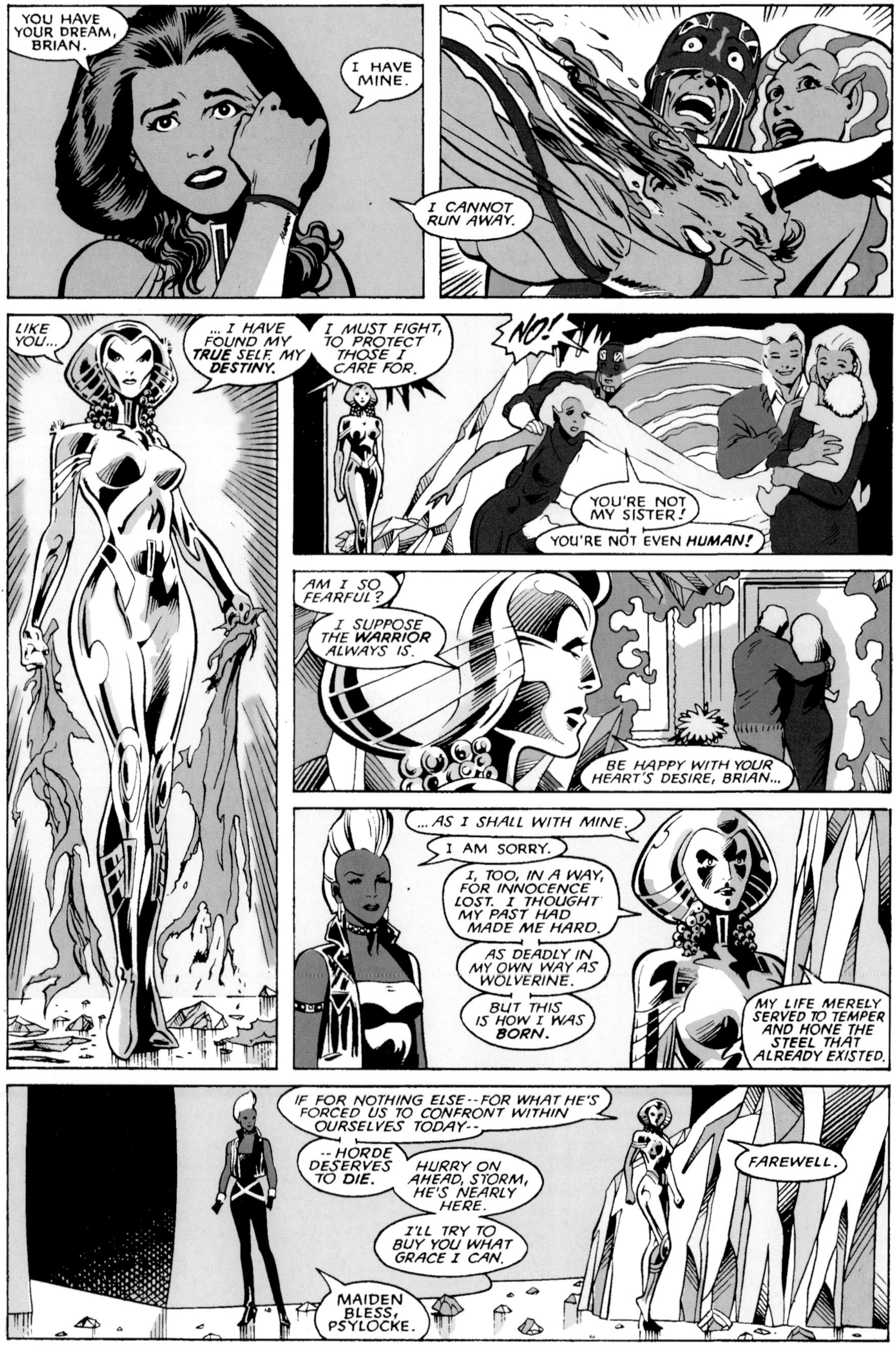
YOU HAVE YOUR DREAM, BRIAN.
I HAVE MINE.
I CANNOT RUN AWAY.
LIKE YOU...
... I HAVE FOUND MY TRUE SELF. MY DESTINY.
I MUST FIGHT, TO PROTECT THOSE I CARE FOR.
NO!
YOU'RE NOT MY SISTER!
YOU'RE NOT EVEN HUMAN!
AM I SO FEARFUL?
I SUPPOSE THE WARRIOR ALWAYS IS.
BE HAPPY WITH YOUR HEART'S DESIRE, BRIAN...
...AS I SHALL WITH MINE.
I AM SORRY.
I, TOO, IN A WAY, FOR INNOCENCE LOST. I THOUGHT MY PAST HAD MADE ME HARD.
AS DEADLY IN MY OWN WAY AS WOLVERINE.
BUT THIS IS HOW I WAS BORN.
MY LIFE MERELY SERVED TO TEMPER AND HONE THE STEEL THAT ALREADY EXISTED.
IF FOR NOTHING ELSE--FOR WHAT HE'S FORCED US TO CONFRONT WITHIN OURSELVES TODAY--
--HORDE DESERVES TO DIE.
HURRY ON AHEAD, STORM, HE'S NEARLY HERE.
I'LL TRY TO BUY YOU WHAT GRACE I CAN.
FAREWELL.
MAIDEN BLESS, PSYLOCKE.

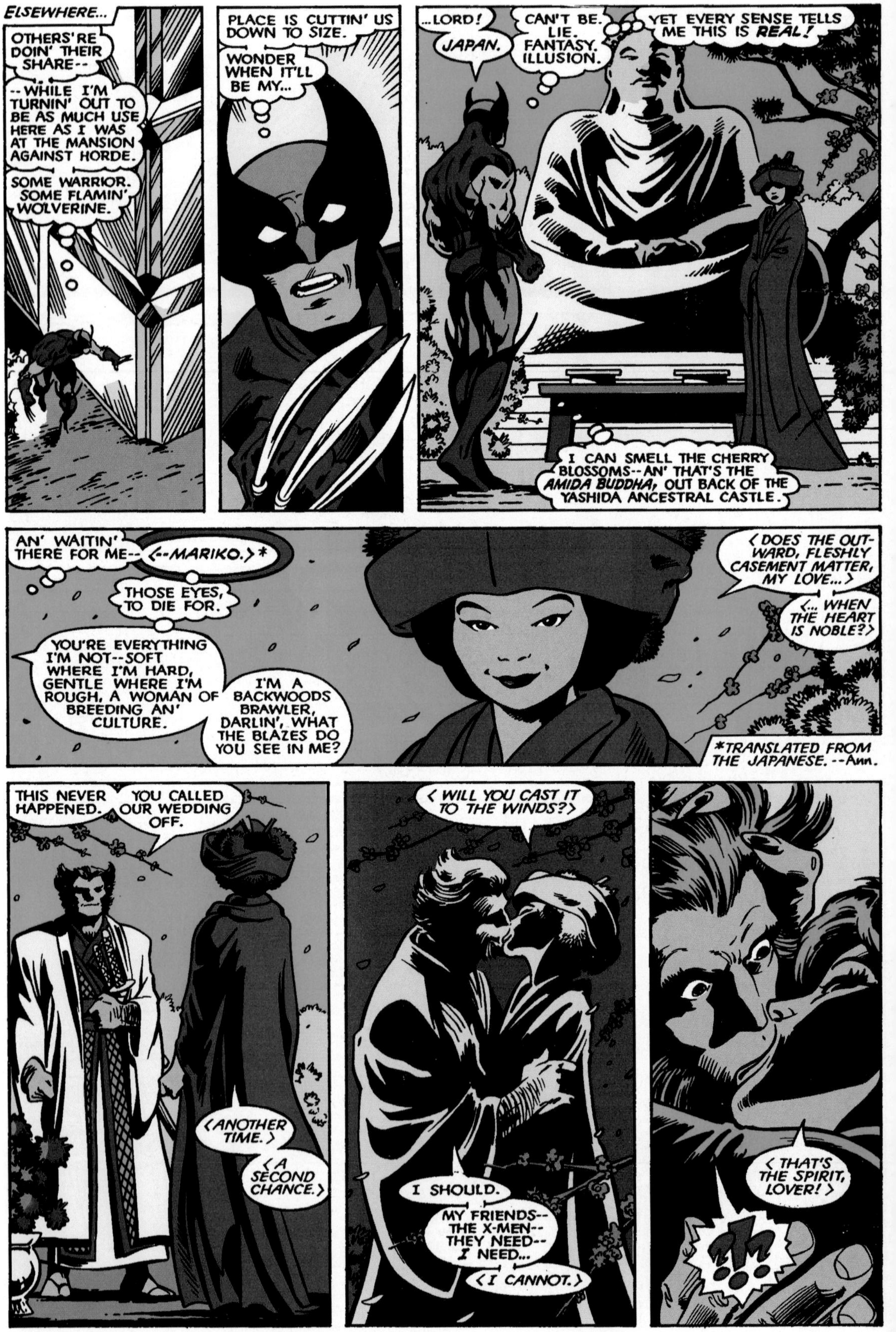
ELSEWHERE...
OTHERS'RE DOIN' THEIR SHARE--
--WHILE I'M TURNIN' OUT TO BE AS MUCH USE HERE AS I WAS AT THE MANSION AGAINST HORDE.
SOME WARRIOR. SOME FLAMIN' WOLVERINE.
PLACE IS CUTTIN' US DOWN TO SIZE.
WONDER WHEN IT'LL BE MY...
...LORD!
JAPAN.
CAN'T BE. LIE. FANTASY. ILLUSION.
YET EVERY SENSE TELLS ME THIS IS REAL!
I CAN SMELL THE CHERRY BLOSSOMS--AN' THAT'S THE AMIDA BUDDHA, OUT BACK OF THE YASHIDA ANCESTRAL CASTLE.
AN' WAITIN' THERE FOR ME--
<--MARIKO.>*
THOSE EYES, TO DIE FOR.
YOU'RE EVERYTHING I'M NOT--SOFT WHERE I'M HARD, GENTLE WHERE I'M ROUGH, A WOMAN OF BREEDING AN' CULTURE.
I'M A BACKWOODS BRAWLER, DARLIN', WHAT THE BLAZES DO YOU SEE IN ME?
<DOES THE OUTWARD, FLESHLY CASEMENT MATTER, MY LOVE...>
<...WHEN THE HEART IS NOBLE?>
*TRANSLATED FROM THE JAPANESE. --Ann.
THIS NEVER HAPPENED.
YOU CALLED OUR WEDDING OFF.
<ANOTHER TIME.>
<A SECOND CHANCE.>
<WILL YOU CAST IT TO THE WINDS?>
I SHOULD.
MY FRIENDS--THE X-MEN--THEY NEED--I NEED...
<I CANNOT.>
<THAT'S THE SPIRIT, LOVER!>
?!!

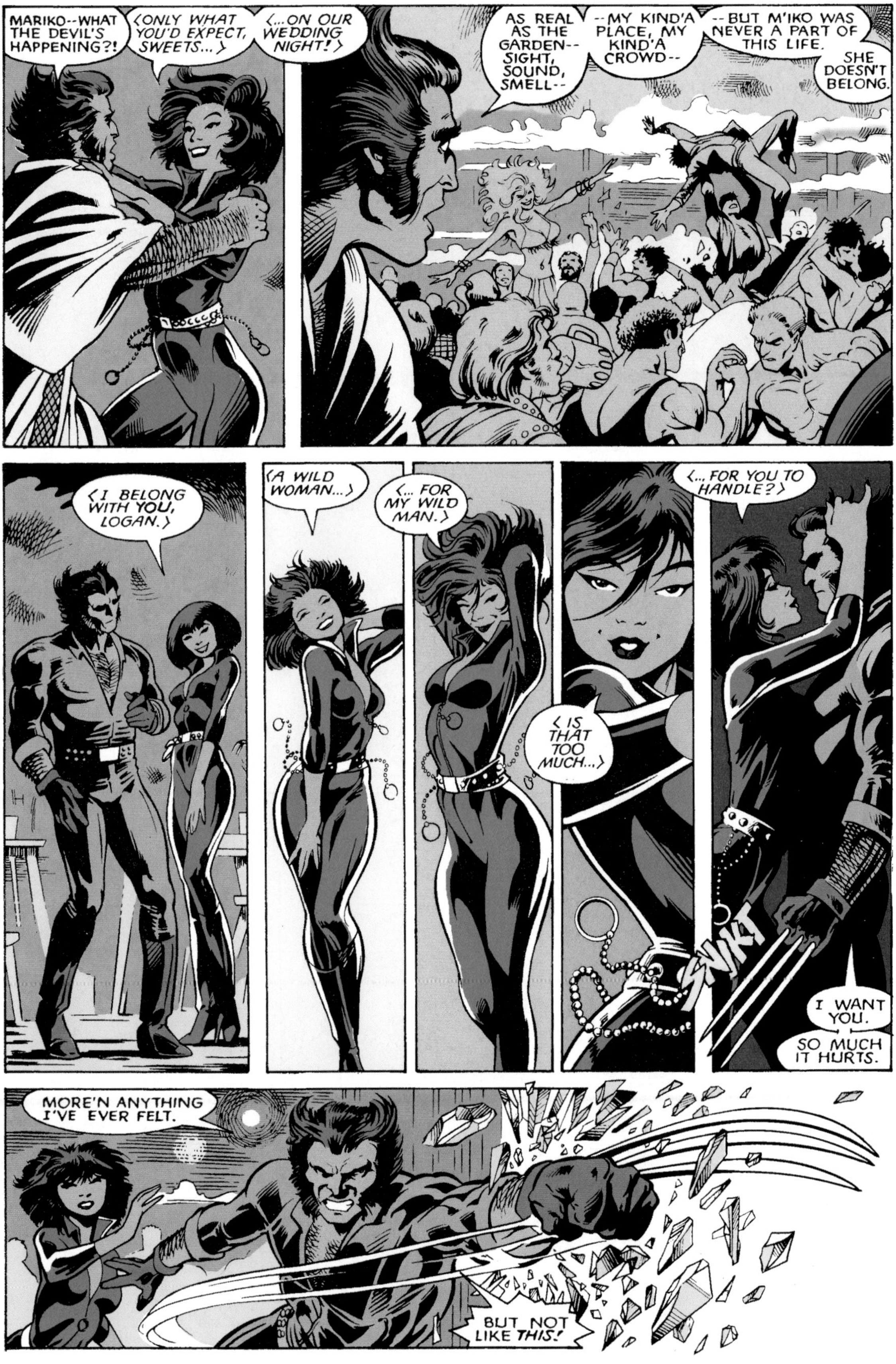
MARIKO--WHAT THE DEVIL'S HAPPENING?!
‹ONLY WHAT YOU'D EXPECT, SWEETS...›
‹...ON OUR WEDDING NIGHT!›
AS REAL AS THE GARDEN-- SIGHT, SOUND, SMELL--
--MY KIND'A PLACE, MY KIND'A CROWD--
--BUT M'IKO WAS NEVER A PART OF THIS LIFE.
SHE DOESN'T BELONG.
‹I BELONG WITH YOU, LOGAN.›
‹A WILD WOMAN...›
‹... FOR MY WILD MAN.›
‹... FOR YOU TO HANDLE?›
‹IS THAT TOO MUCH...›
SNIKT
I WANT YOU.
SO MUCH IT HURTS.
MORE'N ANYTHING I'VE EVER FELT.
BUT NOT LIKE THIS!

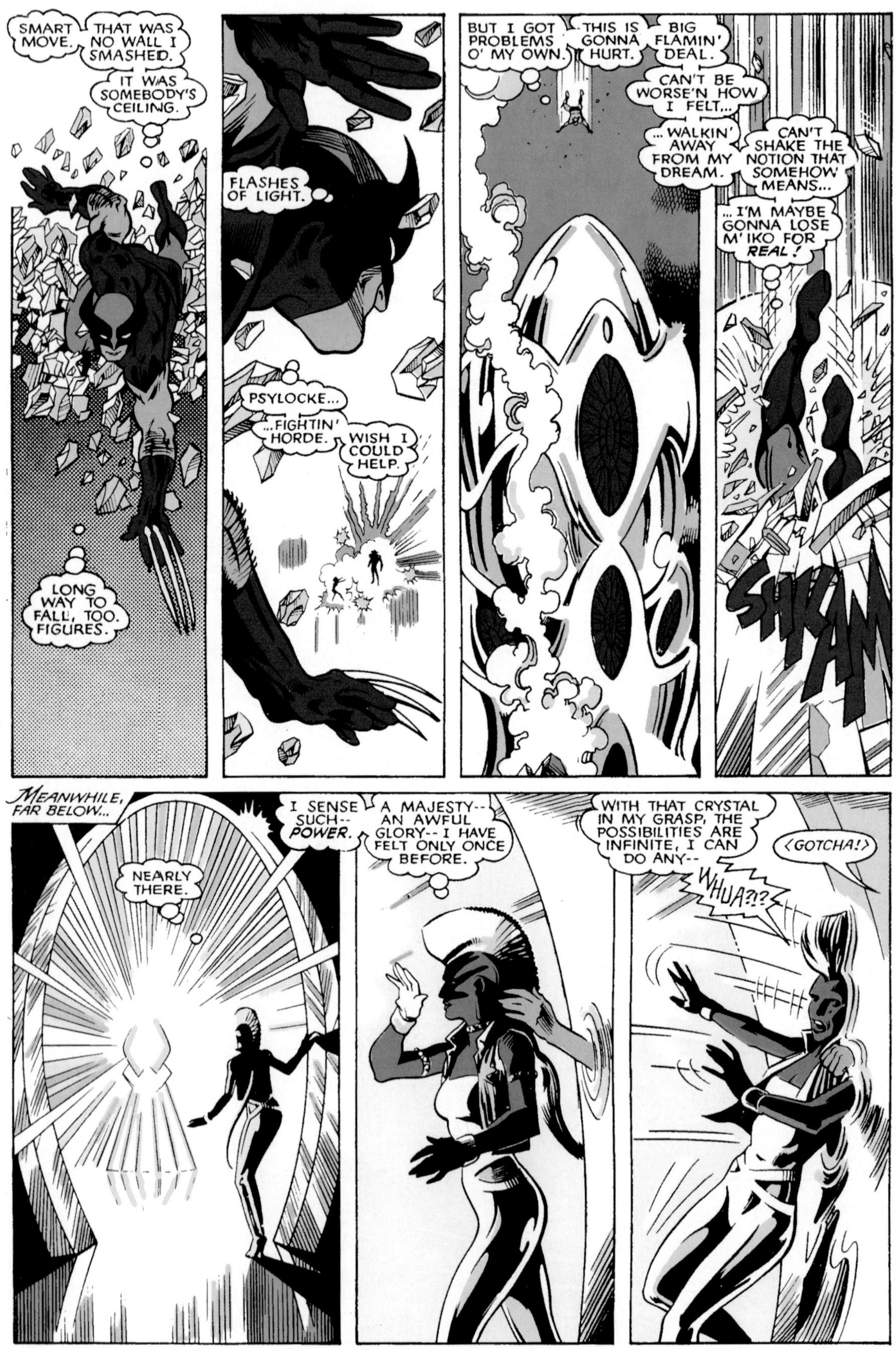
SMART MOVE.
THAT WAS NO WALL I SMASHED.
IT WAS SOMEBODY'S CEILING.
LONG WAY TO FALL, TOO. FIGURES.
FLASHES OF LIGHT.
PSYLOCKE...
...FIGHTIN' HORDE.
WISH I COULD HELP.
BUT I GOT PROBLEMS O' MY OWN.
THIS IS GONNA HURT.
BIG FLAMIN' DEAL.
CAN'T BE WORSE'N HOW I FELT...
... WALKIN' AWAY FROM MY DREAM.
CAN'T SHAKE THE NOTION THAT SOMEHOW MEANS...
... I'M MAYBE GONNA LOSE M'IKO FOR REAL!
SHKAM
MEANWHILE, FAR BELOW...
NEARLY THERE.
I SENSE SUCH-- POWER.
A MAJESTY-- AN AWFUL GLORY-- I HAVE FELT ONLY ONCE BEFORE.
WITH THAT CRYSTAL IN MY GRASP, THE POSSIBILITIES ARE INFINITE, I CAN DO ANY--
WHUA?!?
<GOTCHA!>

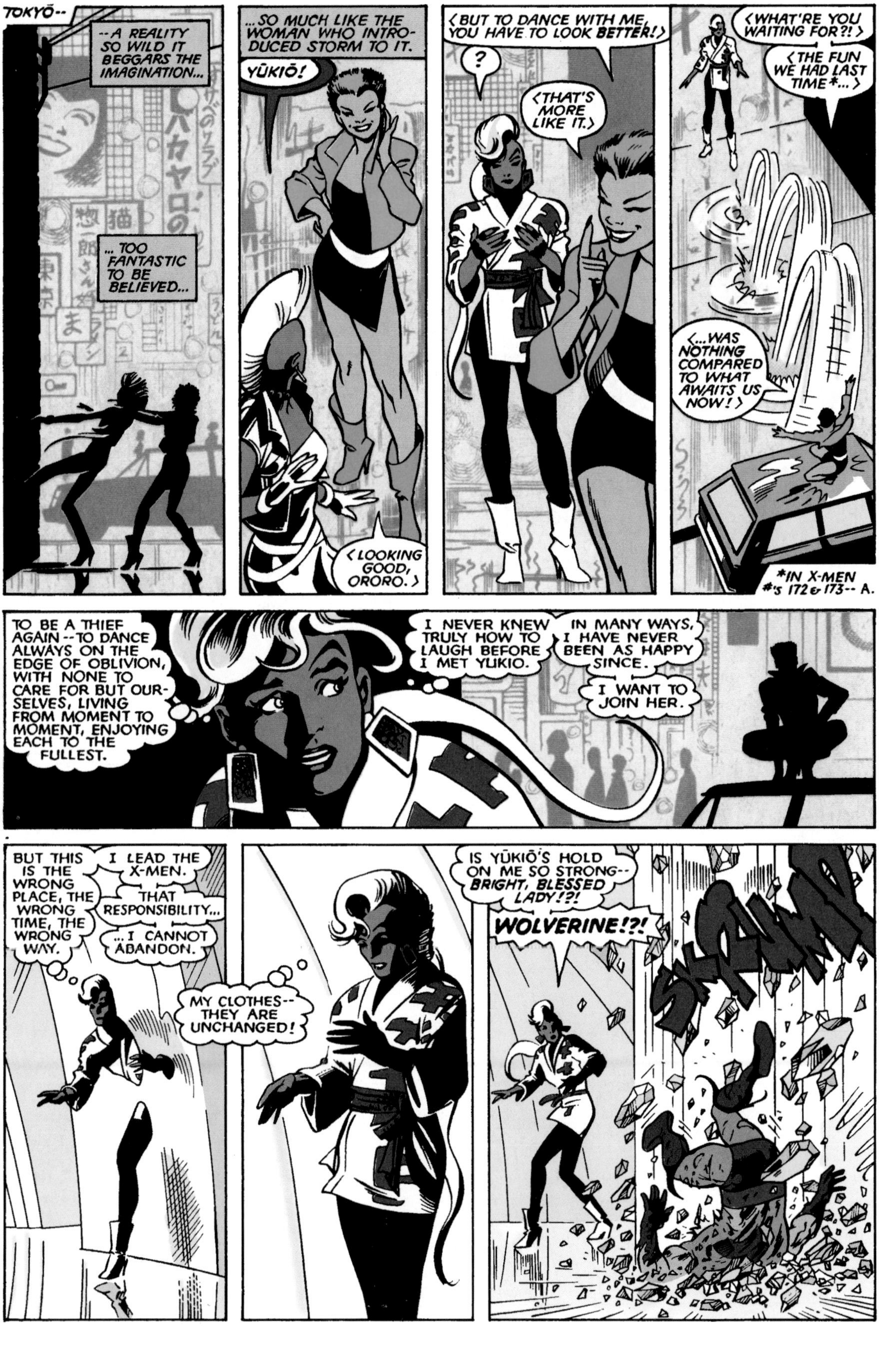
TOKYŌ--
--A REALITY SO WILD IT BEGGARS THE IMAGINATION...
...TOO FANTASTIC TO BE BELIEVED...
...SO MUCH LIKE THE WOMAN WHO INTRODUCED STORM TO IT.
YŪKIŌ!
‹LOOKING GOOD, ORORO.›
‹BUT TO DANCE WITH ME, YOU HAVE TO LOOK BETTER!›
?
‹THAT'S MORE LIKE IT.›
‹WHAT'RE YOU WAITING FOR?!›
‹THE FUN WE HAD LAST TIME*...›
‹...WAS NOTHING COMPARED TO WHAT AWAITS US NOW!›
*IN X-MEN #'S 172 & 173-- A.
TO BE A THIEF AGAIN--TO DANCE ALWAYS ON THE EDGE OF OBLIVION, WITH NONE TO CARE FOR BUT OURSELVES, LIVING FROM MOMENT TO MOMENT, ENJOYING EACH TO THE FULLEST.
I NEVER KNEW TRULY HOW TO LAUGH BEFORE I MET YUKIO.
IN MANY WAYS, I HAVE NEVER BEEN AS HAPPY SINCE.
I WANT TO JOIN HER.
BUT THIS IS THE WRONG PLACE, THE WRONG TIME, THE WRONG WAY.
I LEAD THE X-MEN.
THAT RESPONSIBILITY...
...I CANNOT ABANDON.
MY CLOTHES-- THEY ARE UNCHANGED!
IS YŪKIŌ'S HOLD ON ME SO STRONG-- BRIGHT, BLESSED LADY!?!
WOLVERINE!?!

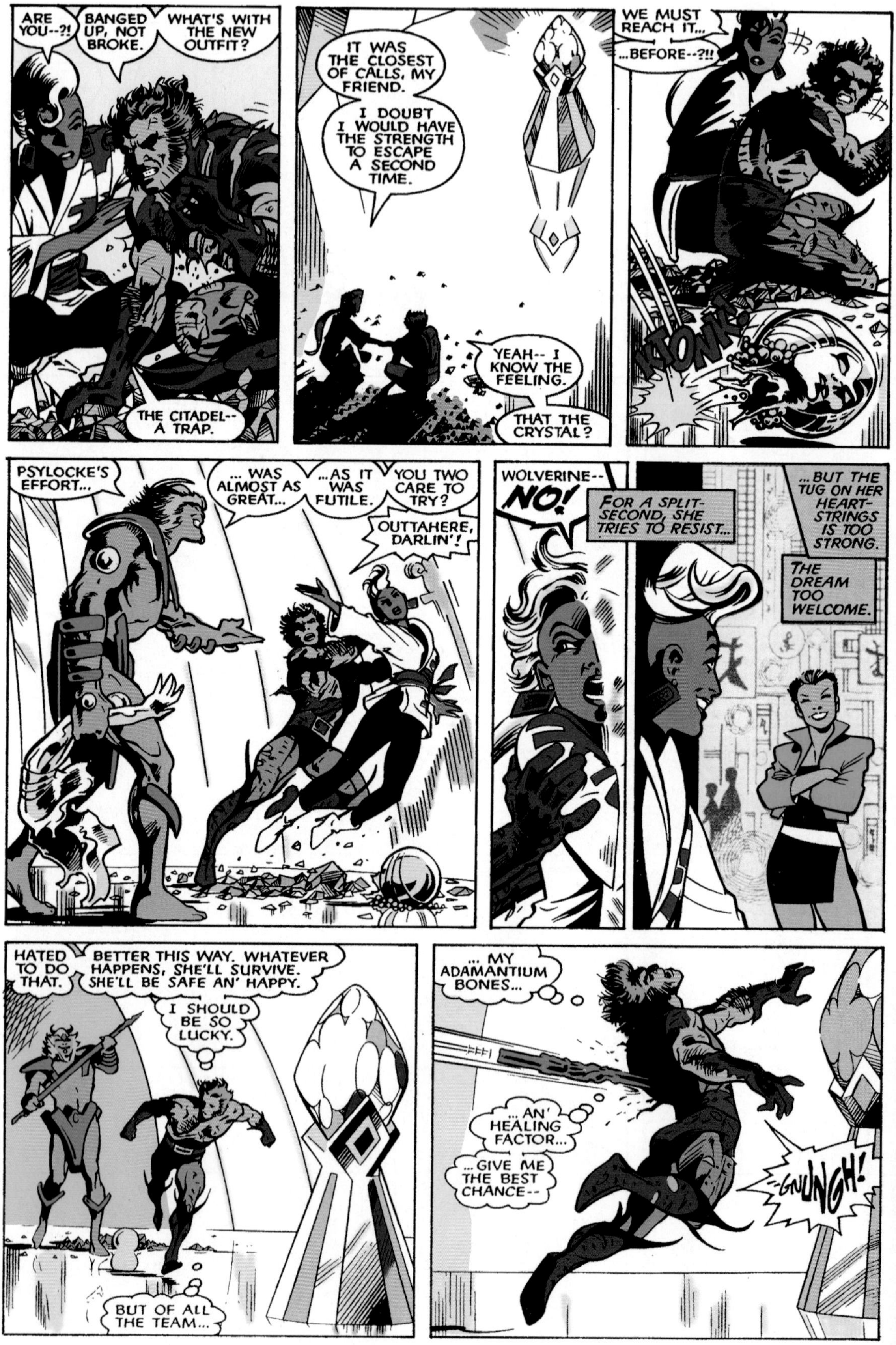

ARE YOU--?!
BANGED UP, NOT BROKE.
WHAT'S WITH THE NEW OUTFIT?
THE CITADEL-- A TRAP.
IT WAS THE CLOSEST OF CALLS, MY FRIEND.
I DOUBT I WOULD HAVE THE STRENGTH TO ESCAPE A SECOND TIME.
YEAH-- I KNOW THE FEELING.
THAT THE CRYSTAL?
WE MUST REACH IT...
...BEFORE--?!!
KTONK!
PSYLOCKE'S EFFORT...
... WAS ALMOST AS GREAT...
...AS IT WAS FUTILE.
YOU TWO CARE TO TRY?
OUTTAHERE, DARLIN'!
WOLVERINE-- NO!
FOR A SPLIT-SECOND, SHE TRIES TO RESIST...
...BUT THE TUG ON HER HEART-STRINGS IS TOO STRONG.
THE DREAM TOO WELCOME.
HATED TO DO THAT.
BETTER THIS WAY. WHATEVER HAPPENS, SHE'LL SURVIVE. SHE'LL BE SAFE AN' HAPPY.
I SHOULD BE SO LUCKY.
BUT OF ALL THE TEAM...
... MY ADAMANTIUM BONES...
... AN' HEALING FACTOR...
...GIVE ME THE BEST CHANCE--
GNUNGH!

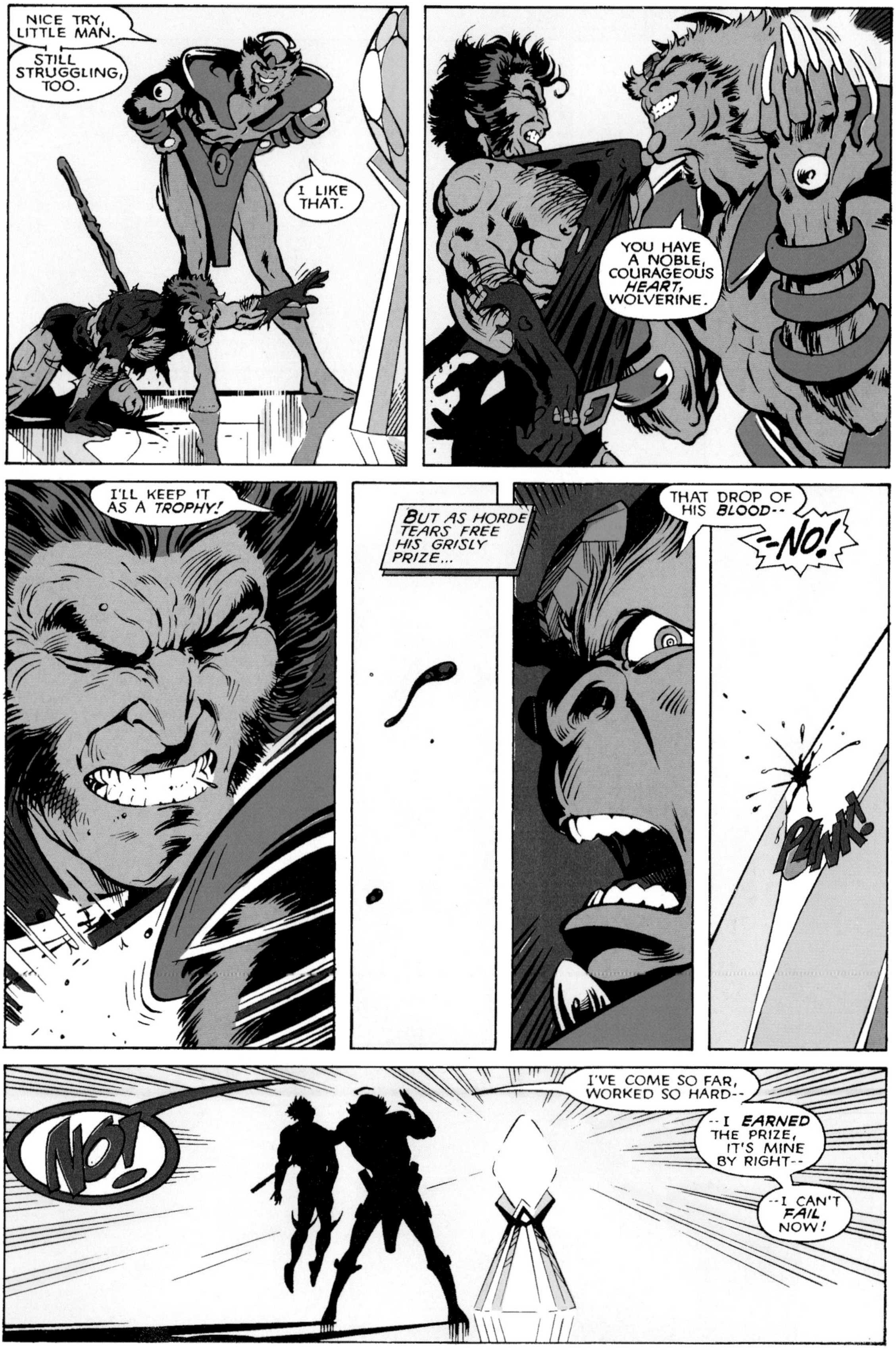
NICE TRY, LITTLE MAN.
STILL STRUGGLING, TOO.
I LIKE THAT.
YOU HAVE A NOBLE, COURAGEOUS HEART, WOLVERINE.
I'LL KEEP IT AS A TROPHY!
BUT AS HORDE TEARS FREE HIS GRISLY PRIZE...
THAT DROP OF HIS BLOOD--
--NO!
PLINK!
NO!
I'VE COME SO FAR, WORKED SO HARD--
--I EARNED THE PRIZE, IT'S MINE BY RIGHT--
--I CAN'T FAIL NOW!

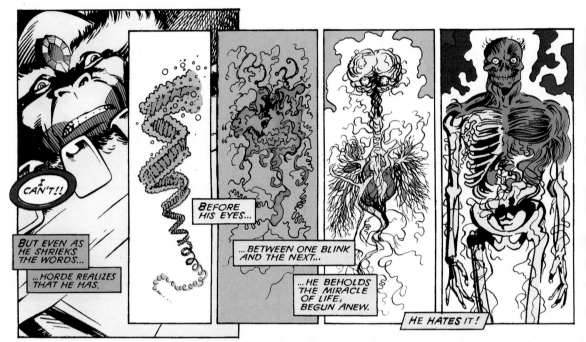

I CAN'T!!

BUT EVEN AS HE SHRIEKS THE WORDS...

...HORDE REALIZES THAT HE HAS.

BEFORE HIS EYES...

...BETWEEN ONE BLINK AND THE NEXT...

...HE BEHOLDS THE MIRACLE OF LIFE, BEGUN ANEW.

HE HATES IT!

HOW?! THIS ISN'T POSSIBLE-- YOU WERE DEAD-- I KILLED YOU!

THAT'S WHAT I THOUGHT.

BUT MY HEALING FACTOR'S IN EVERY CELL OF MY BODY.

SO, I GUESS, IS MY WILL TO LIVE.

GIVEN SUFFICIENT POWER, MY ENTIRE BODY COULD BE REGENERATED FROM THE GENETIC DATA ENCODED IN A SINGLE CELL. OR DROP OF BLOOD.

LOOKS LIKE THE CRYSTAL HAD THE POWER-- TO RESTORE BODY AND MIND BOTH.

THAT SHARD YOU WEAR, BUB.

IT DON'T BELONG TO YOU.

TIME IT WAS RETURNED TO ITS RIGHTFUL HOME.

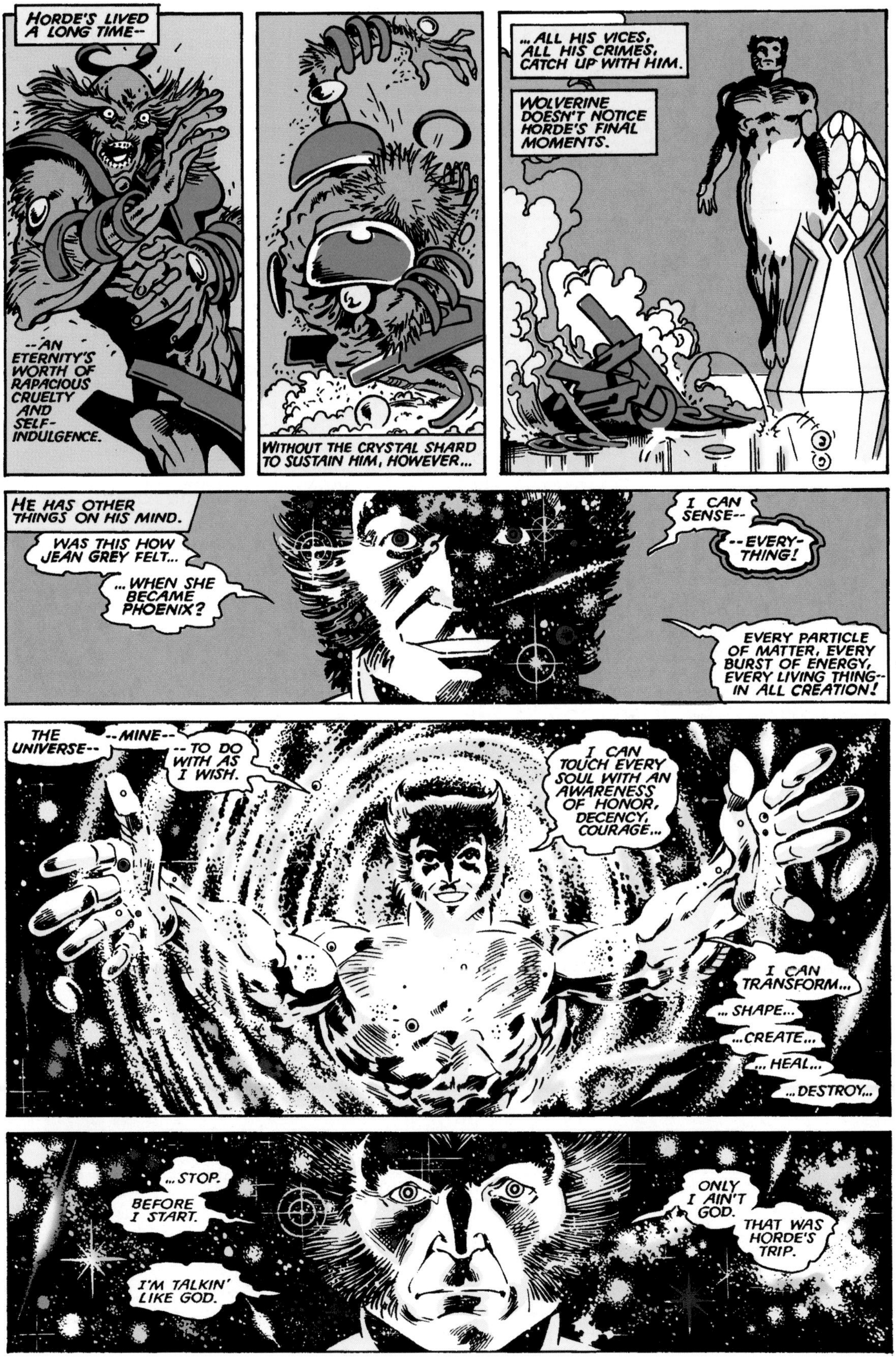
HORDE'S LIVED A LONG TIME--
--AN ETERNITY'S WORTH OF RAPACIOUS CRUELTY AND SELF-INDULGENCE.
WITHOUT THE CRYSTAL SHARD TO SUSTAIN HIM, HOWEVER...
...ALL HIS VICES, ALL HIS CRIMES, CATCH UP WITH HIM.
WOLVERINE DOESN'T NOTICE HORDE'S FINAL MOMENTS.
HE HAS OTHER THINGS ON HIS MIND.
WAS THIS HOW JEAN GREY FELT...
...WHEN SHE BECAME PHOENIX?
I CAN SENSE--
--EVERY-THING!
EVERY PARTICLE OF MATTER, EVERY BURST OF ENERGY, EVERY LIVING THING-- IN ALL CREATION!
THE UNIVERSE--
--MINE--
--TO DO WITH AS I WISH.
I CAN TOUCH EVERY SOUL WITH AN AWARENESS OF HONOR, DECENCY, COURAGE...
I CAN TRANSFORM...
...SHAPE...
...CREATE...
...HEAL...
...DESTROY...
...STOP.
BEFORE I START.
I'M TALKIN' LIKE GOD.
ONLY I AIN'T GOD.
THAT WAS HORDE'S TRIP.

THING I ALWAYS HATED MOST WAS A BODY MUCKIN' WITH MY MIND AN' SOUL.

IF I CAN'T ABIDE THAT BEIN' DONE TO ME...

...I GOT NO RIGHT DOIN' IT TO OTHERS--

--NO MATTER HOW FINE MY RATIONALIZATIONS.

BUT I JUST CAN'T JUST WALK AWAY.

LONG AS THIS CRYSTAL EXISTS, IT'S A THREAT.

BUT THE X-MEN ARE TRAPPED IN THE CITADEL. I SMASH THE CRYSTAL, I COULD BE KILLIN' THEM AS WELL.

WISH THERE WAS A WAY TO SAVE 'EM.

BUT THE LONGER I WAIT...

...THE MORE IRRESISTIBLE THE TEMPTATION GROWS TO USE THE POWER.

SNIKT

LIKE STORM SAID, TODAY'S AS GOOD A DAY AS ANY TO DIE--

--TOO BAD SHE AIN'T HERE...

...SO I COULD RETURN HER KISS--

--AN' THIS, AS GOOD A WAY AS ANY TO GO!

SKASH!

SKARA BOOM!

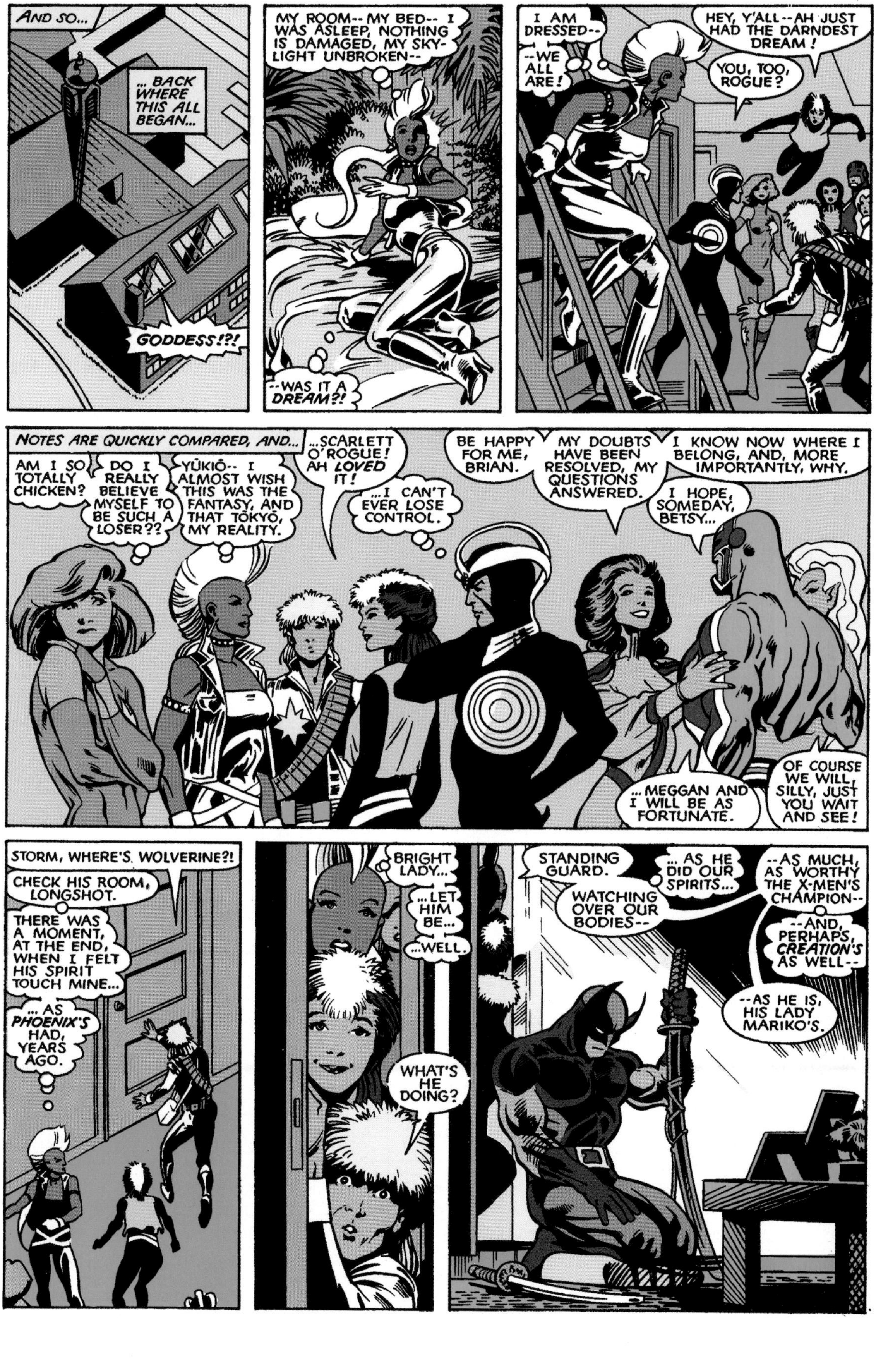
AND SO...
... BACK WHERE THIS ALL BEGAN...
GODDESS!?!
MY ROOM-- MY BED-- I WAS ASLEEP, NOTHING IS DAMAGED, MY SKY-LIGHT UNBROKEN--
--WAS IT A DREAM?!
I AM DRESSED--
--WE ALL ARE!
HEY, Y'ALL--AH JUST HAD THE DARNDEST DREAM!
YOU, TOO, ROGUE?
NOTES ARE QUICKLY COMPARED, AND...
AM I SO TOTALLY CHICKEN?
DO I REALLY BELIEVE MYSELF TO BE SUCH A LOSER??
YŪKIŌ-- I ALMOST WISH THIS WAS THE FANTASY, AND THAT TŌKYŌ, MY REALITY.
...SCARLETT O'ROGUE! AH LOVED IT!
...I CAN'T EVER LOSE CONTROL.
BE HAPPY FOR ME, BRIAN.
MY DOUBTS HAVE BEEN RESOLVED, MY QUESTIONS ANSWERED.
I KNOW NOW WHERE I BELONG, AND, MORE IMPORTANTLY, WHY.
I HOPE, SOMEDAY, BETSY...
...MEGGAN AND I WILL BE AS FORTUNATE.
OF COURSE WE WILL, SILLY, JUST YOU WAIT AND SEE!
STORM, WHERE'S WOLVERINE?!
CHECK HIS ROOM, LONGSHOT.
THERE WAS A MOMENT, AT THE END, WHEN I FELT HIS SPIRIT TOUCH MINE...
... AS PHOENIX'S HAD, YEARS AGO.
BRIGHT LADY...
...LET HIM BE...
...WELL.
WHAT'S HE DOING?
STANDING GUARD.
WATCHING OVER OUR BODIES--
... AS HE DID OUR SPIRITS...
--AS MUCH, AS WORTHY THE X-MEN'S CHAMPION--
--AND, PERHAPS, CREATION'S AS WELL--
--AS HE IS, HIS LADY MARIKO'S.

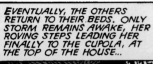

EVENTUALLY, THE OTHERS RETURN TO THEIR BEDS. ONLY STORM REMAINS AWAKE, HER ROVING STEPS LEADING HER FINALLY TO THE CUPOLA, AT THE TOP OF THE HOUSE...

... WHERE SHE STARES WONDERINGLY AT THE STARS.

ALREADY, THE NIGHT'S EVENTS HAVE BEGUN TO FADE FROM HER MEMORY.

SOON, SHE SENSES, IT WILL BE FORGOTTEN, LIKE ANY DREAM.

PERHAPS THAT IS FOR THE BEST.

SOMEHOW, WOLVERINE FOUND A WAY TO DEFEAT HORDE AND BRING THE X-MEN SAFELY HOME.

SHE'LL PROBABLY NEVER KNOW THE PRICE OF THAT VICTORY...

...SAVE THAT IT WAS AS TERRIBLE IN ITS OWN WAY AS THE COST OF DEFEAT.

AND THAT TOO, SHE THINKS, IS FOR THE BEST.

ACROSS THE INFINITE, STATUES STAND TALL AND SILENT BEFORE THEIR SHATTERED CITADEL.

ONLY-- THESE AREN'T STATUES.

EACH CAME IN TURN SEEKING THE CRYSTAL, UNAWARE IT WAS IN REALITY A TEST, AS OLD AND ENDURING AS TIME.

TO ATTAIN THIS ULTIMATE PRIZE...

... YET DENY THE TEMPTATION OF ITS POWER...

... IS THE MARK OF A TRULY MATURE SPECIES. THE QUESTER IS RETURNED HOME, HIS RACE ALLOWED TO EVOLVE TO ITS FULL POTENTIAL.

BUT THOSE WHO TRY TO USE THE CRYSTAL ...

... FIND THEMSELVES TRANSFORMED INTO THESE ETERNAL GUARDIANS.

WORSE THEIR RACES ARE GENETICALLY FROZEN IN PLACE, NEVER TO EVOLVE ANOTHER STEP. FOREVER LEFT BEHIND, WHILE THE REST OF CREATION PASSES THEM BY.

HUMANITY WILL NEVER KNOW THE DEBT IT OWES.

FOR TONIGHT, THE RACE FACED ITS ULTIMATE TEST.

AND THANKS TO ITS WAYWARD, OUTCAST CHILDREN-- THE X-MEN-- PASSED.

FIN

Cover to X-Men: The Fall of the Mutants TPB

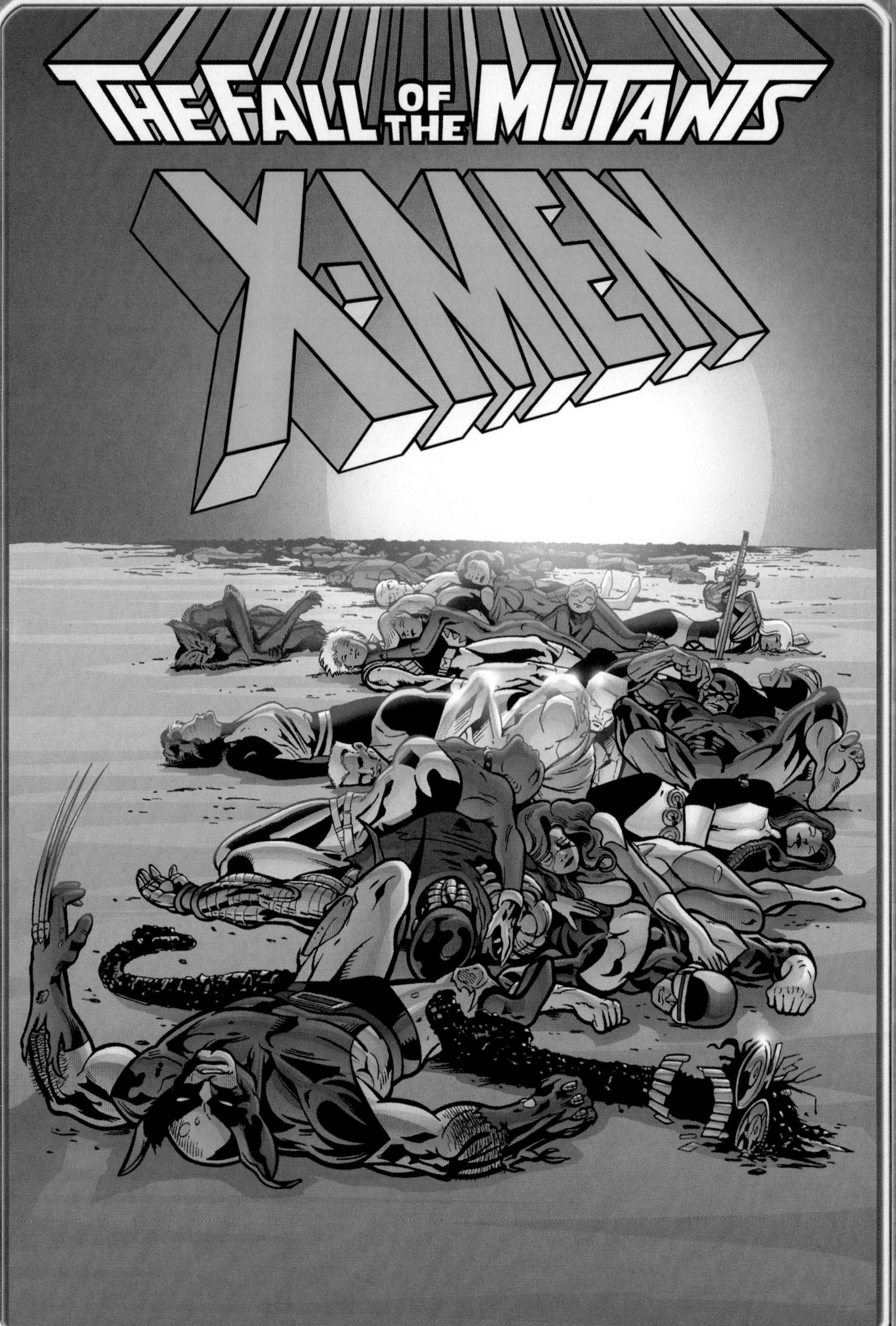

THE FALL OF THE MUTANTS
X-MEN

Cover to X-Men: Danger Room Battle Archive TPB

NOTES:

Downloaded straight from the battle computer in the X-Men's Danger Room at their headquarters in Westchester, New York, we are proud to re-present these five classic X-Men battles which are some of the finest examples of the X-Men as a combat team.

•

FILES:

•

Uncanny X-Men Annual № 3

•

Uncanny X-Men Annual № 10

•

Uncanny X-Men Annual № 17

•

New Mutants Annual № 2

•

Incredible Hulk Annual № 7

•

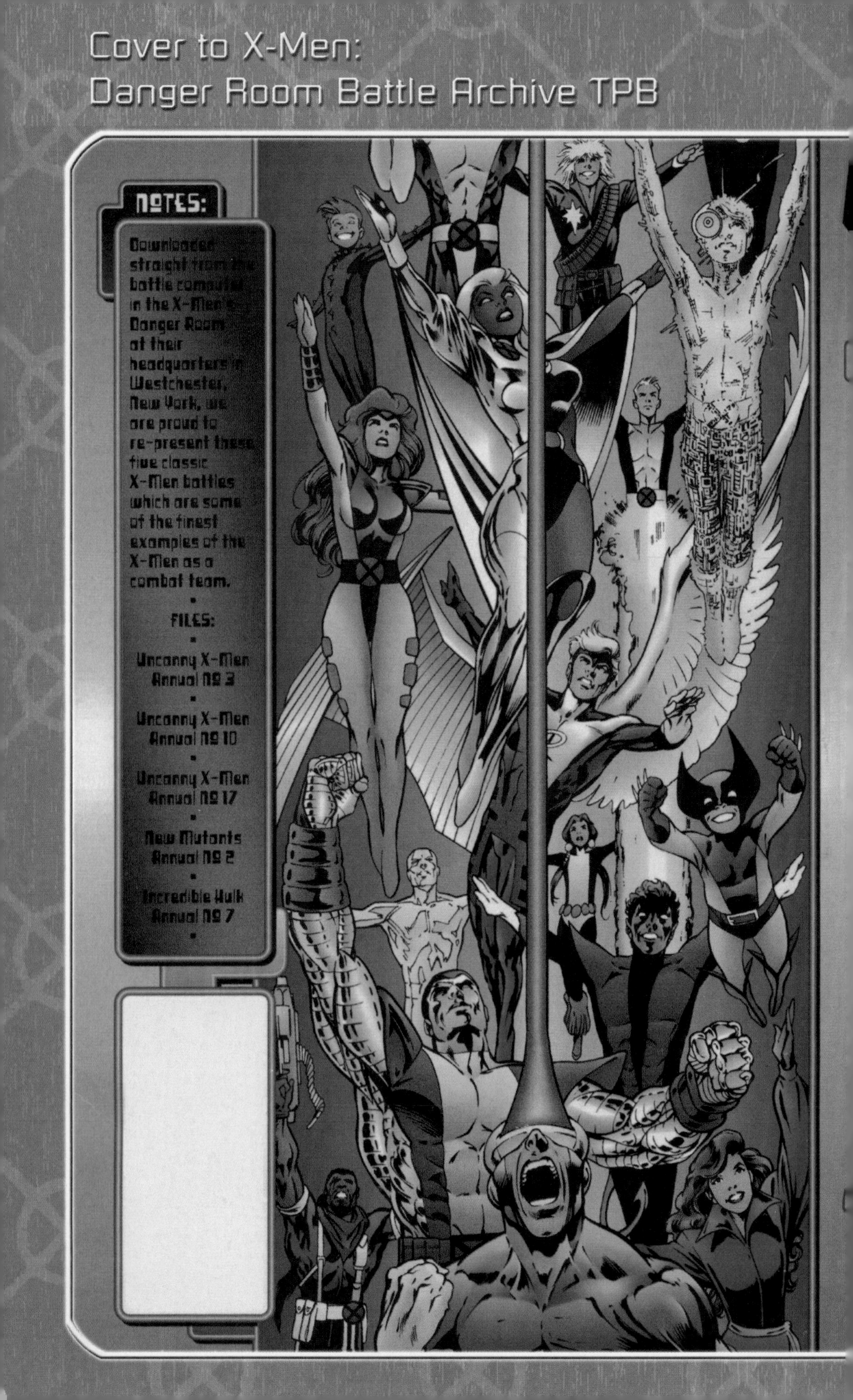

X-MEN®

FILE:

DANGER ROOM™
BATTLE ARCHIVES

ENTER:

MARVEL COMICS

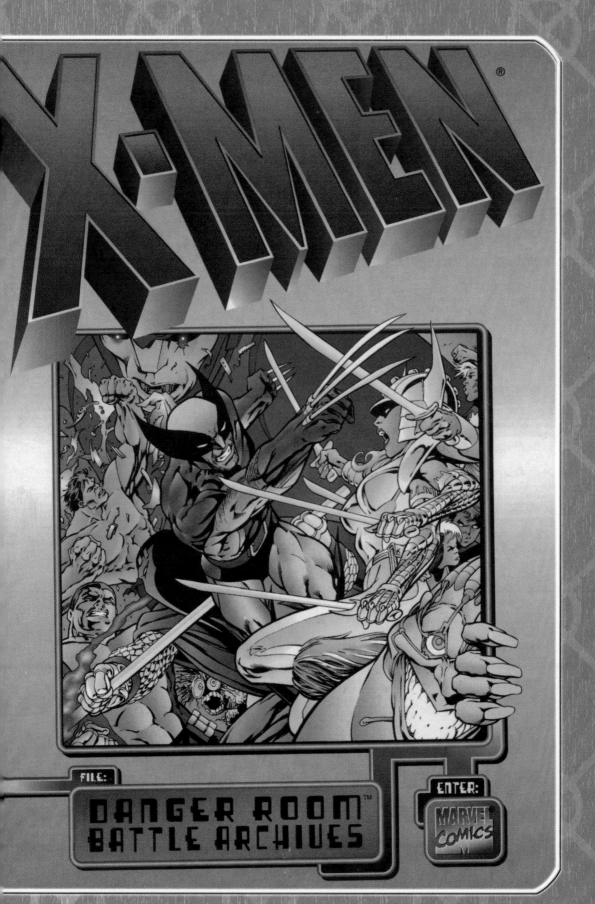

Cover to Uncanny X-Men #445

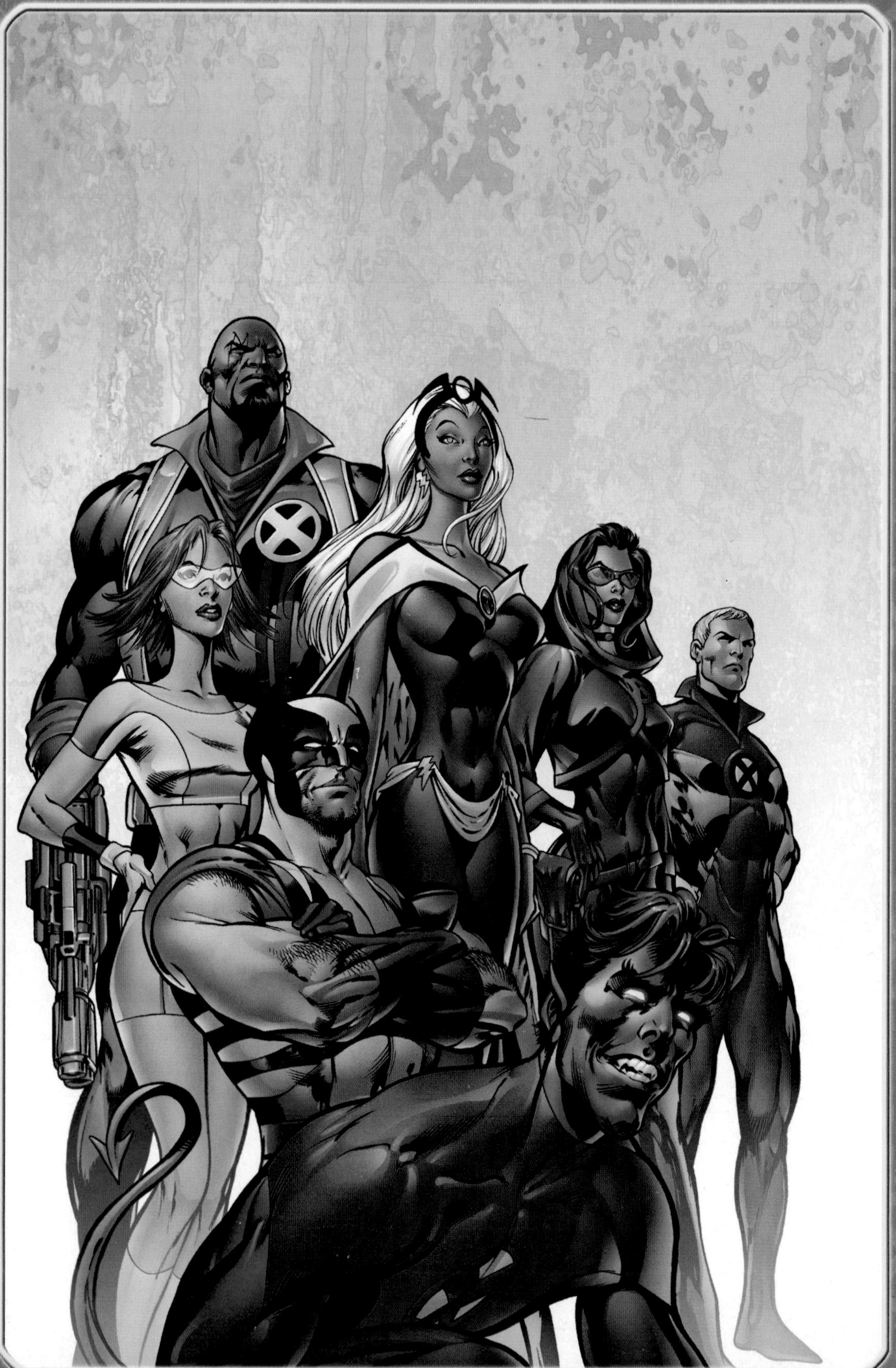